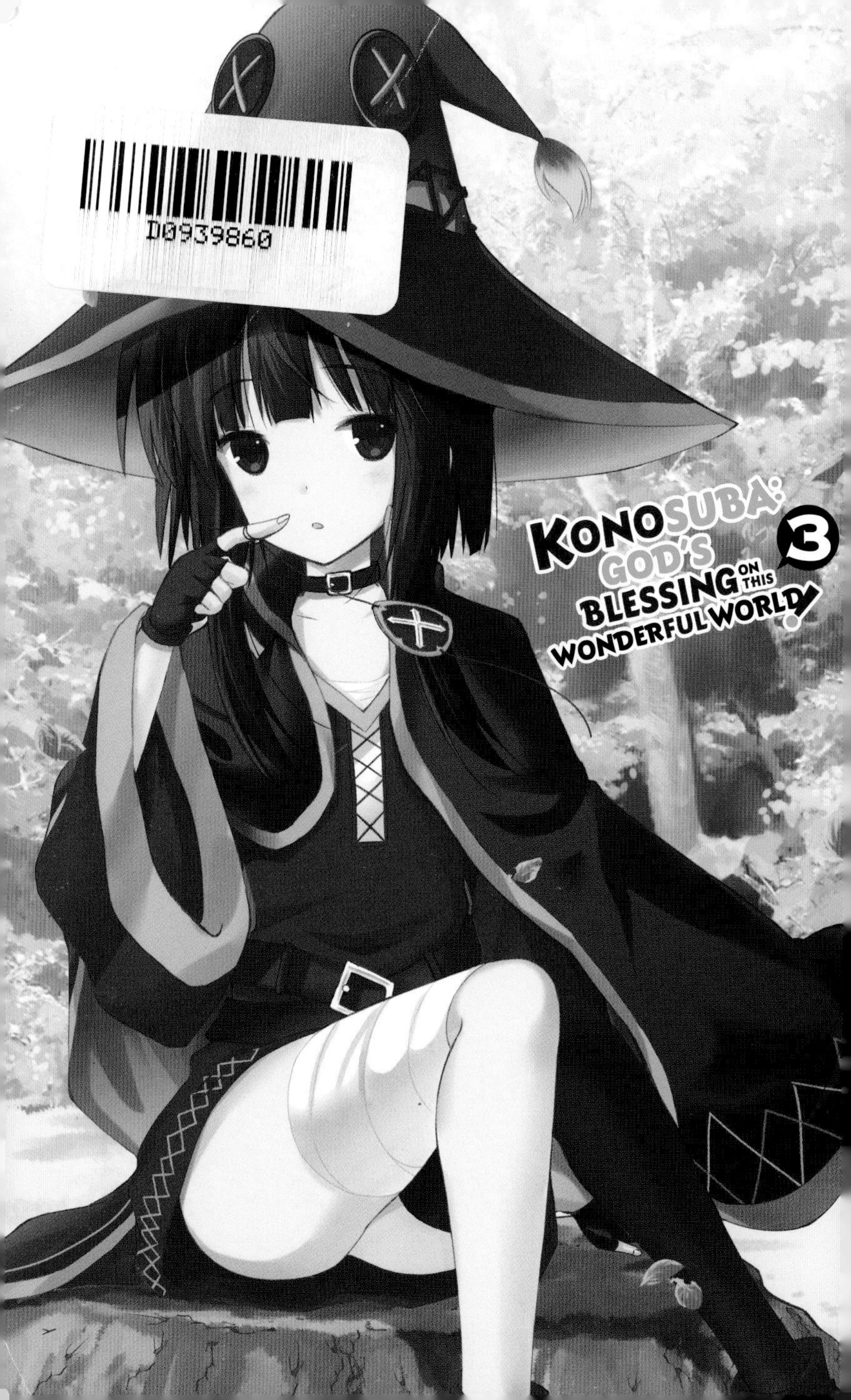
KONOSUBA: GOD'S BLESSING ON THIS WONDERFUL WORLD!
3

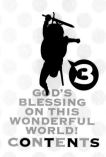

## 3
### GOD'S BLESSING ON THIS WONDERFUL WORLD!
# CONTENTS

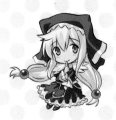

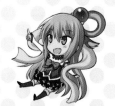

# CHAPTER 13 MAY I TRADE WITH THESE TRUE FRIENDS!

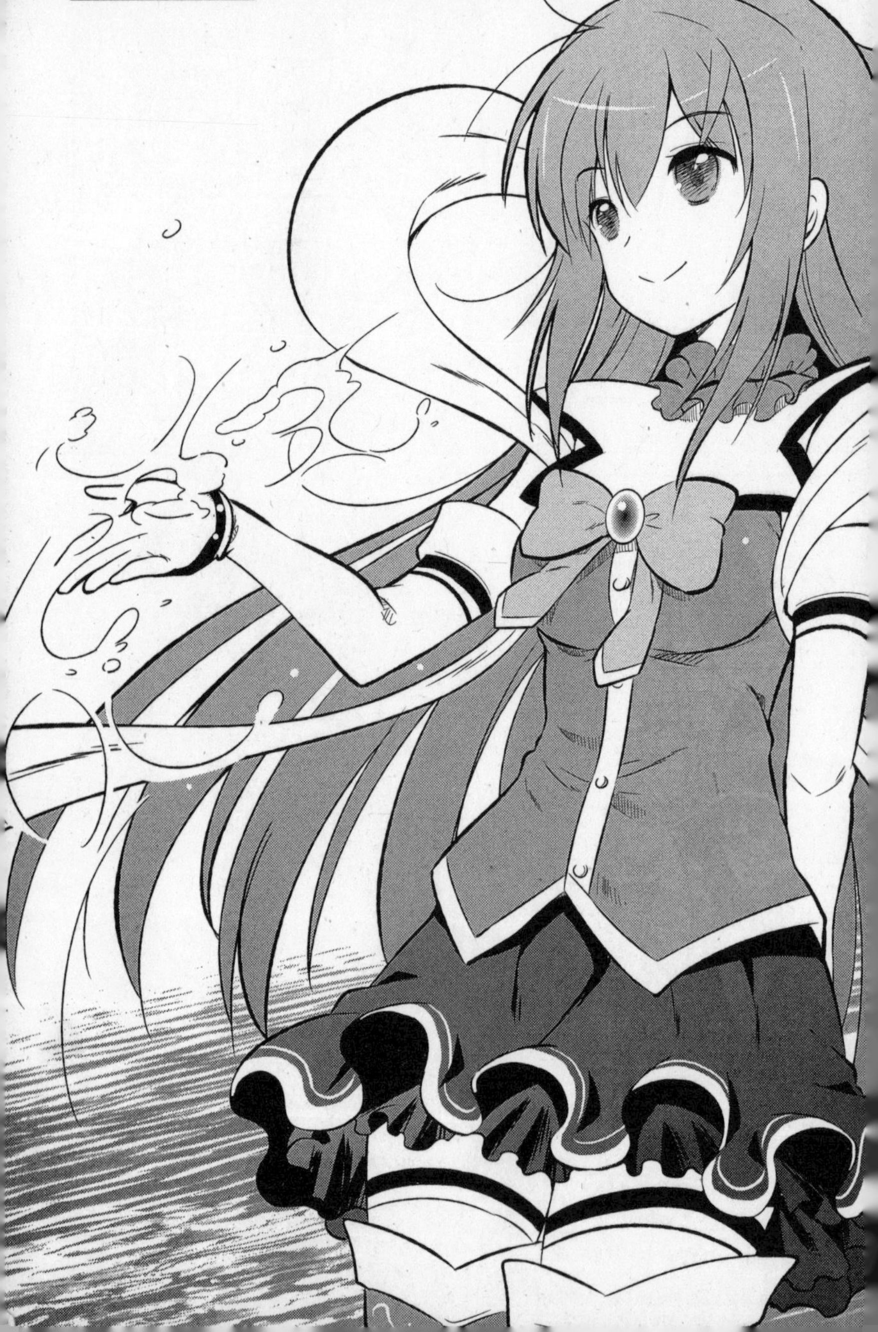

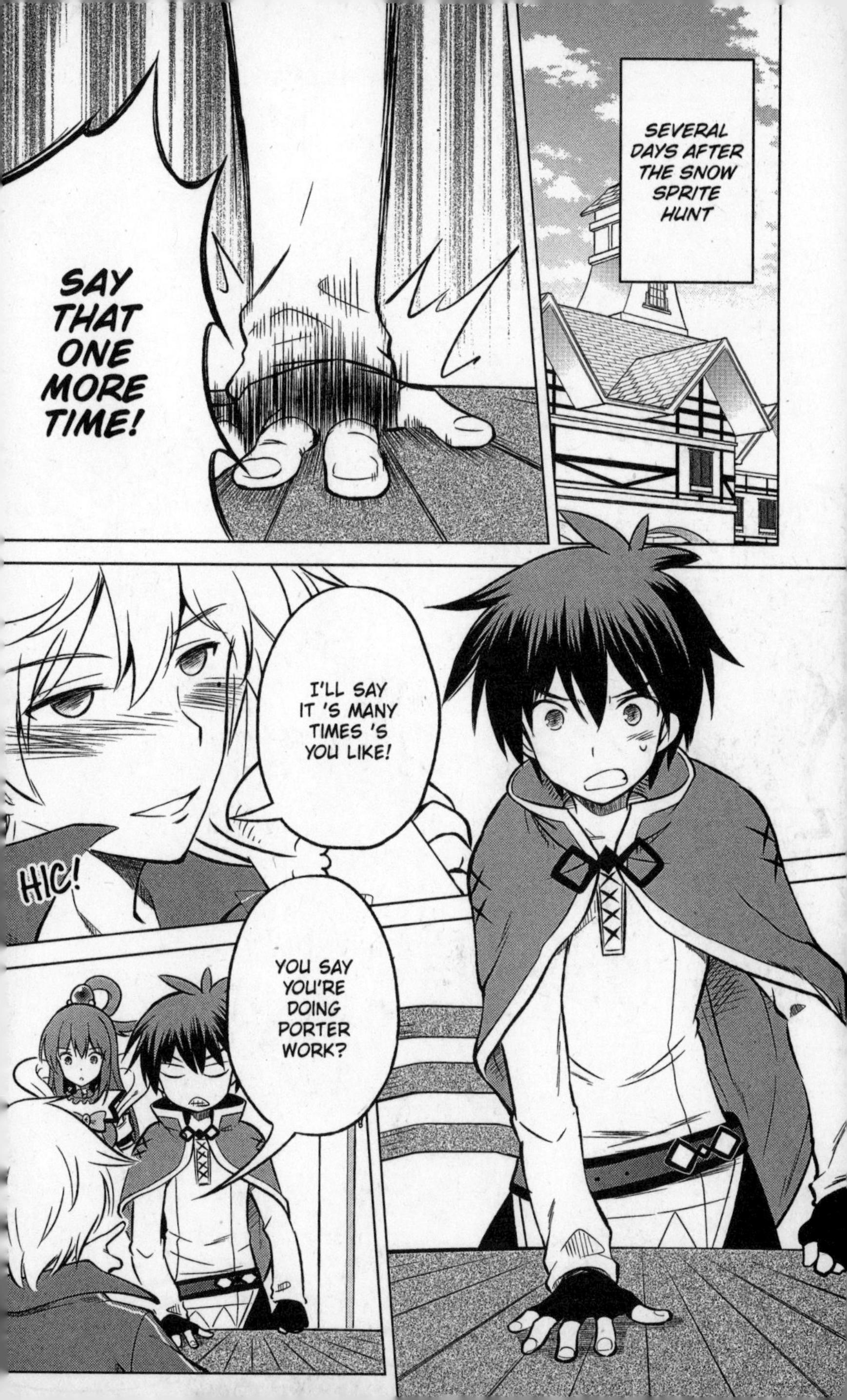
SEVERAL DAYS AFTER THE SNOW SPRITE HUNT
SAY THAT ONE MORE TIME!
I'LL SAY IT 'S MANY TIMES 'S YOU LIKE!
HIC!
YOU SAY YOU'RE DOING PORTER WORK?

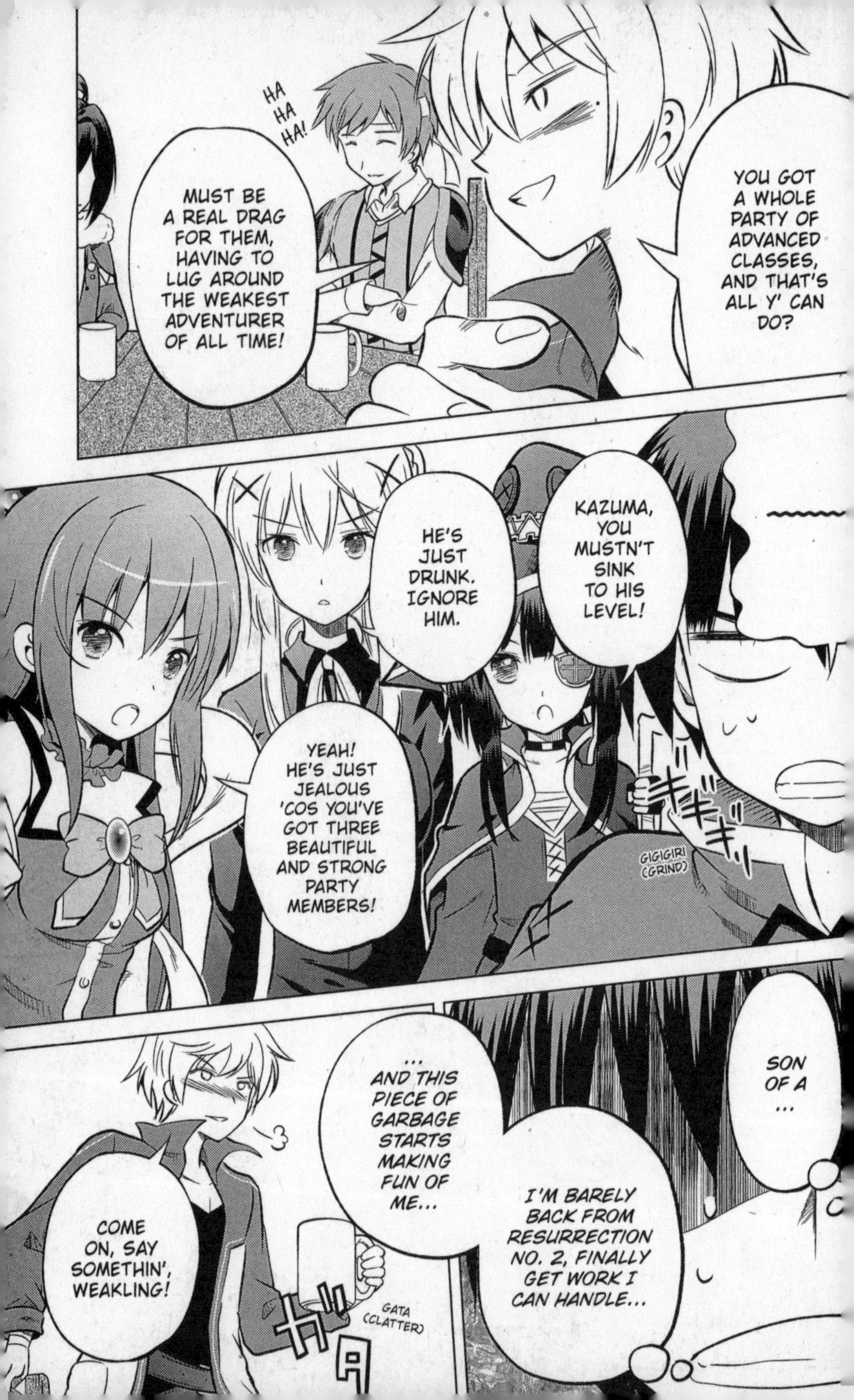
YOU GOT A WHOLE PARTY OF ADVANCED CLASSES, AND THAT'S ALL Y' CAN DO?
HA HA HA!
MUST BE A REAL DRAG FOR THEM, HAVING TO LUG AROUND THE WEAKEST ADVENTURER OF ALL TIME!
~~~~
KAZUMA, YOU MUSTN'T SINK TO HIS LEVEL!
HE'S JUST DRUNK. IGNORE HIM.
GIGIGIRI (GRIND)
YEAH! HE'S JUST JEALOUS 'COS YOU'VE GOT THREE BEAUTIFUL AND STRONG PARTY MEMBERS!
SON OF A ...
I'M BARELY BACK FROM RESURRECTION NO. 2, FINALLY GET WORK I CAN HANDLE...
... AND THIS PIECE OF GARBAGE STARTS MAKING FUN OF ME...
GATA (CLATTER)
COME ON, SAY SOMETHIN', WEAKLING!
~~~~

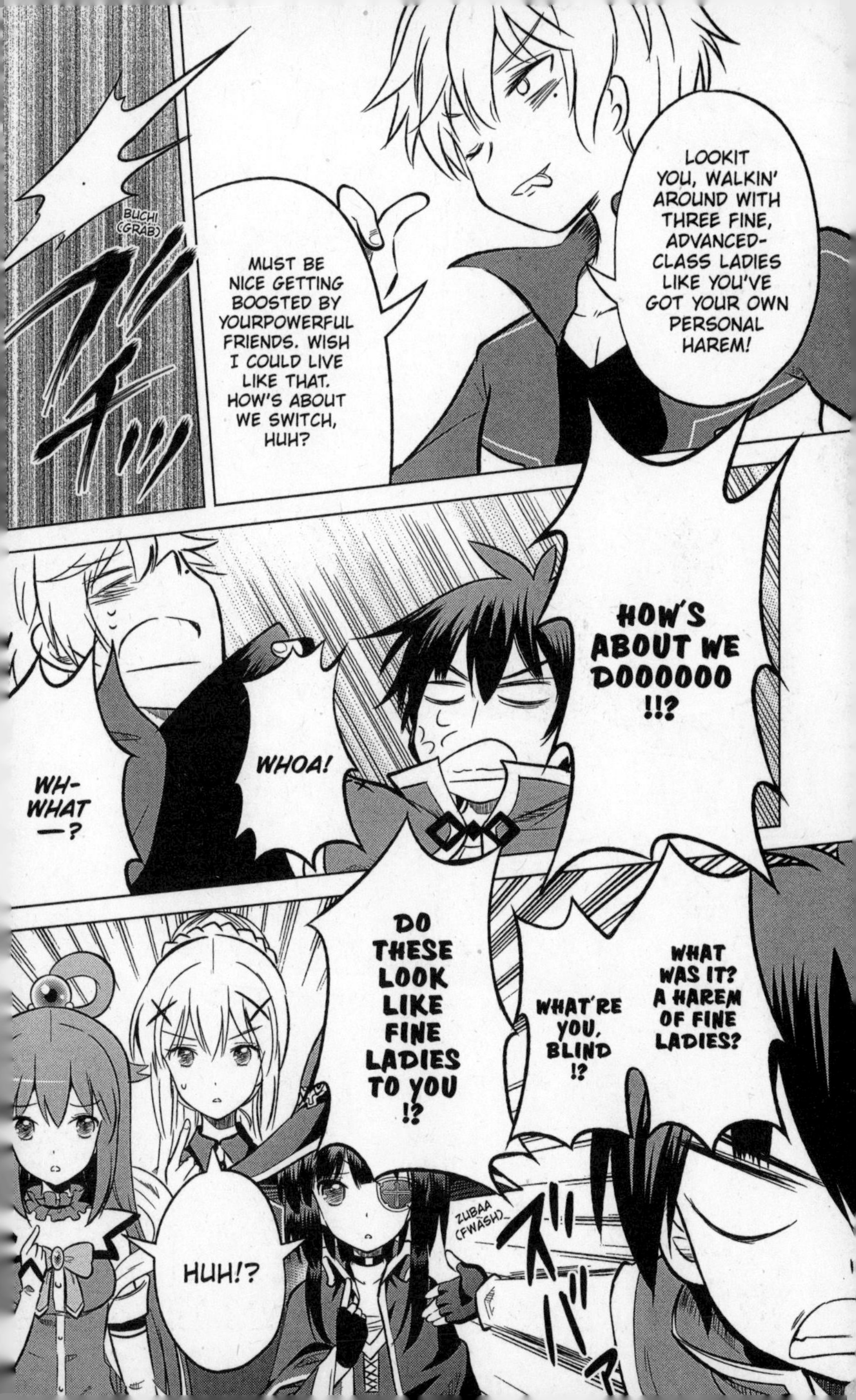
LOOKIT YOU, WALKIN' AROUND WITH THREE FINE, ADVANCED-CLASS LADIES LIKE YOU'VE GOT YOUR OWN PERSONAL HAREM!
MUST BE NICE GETTING BOOSTED BY YOURPOWERFUL FRIENDS. WISH I COULD LIVE LIKE THAT. HOW'S ABOUT WE SWITCH, HUH?
BUCHI (GRAB)
HOW'S ABOUT WE DOOOOOO !!?
WHOA!
WH-WHAT—?
WHAT WAS IT? A HAREM OF FINE LADIES?
WHAT'RE YOU, BLIND !?
DO THESE LOOK LIKE FINE LADIES TO YOU !?
ZUBAA (FWASH)
HUH!?

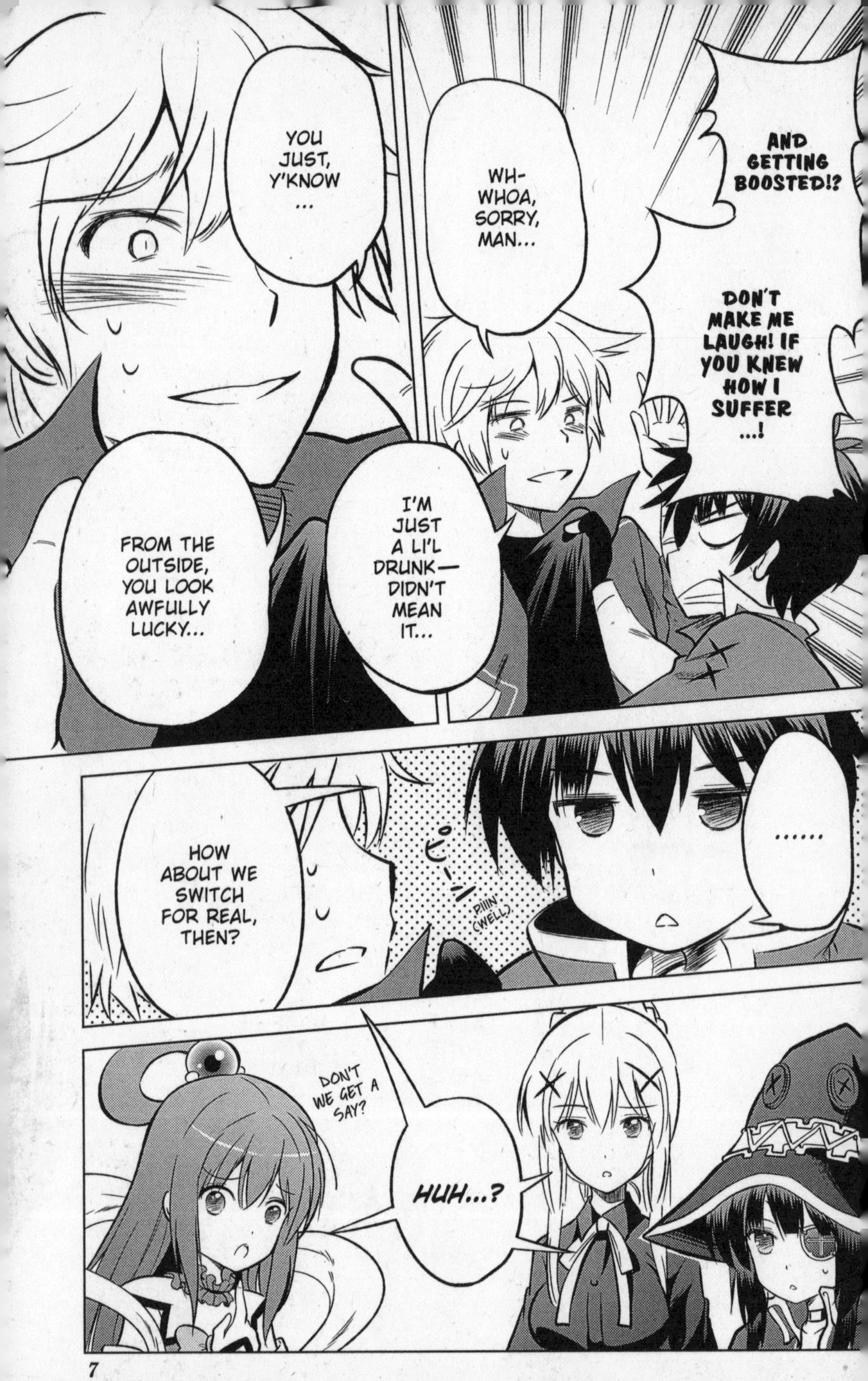
AND GETTING BOOSTED!?
DON'T MAKE ME LAUGH! IF YOU KNEW HOW I SUFFER ...!
WH-WHOA, SORRY, MAN...
I'M JUST A LI'L DRUNK—DIDN'T MEAN IT...
YOU JUST, Y'KNOW ...
FROM THE OUTSIDE, YOU LOOK AWFULLY LUCKY...
......
PIIIN (WELL)
HOW ABOUT WE SWITCH FOR REAL, THEN?
HUH...?
DON'T WE GET A SAY?

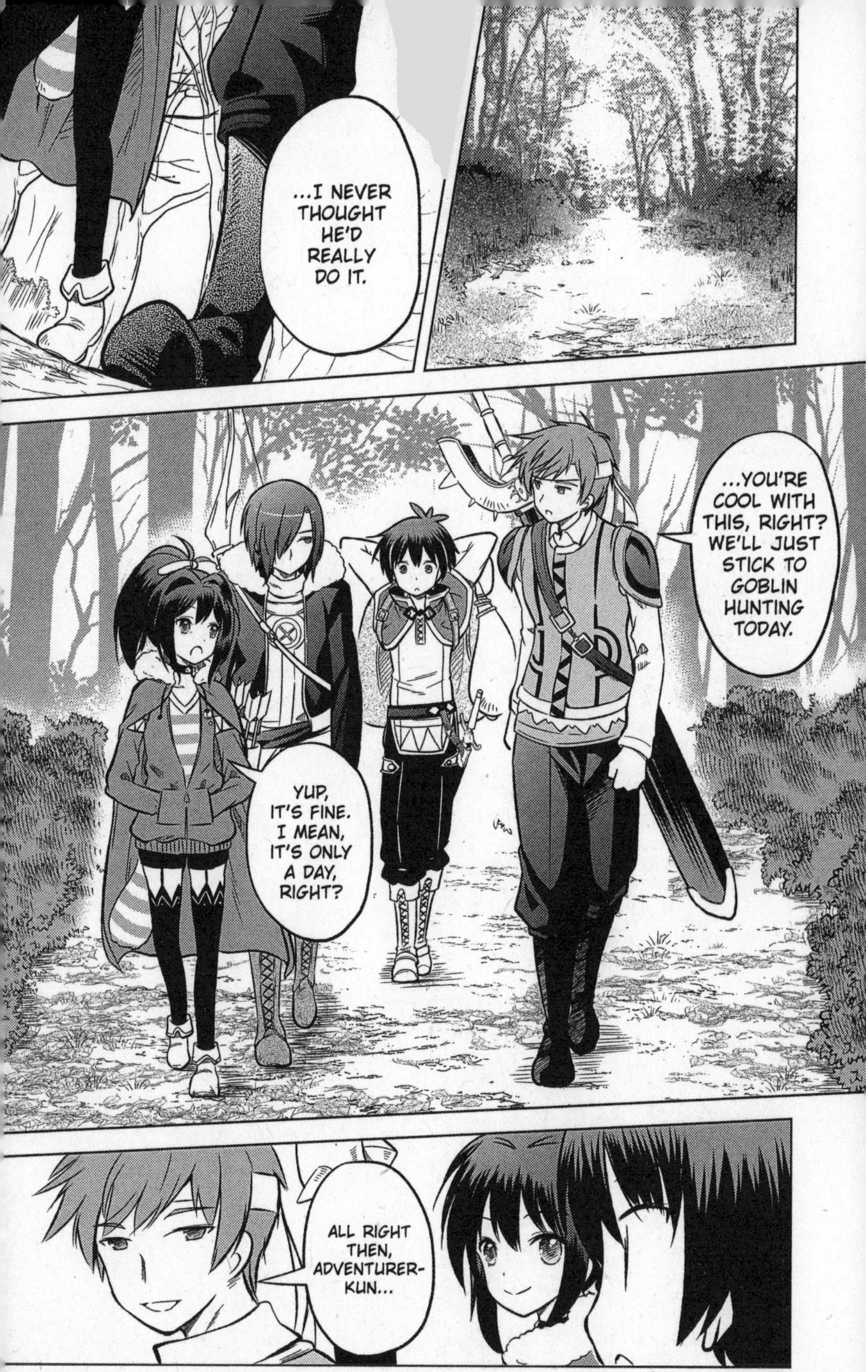
...I NEVER THOUGHT HE'D REALLY DO IT.
...YOU'RE COOL WITH THIS, RIGHT? WE'LL JUST STICK TO GOBLIN HUNTING TODAY.
YUP, IT'S FINE. I MEAN, IT'S ONLY A DAY, RIGHT?
ALL RIGHT THEN, ADVENTURER-KUN...

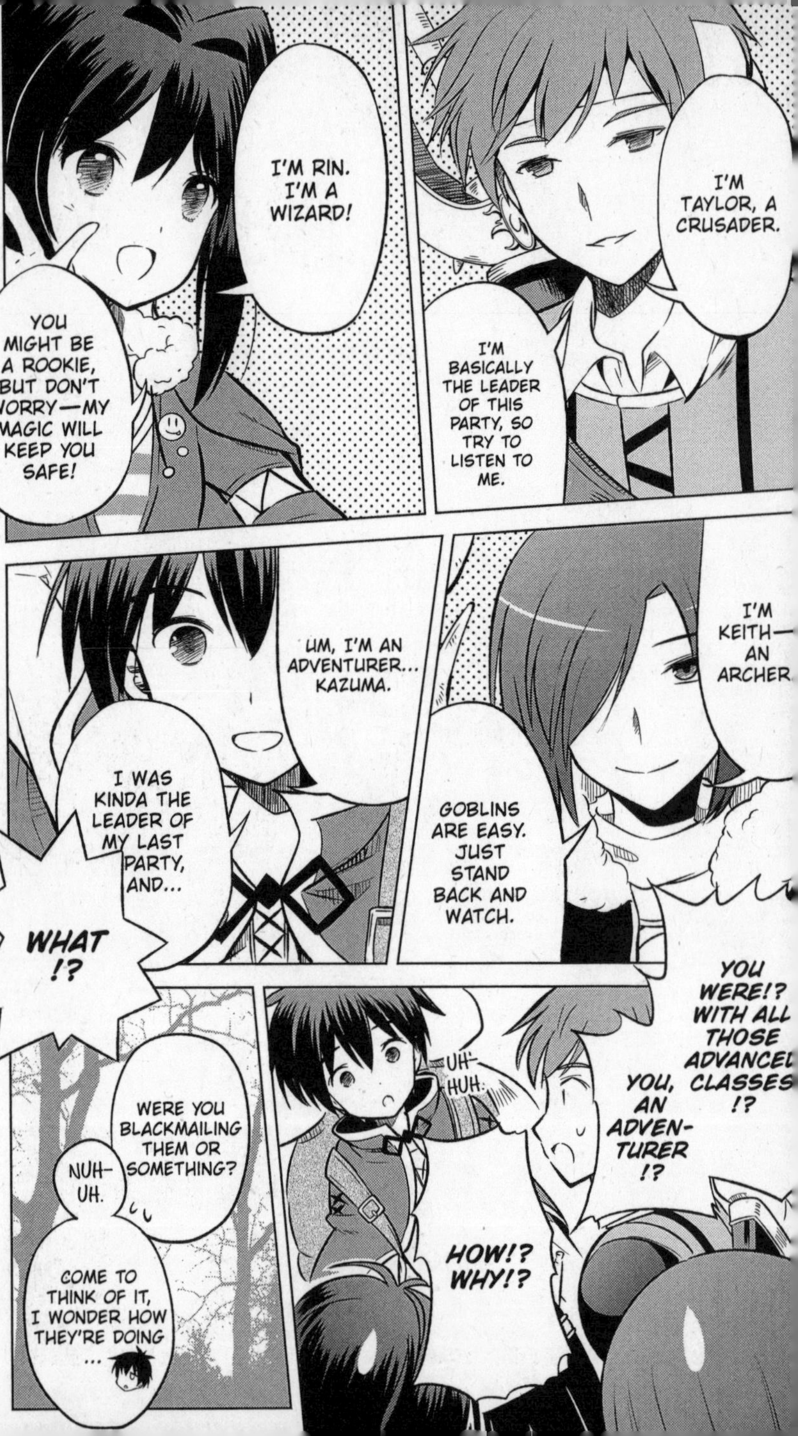
I'M TAYLOR, A CRUSADER.
I'M BASICALLY THE LEADER OF THIS PARTY, SO TRY TO LISTEN TO ME.
I'M RIN. I'M A WIZARD!
YOU MIGHT BE A ROOKIE, BUT DON'T WORRY—MY MAGIC WILL KEEP YOU SAFE!
I'M KEITH—AN ARCHER.
GOBLINS ARE EASY. JUST STAND BACK AND WATCH.
UM, I'M AN ADVENTURER... KAZUMA.
I WAS KINDA THE LEADER OF MY LAST PARTY, AND...
WHAT!?
YOU WERE!? WITH ALL THOSE ADVANCED CLASSES!?
YOU, AN ADVENTURER!?
UH-HUH.
HOW!? WHY!?
WERE YOU BLACKMAILING THEM OR SOMETHING?
NUH-UH.
COME TO THINK OF IT, I WONDER HOW THEY'RE DOING...

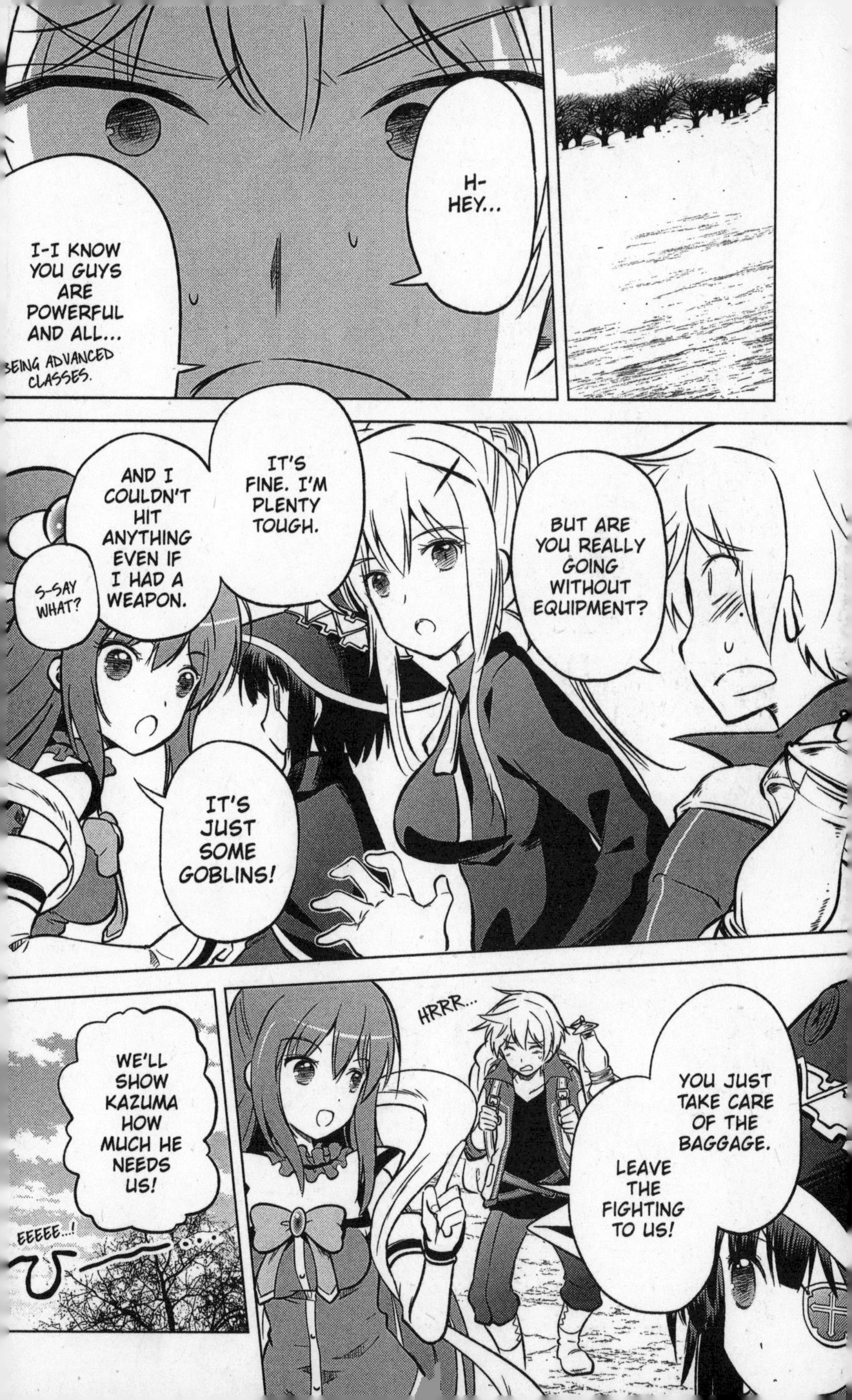
H-HEY...
I-I KNOW YOU GUYS ARE POWERFUL AND ALL...
BEING ADVANCED CLASSES.
BUT ARE YOU REALLY GOING WITHOUT EQUIPMENT?
IT'S FINE. I'M PLENTY TOUGH.
AND I COULDN'T HIT ANYTHING EVEN IF I HAD A WEAPON.
S-SAY WHAT?
IT'S JUST SOME GOBLINS!
YOU JUST TAKE CARE OF THE BAGGAGE.
LEAVE THE FIGHTING TO US!
HRRR...
WE'LL SHOW KAZUMA HOW MUCH HE NEEDS US!
EEEEE...!

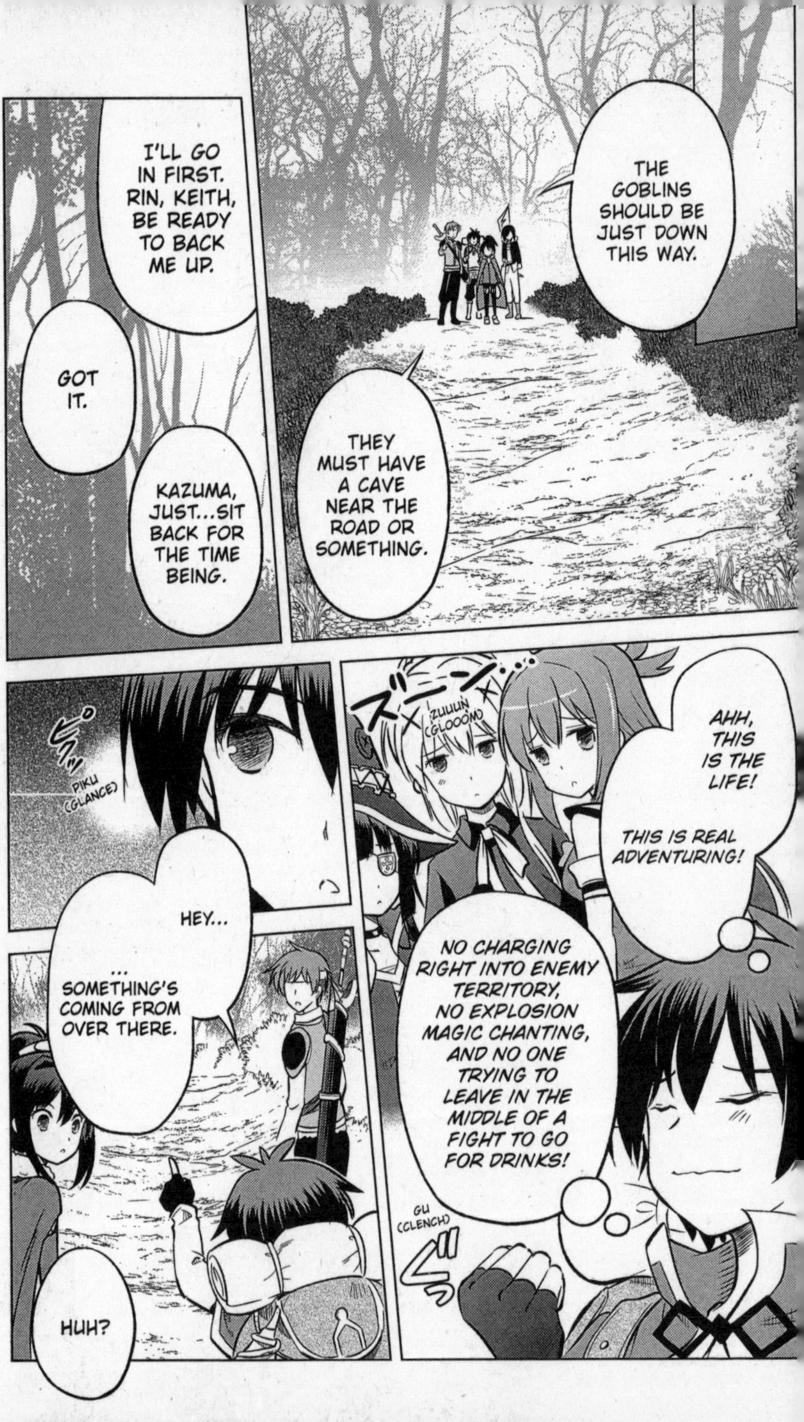
THE GOBLINS SHOULD BE JUST DOWN THIS WAY.
THEY MUST HAVE A CAVE NEAR THE ROAD OR SOMETHING.
I'LL GO IN FIRST. RIN, KEITH, BE READY TO BACK ME UP.
GOT IT.
KAZUMA, JUST...SIT BACK FOR THE TIME BEING.
AHH, THIS IS THE LIFE!
THIS IS REAL ADVENTURING!
ZUUUN (GLOOOM)
NO CHARGING RIGHT INTO ENEMY TERRITORY, NO EXPLOSION MAGIC CHANTING, AND NO ONE TRYING TO LEAVE IN THE MIDDLE OF A FIGHT TO GO FOR DRINKS!
GU (CLENCH)
PIKU (GLANCE)
HEY...
...SOMETHING'S COMING FROM OVER THERE.
HUH?

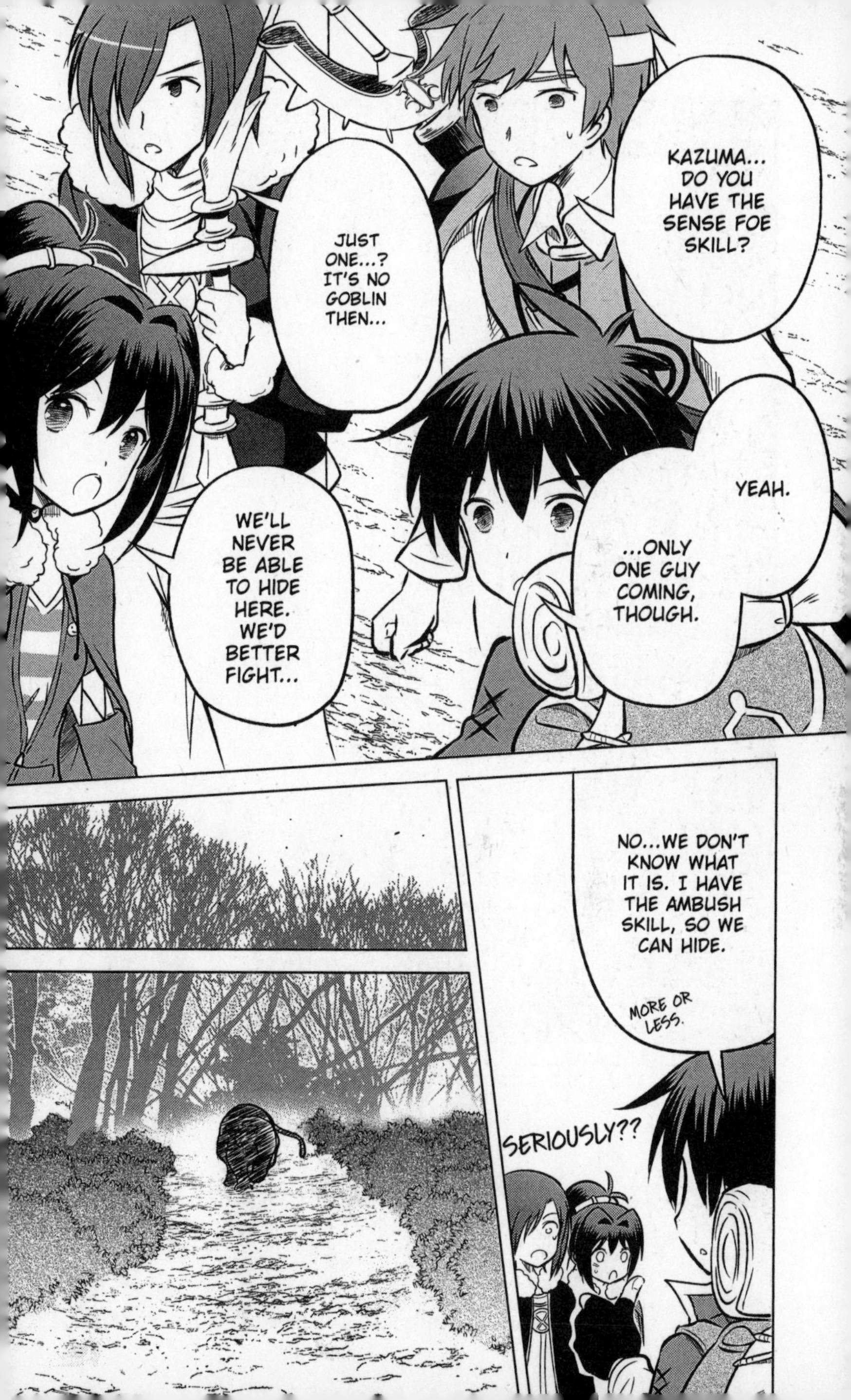
KAZUMA... DO YOU HAVE THE SENSE FOE SKILL?
YEAH.
...ONLY ONE GUY COMING, THOUGH.
JUST ONE...? IT'S NO GOBLIN THEN...
WE'LL NEVER BE ABLE TO HIDE HERE. WE'D BETTER FIGHT...
NO...WE DON'T KNOW WHAT IT IS. I HAVE THE AMBUSH SKILL, SO WE CAN HIDE.
MORE OR LESS.
SERIOUSLY??

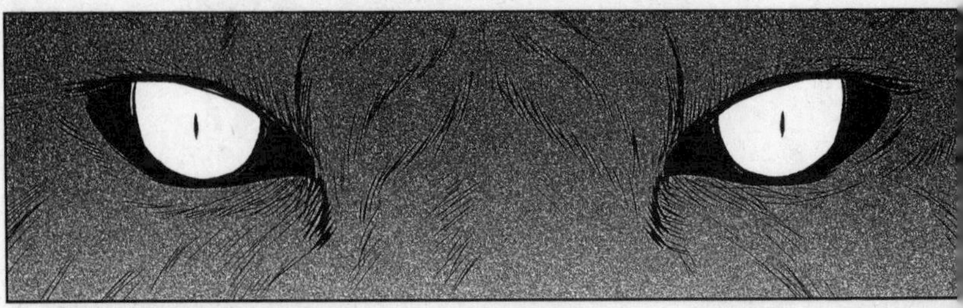

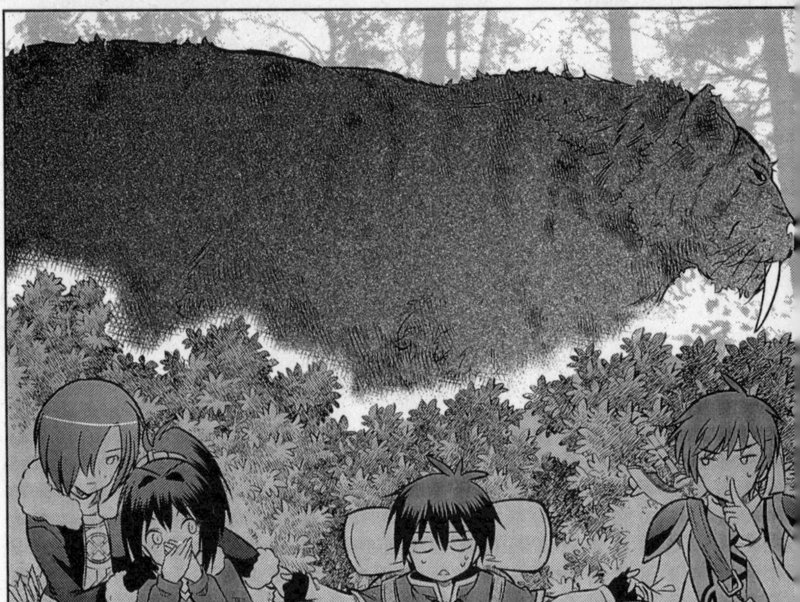

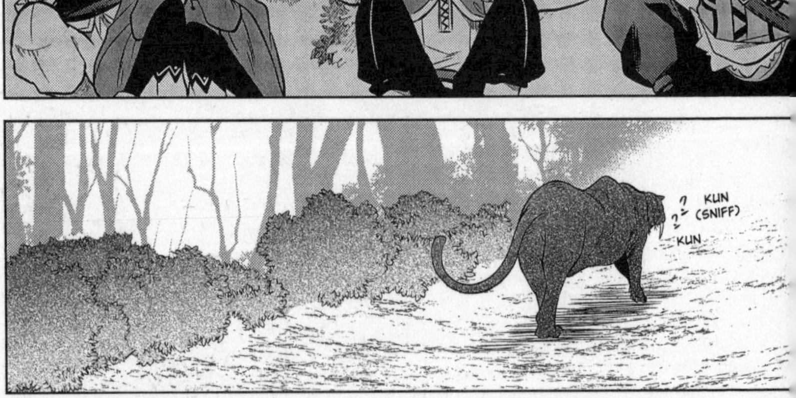
KUN
(SNIFF)
KUN

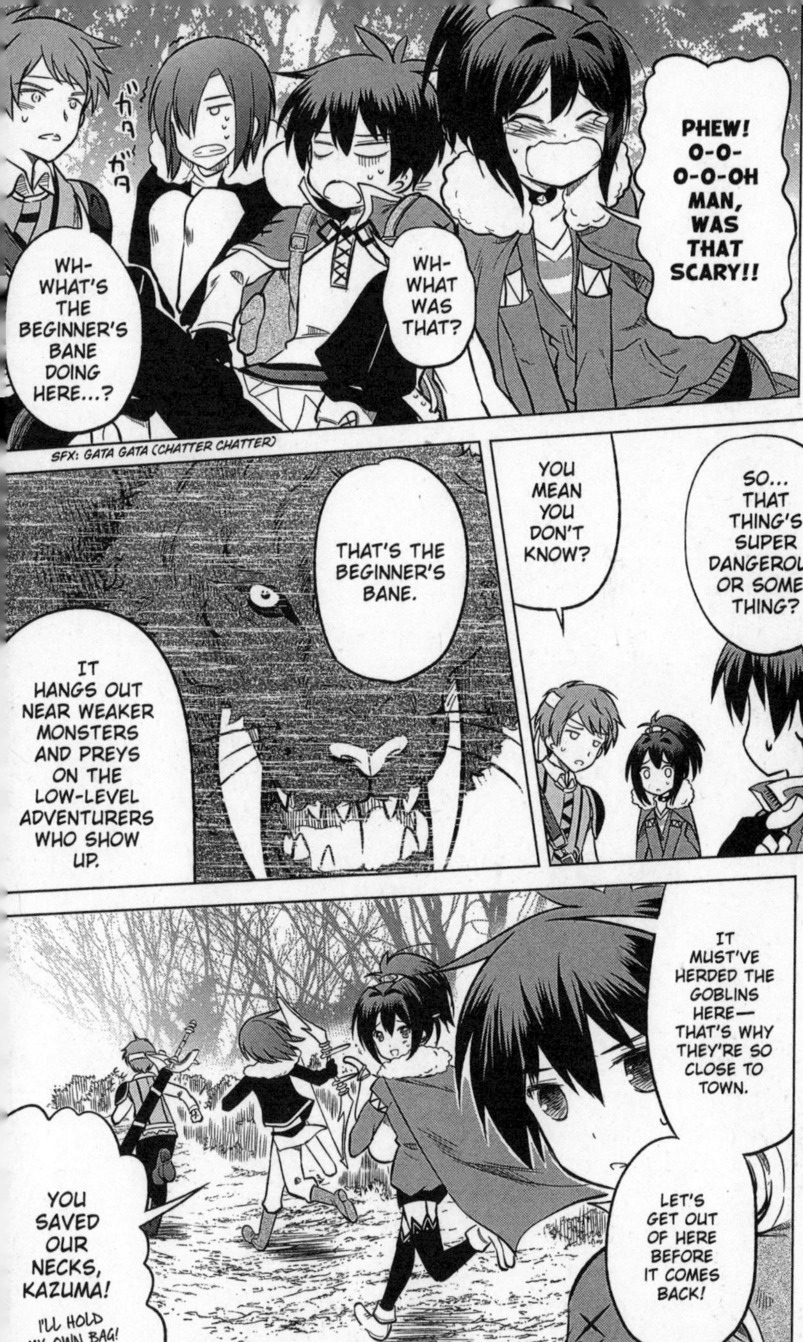
PHEW! O-O-O-O-OH MAN, WAS THAT SCARY!!
WH-WHAT WAS THAT?
WH-WHAT'S THE BEGINNER'S BANE DOING HERE...?
SFX: GATA GATA (CHATTER CHATTER)
SO... THAT THING'S SUPER DANGEROUS OR SOME-THING?
YOU MEAN YOU DON'T KNOW?
THAT'S THE BEGINNER'S BANE.
IT HANGS OUT NEAR WEAKER MONSTERS AND PREYS ON THE LOW-LEVEL ADVENTURERS WHO SHOW UP.
IT MUST'VE HERDED THE GOBLINS HERE—THAT'S WHY THEY'RE SO CLOSE TO TOWN.
LET'S GET OUT OF HERE BEFORE IT COMES BACK!
YOU SAVED OUR NECKS, KAZUMA!
I'LL HOLD MY OWN BAG!

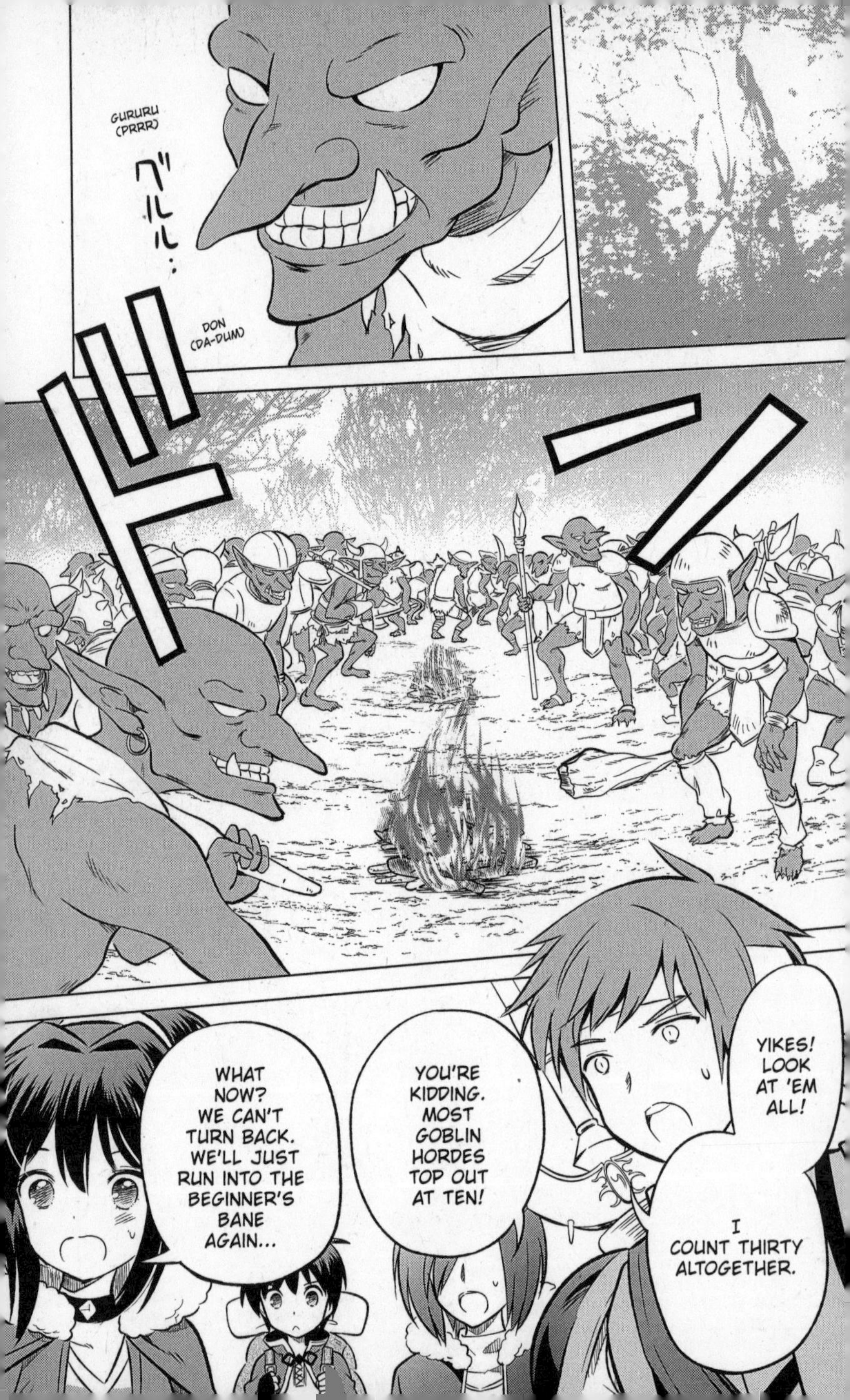
GURURU (PRRR)
ベルル…
DON (DA-DUM)
ドーン
YIKES! LOOK AT 'EM ALL!
I COUNT THIRTY ALTOGETHER.
YOU'RE KIDDING. MOST GOBLIN HORDES TOP OUT AT TEN!
WHAT NOW? WE CAN'T TURN BACK. WE'LL JUST RUN INTO THE BEGINNER'S BANE AGAIN...

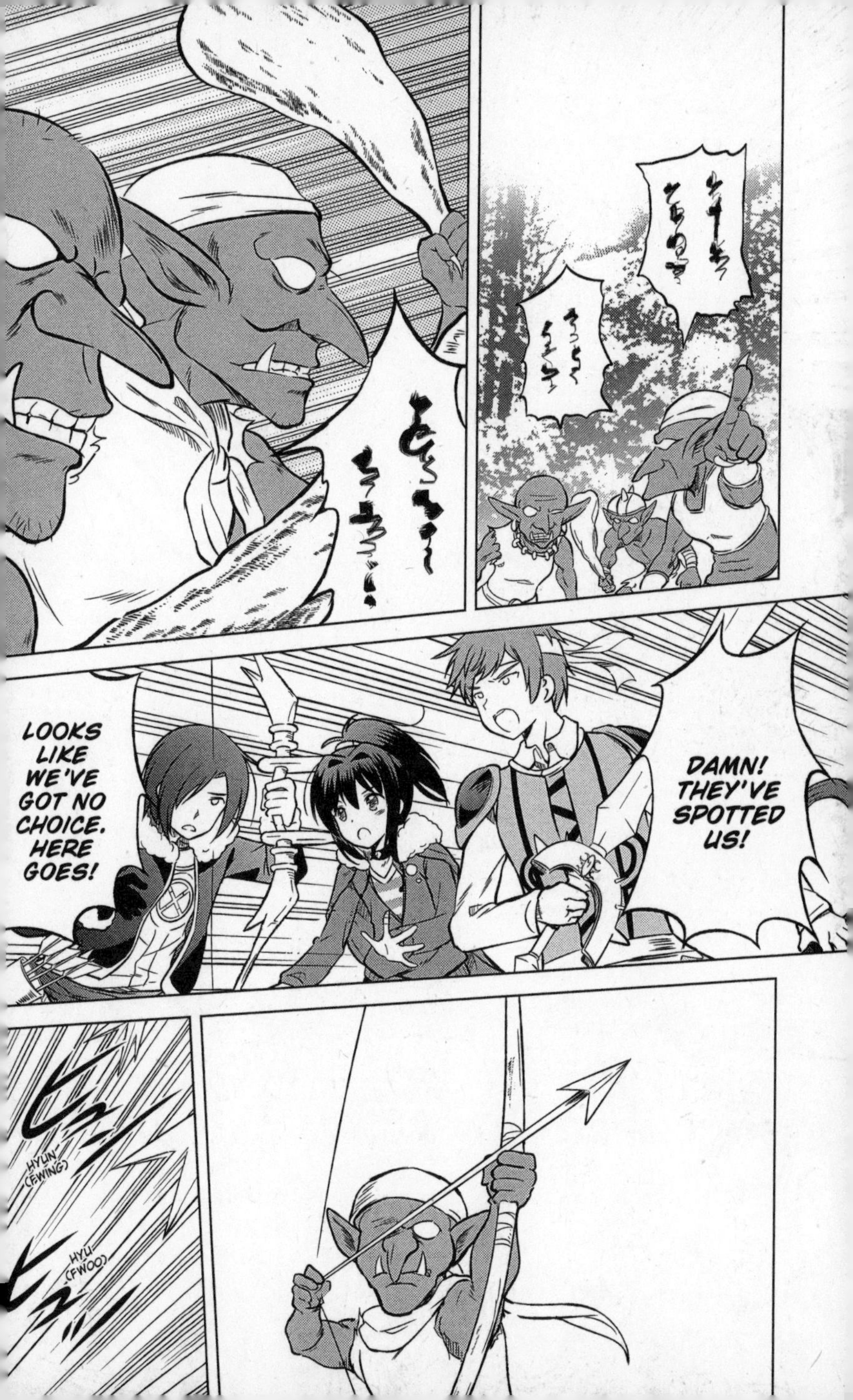
DAMN! THEY'VE SPOTTED US!
LOOKS LIKE WE'VE GOT NO CHOICE. HERE GOES!
HYUN- (FWING)
HYU (FWOO)

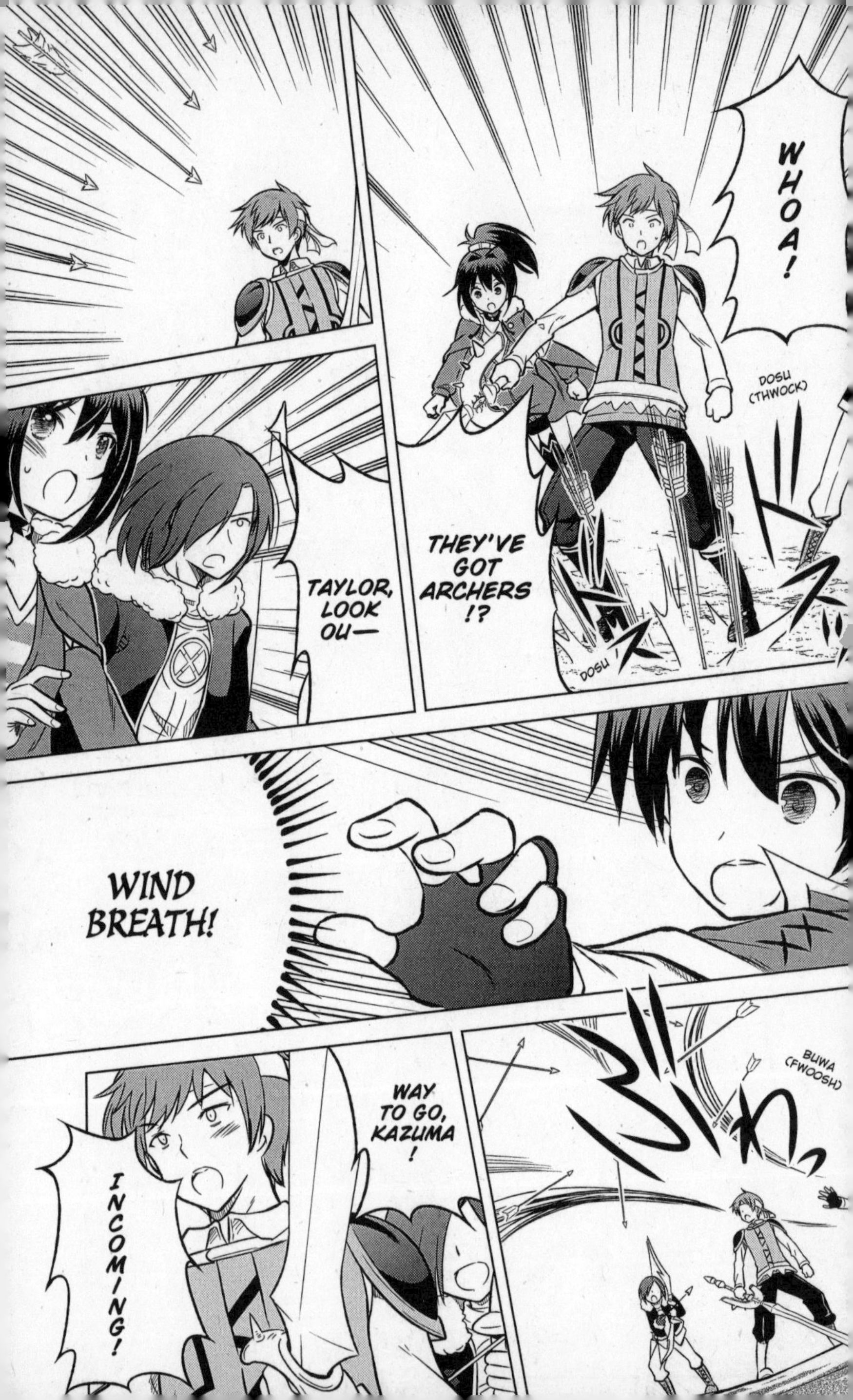
WHOA!
DOSU (THWOCK)
THEY'VE GOT ARCHERS!?
DOSU
TAYLOR, LOOK OU—
WIND BREATH!
BUWA (FWOOSH)
WAY TO GO, KAZUMA!
INCOMING!

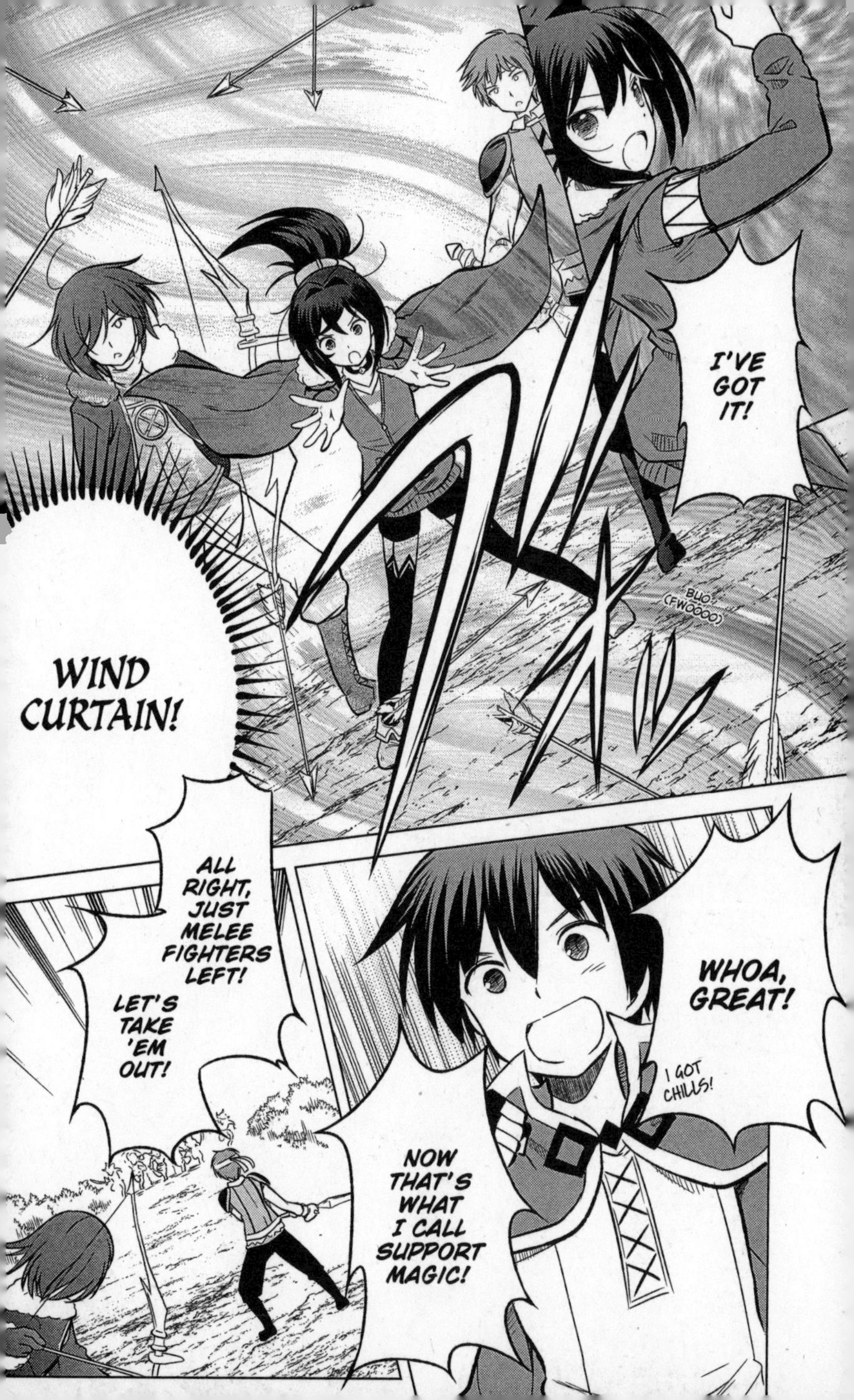
I'VE GOT IT!
BUO... (FWOOOO)
WIND CURTAIN!
WHOA, GREAT!
I GOT CHILLS!
NOW THAT'S WHAT I CALL SUPPORT MAGIC!
ALL RIGHT, JUST MELEE FIGHTERS LEFT!
LET'S TAKE 'EM OUT!

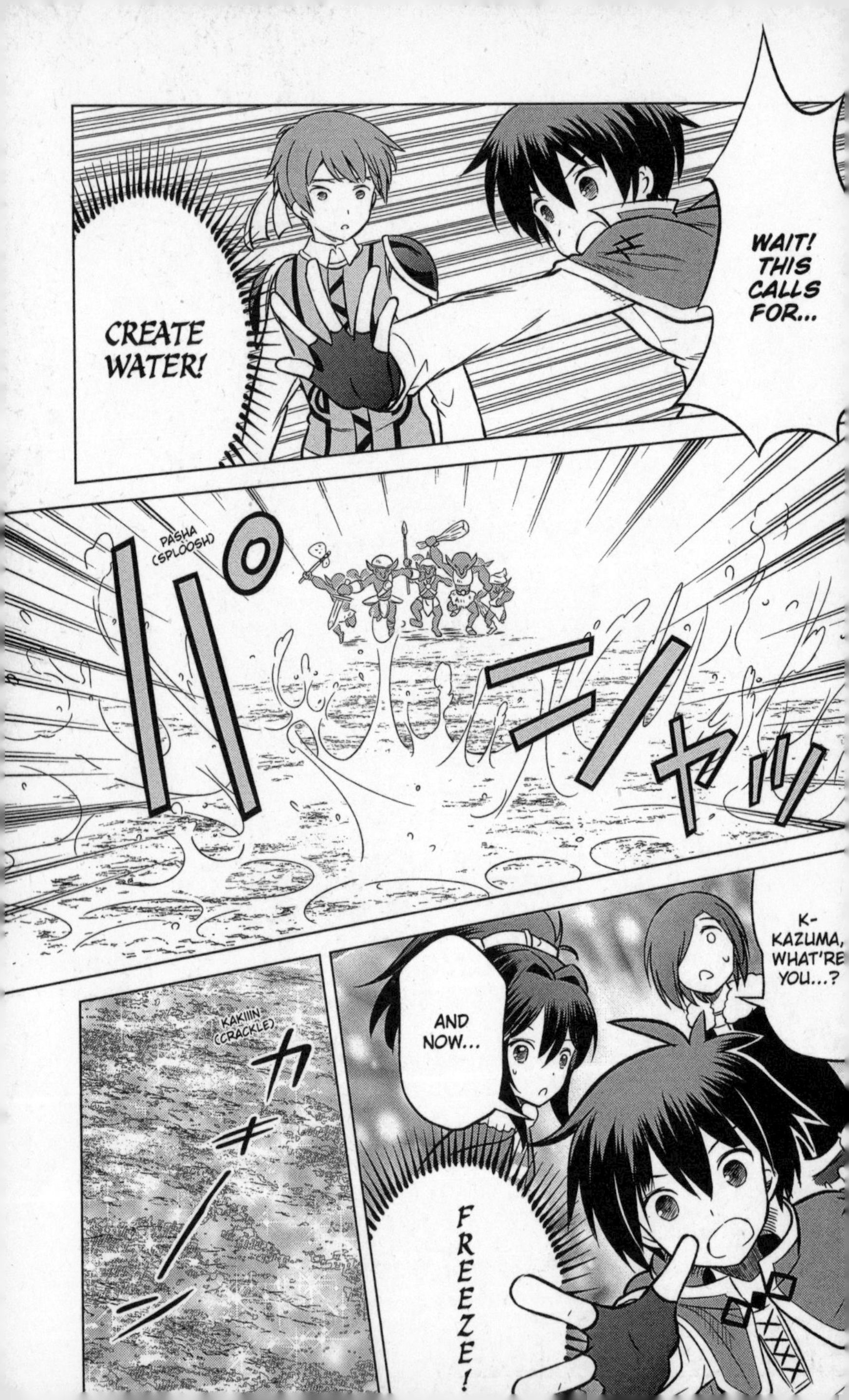
WAIT! THIS CALLS FOR...
CREATE WATER!
PASHA (SPLOOSH)
パシャッ
K-KAZUMA, WHAT'RE YOU...?
AND NOW...
FREEZE!
KAKIIN (CRACKLE)
カキーン

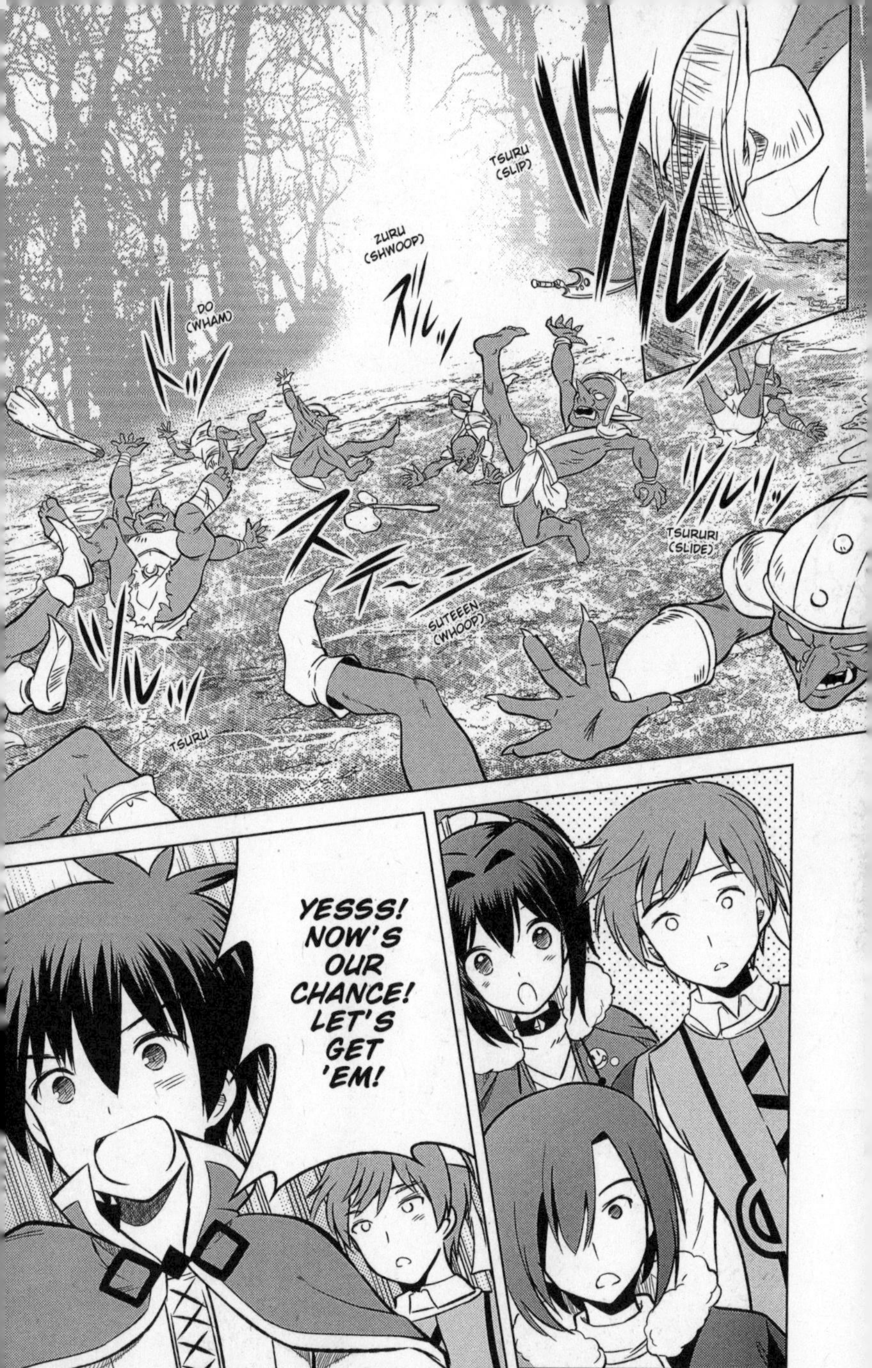
TSURU (SLIP)
ZURU (SHWOOP)
DO (WHAM)
TSURURI (SLIDE)
SUTEEEN (WHOOP)
TSURU
YESSS! NOW'S OUR CHANCE! LET'S GET 'EM!

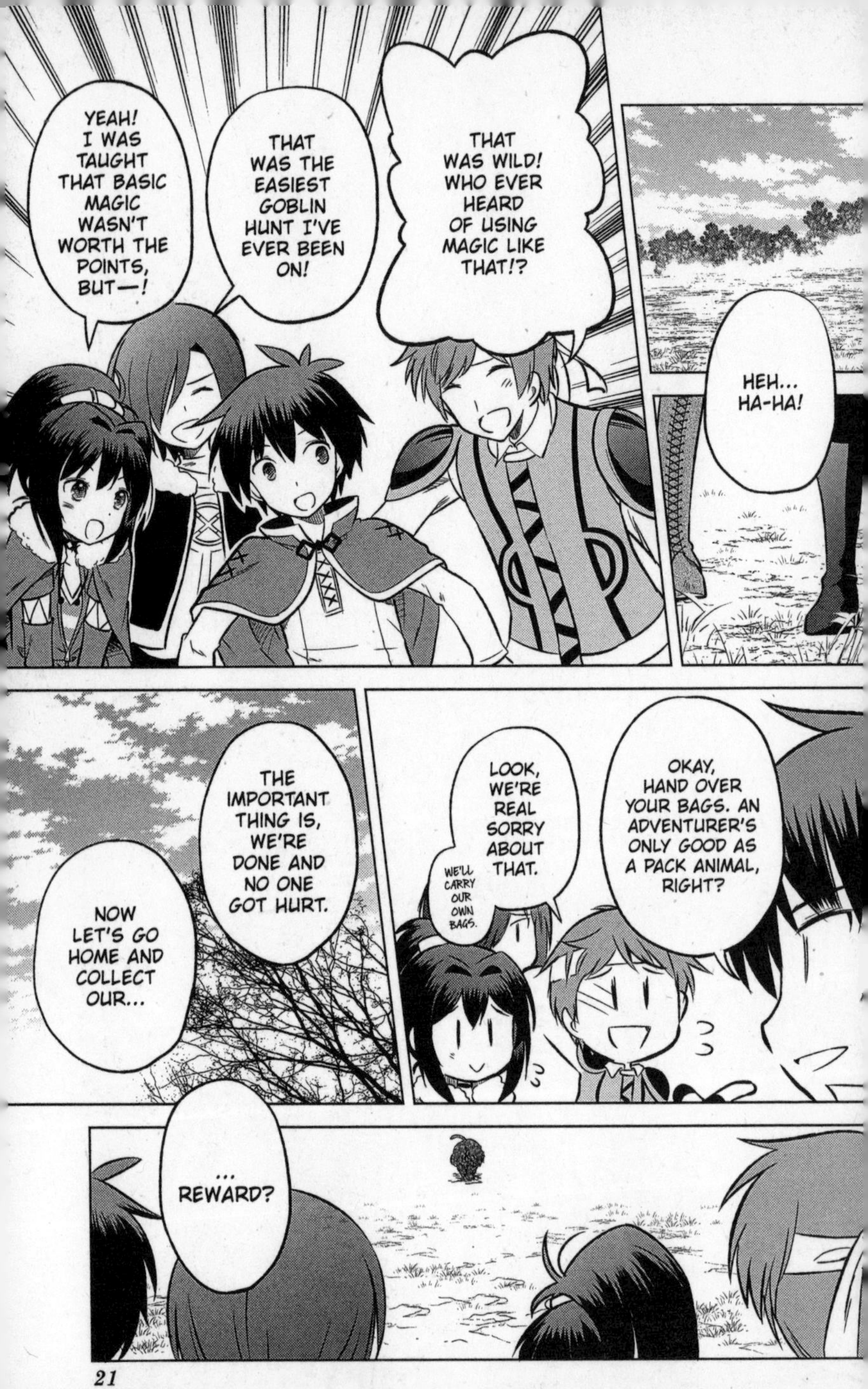
HEH... HA-HA!
THAT WAS WILD! WHO EVER HEARD OF USING MAGIC LIKE THAT!?
THAT WAS THE EASIEST GOBLIN HUNT I'VE EVER BEEN ON!
YEAH! I WAS TAUGHT THAT BASIC MAGIC WASN'T WORTH THE POINTS, BUT—!
OKAY, HAND OVER YOUR BAGS. AN ADVENTURER'S ONLY GOOD AS A PACK ANIMAL, RIGHT?
LOOK, WE'RE REAL SORRY ABOUT THAT.
WE'LL CARRY OUR OWN BAGS.
THE IMPORTANT THING IS, WE'RE DONE AND NO ONE GOT HURT.
NOW LET'S GO HOME AND COLLECT OUR...
... REWARD?

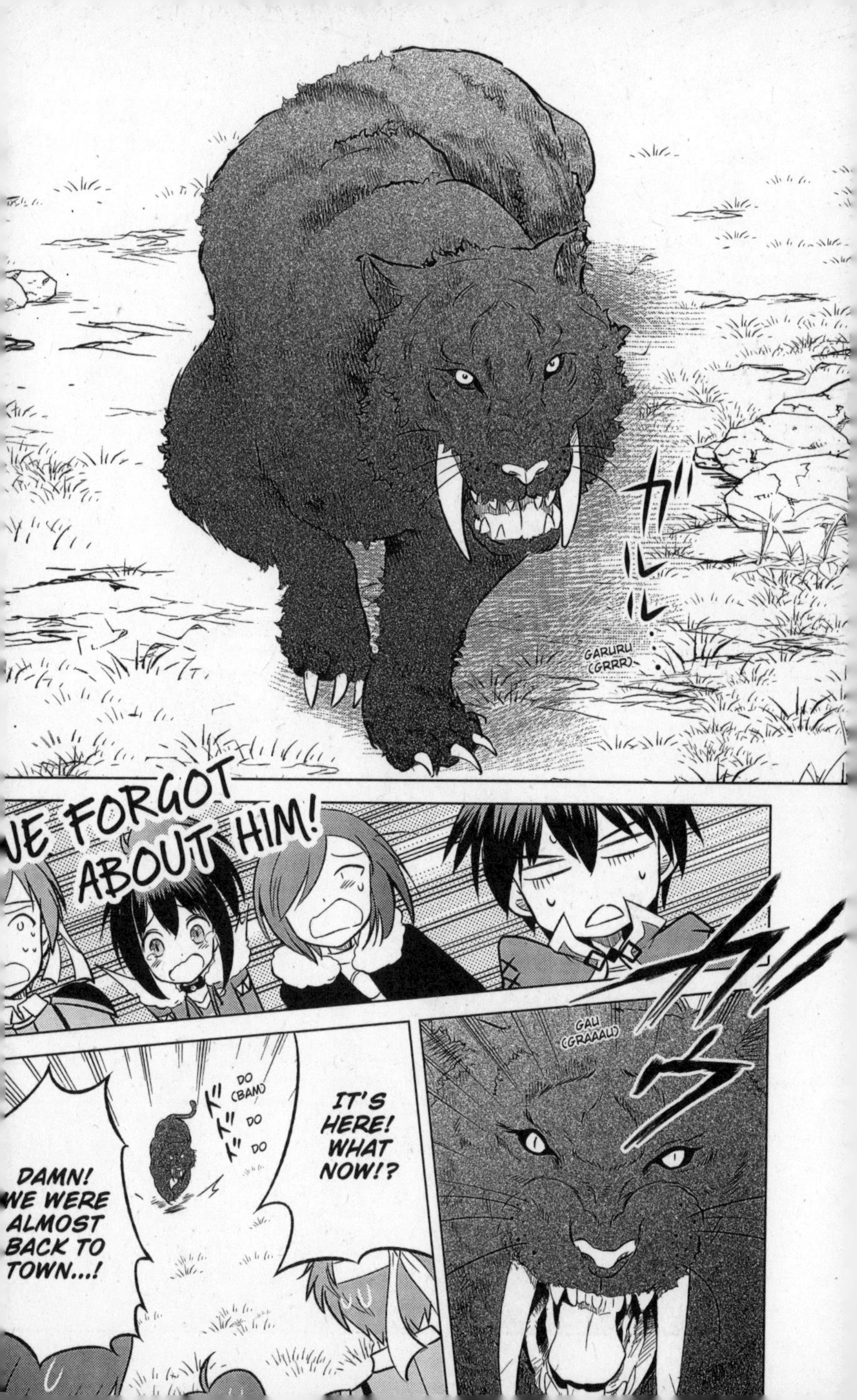

ガルル
GARURU (GRRR)
WE FORGOT ABOUT HIM!
ガウ
GAU (GRAAAU)
IT'S HERE! WHAT NOW!?
ドドド
DO (BAM) DO DO
DAMN! WE WERE ALMOST BACK TO TOWN...!

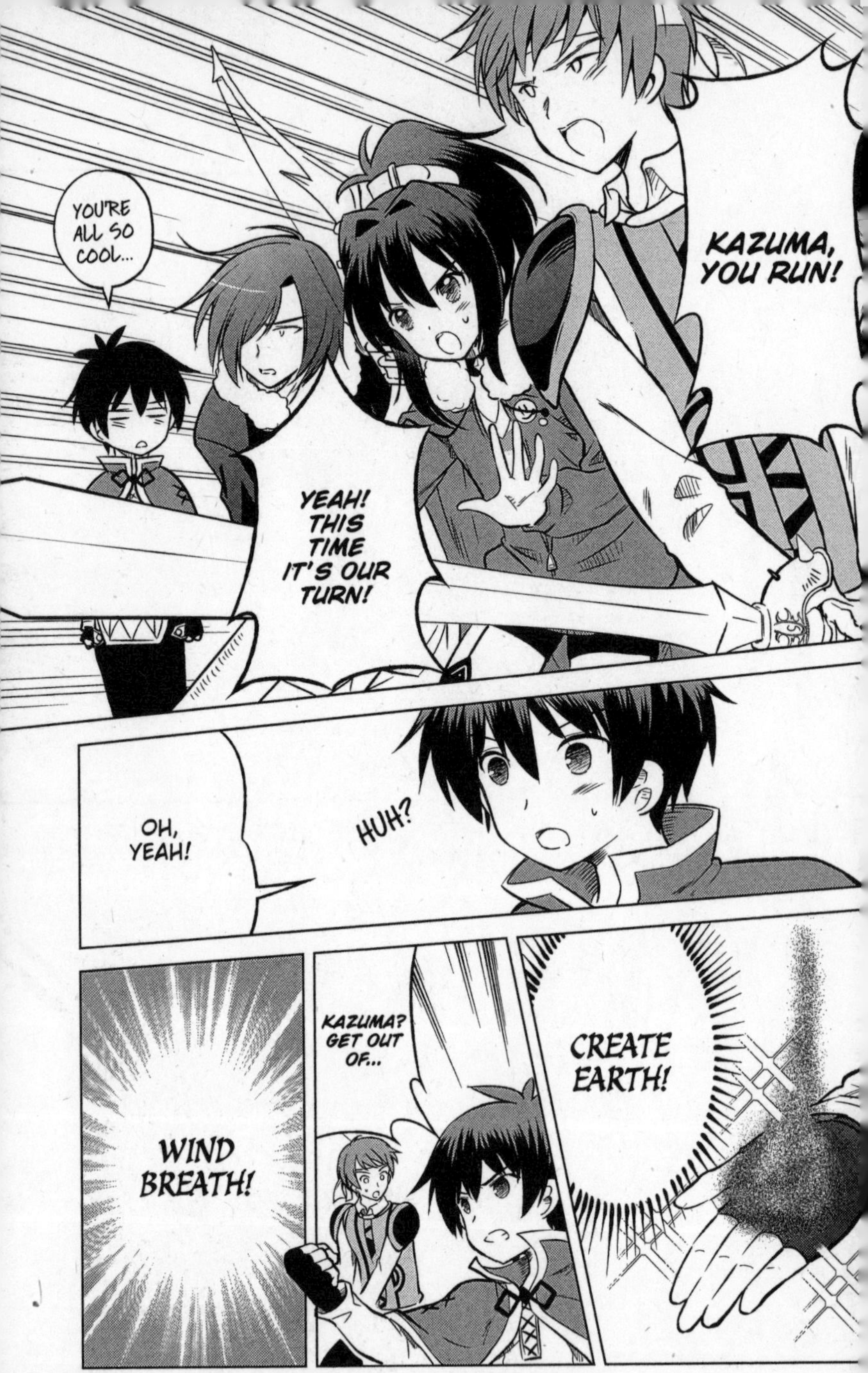
KAZUMA, YOU RUN!
YEAH! THIS TIME IT'S OUR TURN!
YOU'RE ALL SO COOL...
HUH?
OH, YEAH!
CREATE EARTH!
KAZUMA? GET OUT OF...
WIND BREATH!

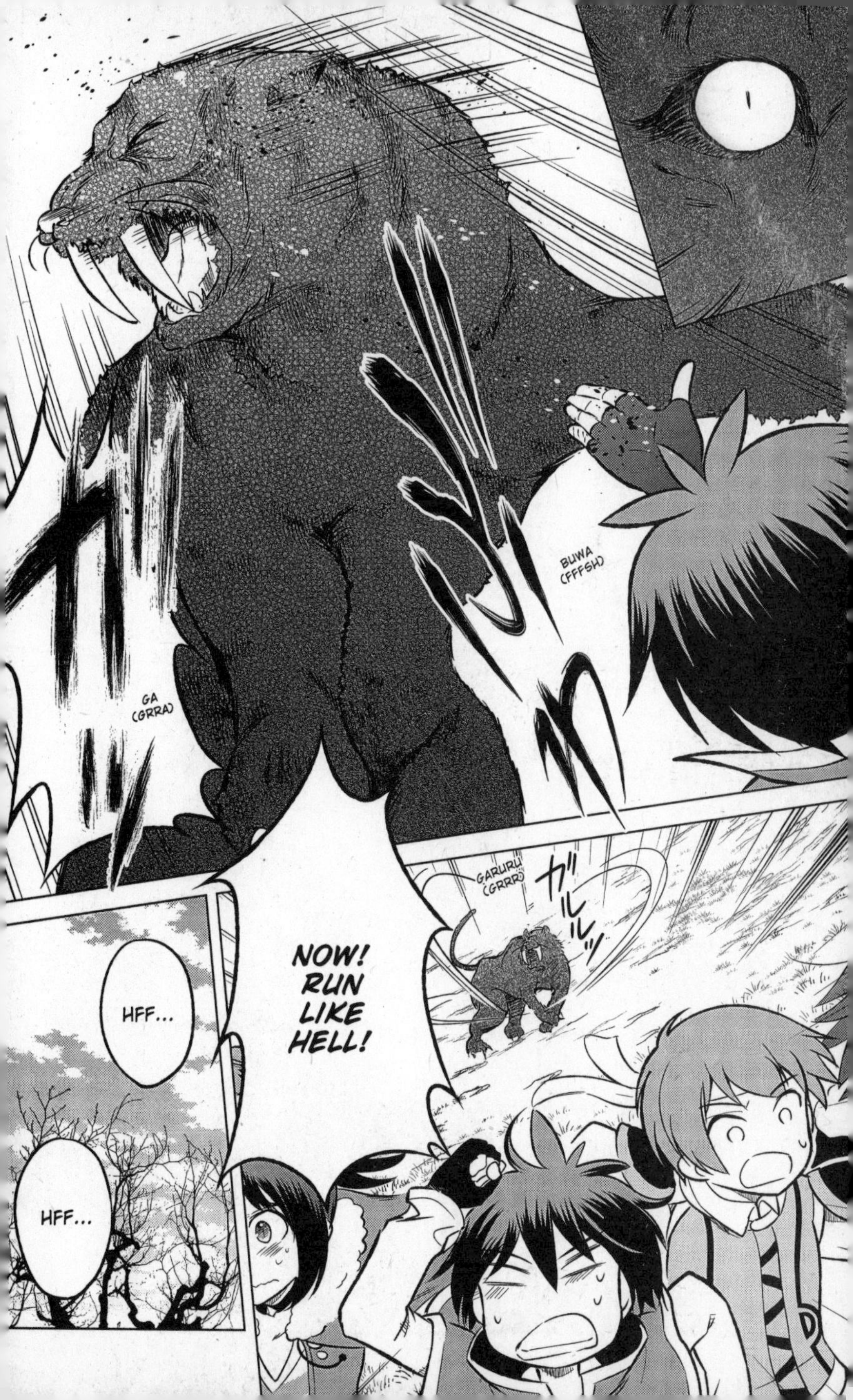
BUWA (FFFSH)
GA (GRRA)
GARURU (GRRR)
ガルルッ
NOW! RUN LIKE HELL!
HFF...
HFF...

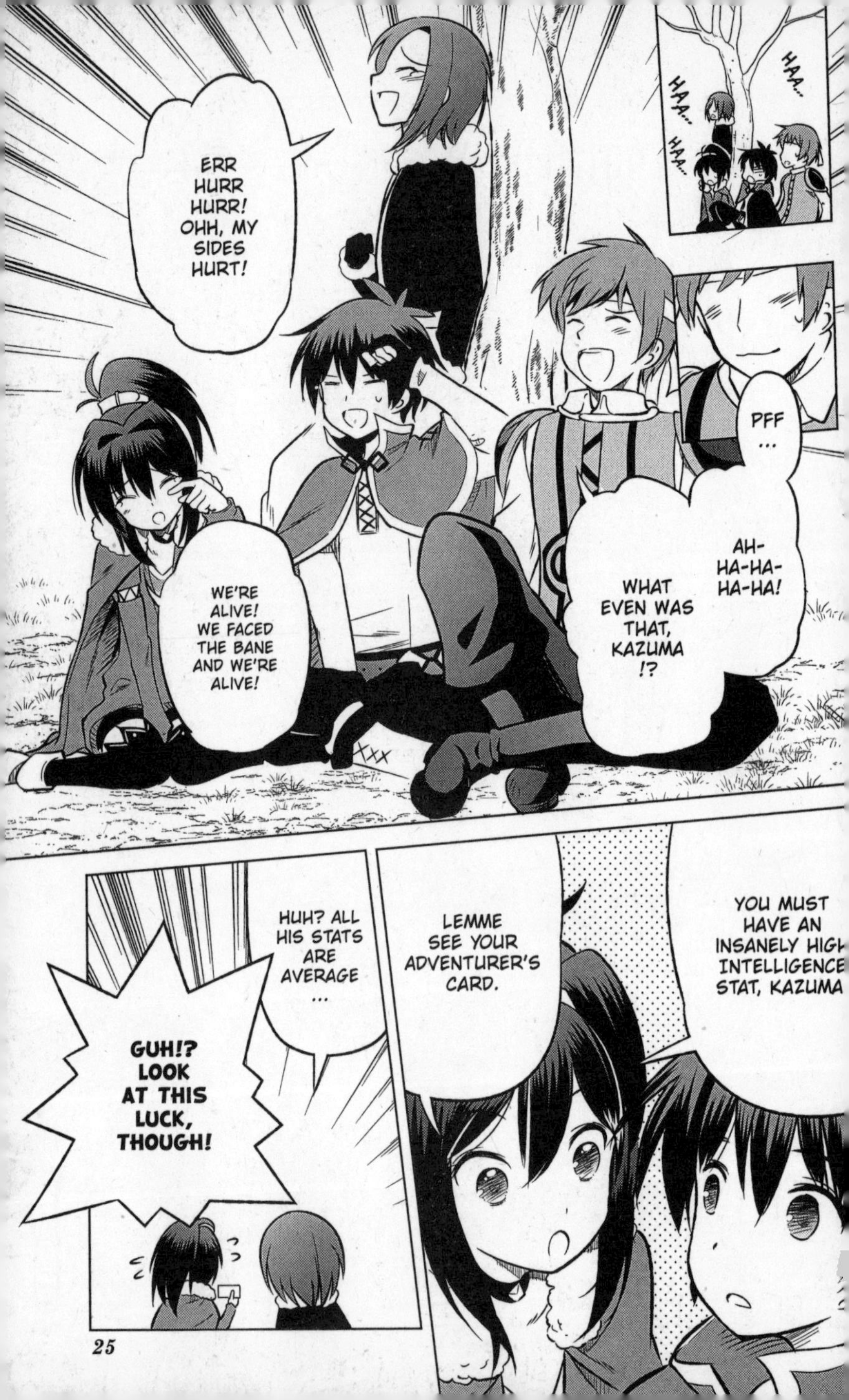
HAA... HAA... HAA... HAA...
PFF...
AH-HA-HA-HA!
WHAT EVEN WAS THAT, KAZUMA!?
ERR HURR HURR! OHH, MY SIDES HURT!
WE'RE ALIVE! WE FACED THE BANE AND WE'RE ALIVE!
YOU MUST HAVE AN INSANELY HIGH INTELLIGENCE STAT, KAZUMA
LEMME SEE YOUR ADVENTURER'S CARD.
HUH? ALL HIS STATS ARE AVERAGE...
GUH!? LOOK AT THIS LUCK, THOUGH!

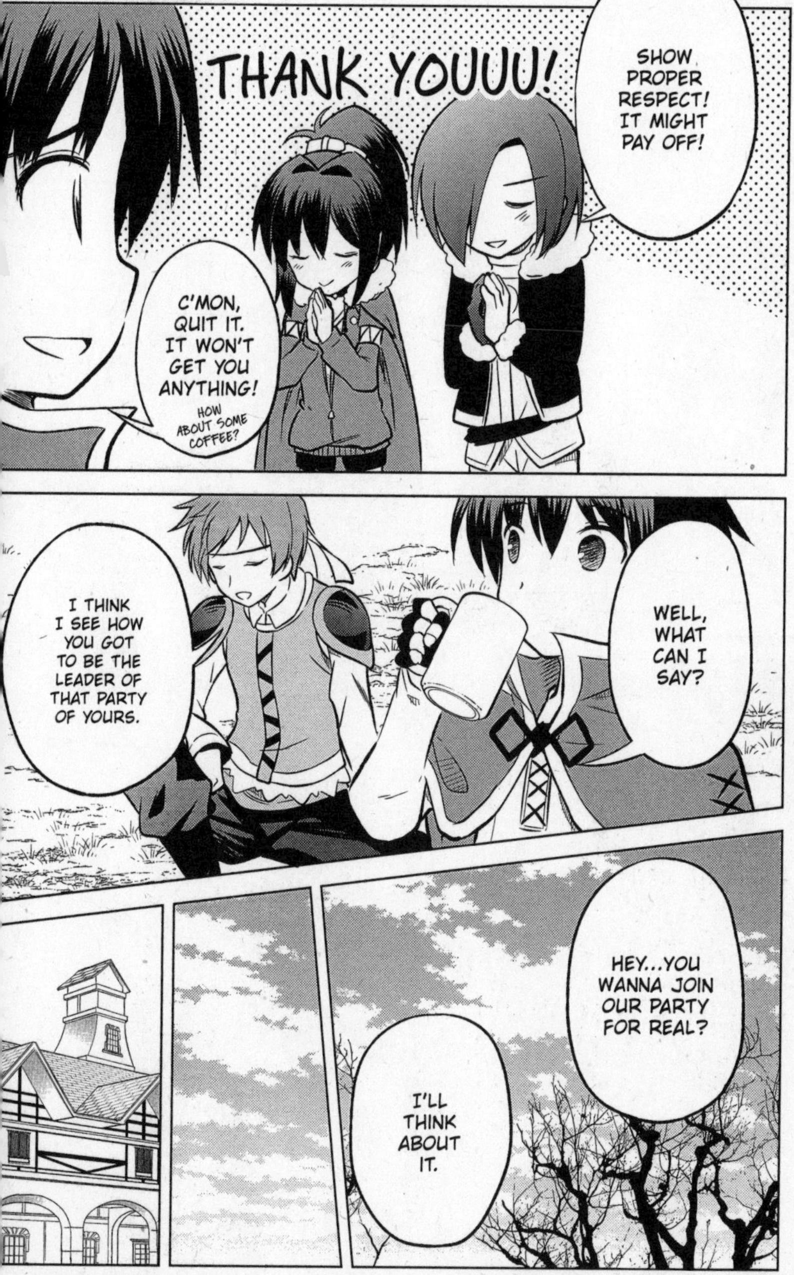
SHOW PROPER RESPECT! IT MIGHT PAY OFF!
THANK YOUUU!
C'MON, QUIT IT. IT WON'T GET YOU ANYTHING!
HOW ABOUT SOME COFFEE?
WELL, WHAT CAN I SAY?
I THINK I SEE HOW YOU GOT TO BE THE LEADER OF THAT PARTY OF YOURS.
HEY...YOU WANNA JOIN OUR PARTY FOR REAL?
I'LL THINK ABOUT IT.

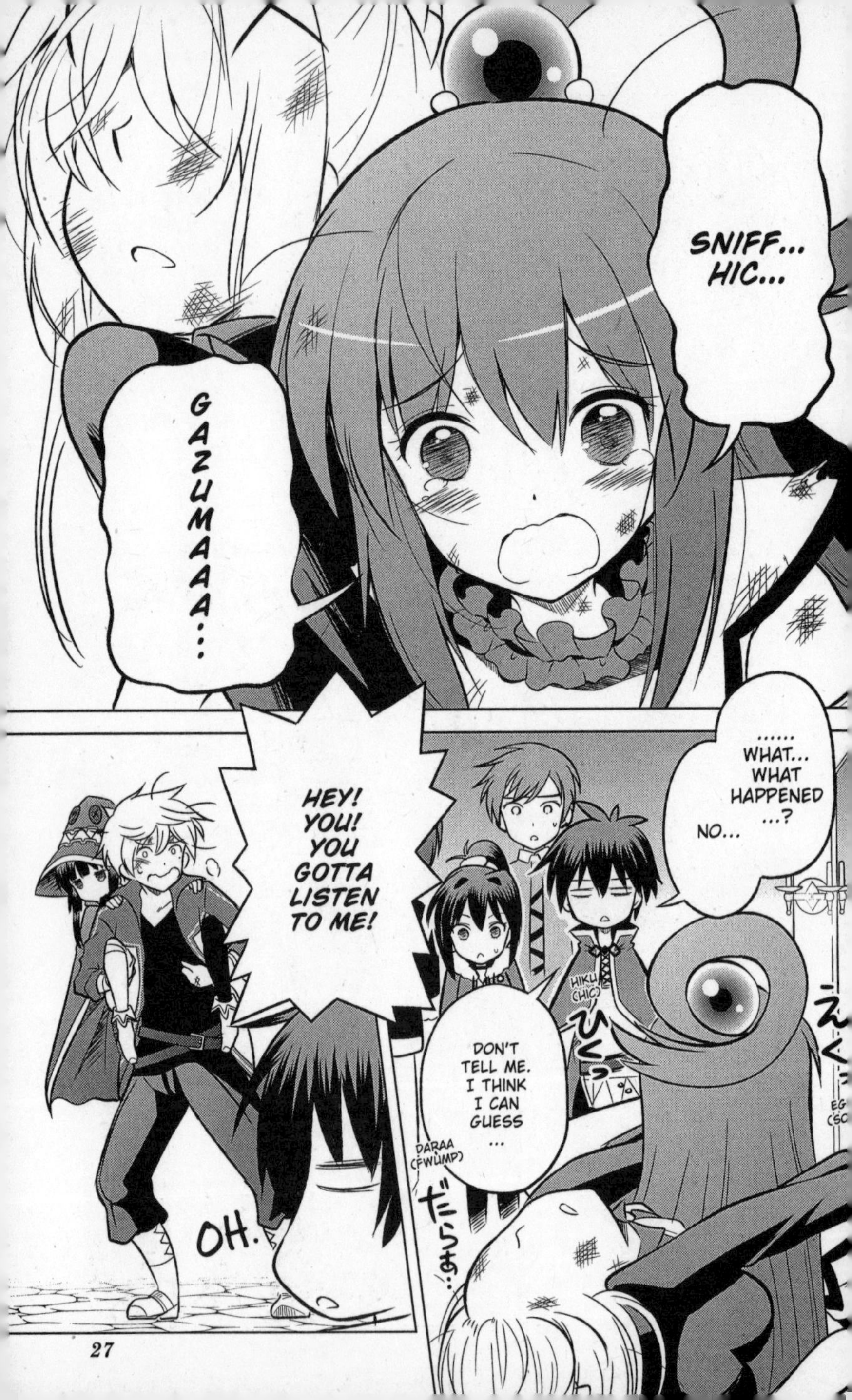
SNIFF... HIC...
GAZUMAAAA...
...... WHAT... WHAT HAPPENED ...?
NO...
HEY! YOU! YOU GOTTA LISTEN TO ME!
えぐっ
HIKU (HIC)
ひくっ
DON'T TELL ME. I THINK I CAN GUESS ...
DARAA (FWUMP)
だらぁ…
OH.

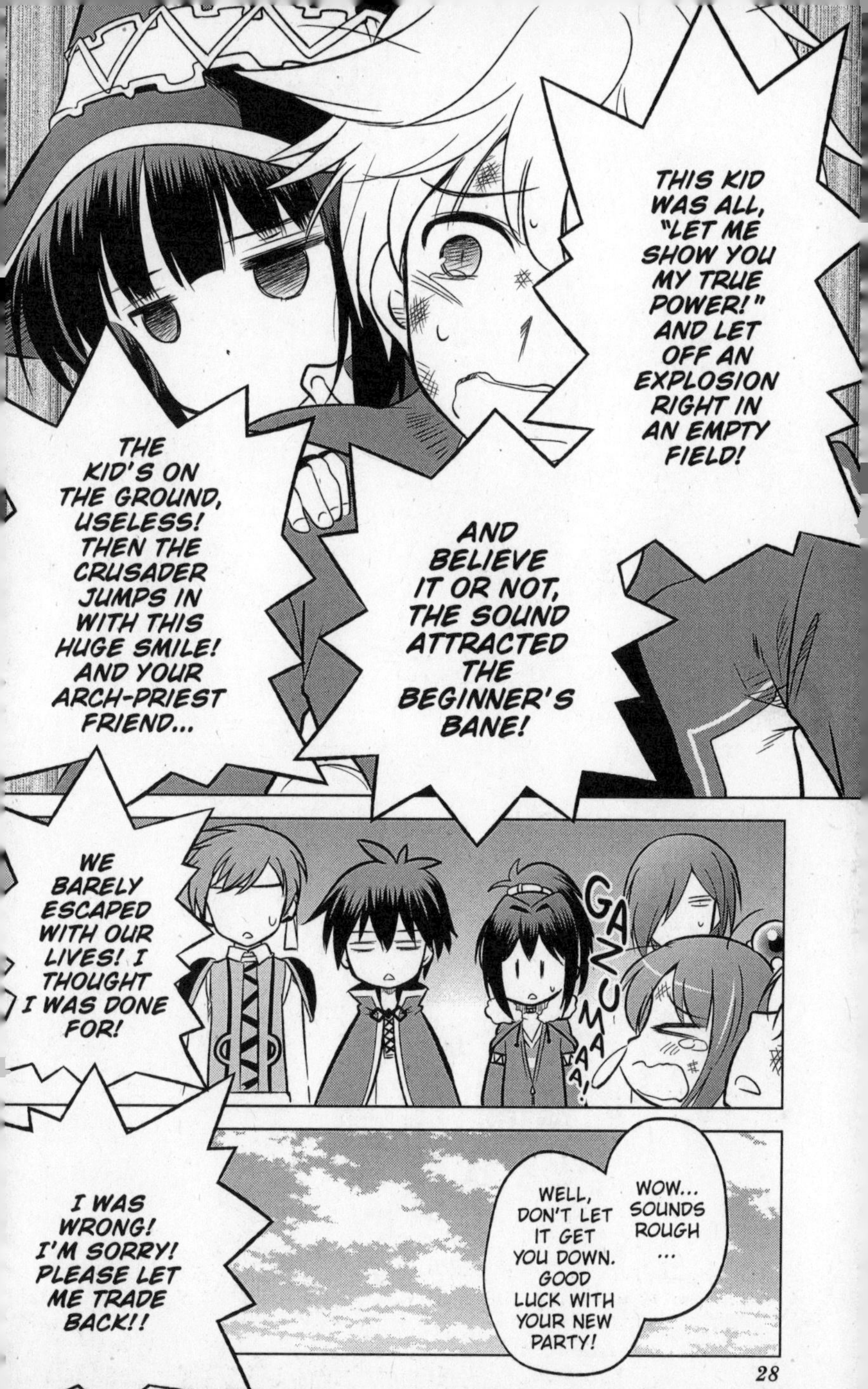
THIS KID WAS ALL, "LET ME SHOW YOU MY TRUE POWER!" AND LET OFF AN EXPLOSION RIGHT IN AN EMPTY FIELD!
THE KID'S ON THE GROUND, USELESS! THEN THE CRUSADER JUMPS IN WITH THIS HUGE SMILE! AND YOUR ARCH-PRIEST FRIEND...
AND BELIEVE IT OR NOT, THE SOUND ATTRACTED THE BEGINNER'S BANE!
GAZUMAAA!
WE BARELY ESCAPED WITH OUR LIVES! I THOUGHT I WAS DONE FOR!
WOW... SOUNDS ROUGH...
WELL, DON'T LET IT GET YOU DOWN. GOOD LUCK WITH YOUR NEW PARTY!
I WAS WRONG! I'M SORRY! PLEASE LET ME TRADE BACK!!

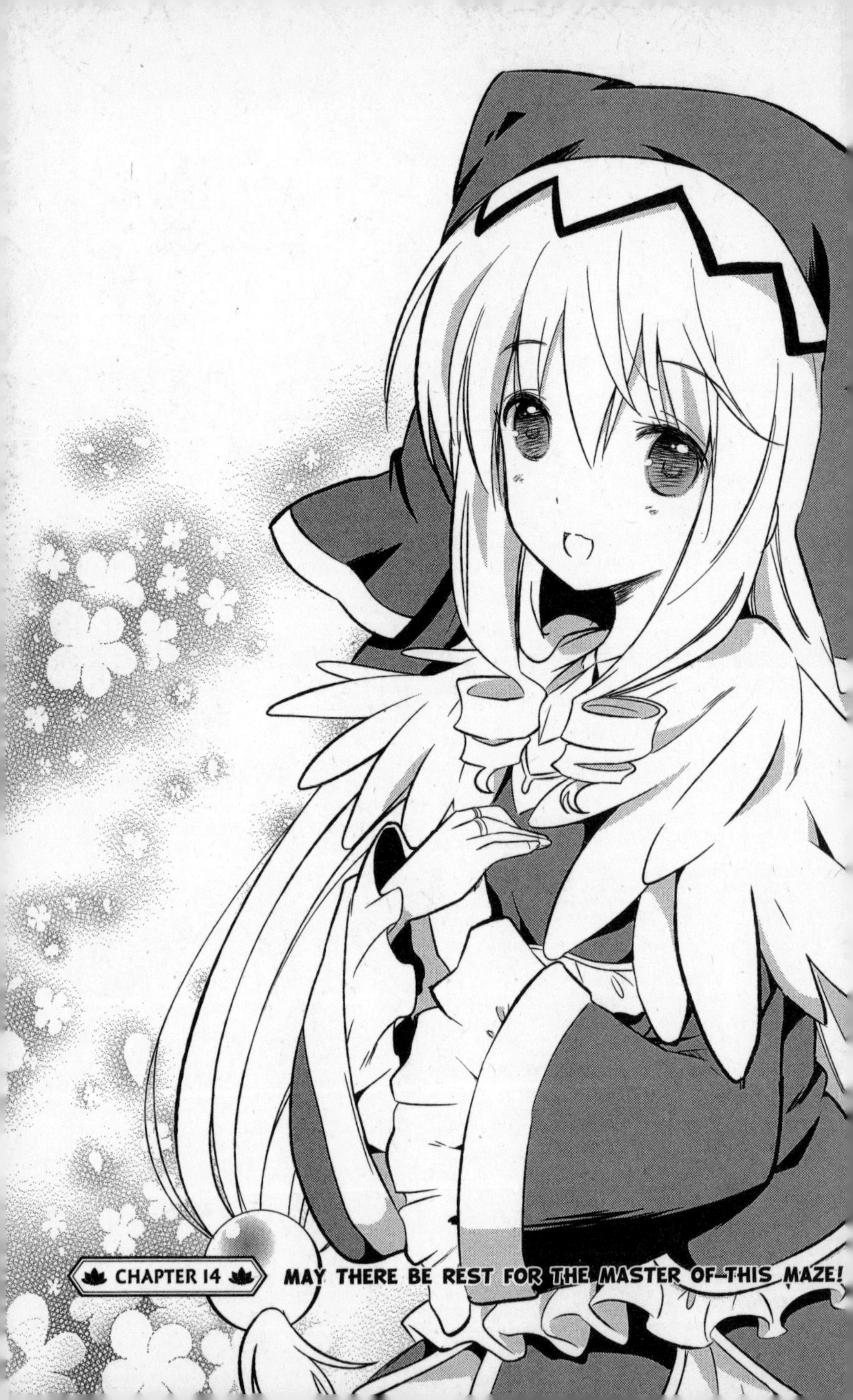
CHAPTER 14
MAY THERE BE REST FOR THE MASTER OF THIS MAZE!

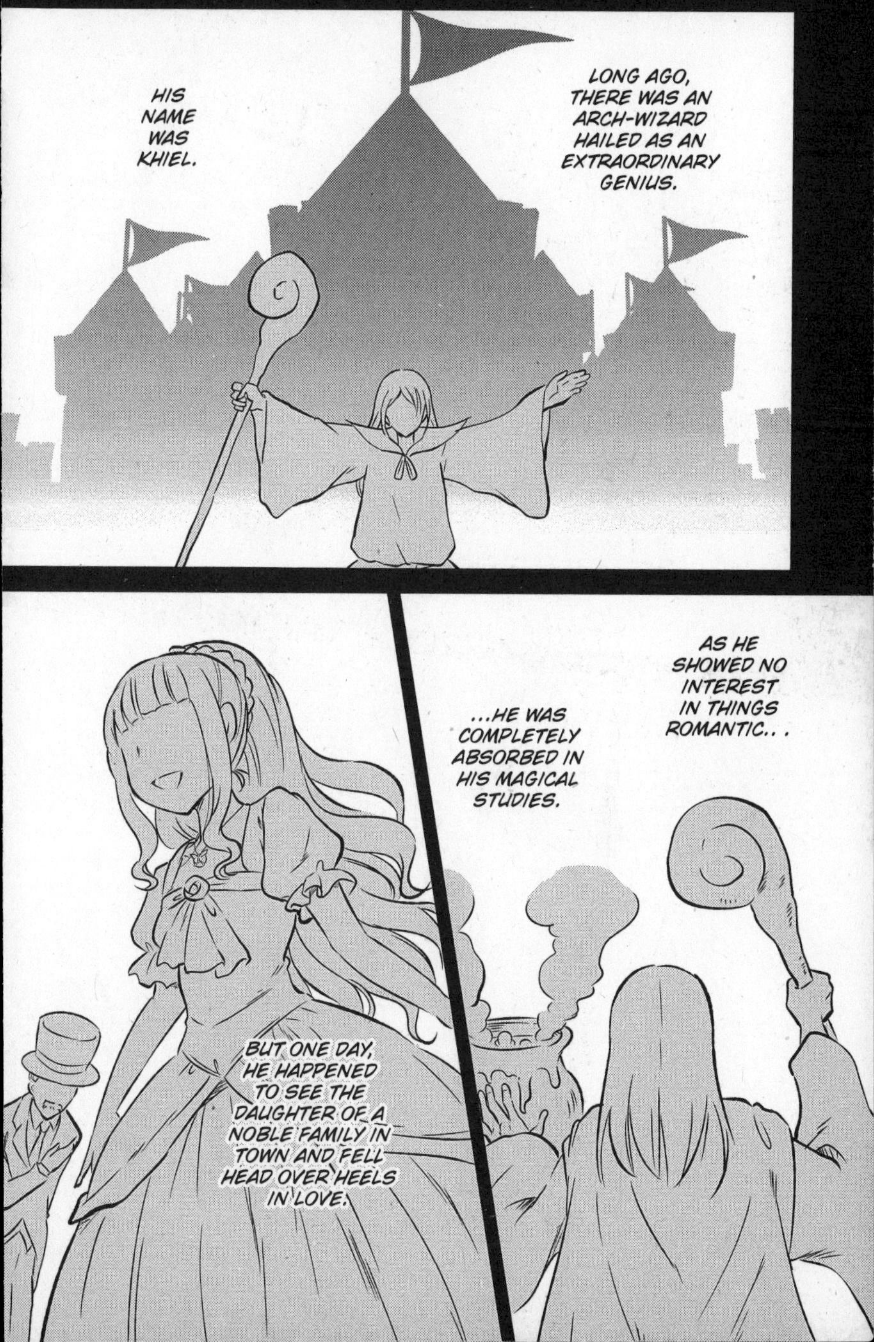
LONG AGO, THERE WAS AN ARCH-WIZARD HAILED AS AN EXTRAORDINARY GENIUS.
HIS NAME WAS KHIEL.
AS HE SHOWED NO INTEREST IN THINGS ROMANTIC. . .
...HE WAS COMPLETELY ABSORBED IN HIS MAGICAL STUDIES.
BUT ONE DAY, HE HAPPENED TO SEE THE DAUGHTER OF A NOBLE FAMILY IN TOWN AND FELL HEAD OVER HEELS IN LOVE.

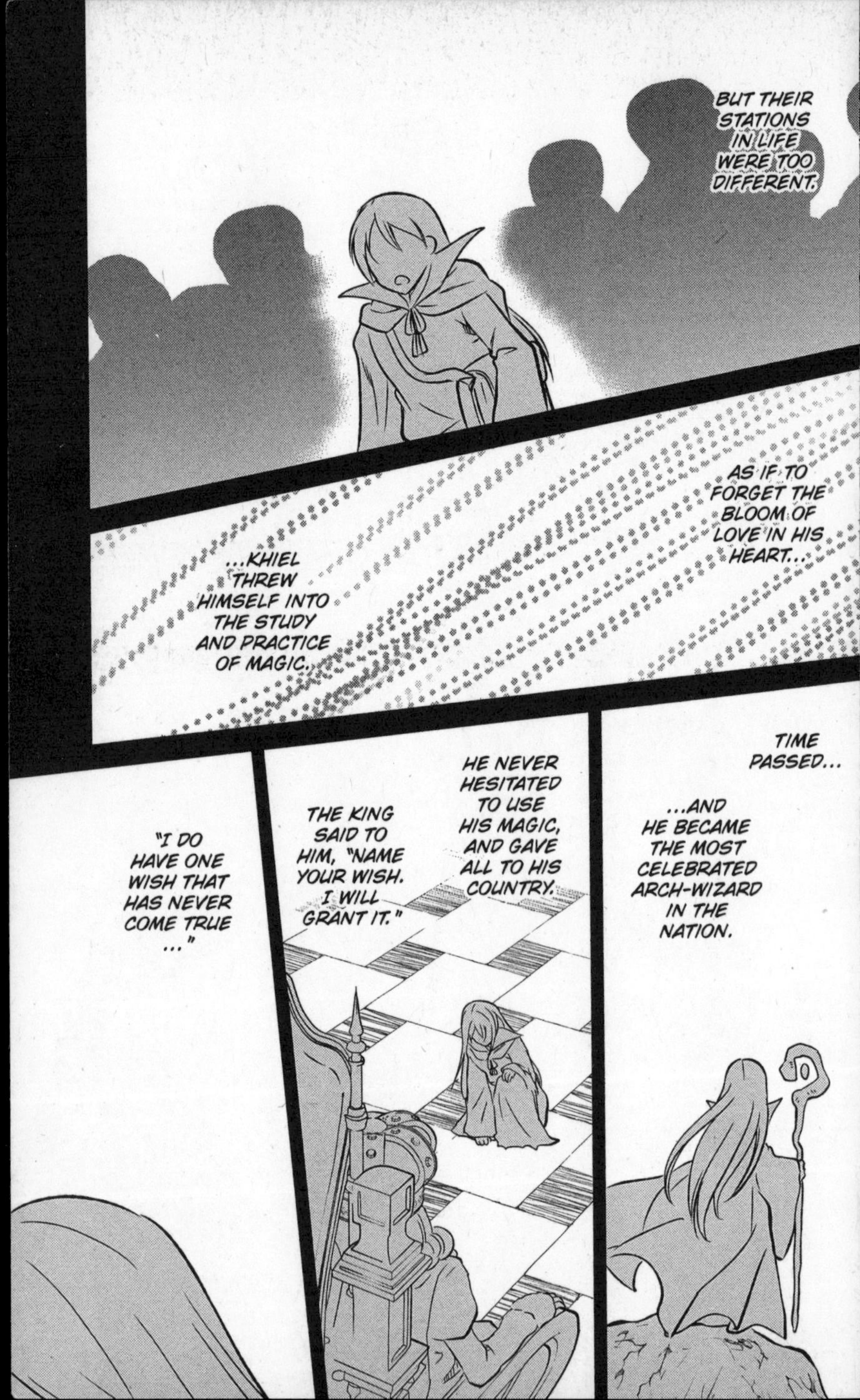
BUT THEIR STATIONS IN LIFE WERE TOO DIFFERENT.
AS IF TO FORGET THE BLOOM OF LOVE IN HIS HEART...
...KHIEL THREW HIMSELF INTO THE STUDY AND PRACTICE OF MAGIC.
TIME PASSED...
...AND HE BECAME THE MOST CELEBRATED ARCH-WIZARD IN THE NATION.
HE NEVER HESITATED TO USE HIS MAGIC, AND GAVE ALL TO HIS COUNTRY.
THE KING SAID TO HIM, "NAME YOUR WISH. I WILL GRANT IT."
"I DO HAVE ONE WISH THAT HAS NEVER COME TRUE ..."

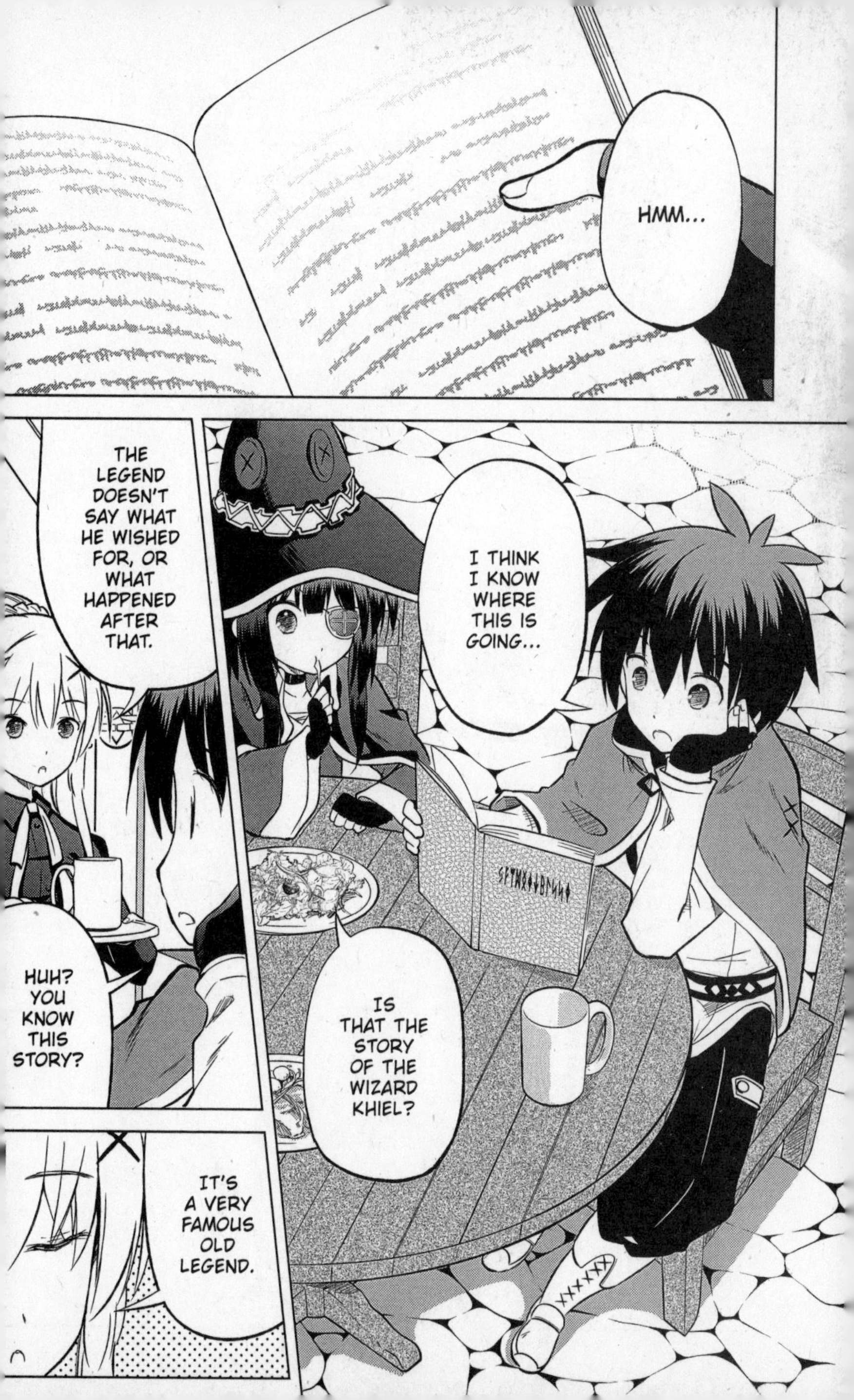
HMM...
I THINK I KNOW WHERE THIS IS GOING...
IS THAT THE STORY OF THE WIZARD KHIEL?
THE LEGEND DOESN'T SAY WHAT HE WISHED FOR, OR WHAT HAPPENED AFTER THAT.
HUH? YOU KNOW THIS STORY?
IT'S A VERY FAMOUS OLD LEGEND.

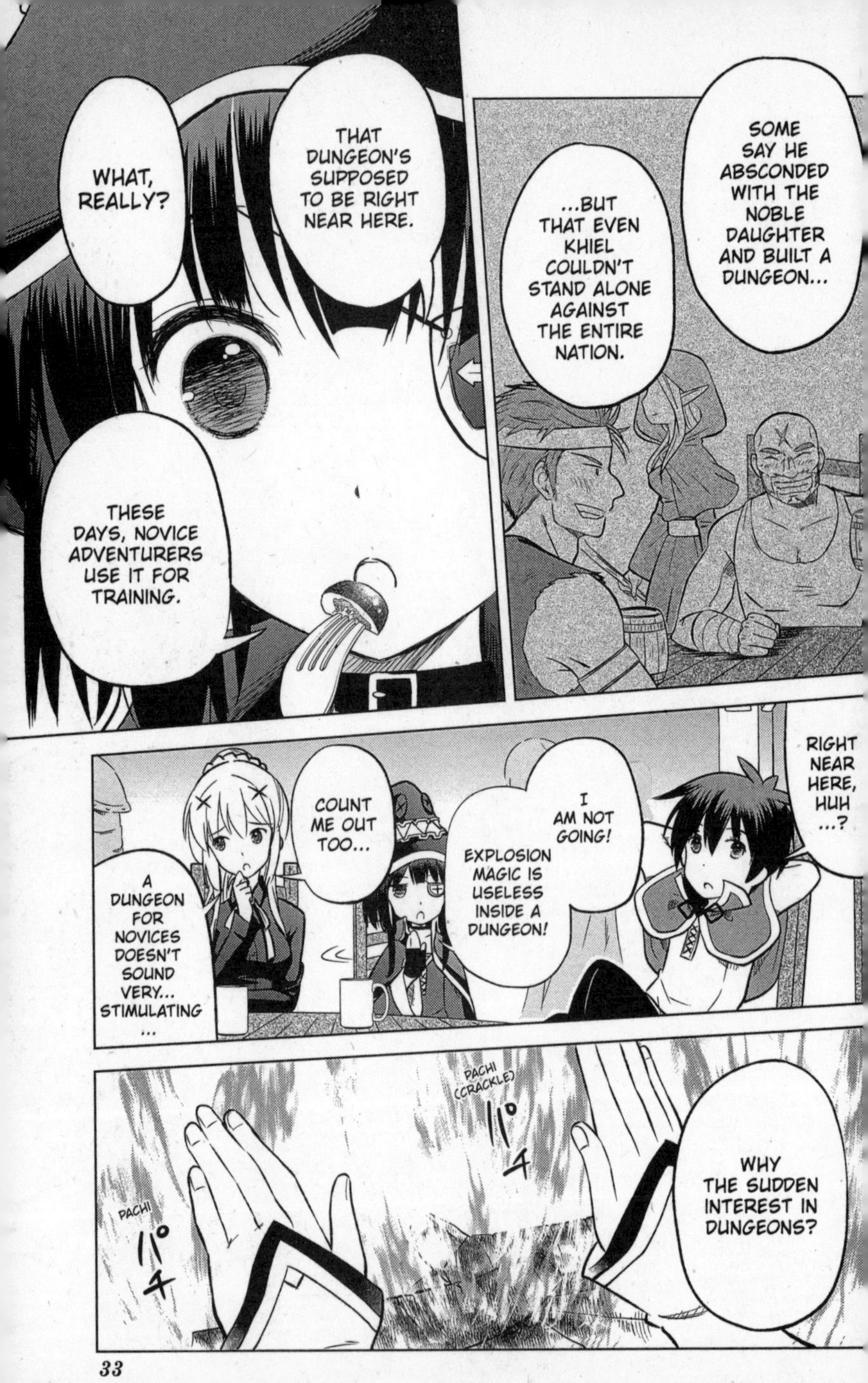
SOME SAY HE ABSCONDED WITH THE NOBLE DAUGHTER AND BUILT A DUNGEON...
...BUT THAT EVEN KHIEL COULDN'T STAND ALONE AGAINST THE ENTIRE NATION.
THAT DUNGEON'S SUPPOSED TO BE RIGHT NEAR HERE.
WHAT, REALLY?
THESE DAYS, NOVICE ADVENTURERS USE IT FOR TRAINING.
RIGHT NEAR HERE, HUH ...?
I AM NOT GOING!
EXPLOSION MAGIC IS USELESS INSIDE A DUNGEON!
COUNT ME OUT TOO...
A DUNGEON FOR NOVICES DOESN'T SOUND VERY... STIMULATING ...
WHY THE SUDDEN INTEREST IN DUNGEONS?
PACHI (CRACKLE)
パチ
PACHI
パチ

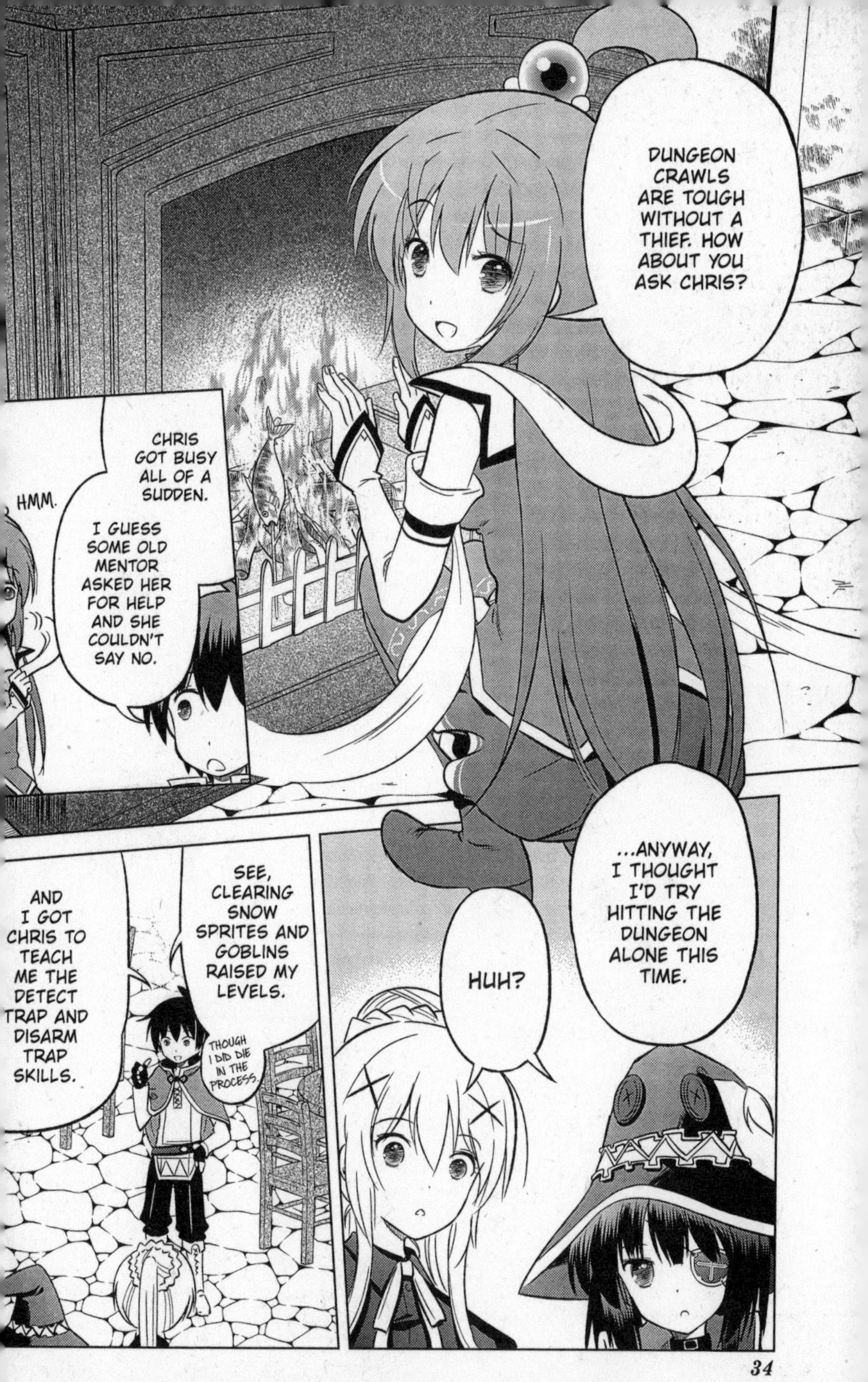
DUNGEON CRAWLS ARE TOUGH WITHOUT A THIEF. HOW ABOUT YOU ASK CHRIS?
CHRIS GOT BUSY ALL OF A SUDDEN.
I GUESS SOME OLD MENTOR ASKED HER FOR HELP AND SHE COULDN'T SAY NO.
HMM.
...ANYWAY, I THOUGHT I'D TRY HITTING THE DUNGEON ALONE THIS TIME.
HUH?
SEE, CLEARING SNOW SPRITES AND GOBLINS RAISED MY LEVELS.
THOUGH I DID DIE IN THE PROCESS.
AND I GOT CHRIS TO TEACH ME THE DETECT TRAP AND DISARM TRAP SKILLS.

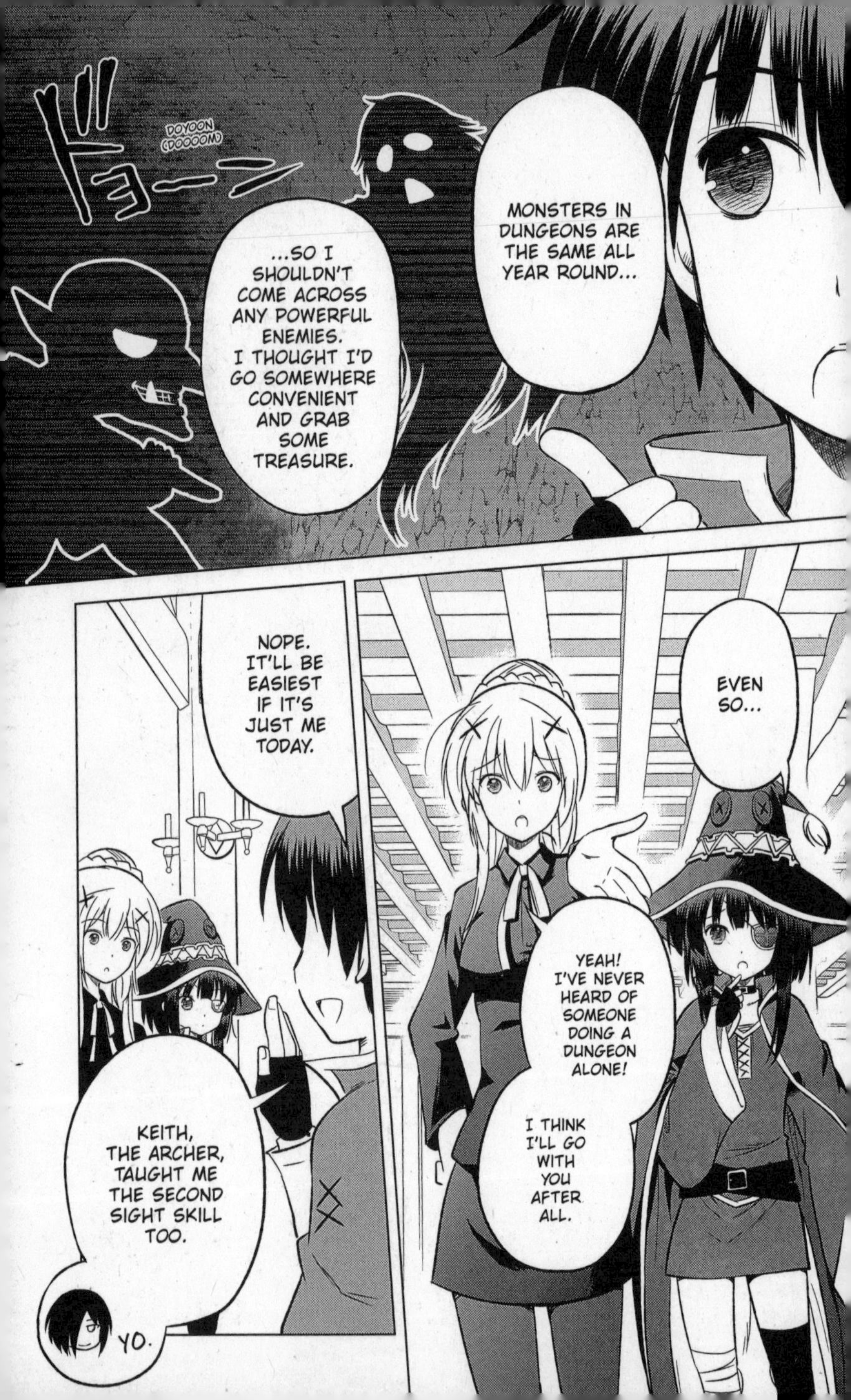
MONSTERS IN DUNGEONS ARE THE SAME ALL YEAR ROUND...
...SO I SHOULDN'T COME ACROSS ANY POWERFUL ENEMIES. I THOUGHT I'D GO SOMEWHERE CONVENIENT AND GRAB SOME TREASURE.
DOYOON (DOOOOM)
EVEN SO...
YEAH! I'VE NEVER HEARD OF SOMEONE DOING A DUNGEON ALONE!
I THINK I'LL GO WITH YOU AFTER ALL.
NOPE. IT'LL BE EASIEST IF IT'S JUST ME TODAY.
KEITH, THE ARCHER, TAUGHT ME THE SECOND SIGHT SKILL TOO.
YO.

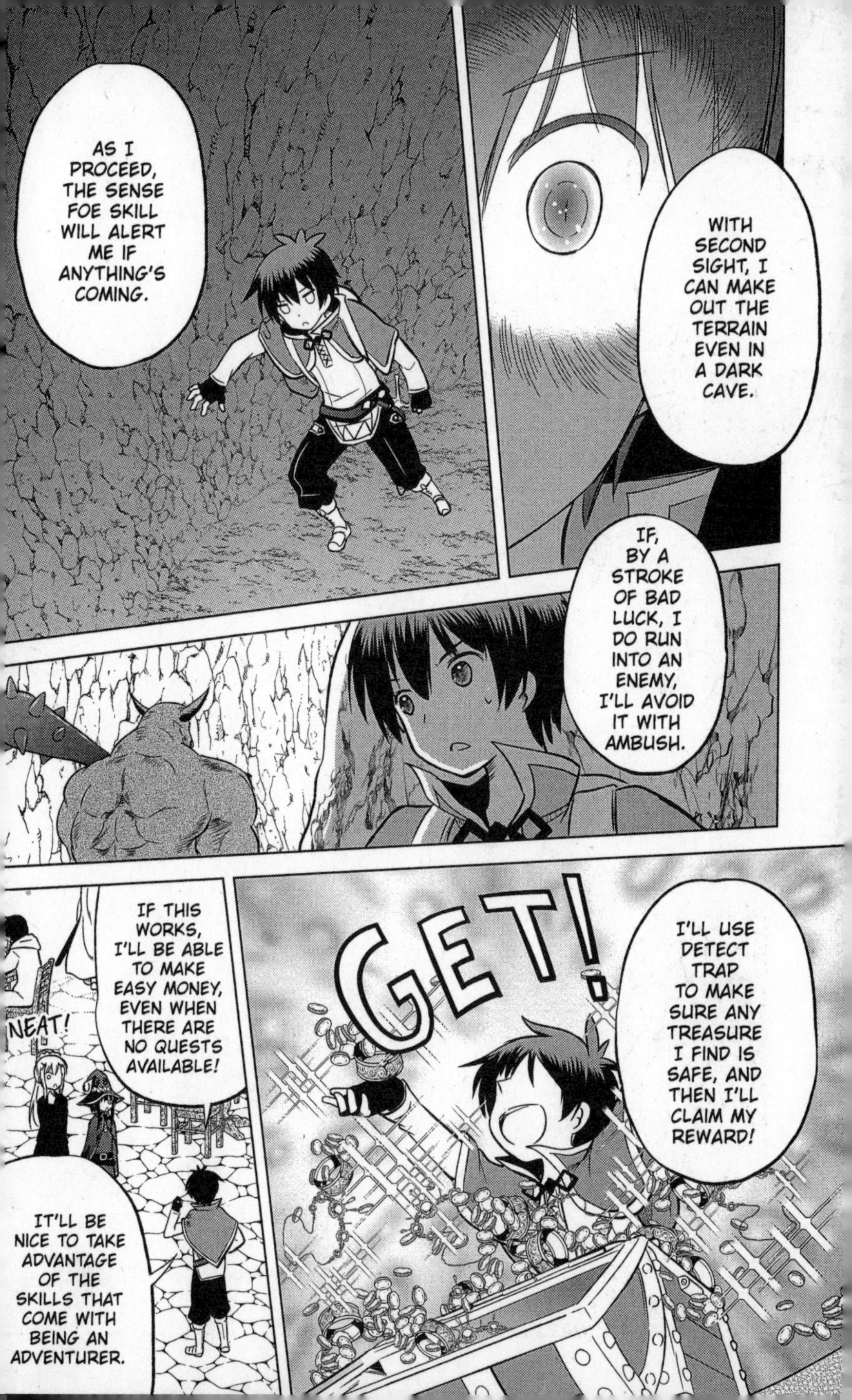
WITH SECOND SIGHT, I CAN MAKE OUT THE TERRAIN EVEN IN A DARK CAVE.
AS I PROCEED, THE SENSE FOE SKILL WILL ALERT ME IF ANYTHING'S COMING.
IF, BY A STROKE OF BAD LUCK, I DO RUN INTO AN ENEMY, I'LL AVOID IT WITH AMBUSH.
GET!
I'LL USE DETECT TRAP TO MAKE SURE ANY TREASURE I FIND IS SAFE, AND THEN I'LL CLAIM MY REWARD!
IF THIS WORKS, I'LL BE ABLE TO MAKE EASY MONEY, EVEN WHEN THERE ARE NO QUESTS AVAILABLE!
NEAT!
IT'LL BE NICE TO TAKE ADVANTAGE OF THE SKILLS THAT COME WITH BEING AN ADVENTURER.

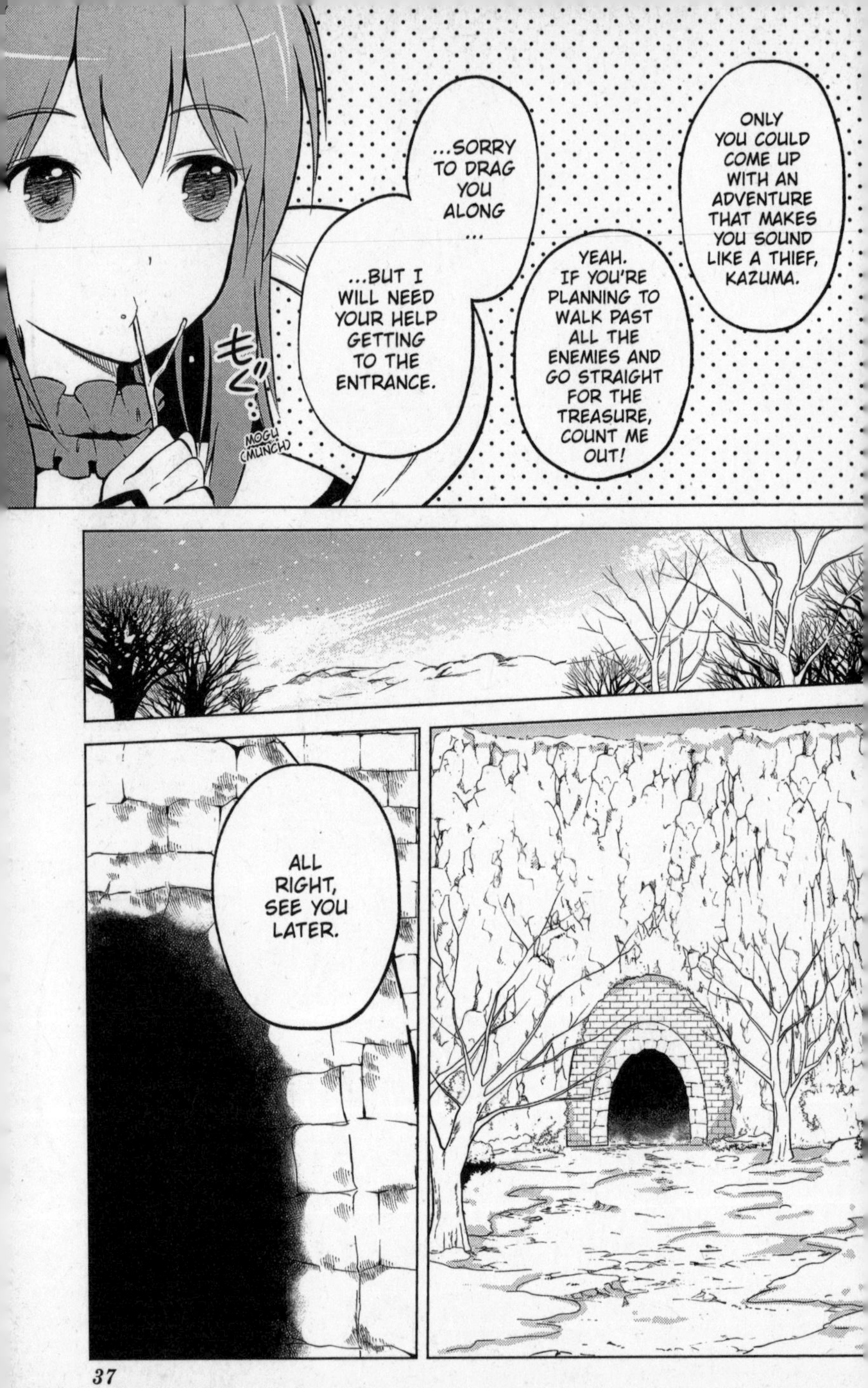
ONLY YOU COULD COME UP WITH AN ADVENTURE THAT MAKES YOU SOUND LIKE A THIEF, KAZUMA.
YEAH. IF YOU'RE PLANNING TO WALK PAST ALL THE ENEMIES AND GO STRAIGHT FOR THE TREASURE, COUNT ME OUT!
...SORRY TO DRAG YOU ALONG ...
...BUT I WILL NEED YOUR HELP GETTING TO THE ENTRANCE.
もぐ…
MOGU (MUNCH)
ALL RIGHT, SEE YOU LATER.

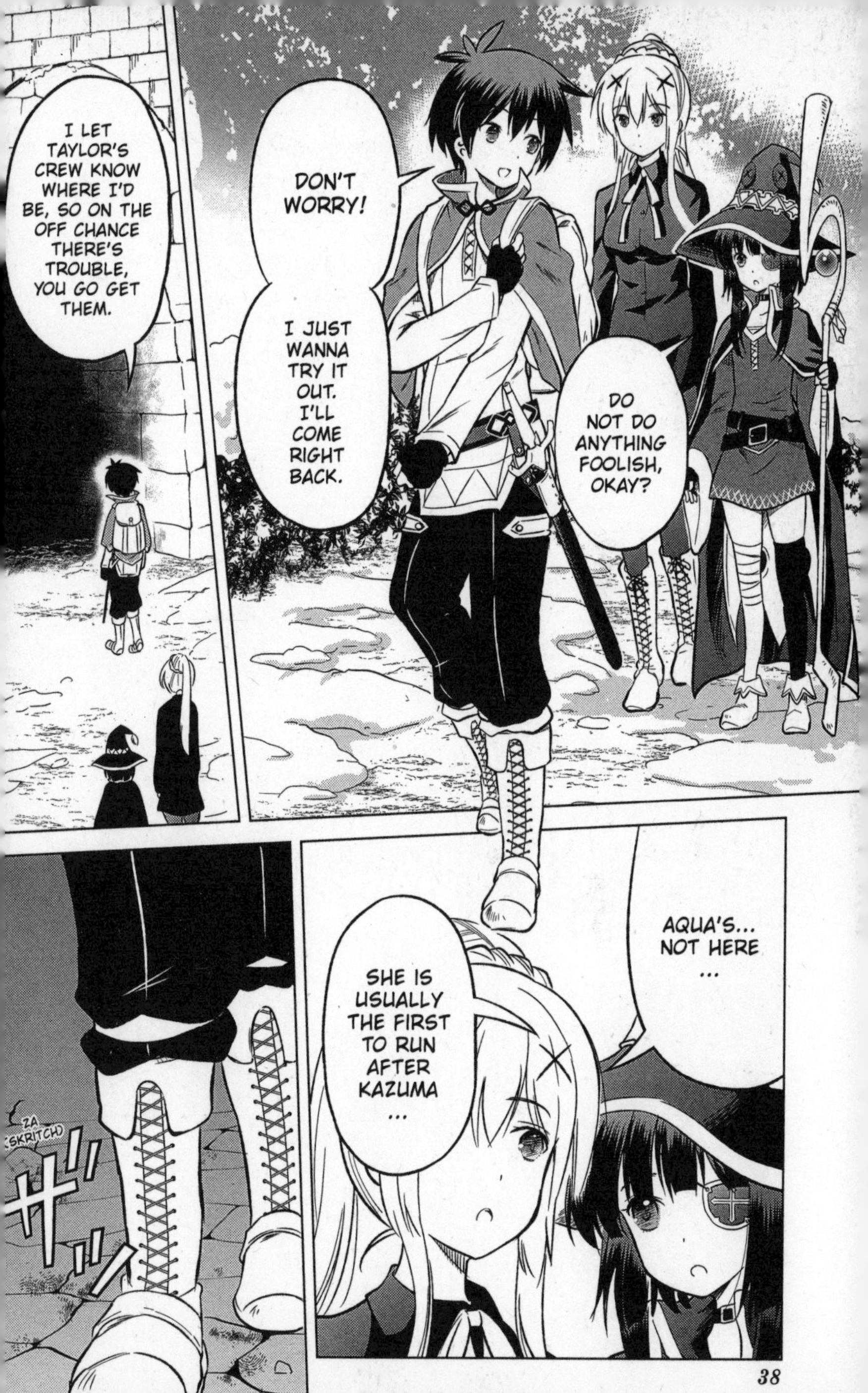
DO NOT DO ANYTHING FOOLISH, OKAY?
DON'T WORRY!
I JUST WANNA TRY IT OUT. I'LL COME RIGHT BACK.
I LET TAYLOR'S CREW KNOW WHERE I'D BE, SO ON THE OFF CHANCE THERE'S TROUBLE, YOU GO GET THEM.
AQUA'S... NOT HERE ...
SHE IS USUALLY THE FIRST TO RUN AFTER KAZUMA ...
ZA (SKRITCH)

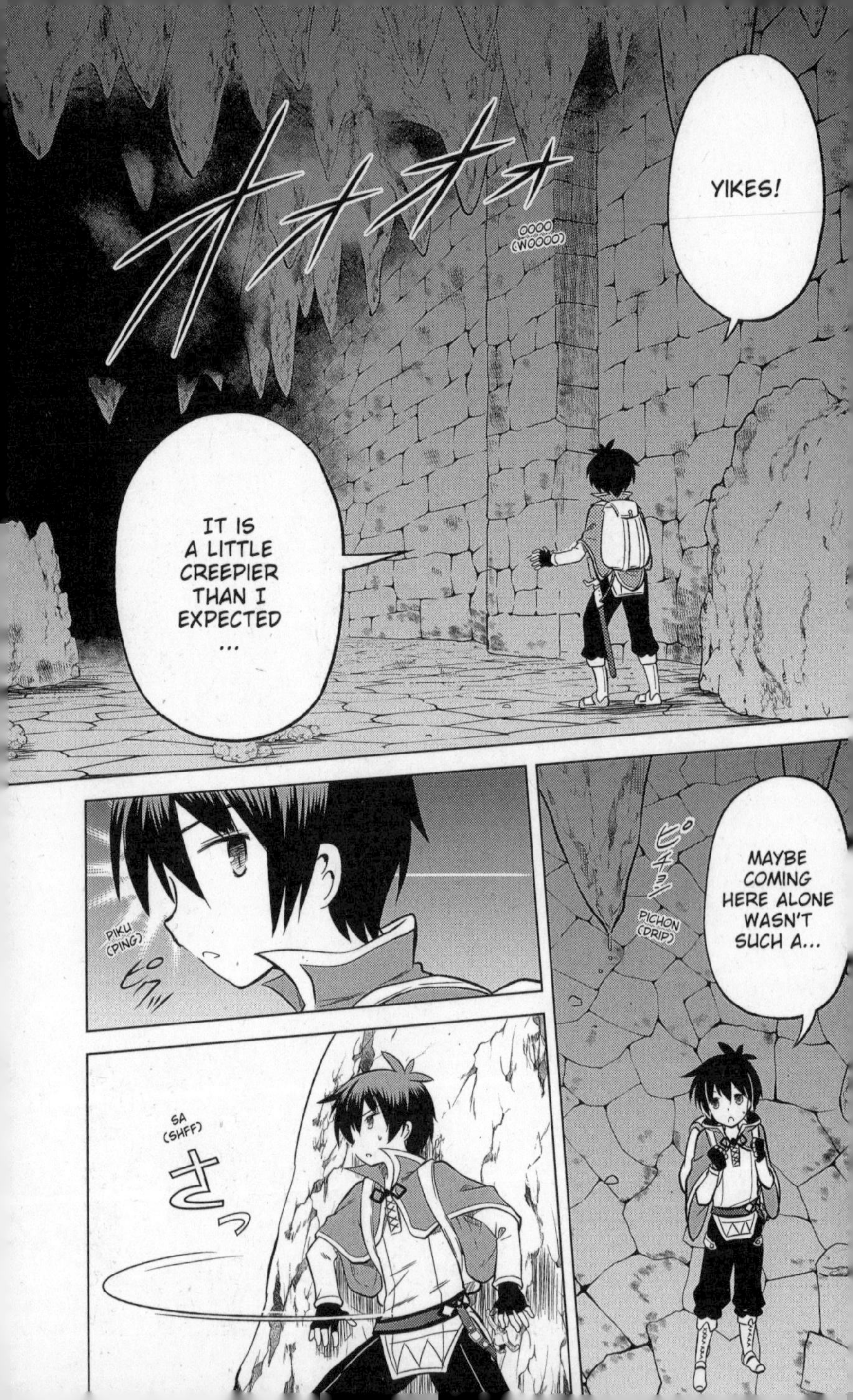
YIKES!
オォォォォ
OOOO (WOOOO)
IT IS A LITTLE CREEPIER THAN I EXPECTED ...
MAYBE COMING HERE ALONE WASN'T SUCH A...
ピチョン
PICHON (DRIP)
PIKU (PING)
SA (SHFF)
さっ

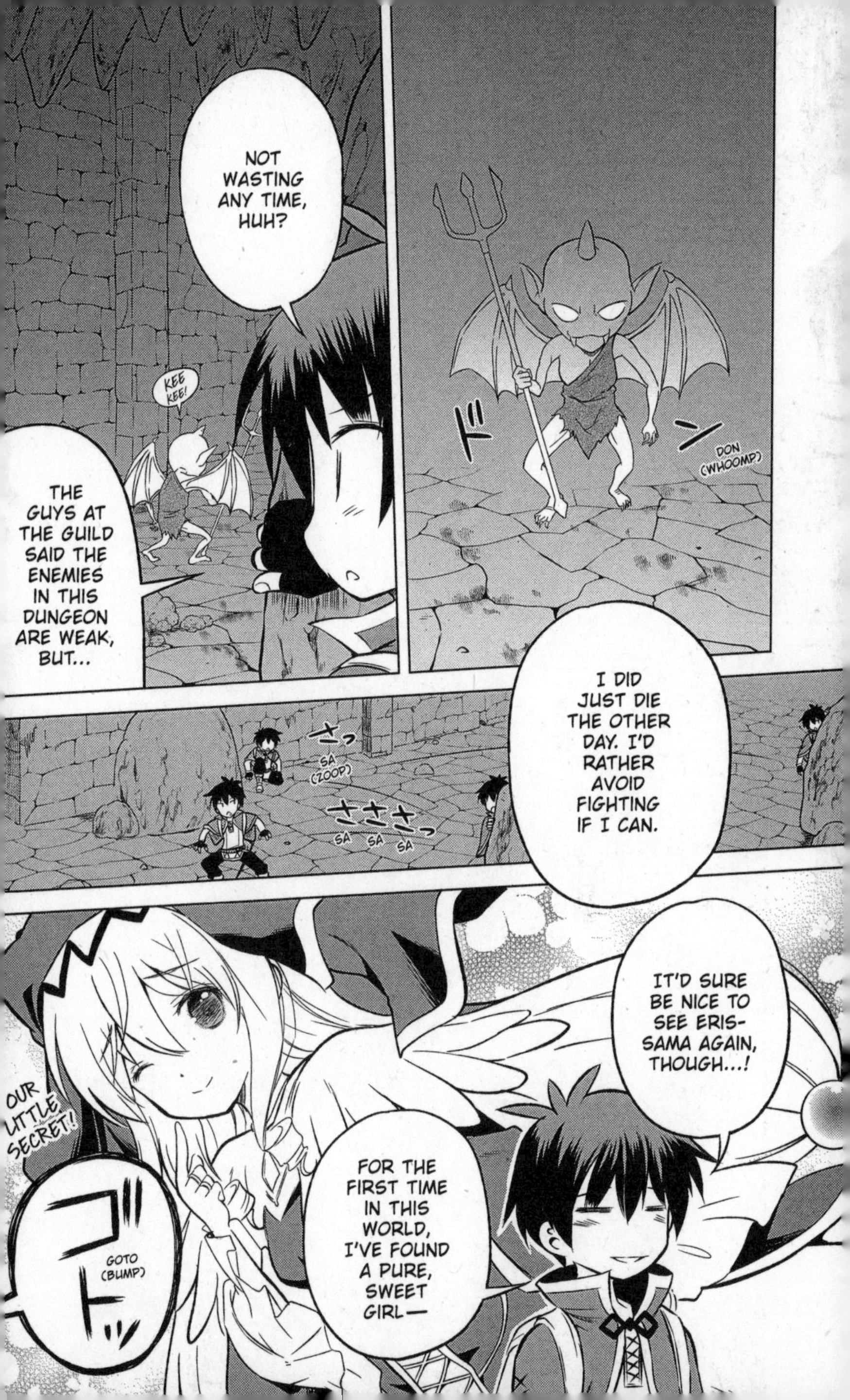

ドン
DON (WHOOMP)
NOT WASTING ANY TIME, HUH?
KEE KEE!
THE GUYS AT THE GUILD SAID THE ENEMIES IN THIS DUNGEON ARE WEAK, BUT...
I DID JUST DIE THE OTHER DAY. I'D RATHER AVOID FIGHTING IF I CAN.
さっ
SA (ZOOP)
さささっ
SA SA SA
IT'D SURE BE NICE TO SEE ERIS-SAMA AGAIN, THOUGH...!
FOR THE FIRST TIME IN THIS WORLD, I'VE FOUND A PURE, SWEET GIRL—
OUR LITTLE SECRET!
ゴトッ
GOTO (BUMP)

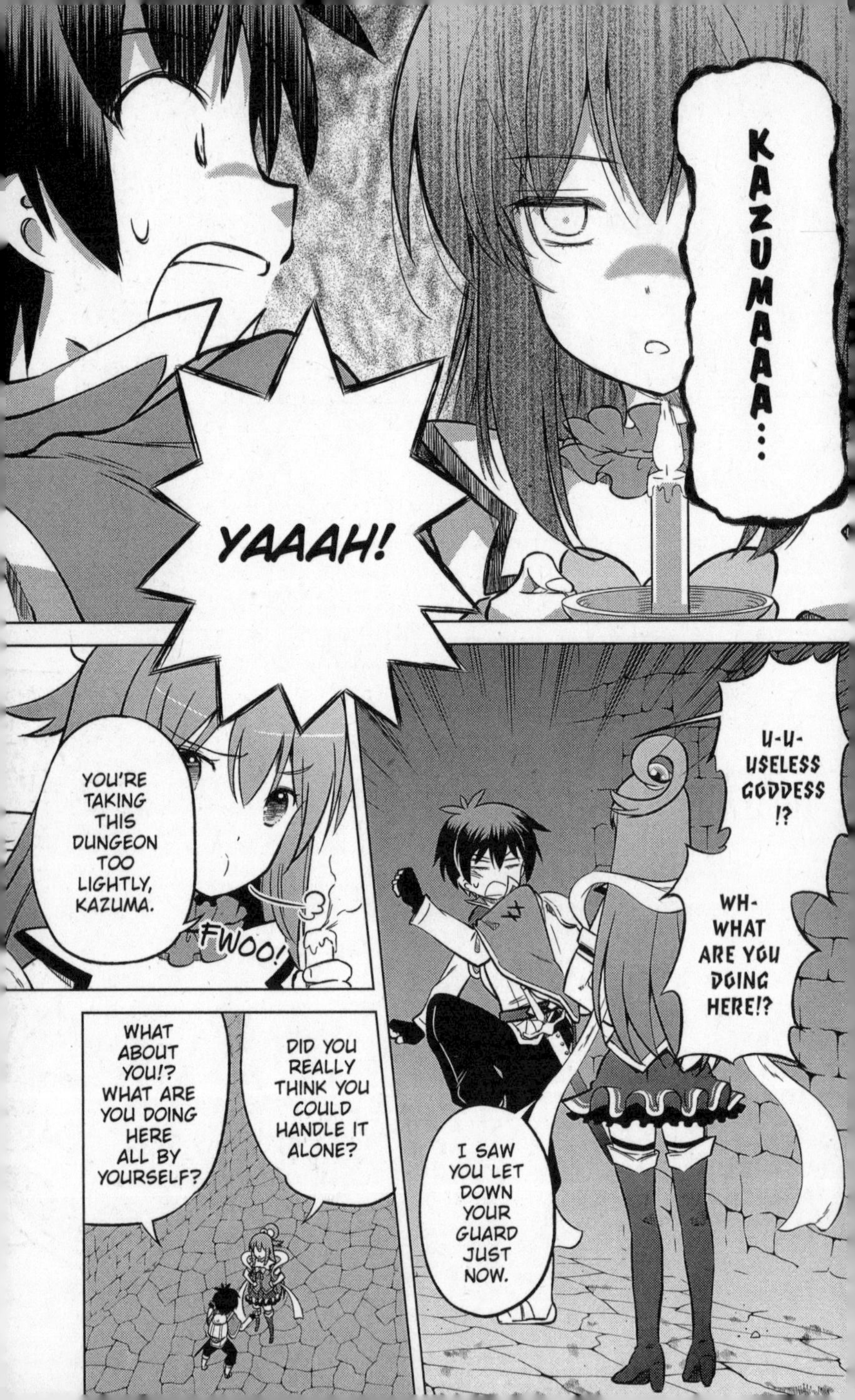
KAZUMAAA...
YAAAH!
U-U-USELESS GODDESS!?
WH-WHAT ARE YOU DOING HERE!?
I SAW YOU LET DOWN YOUR GUARD JUST NOW.
YOU'RE TAKING THIS DUNGEON TOO LIGHTLY, KAZUMA.
FWOO!
DID YOU REALLY THINK YOU COULD HANDLE IT ALONE?
WHAT ABOUT YOU!? WHAT ARE YOU DOING HERE ALL BY YOURSELF?

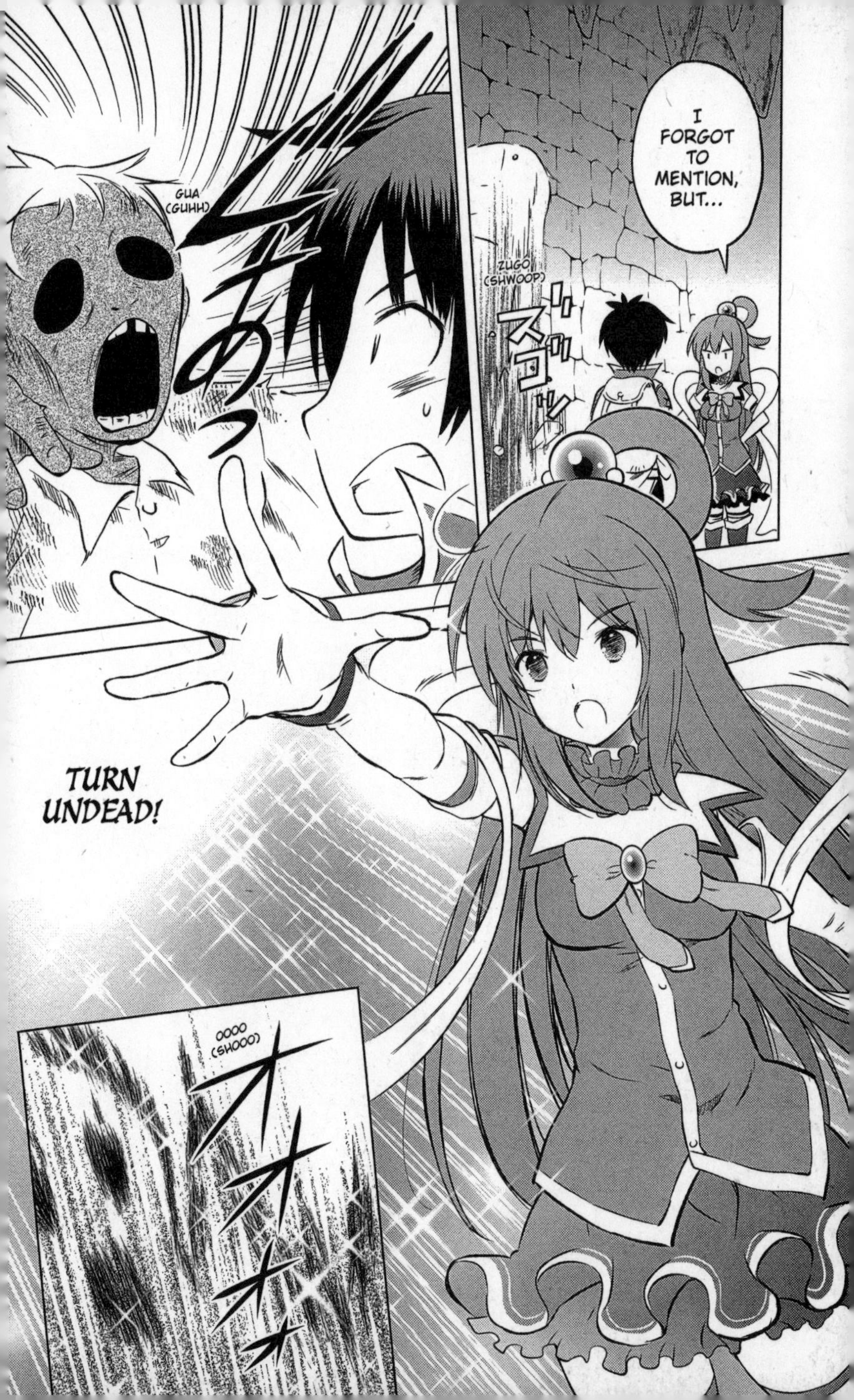
I FORGOT TO MENTION, BUT...
ZUGO (SHWOOP)
GUA (GUHH)
TURN UNDEAD!
OOOO (SHOOO)

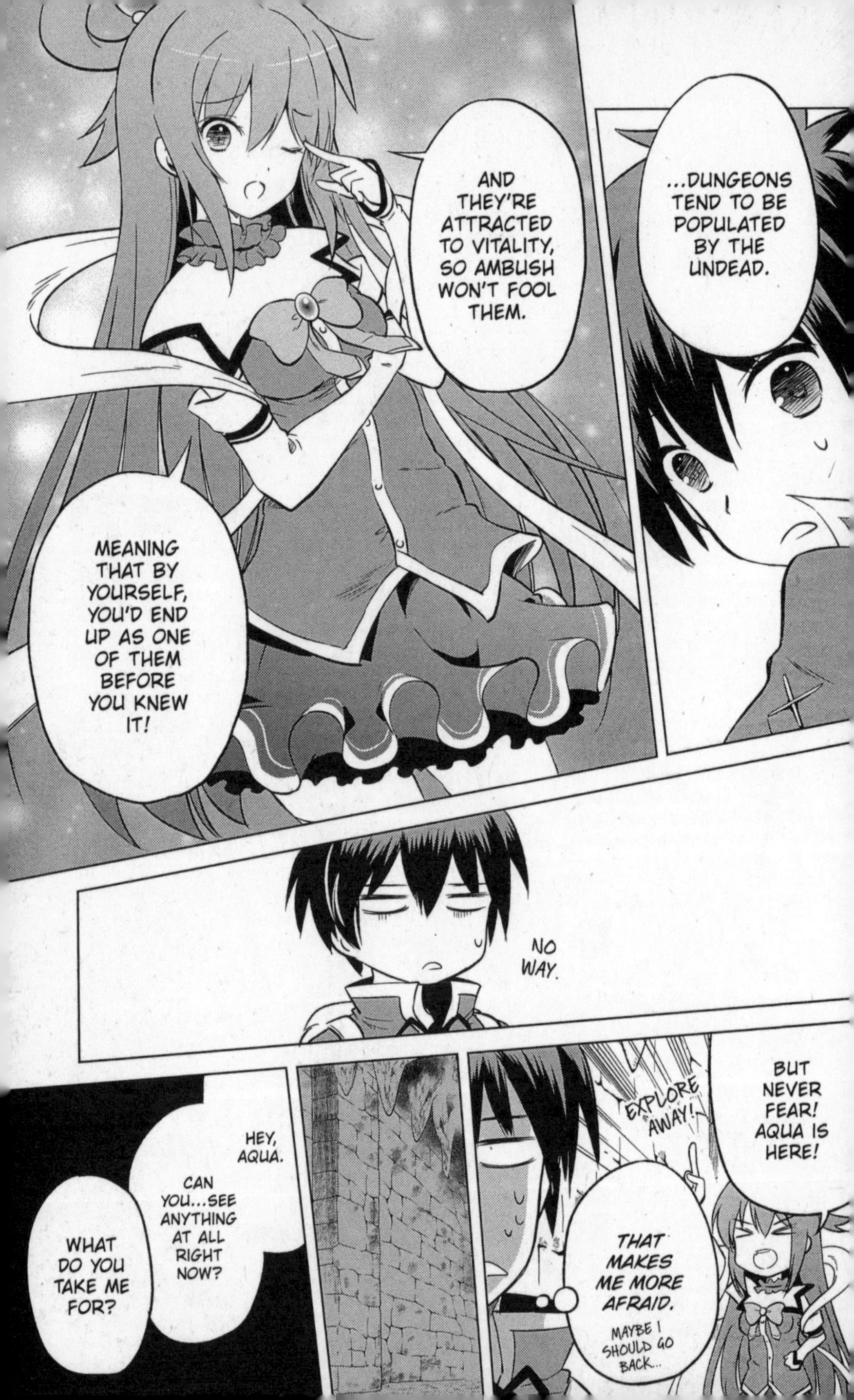
...DUNGEONS TEND TO BE POPULATED BY THE UNDEAD.
AND THEY'RE ATTRACTED TO VITALITY, SO AMBUSH WON'T FOOL THEM.
MEANING THAT BY YOURSELF, YOU'D END UP AS ONE OF THEM BEFORE YOU KNEW IT!
NO WAY.
BUT NEVER FEAR! AQUA IS HERE!
EXPLORE AWAY!
THAT MAKES ME MORE AFRAID.
MAYBE I SHOULD GO BACK...
HEY, AQUA.
CAN YOU...SEE ANYTHING AT ALL RIGHT NOW?
WHAT DO YOU TAKE ME FOR?

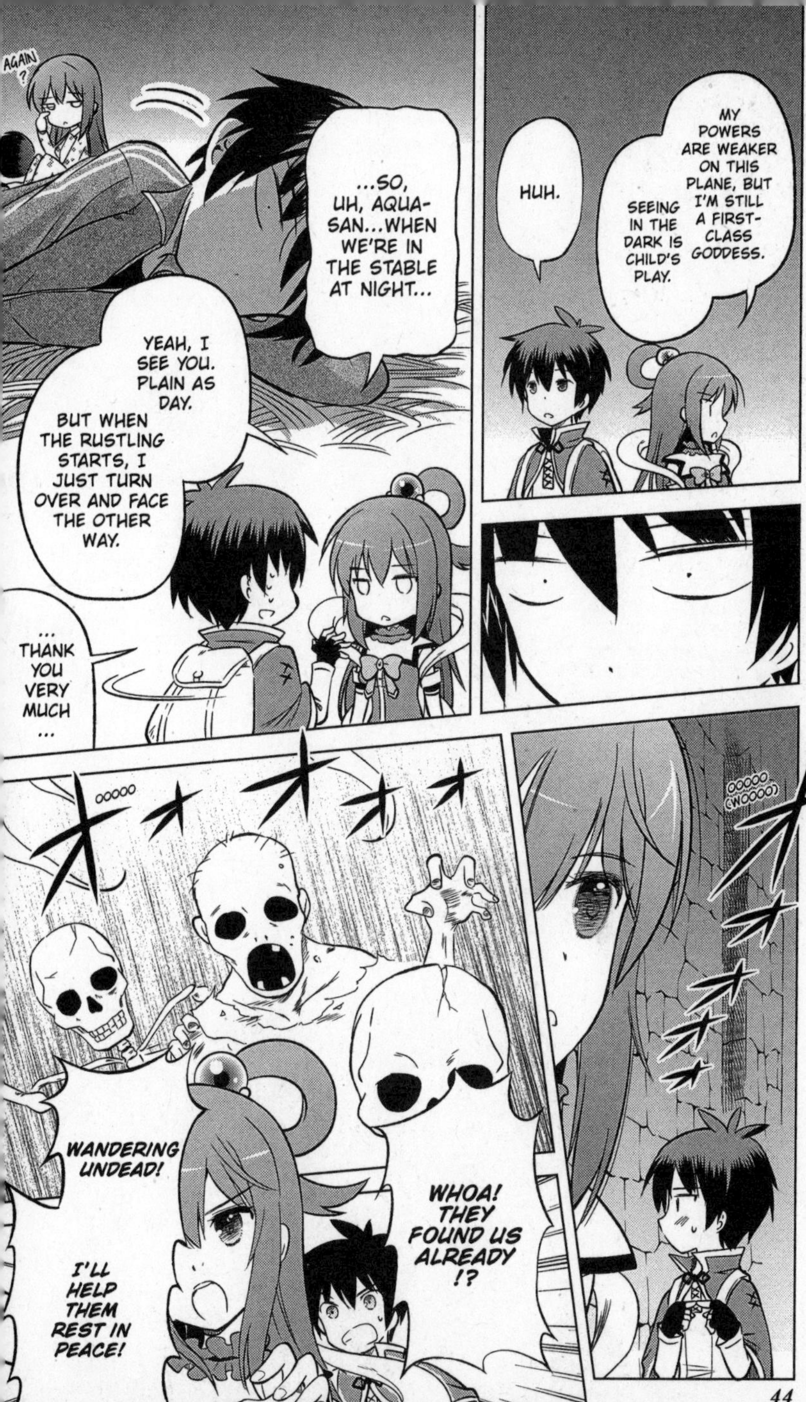

MY POWERS ARE WEAKER ON THIS PLANE, BUT I'M STILL A FIRST-CLASS GODDESS.
SEEING IN THE DARK IS CHILD'S PLAY.
HUH.
...SO, UH, AQUA-SAN...WHEN WE'RE IN THE STABLE AT NIGHT...
AGAIN?
YEAH, I SEE YOU. PLAIN AS DAY.
BUT WHEN THE RUSTLING STARTS, I JUST TURN OVER AND FACE THE OTHER WAY.
...THANK YOU VERY MUCH...
OOOOO (WOOOO)
OOOOO
WANDERING UNDEAD!
WHOA! THEY FOUND US ALREADY!?
I'LL HELP THEM REST IN PEACE!

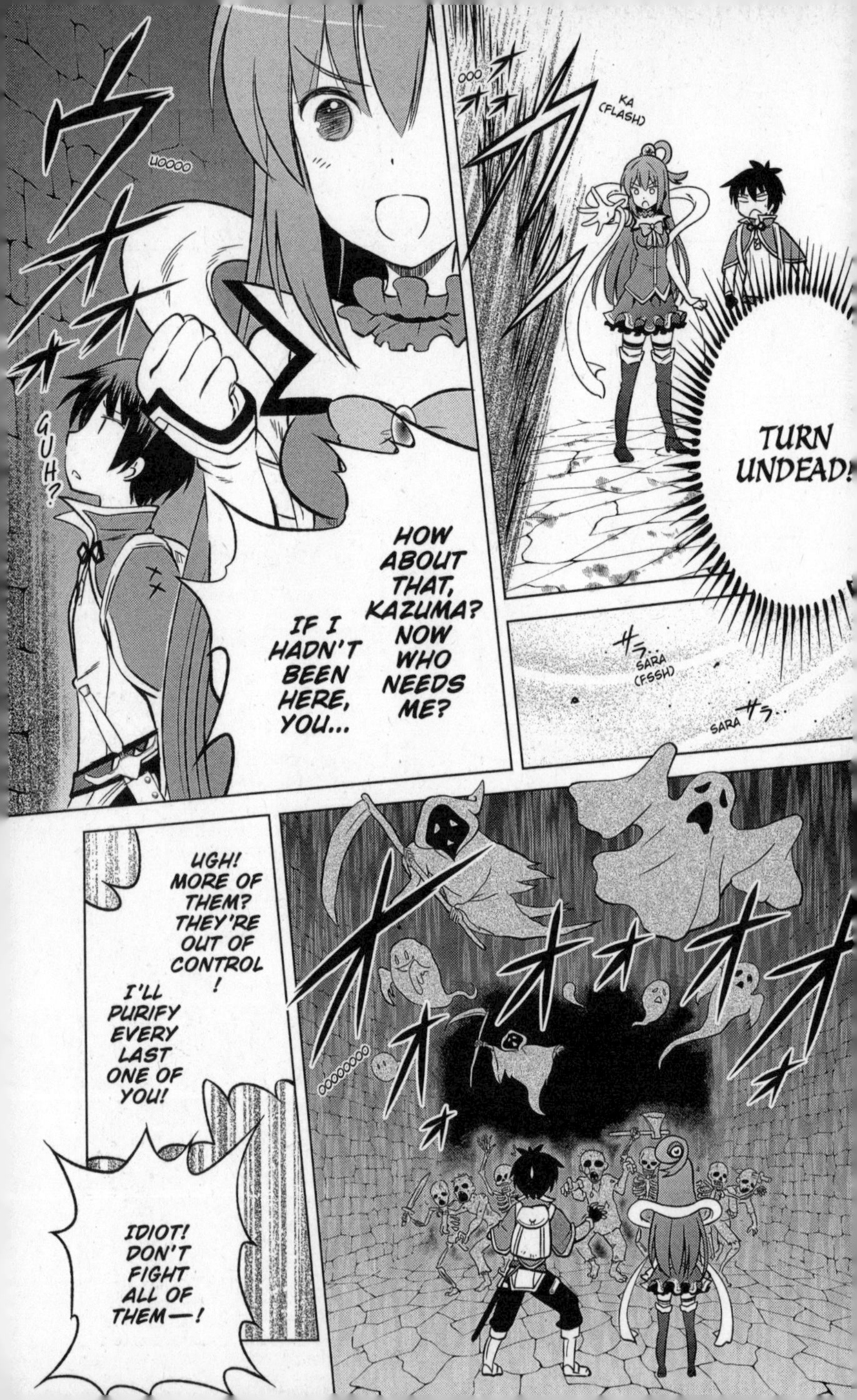
OOO
KA (FLASH)
TURN UNDEAD!
SARA (FSSH)
SARA
UOOOO
GUH?
HOW ABOUT THAT, KAZUMA? NOW WHO NEEDS ME?
IF I HADN'T BEEN HERE, YOU...
OOOOOOOO
UGH! MORE OF THEM? THEY'RE OUT OF CONTROL!
I'LL PURIFY EVERY LAST ONE OF YOU!
IDIOT! DON'T FIGHT ALL OF THEM—!

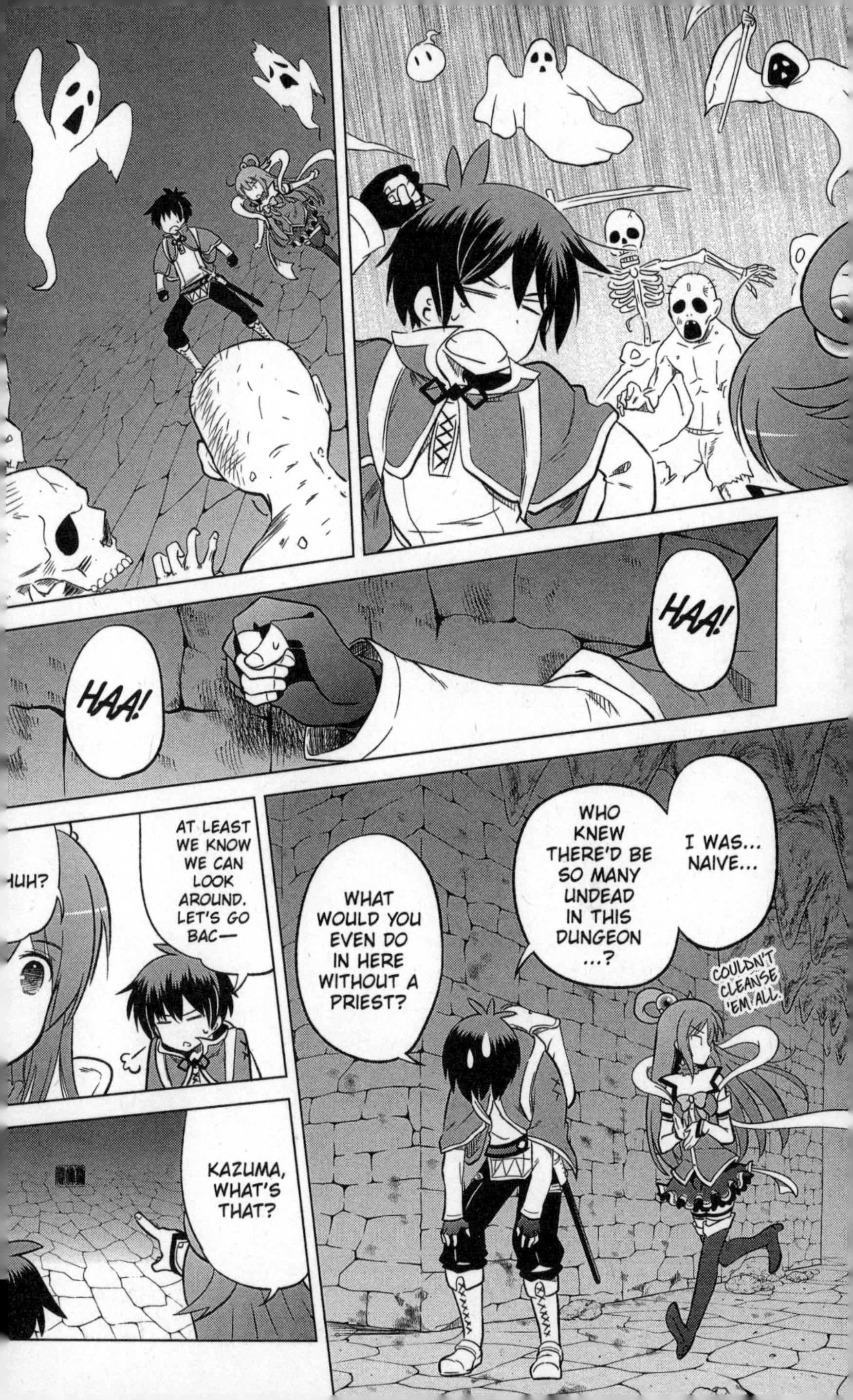
HAA!
HAA!
I WAS... NAIVE...
WHO KNEW THERE'D BE SO MANY UNDEAD IN THIS DUNGEON ...?
COULDN'T CLEANSE 'EM ALL.
WHAT WOULD YOU EVEN DO IN HERE WITHOUT A PRIEST?
AT LEAST WE KNOW WE CAN LOOK AROUND. LET'S GO BAC—
HUH?
KAZUMA, WHAT'S THAT?

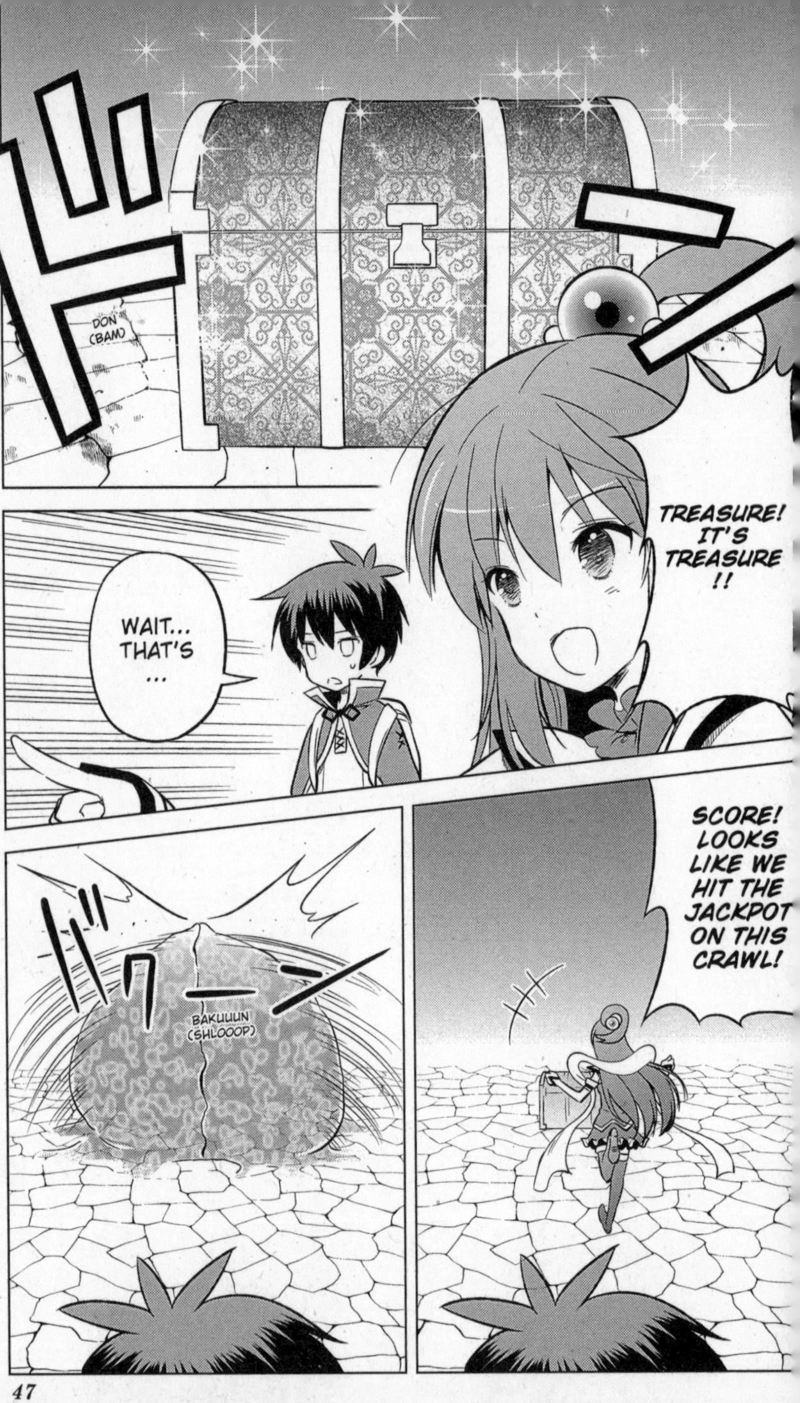
DON (BAM)
TREASURE! IT'S TREASURE!!
WAIT... THAT'S...
SCORE! LOOKS LIKE WE HIT THE JACKPOT ON THIS CRAWL!
BAKUUUN (SHLOOOP)

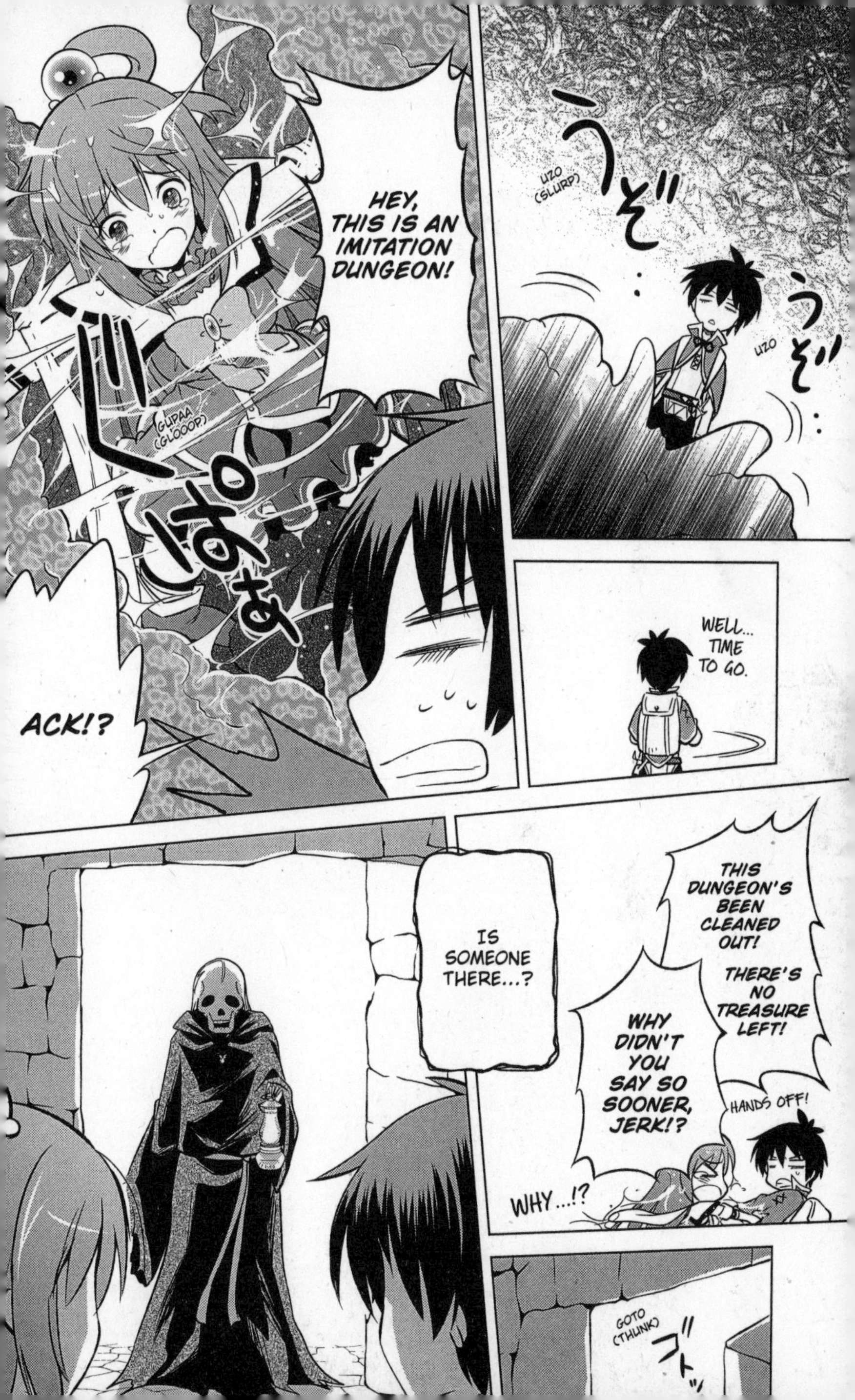

UZO (SLURP)
UZO
WELL... TIME TO GO.
HEY, THIS IS AN IMITATION DUNGEON!
GUPAA (GLOOOP)
ACK!?
THIS DUNGEON'S BEEN CLEANED OUT!
THERE'S NO TREASURE LEFT!
WHY DIDN'T YOU SAY SO SOONER, JERK!?
HANDS OFF!
WHY...!?
GOTO (THUNK)
IS SOMEONE THERE...?

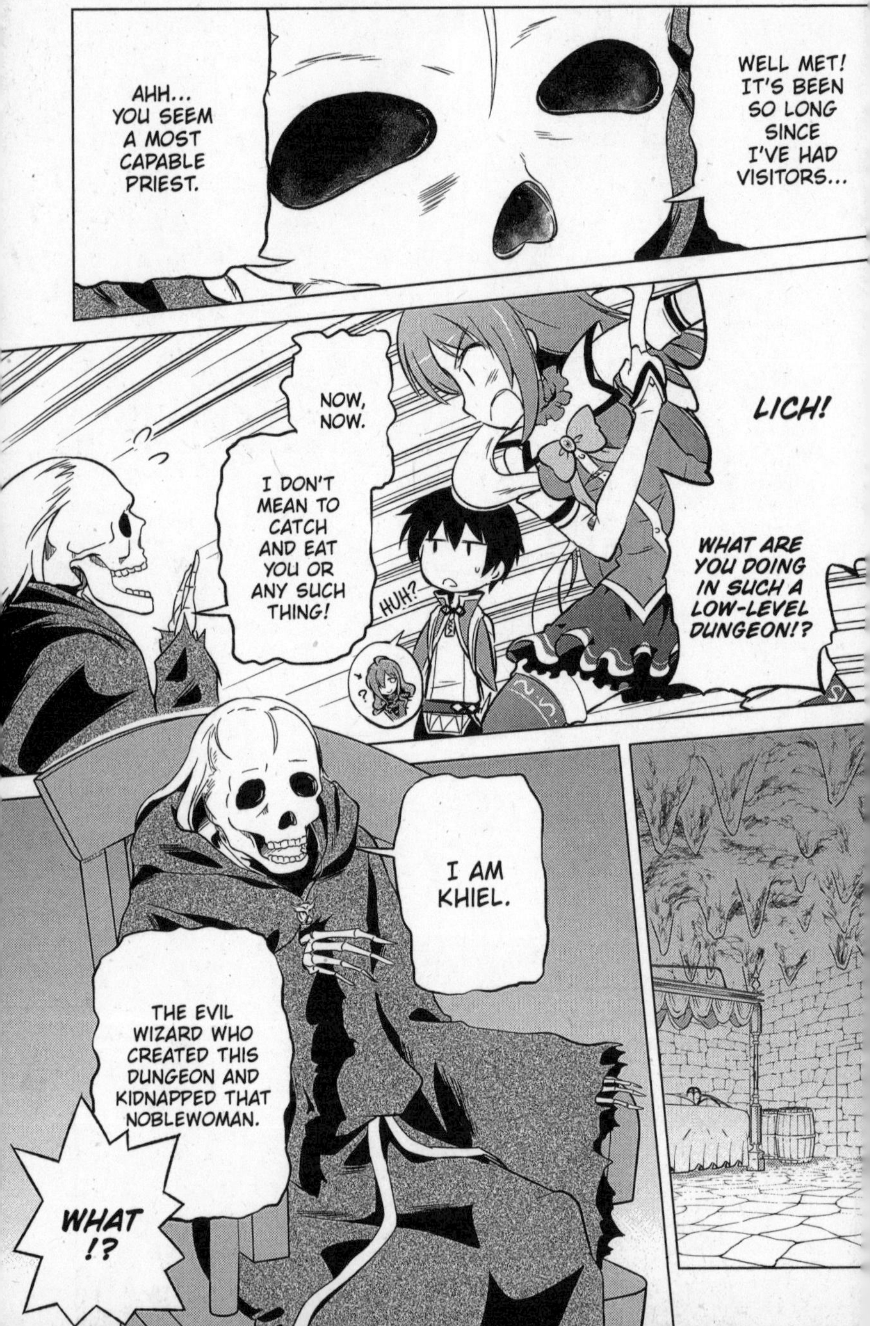
WELL MET! IT'S BEEN SO LONG SINCE I'VE HAD VISITORS...
AHH... YOU SEEM A MOST CAPABLE PRIEST.
LICH!
WHAT ARE YOU DOING IN SUCH A LOW-LEVEL DUNGEON!?
NOW, NOW.
I DON'T MEAN TO CATCH AND EAT YOU OR ANY SUCH THING!
HUH?
I AM KHIEL.
THE EVIL WIZARD WHO CREATED THIS DUNGEON AND KIDNAPPED THAT NOBLEWOMAN.
WHAT !?

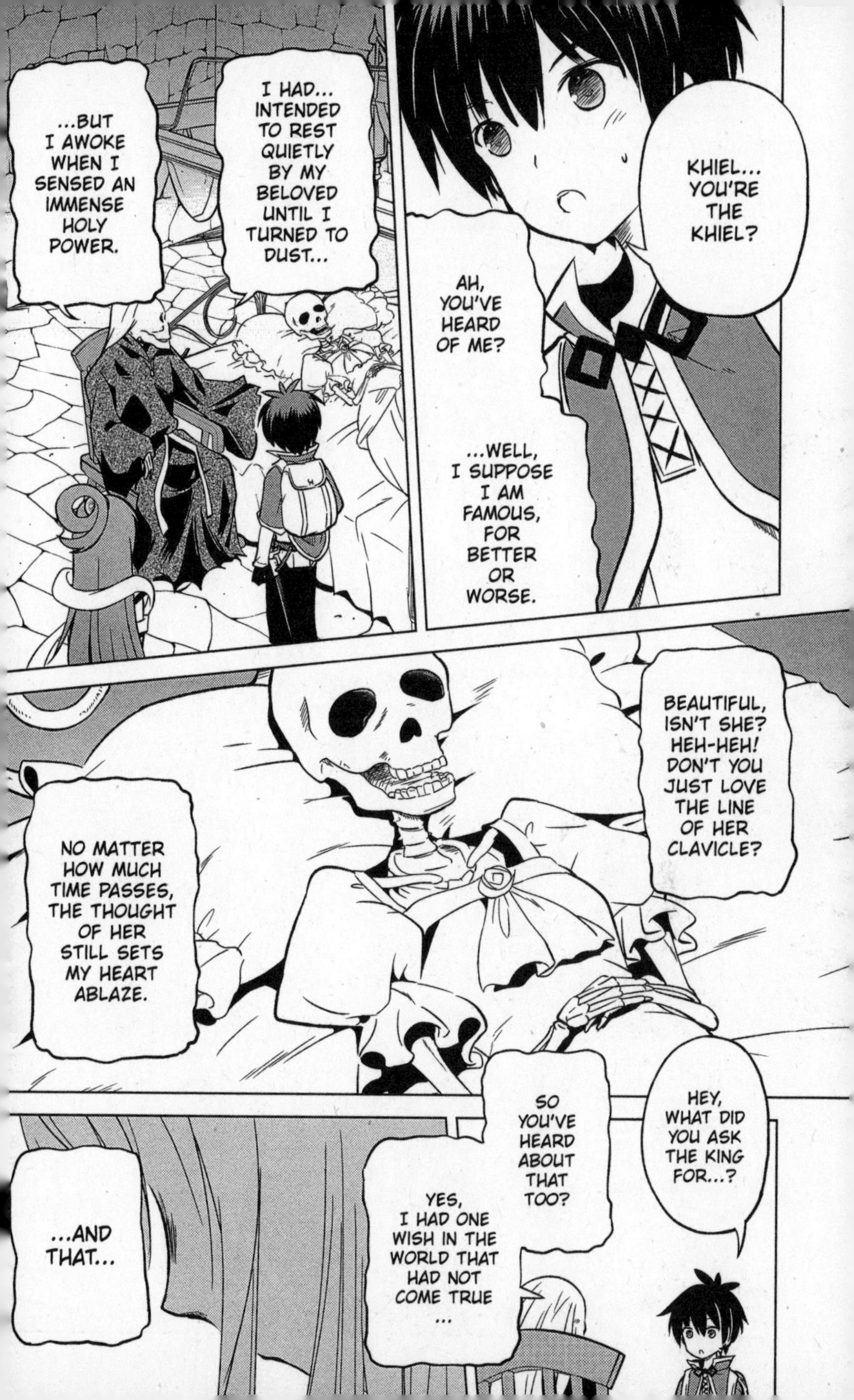
KHIEL... YOU'RE THE KHIEL?
AH, YOU'VE HEARD OF ME?
...WELL, I SUPPOSE I AM FAMOUS, FOR BETTER OR WORSE.
I HAD... INTENDED TO REST QUIETLY BY MY BELOVED UNTIL I TURNED TO DUST...
...BUT I AWOKE WHEN I SENSED AN IMMENSE HOLY POWER.
BEAUTIFUL, ISN'T SHE? HEH-HEH! DON'T YOU JUST LOVE THE LINE OF HER CLAVICLE?
NO MATTER HOW MUCH TIME PASSES, THE THOUGHT OF HER STILL SETS MY HEART ABLAZE.
HEY, WHAT DID YOU ASK THE KING FOR...?
SO YOU'VE HEARD ABOUT THAT TOO?
YES, I HAD ONE WISH IN THE WORLD THAT HAD NOT COME TRUE ...
...AND THAT...

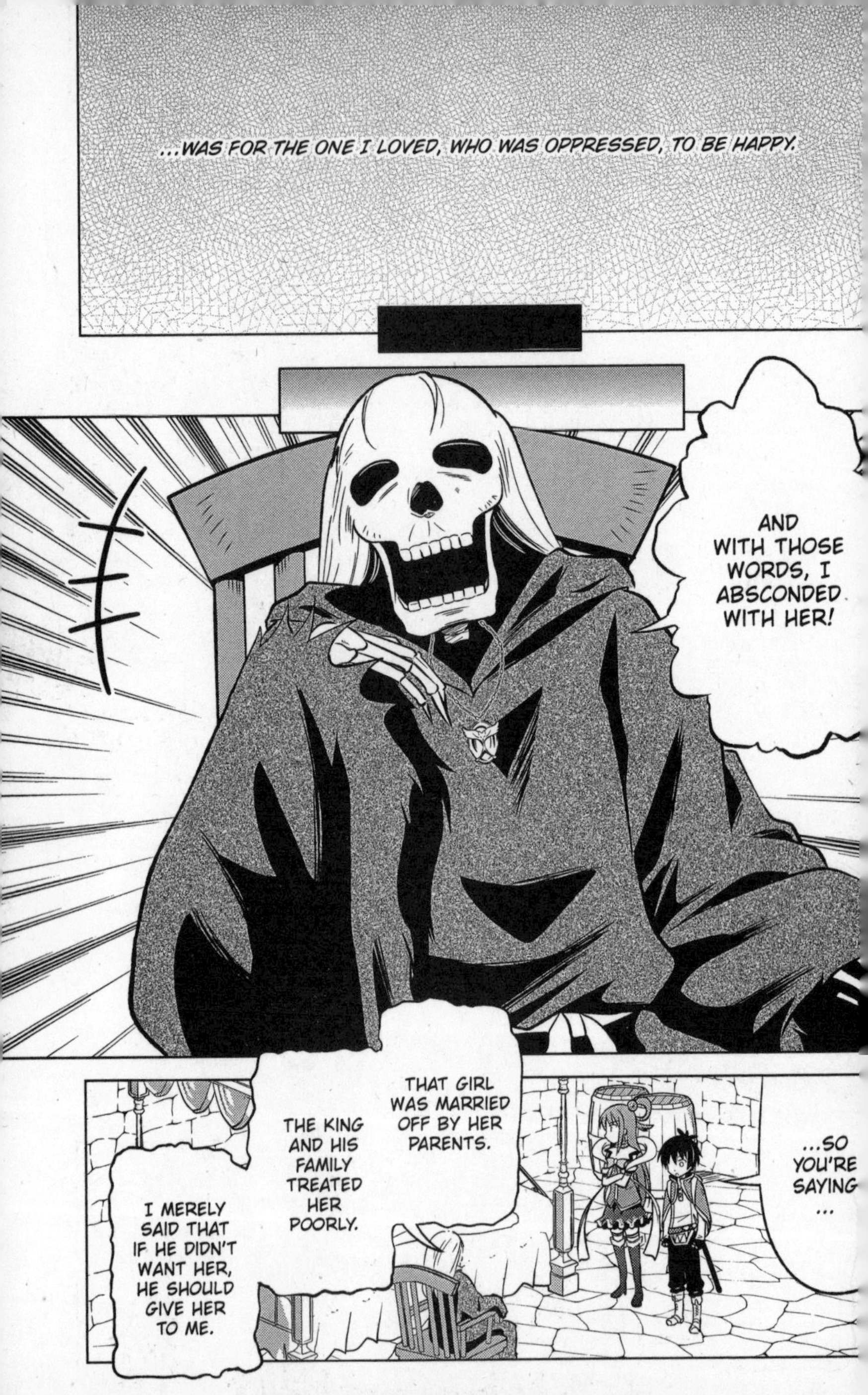
...WAS FOR THE ONE I LOVED, WHO WAS OPPRESSED, TO BE HAPPY.
AND WITH THOSE WORDS, I ABSCONDED WITH HER!
...SO YOU'RE SAYING...
THAT GIRL WAS MARRIED OFF BY HER PARENTS.
THE KING AND HIS FAMILY TREATED HER POORLY.
I MERELY SAID THAT IF HE DIDN'T WANT HER, HE SHOULD GIVE HER TO ME.

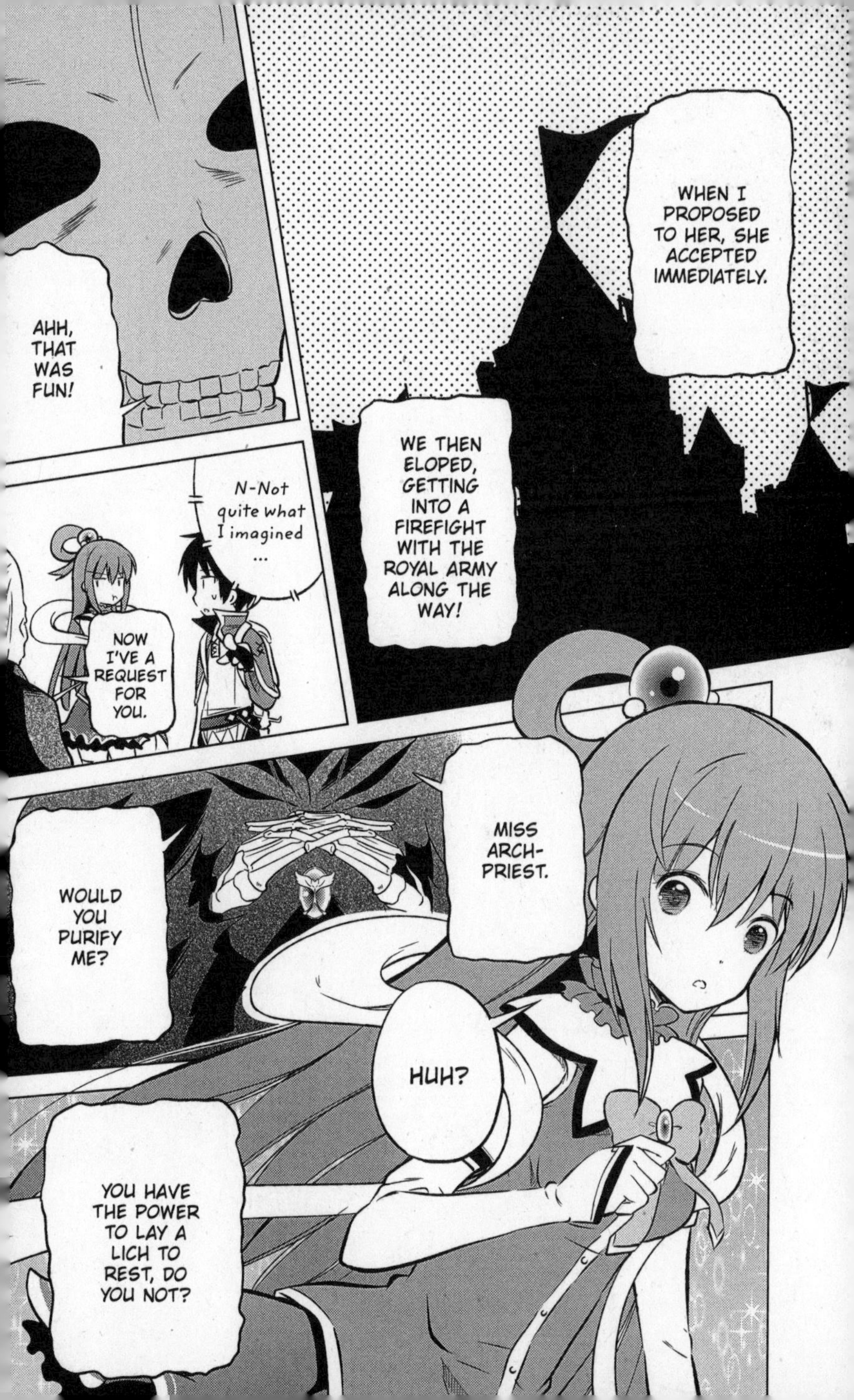
WHEN I PROPOSED TO HER, SHE ACCEPTED IMMEDIATELY.
WE THEN ELOPED, GETTING INTO A FIREFIGHT WITH THE ROYAL ARMY ALONG THE WAY!
AHH, THAT WAS FUN!
N-Not quite what I imagined...
NOW I'VE A REQUEST FOR YOU.
MISS ARCH-PRIEST.
WOULD YOU PURIFY ME?
HUH?
YOU HAVE THE POWER TO LAY A LICH TO REST, DO YOU NOT?

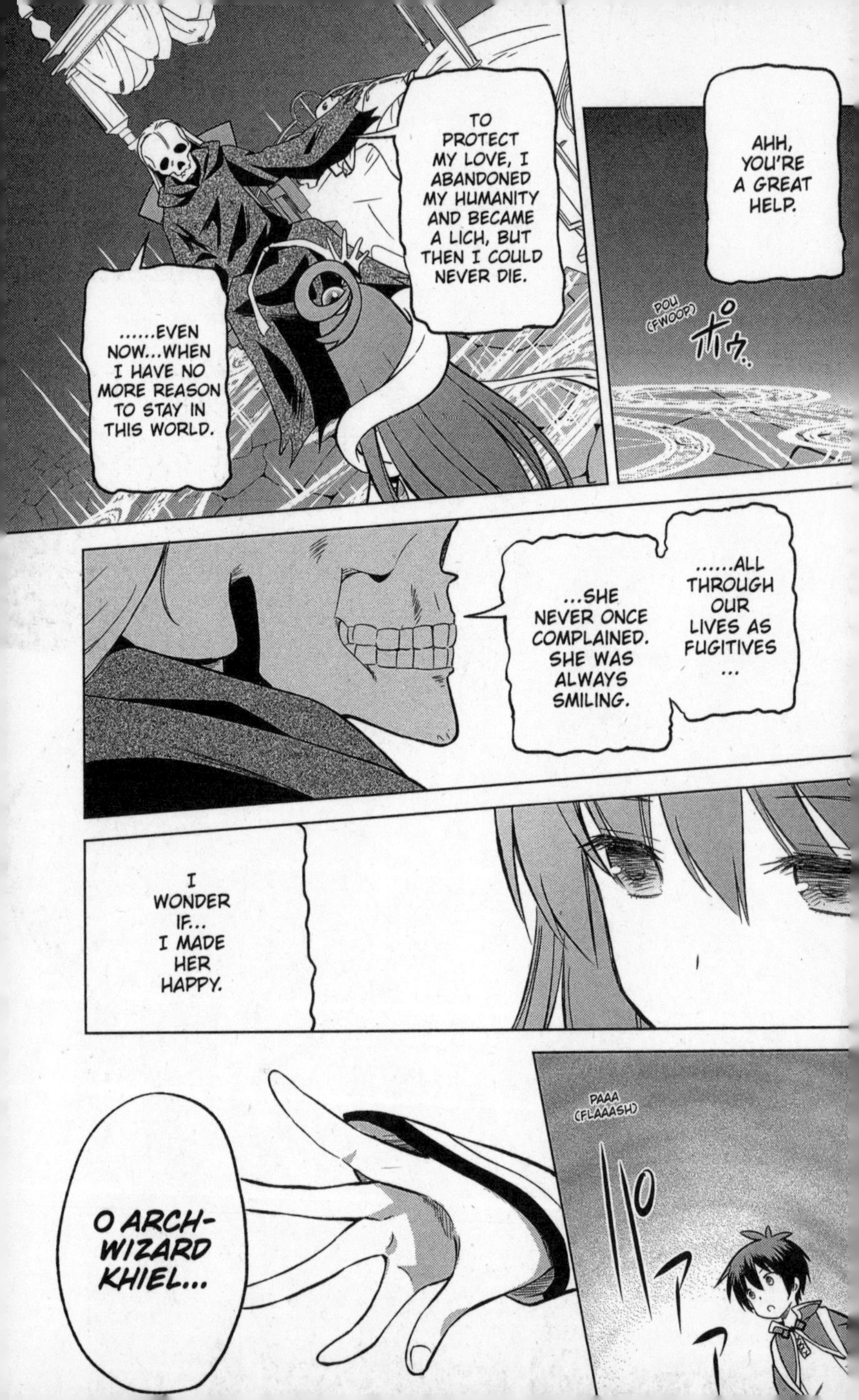
AHH, YOU'RE A GREAT HELP.
POU (FWOOP)
ポゥ..
TO PROTECT MY LOVE, I ABANDONED MY HUMANITY AND BECAME A LICH, BUT THEN I COULD NEVER DIE.
......EVEN NOW...WHEN I HAVE NO MORE REASON TO STAY IN THIS WORLD.
......ALL THROUGH OUR LIVES AS FUGITIVES ...
...SHE NEVER ONCE COMPLAINED. SHE WAS ALWAYS SMILING.
I WONDER IF... I MADE HER HAPPY.
PAAA (FLAAASH)
パァ
O ARCH-WIZARD KHIEL...

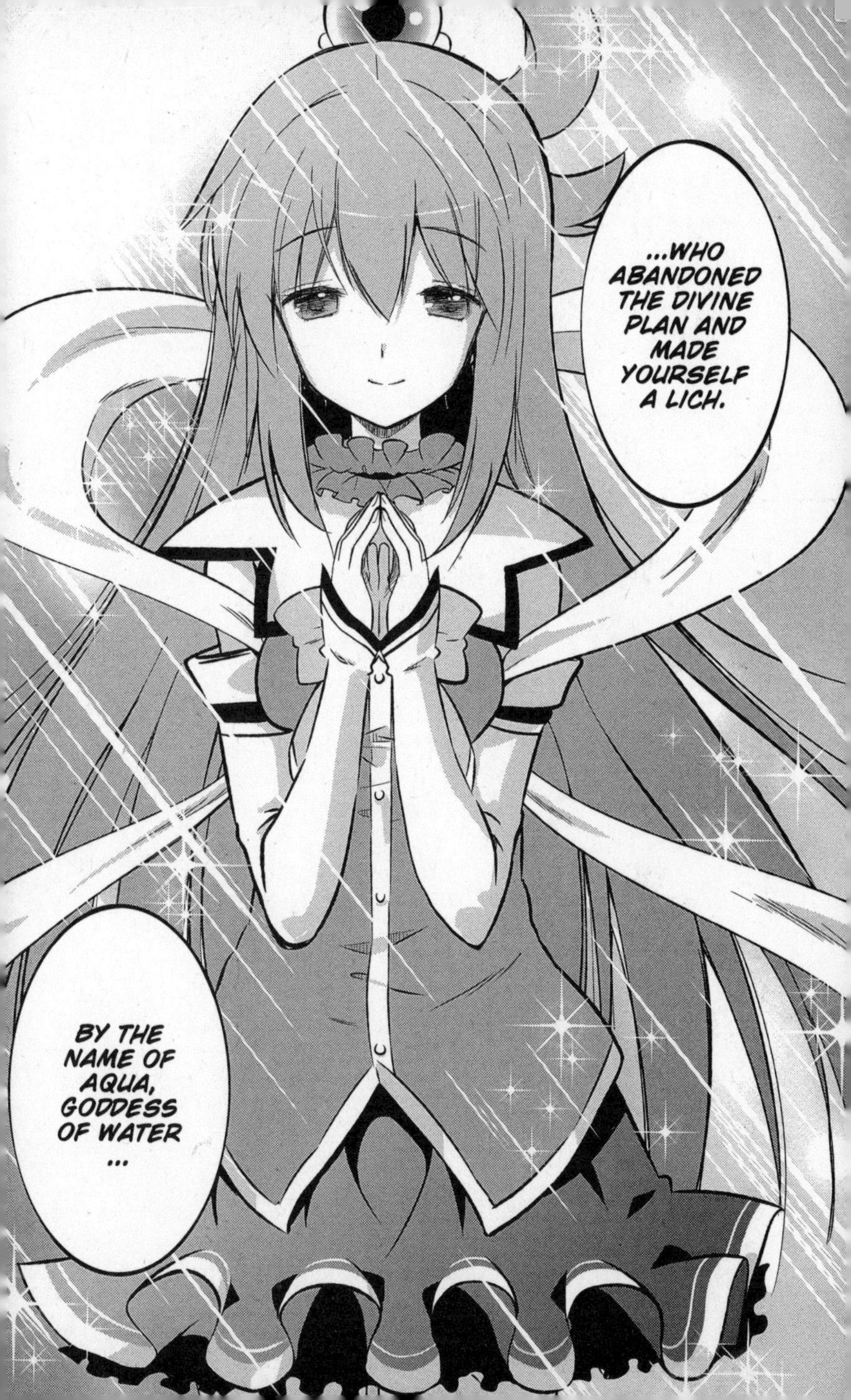
...WHO ABANDONED THE DIVINE PLAN AND MADE YOURSELF A LICH.
BY THE NAME OF AQUA, GODDESS OF WATER ...

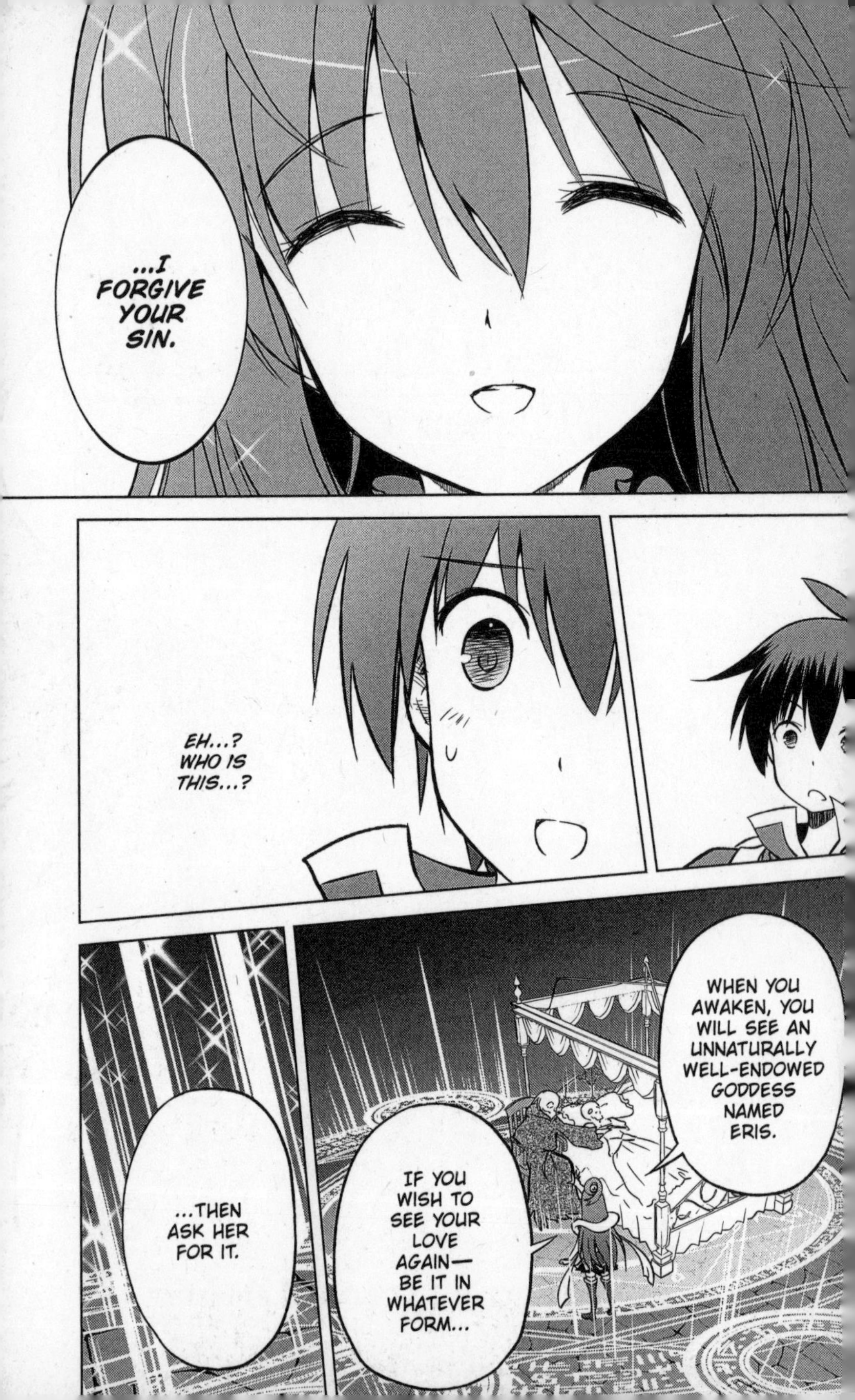
...I FORGIVE YOUR SIN.
EH...? WHO IS THIS...?
WHEN YOU AWAKEN, YOU WILL SEE AN UNNATURALLY WELL-ENDOWED GODDESS NAMED ERIS.
IF YOU WISH TO SEE YOUR LOVE AGAIN—BE IT IN WHATEVER FORM...
...THEN ASK HER FOR IT.

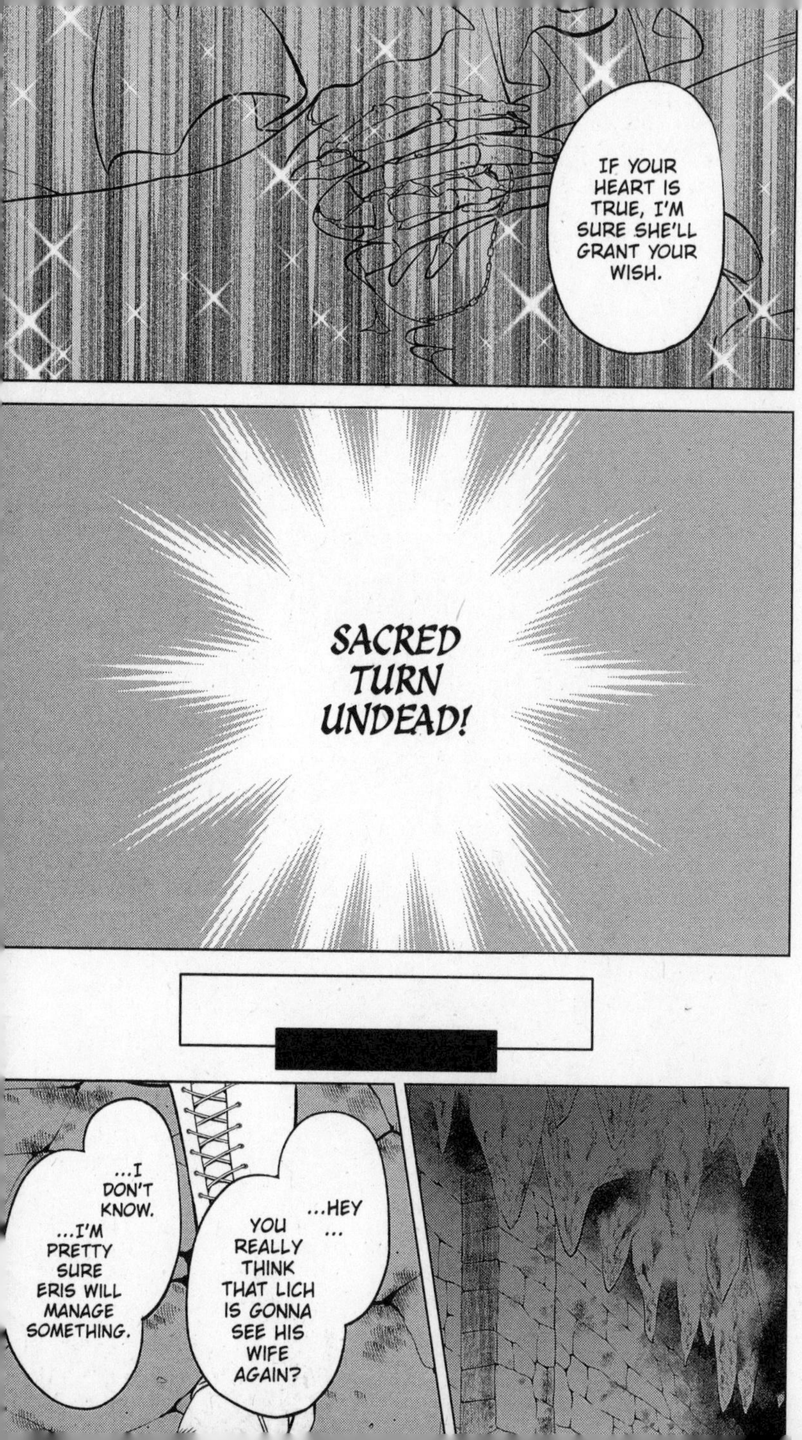
IF YOUR HEART IS TRUE, I'M SURE SHE'LL GRANT YOUR WISH.
SACRED TURN UNDEAD!
...HEY ... YOU REALLY THINK THAT LICH IS GONNA SEE HIS WIFE AGAIN?
...I DON'T KNOW. ...I'M PRETTY SURE ERIS WILL MANAGE SOMETHING.

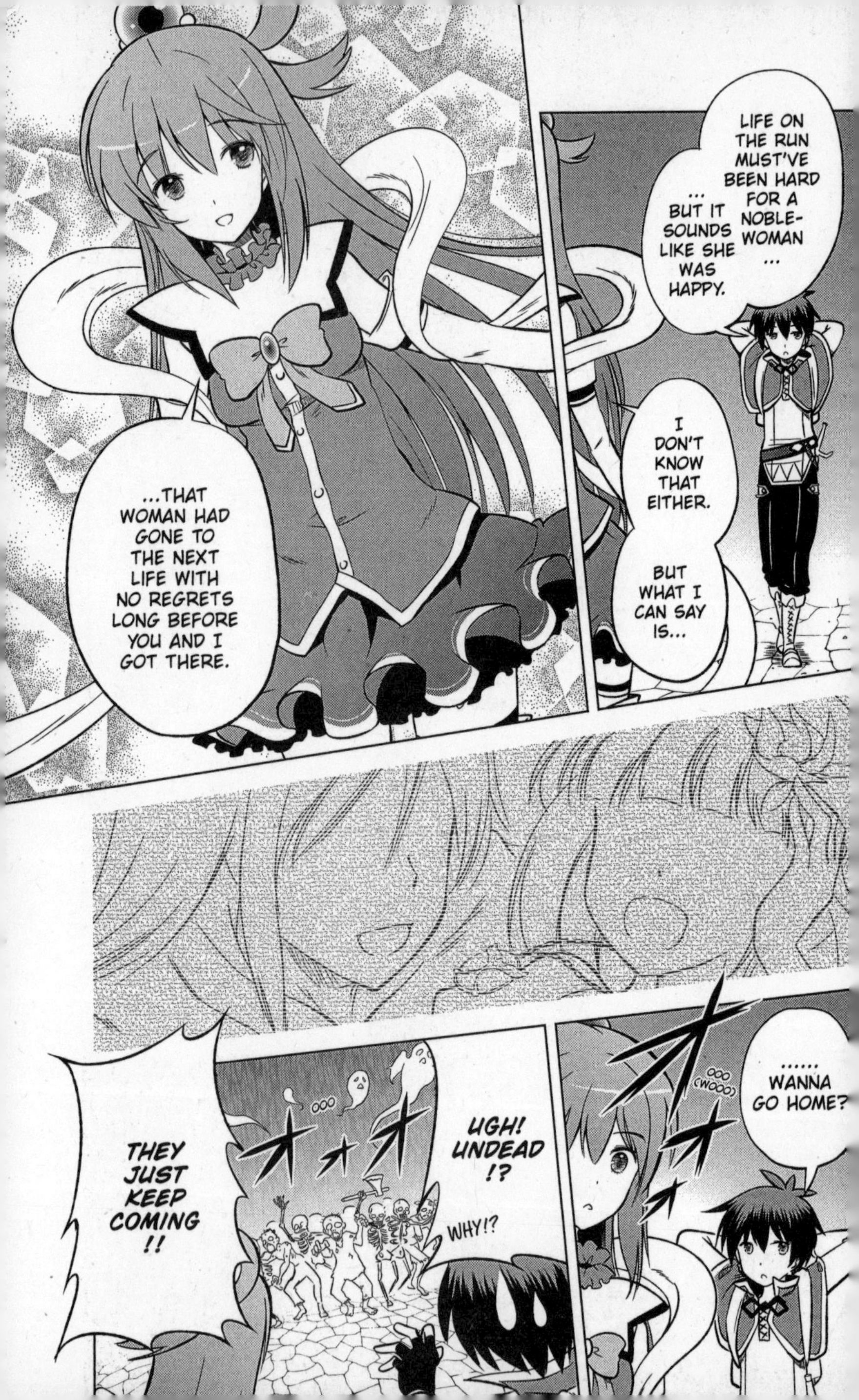
LIFE ON THE RUN MUST'VE BEEN HARD FOR A NOBLE-WOMAN...
...BUT IT SOUNDS LIKE SHE WAS HAPPY.
I DON'T KNOW THAT EITHER.
BUT WHAT I CAN SAY IS...
...THAT WOMAN HAD GONE TO THE NEXT LIFE WITH NO REGRETS LONG BEFORE YOU AND I GOT THERE.
...... WANNA GO HOME?
OOO (WOOO)
OOO
UGH! UNDEAD!?
WHY!?
THEY JUST KEEP COMING!!

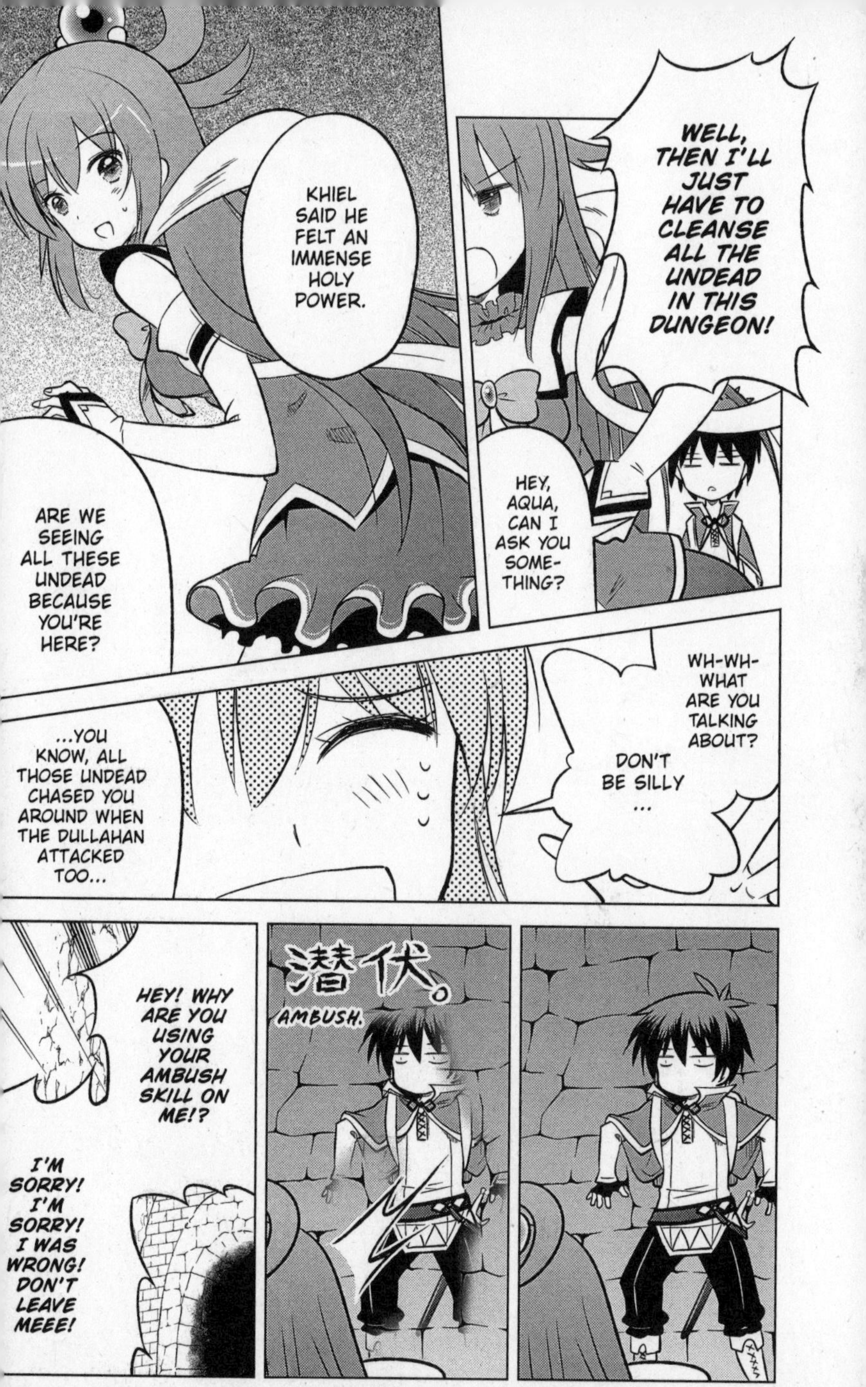
WELL, THEN I'LL JUST HAVE TO CLEANSE ALL THE UNDEAD IN THIS DUNGEON!
HEY, AQUA, CAN I ASK YOU SOME-THING?
KHIEL SAID HE FELT AN IMMENSE HOLY POWER.
ARE WE SEEING ALL THESE UNDEAD BECAUSE YOU'RE HERE?
WH-WH-WHAT ARE YOU TALKING ABOUT?
DON'T BE SILLY...
...YOU KNOW, ALL THOSE UNDEAD CHASED YOU AROUND WHEN THE DULLAHAN ATTACKED TOO...
潜伏。
AMBUSH.
HEY! WHY ARE YOU USING YOUR AMBUSH SKILL ON ME!?
I'M SORRY! I'M SORRY! I WAS WRONG! DON'T LEAVE MEEE!

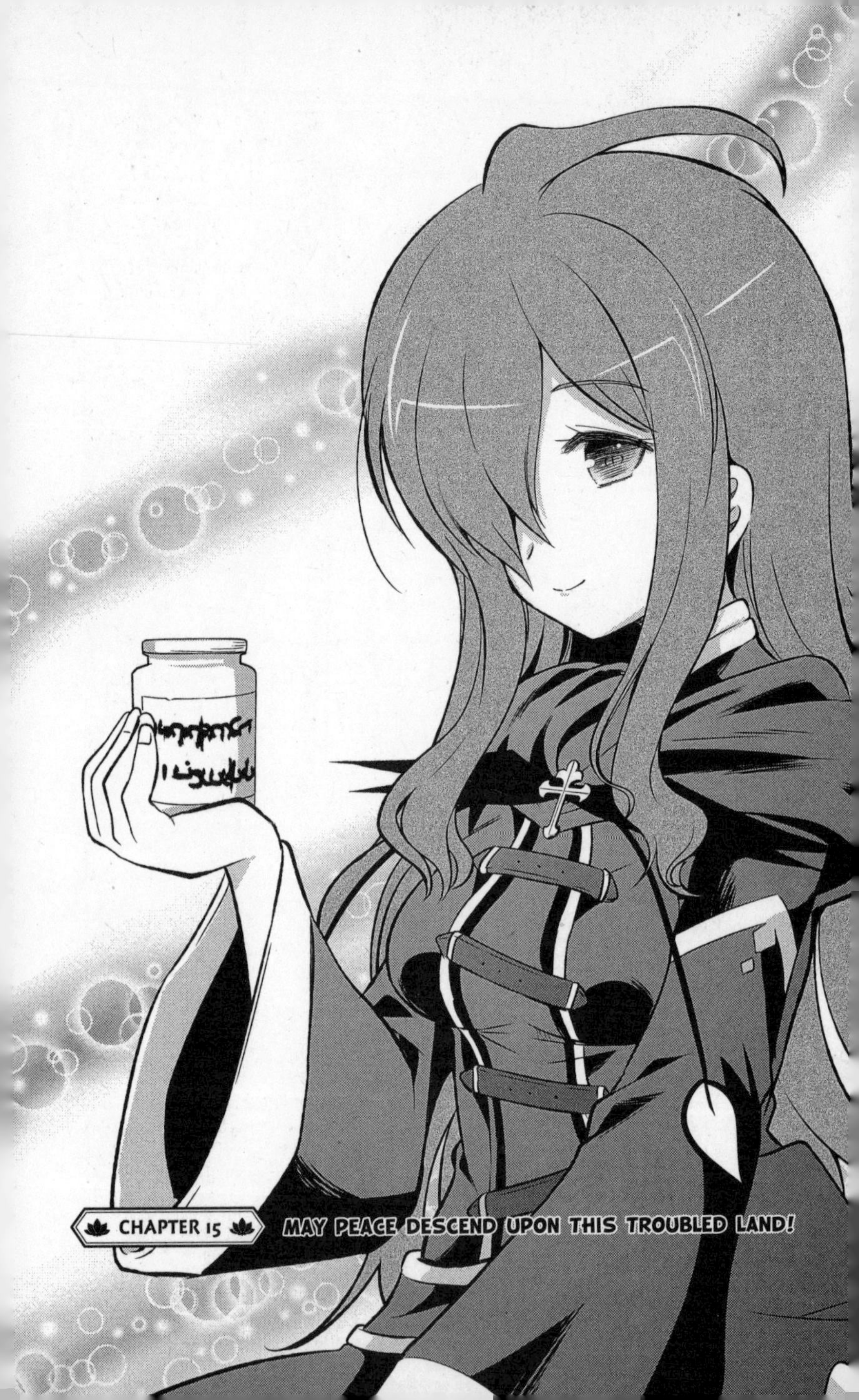
CHAPTER 15
MAY PEACE DESCEND UPON THIS TROUBLED LAND!

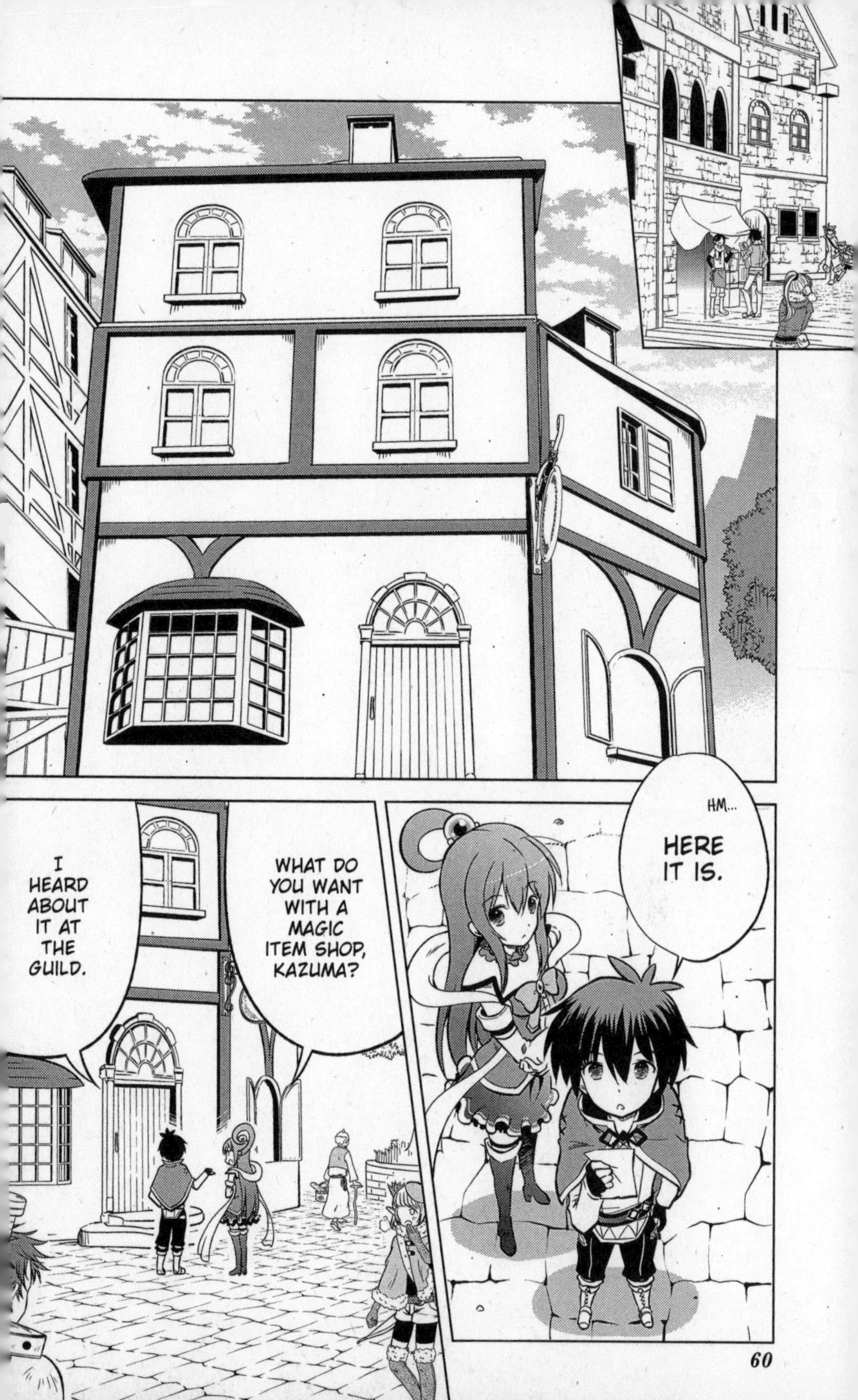
HM... HERE IT IS.
WHAT DO YOU WANT WITH A MAGIC ITEM SHOP, KAZUMA?
I HEARD ABOUT IT AT THE GUILD.

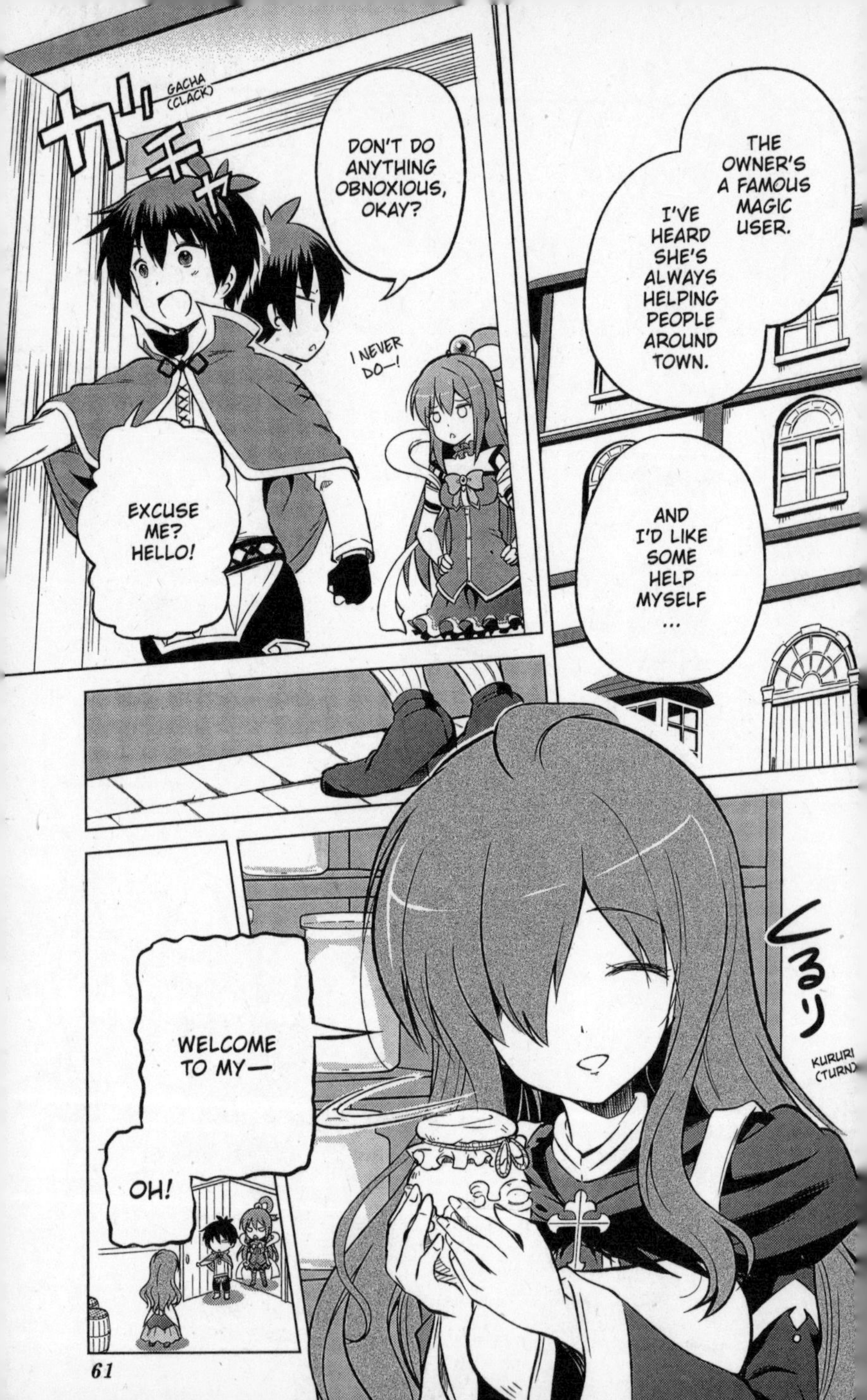
THE OWNER'S A FAMOUS MAGIC USER.
I'VE HEARD SHE'S ALWAYS HELPING PEOPLE AROUND TOWN.
AND I'D LIKE SOME HELP MYSELF...
DON'T DO ANYTHING OBNOXIOUS, OKAY?
I NEVER DO—!
ガチャ
GACHA (CLACK)
EXCUSE ME? HELLO!
くるり
KURURI (TURN)
WELCOME TO MY—
OH!

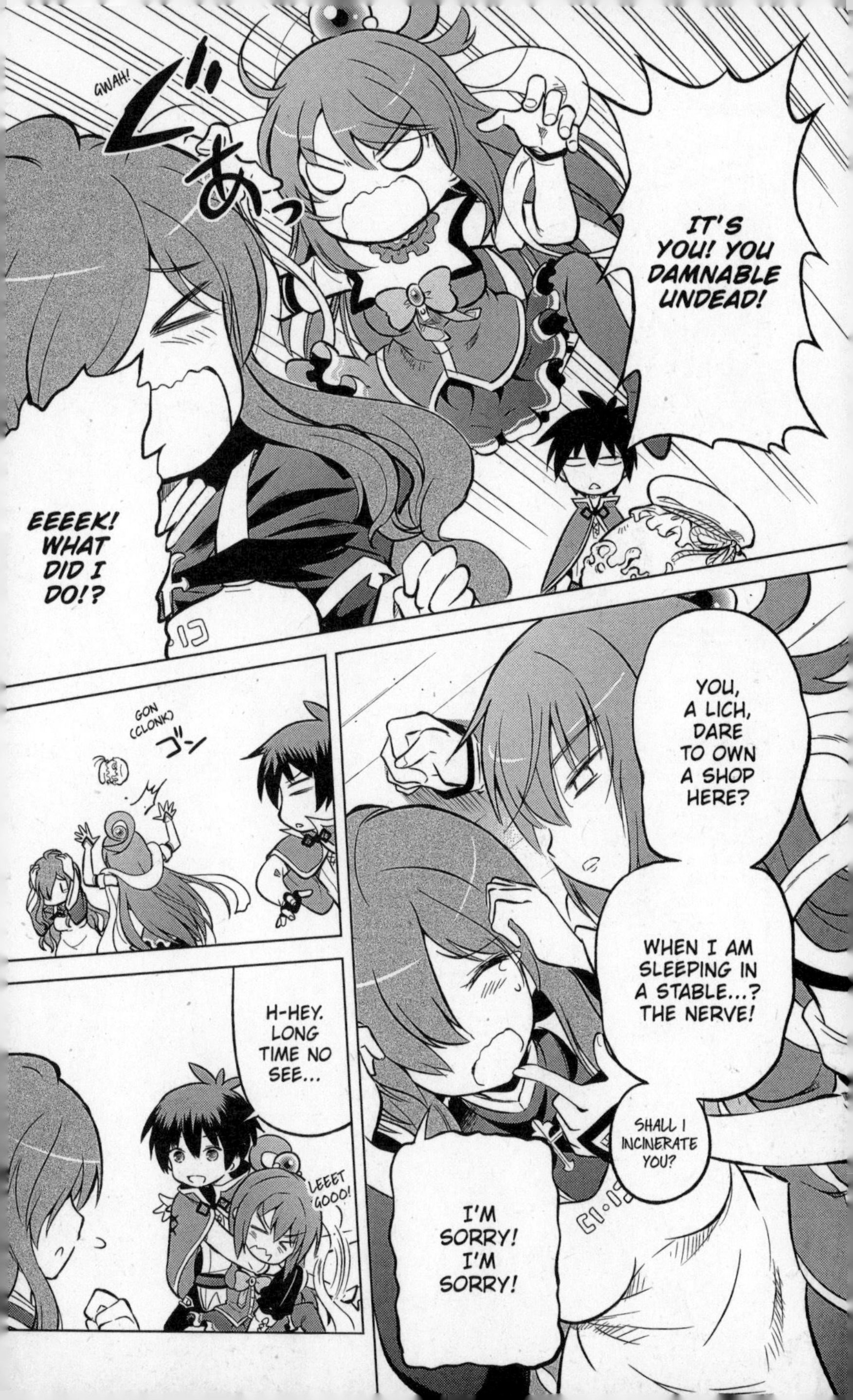
IT'S YOU! YOU DAMNABLE UNDEAD!
GWAH!
ぐあっ
EEEEK! WHAT DID I DO!?
YOU, A LICH, DARE TO OWN A SHOP HERE?
WHEN I AM SLEEPING IN A STABLE...? THE NERVE!
SHALL I INCINERATE YOU?
I'M SORRY! I'M SORRY!
GON (CLONK)
ゴン
H-HEY. LONG TIME NO SEE...
LEEET GOOO!

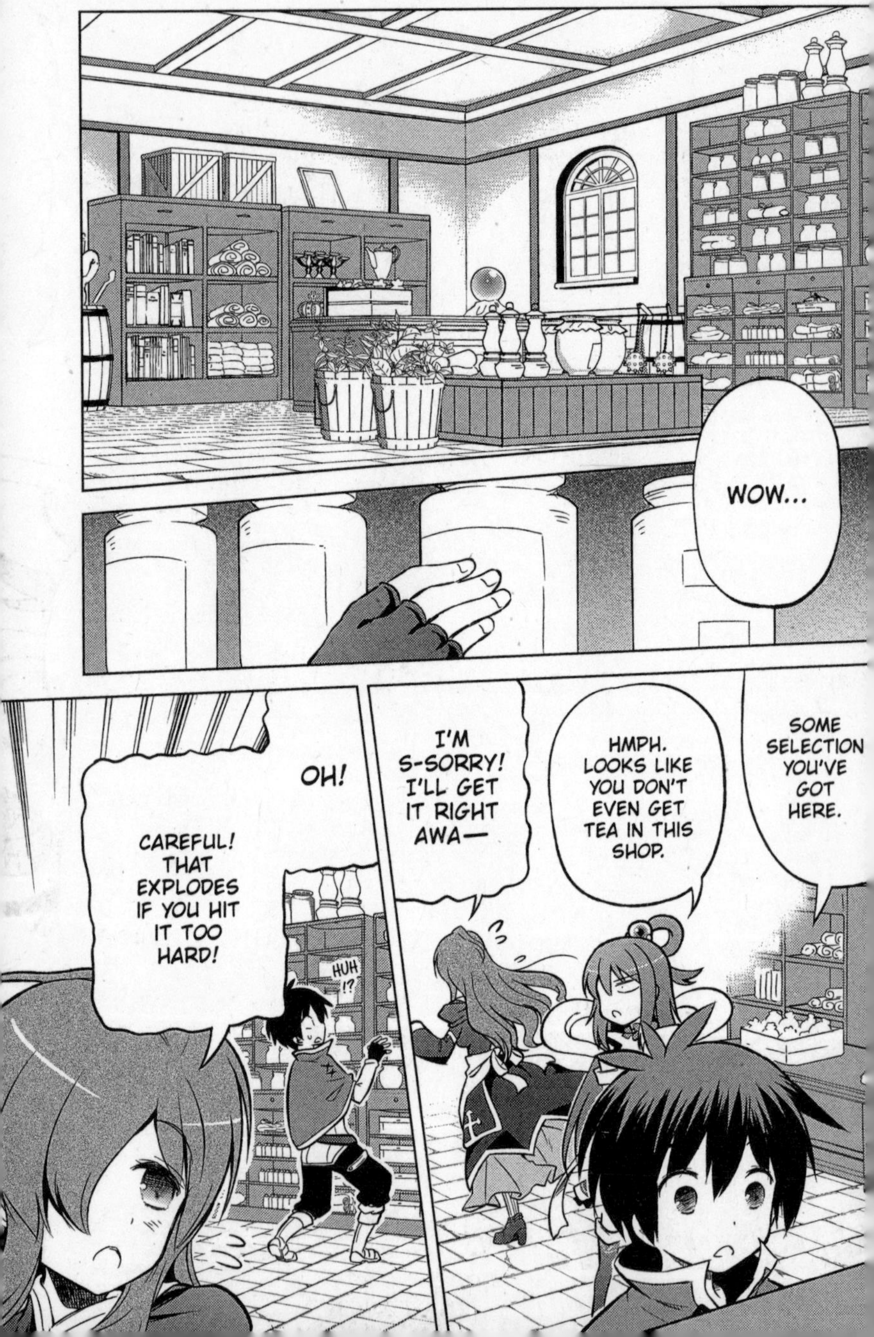
WOW...
SOME SELECTION YOU'VE GOT HERE.
HMPH. LOOKS LIKE YOU DON'T EVEN GET TEA IN THIS SHOP.
I'M S-SORRY! I'LL GET IT RIGHT AWA—
OH!
CAREFUL! THAT EXPLODES IF YOU HIT IT TOO HARD!
HUH !?

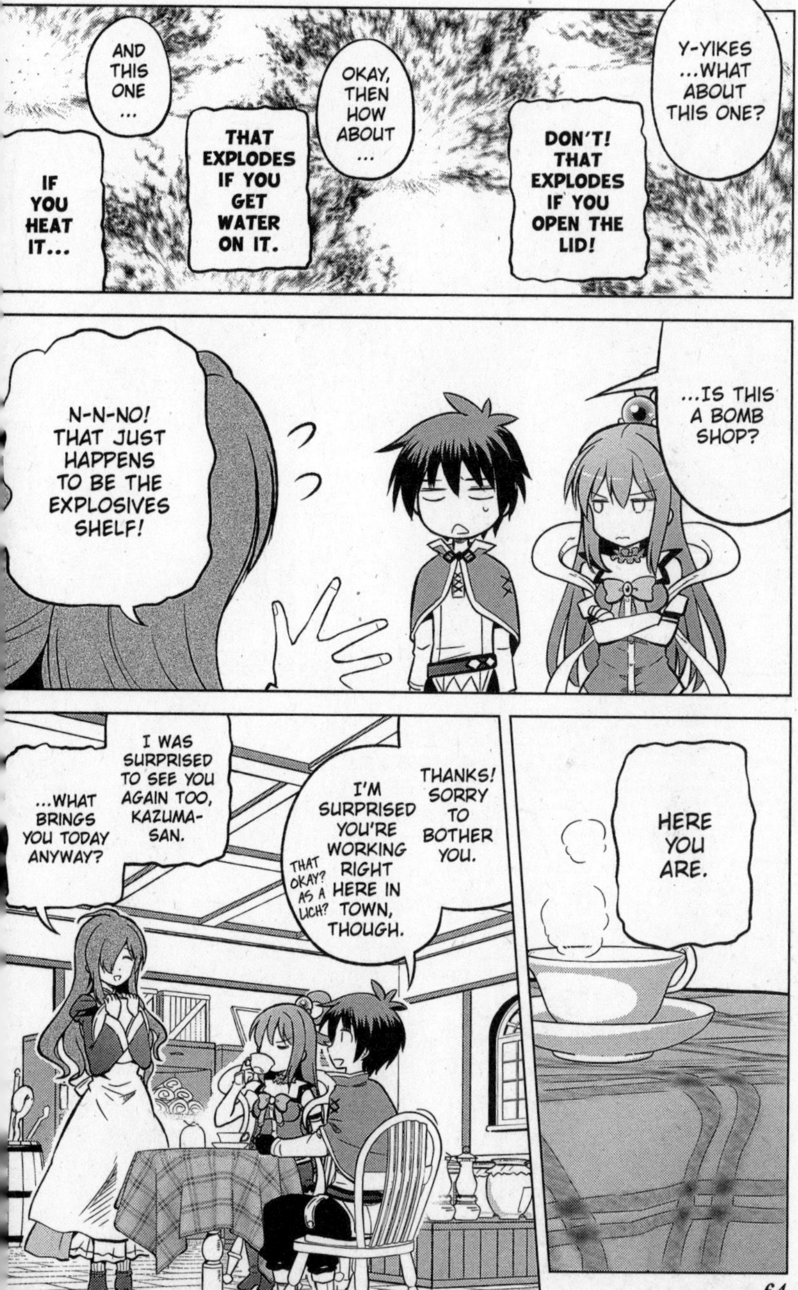
Y-YIKES ...WHAT ABOUT THIS ONE?
DON'T! THAT EXPLODES IF YOU OPEN THE LID!
OKAY, THEN HOW ABOUT ...
THAT EXPLODES IF YOU GET WATER ON IT.
AND THIS ONE ...
IF YOU HEAT IT...
...IS THIS A BOMB SHOP?
N-N-NO! THAT JUST HAPPENS TO BE THE EXPLOSIVES SHELF!
HERE YOU ARE.
THANKS! SORRY TO BOTHER YOU.
I'M SURPRISED YOU'RE WORKING RIGHT HERE IN TOWN, THOUGH.
THAT OKAY? AS A LICH?
I WAS SURPRISED TO SEE YOU AGAIN TOO, KAZUMA-SAN.
...WHAT BRINGS YOU TODAY ANYWAY?

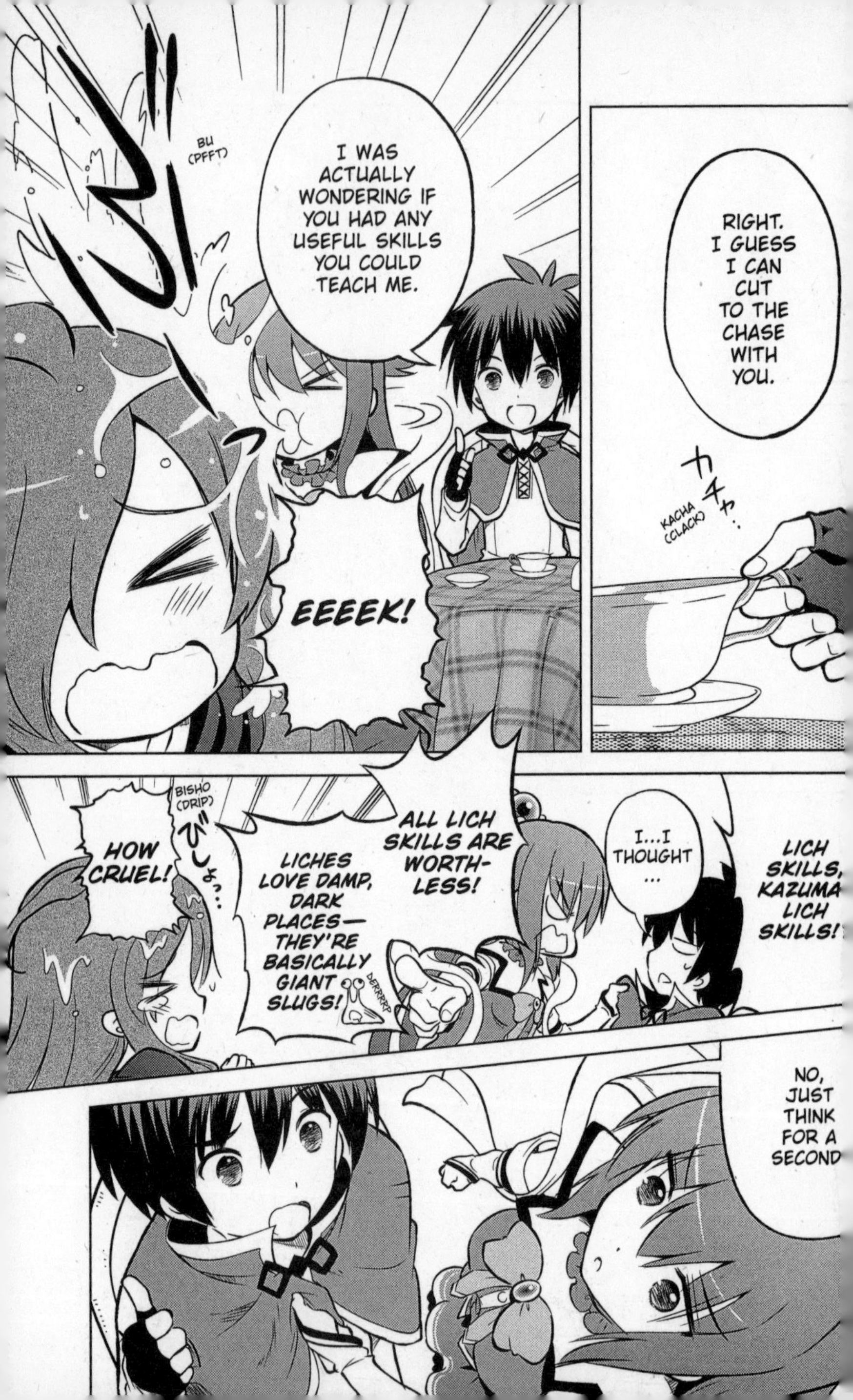
RIGHT. I GUESS I CAN CUT TO THE CHASE WITH YOU.
カチャ…
KACHA (CLACK)
I WAS ACTUALLY WONDERING IF YOU HAD ANY USEFUL SKILLS YOU COULD TEACH ME.
BU (PFFT)
EEEEK!
LICH SKILLS, KAZUMA LICH SKILLS!
I...I THOUGHT...
ALL LICH SKILLS ARE WORTH-LESS!
LICHES LOVE DAMP, DARK PLACES—THEY'RE BASICALLY GIANT SLUGS!
DERRRP
HOW CRUEL!
BISHO (DRIP)
びしょっ…
NO, JUST THINK FOR A SECOND

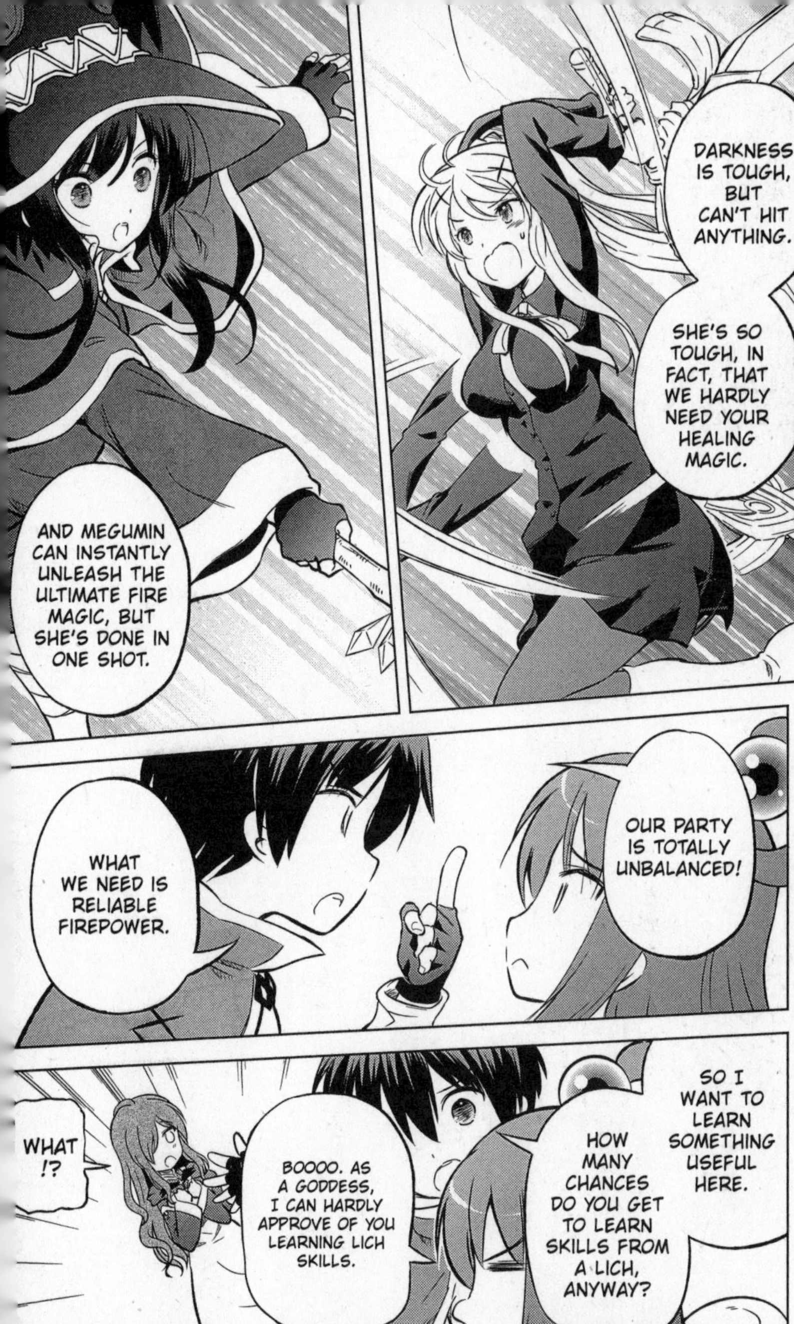
DARKNESS IS TOUGH, BUT CAN'T HIT ANYTHING.
SHE'S SO TOUGH, IN FACT, THAT WE HARDLY NEED YOUR HEALING MAGIC.
AND MEGUMIN CAN INSTANTLY UNLEASH THE ULTIMATE FIRE MAGIC, BUT SHE'S DONE IN ONE SHOT.
OUR PARTY IS TOTALLY UNBALANCED!
WHAT WE NEED IS RELIABLE FIREPOWER.
SO I WANT TO LEARN SOMETHING USEFUL HERE.
HOW MANY CHANCES DO YOU GET TO LEARN SKILLS FROM A LICH, ANYWAY?
BOOOO. AS A GODDESS, I CAN HARDLY APPROVE OF YOU LEARNING LICH SKILLS.
WHAT !?

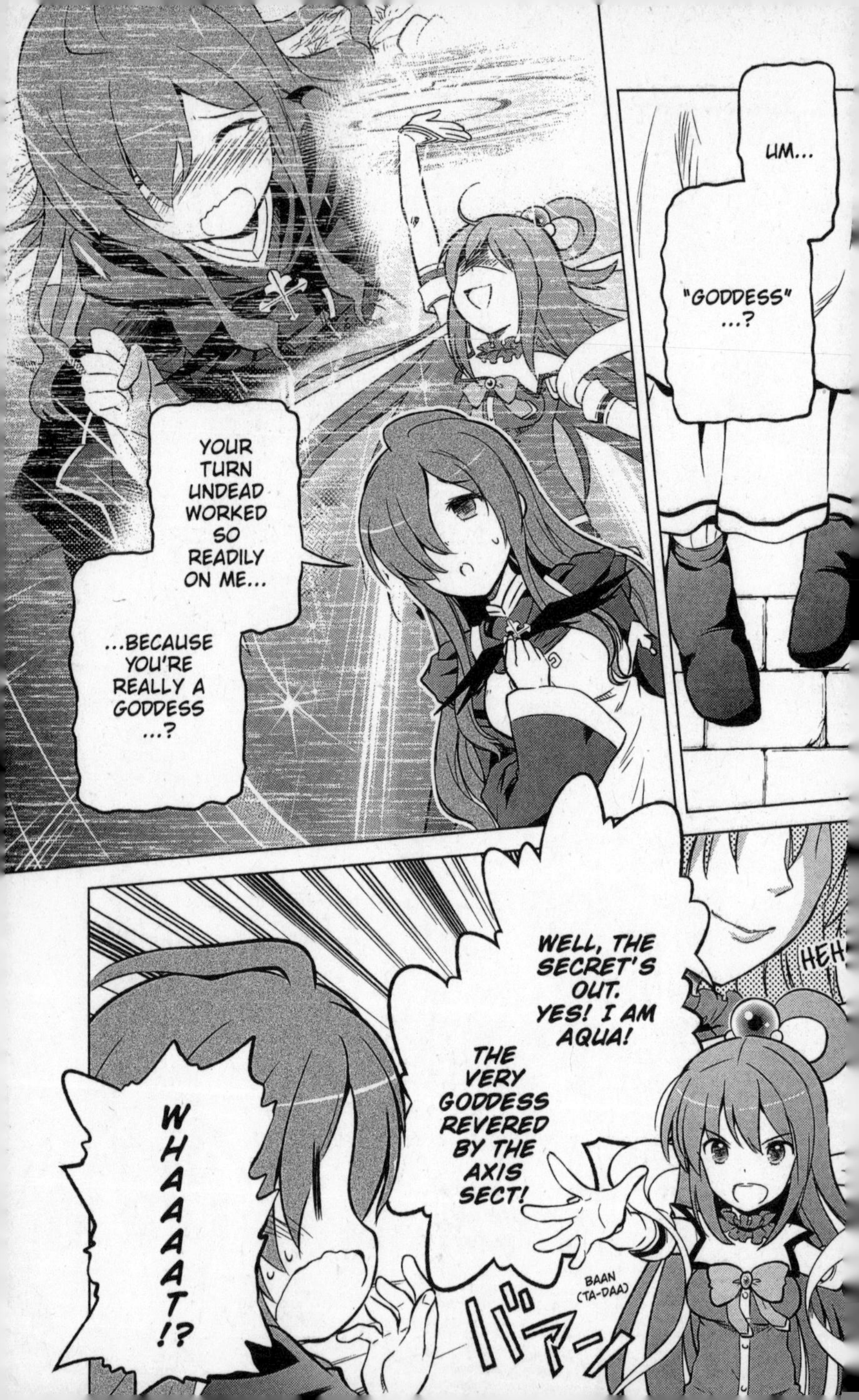
UM...
"GODDESS" ...?
YOUR TURN UNDEAD WORKED SO READILY ON ME...
...BECAUSE YOU'RE REALLY A GODDESS ...?
HEH
WELL, THE SECRET'S OUT. YES! I AM AQUA!
THE VERY GODDESS REVERED BY THE AXIS SECT!
BAAN (TA-DAA)
WHAAAAAT!?

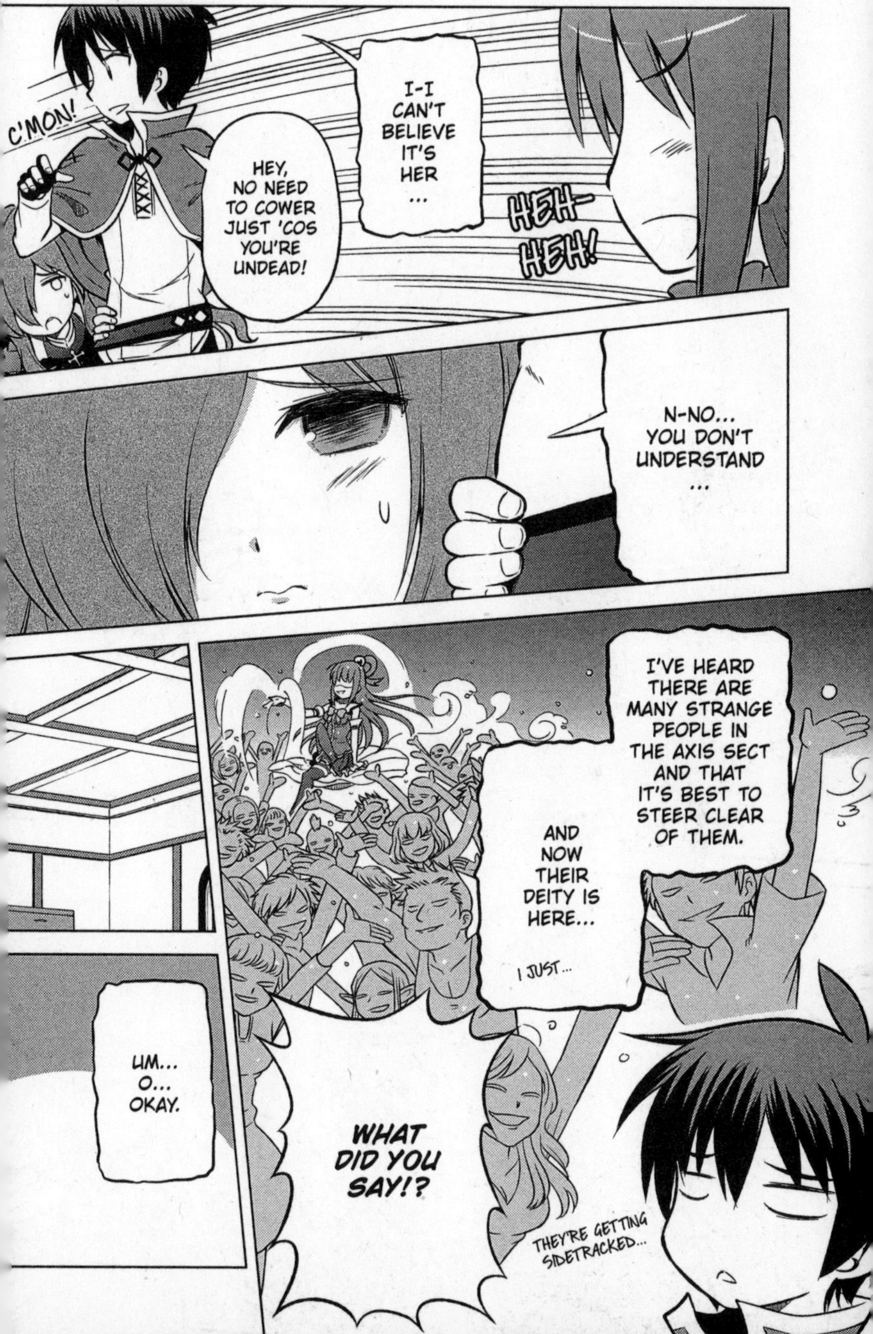
I-I CAN'T BELIEVE IT'S HER ...
HEH-HEH!
C'MON!
HEY, NO NEED TO COWER JUST 'COS YOU'RE UNDEAD!
N-NO... YOU DON'T UNDERSTAND ...
I'VE HEARD THERE ARE MANY STRANGE PEOPLE IN THE AXIS SECT AND THAT IT'S BEST TO STEER CLEAR OF THEM.
AND NOW THEIR DEITY IS HERE...
I JUST...
WHAT DID YOU SAY!?
THEY'RE GETTING SIDETRACKED...
UM... O... OKAY.

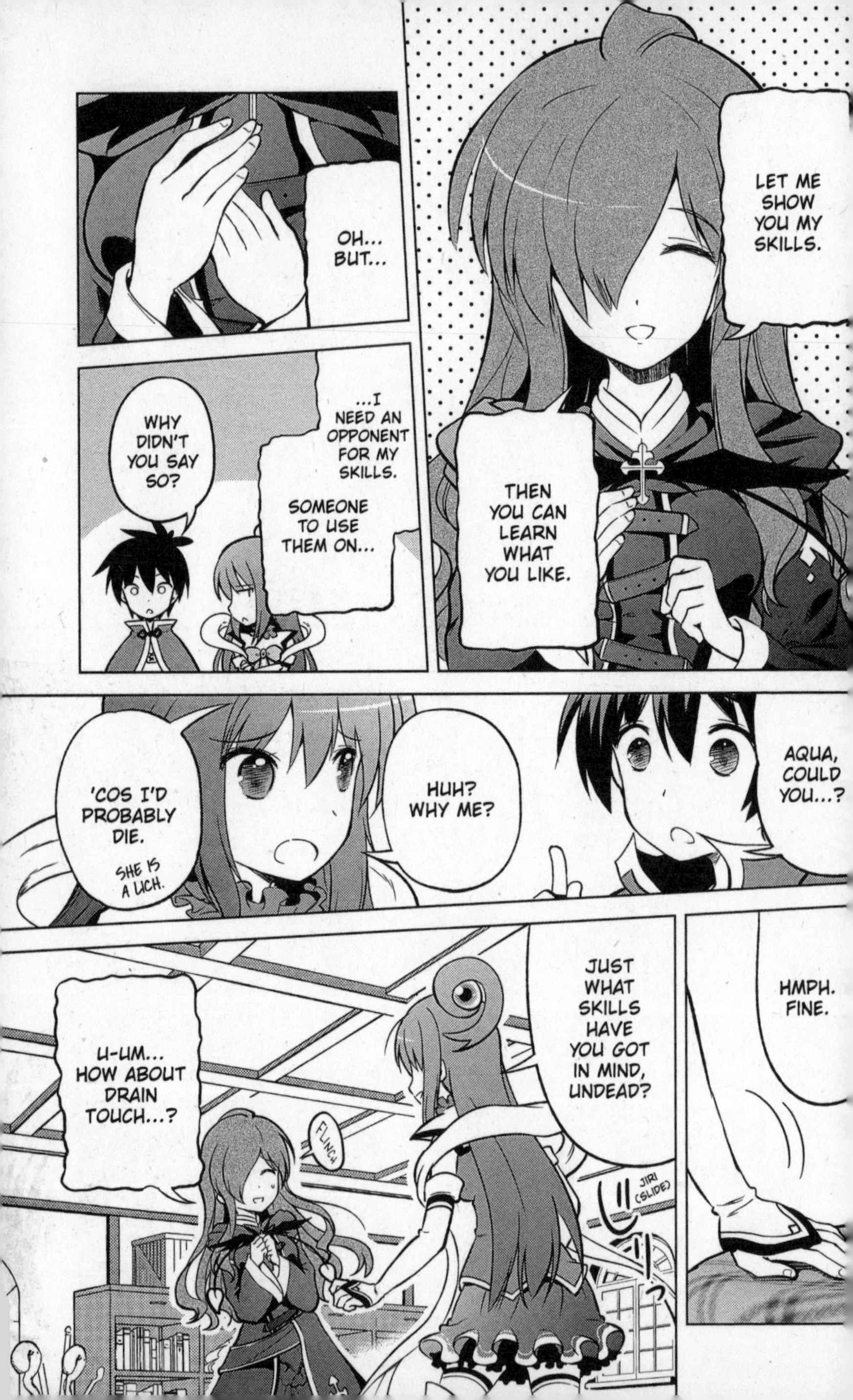
LET ME SHOW YOU MY SKILLS.
THEN YOU CAN LEARN WHAT YOU LIKE.
OH... BUT...
...I NEED AN OPPONENT FOR MY SKILLS.
SOMEONE TO USE THEM ON...
WHY DIDN'T YOU SAY SO?
AQUA, COULD YOU...?
HUH? WHY ME?
'COS I'D PROBABLY DIE.
SHE IS A LICH.
HMPH. FINE.
JUST WHAT SKILLS HAVE YOU GOT IN MIND, UNDEAD?
JIRI (SLIDE)
FLINCH
U-UM... HOW ABOUT DRAIN TOUCH...?

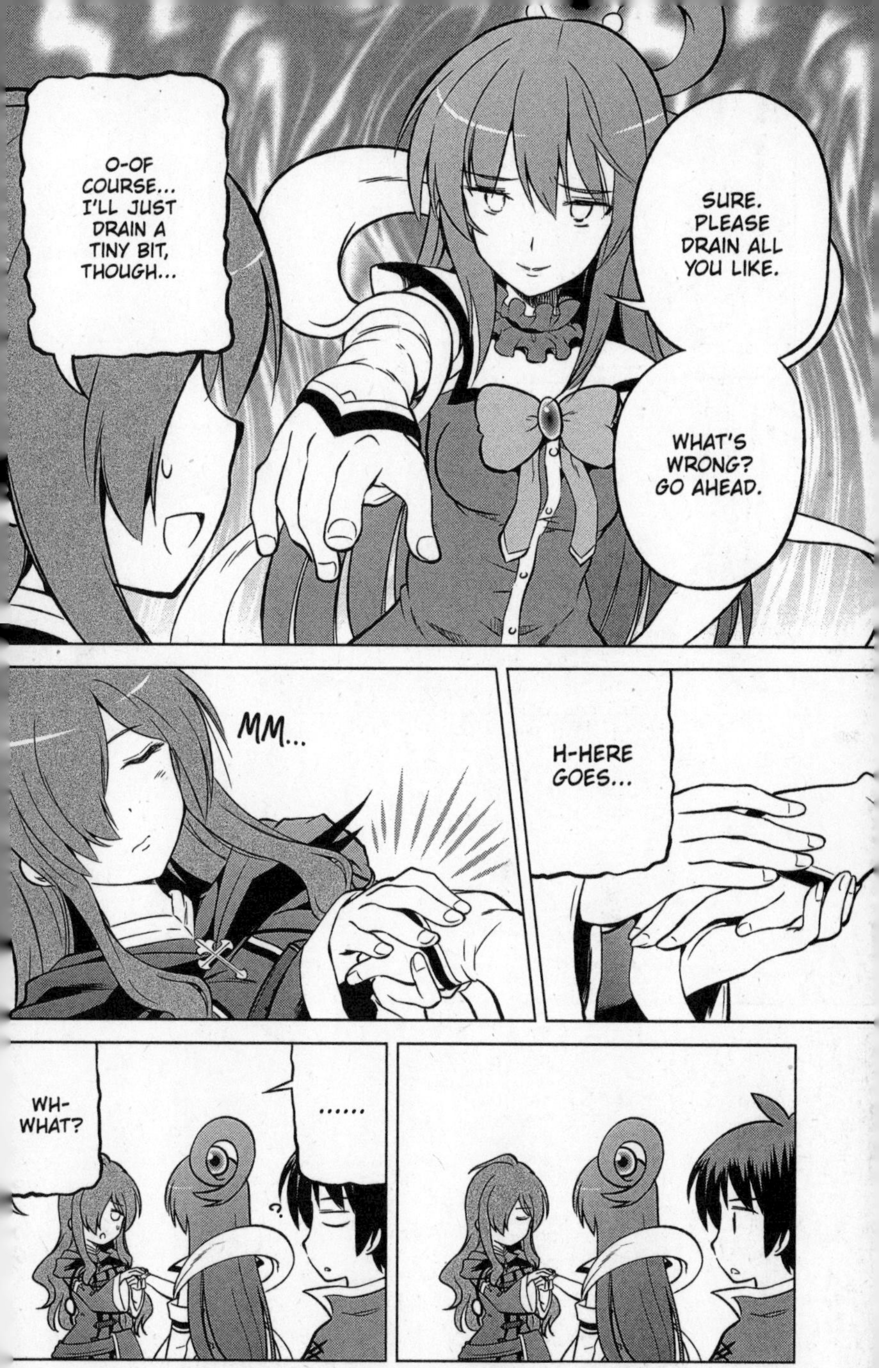
SURE. PLEASE DRAIN ALL YOU LIKE.
WHAT'S WRONG? GO AHEAD.
O-OF COURSE... I'LL JUST DRAIN A TINY BIT, THOUGH...
H-HERE GOES...
MM...
......
WH- WHAT?

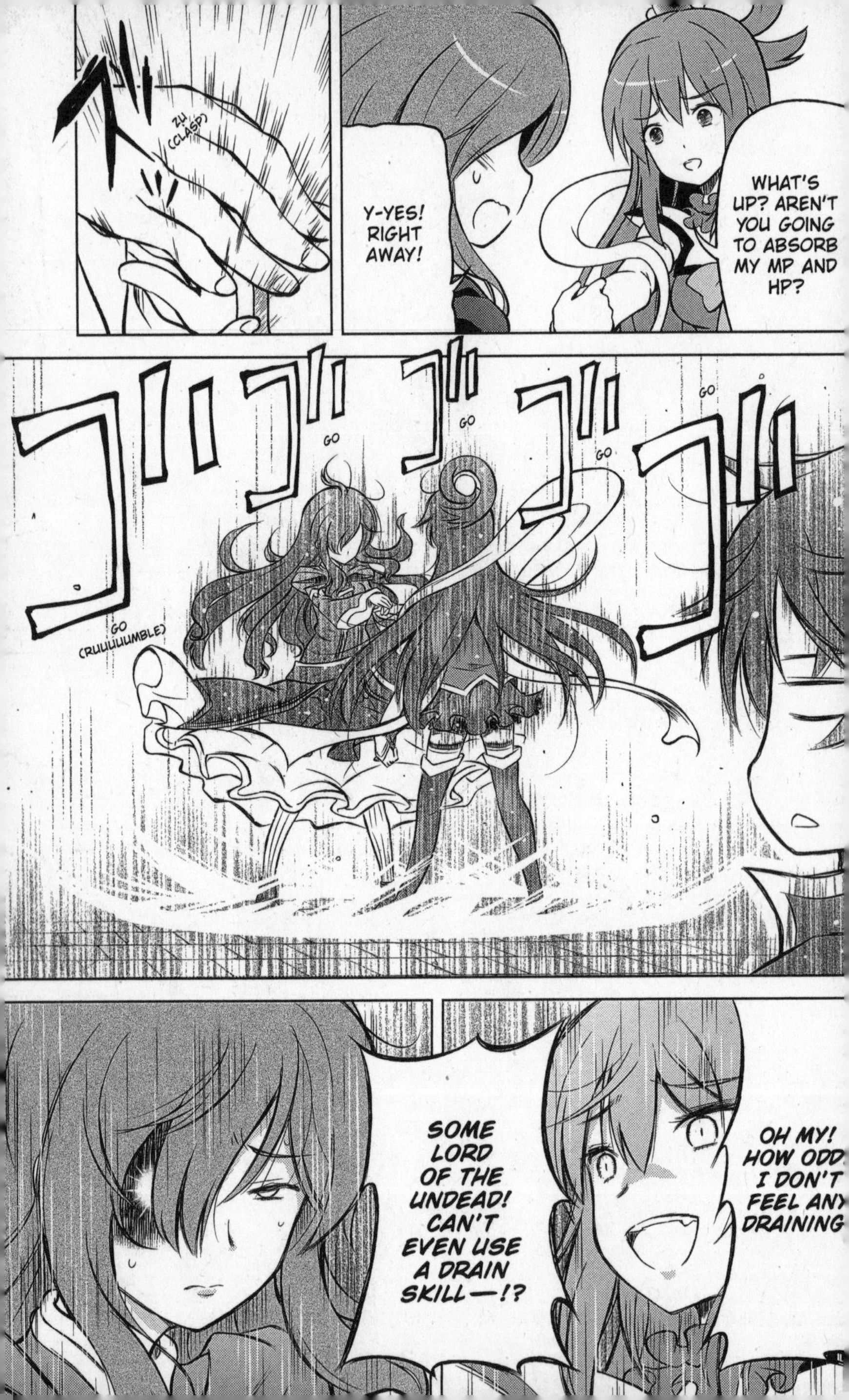
WHAT'S UP? AREN'T YOU GOING TO ABSORB MY MP AND HP?
Y-YES! RIGHT AWAY!
ZU (CLASP)
GO
GO
GO
GO
GO (RUUUUUMBLE)
OH MY! HOW ODD I DON'T FEEL AN DRAINING
SOME LORD OF THE UNDEAD! CAN'T EVEN USE A DRAIN SKILL—!?

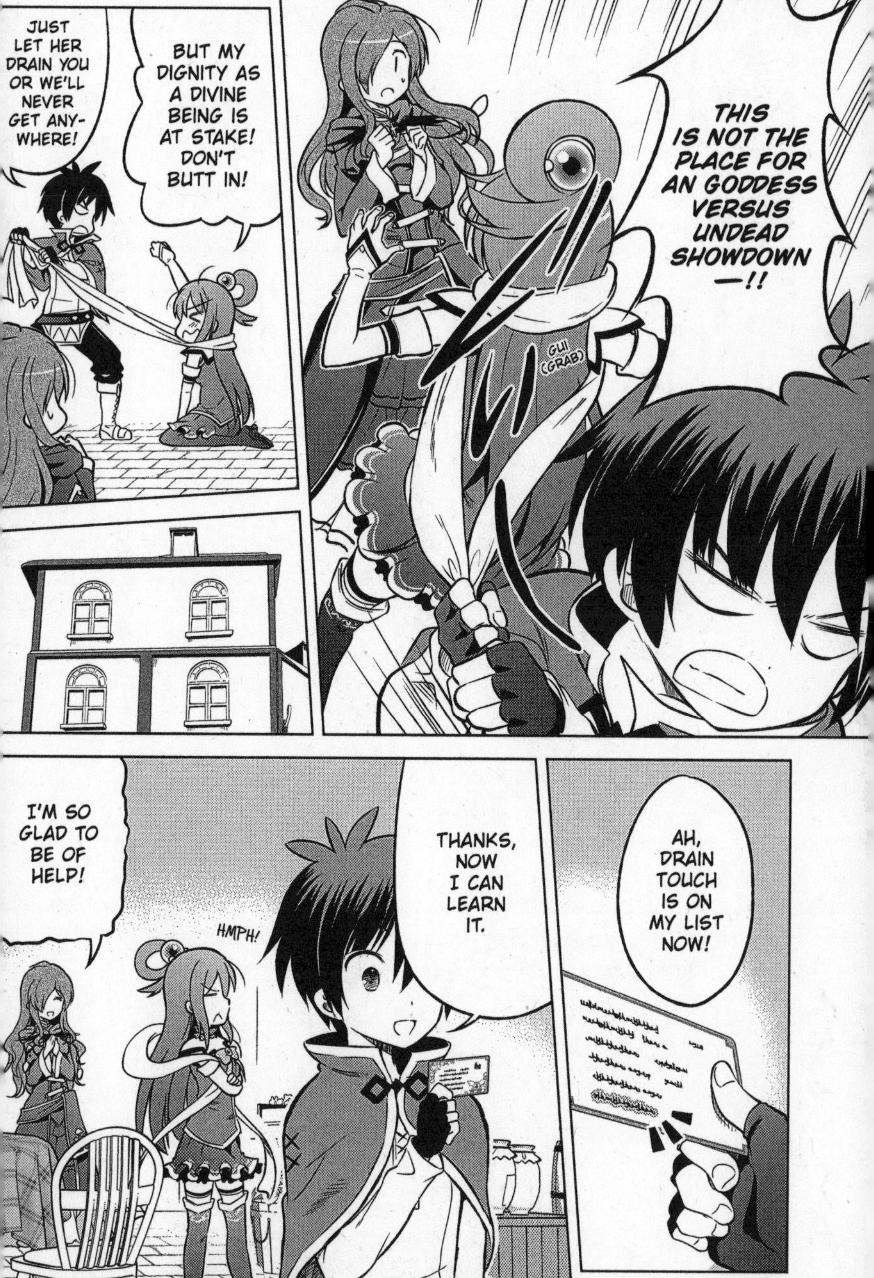
THIS IS NOT THE PLACE FOR AN GODDESS VERSUS UNDEAD SHOWDOWN—!!
GUI (GRAB)
BUT MY DIGNITY AS A DIVINE BEING IS AT STAKE! DON'T BUTT IN!
JUST LET HER DRAIN YOU OR WE'LL NEVER GET ANY-WHERE!
AH, DRAIN TOUCH IS ON MY LIST NOW!
THANKS, NOW I CAN LEARN IT.
I'M SO GLAD TO BE OF HELP!
HMPH!

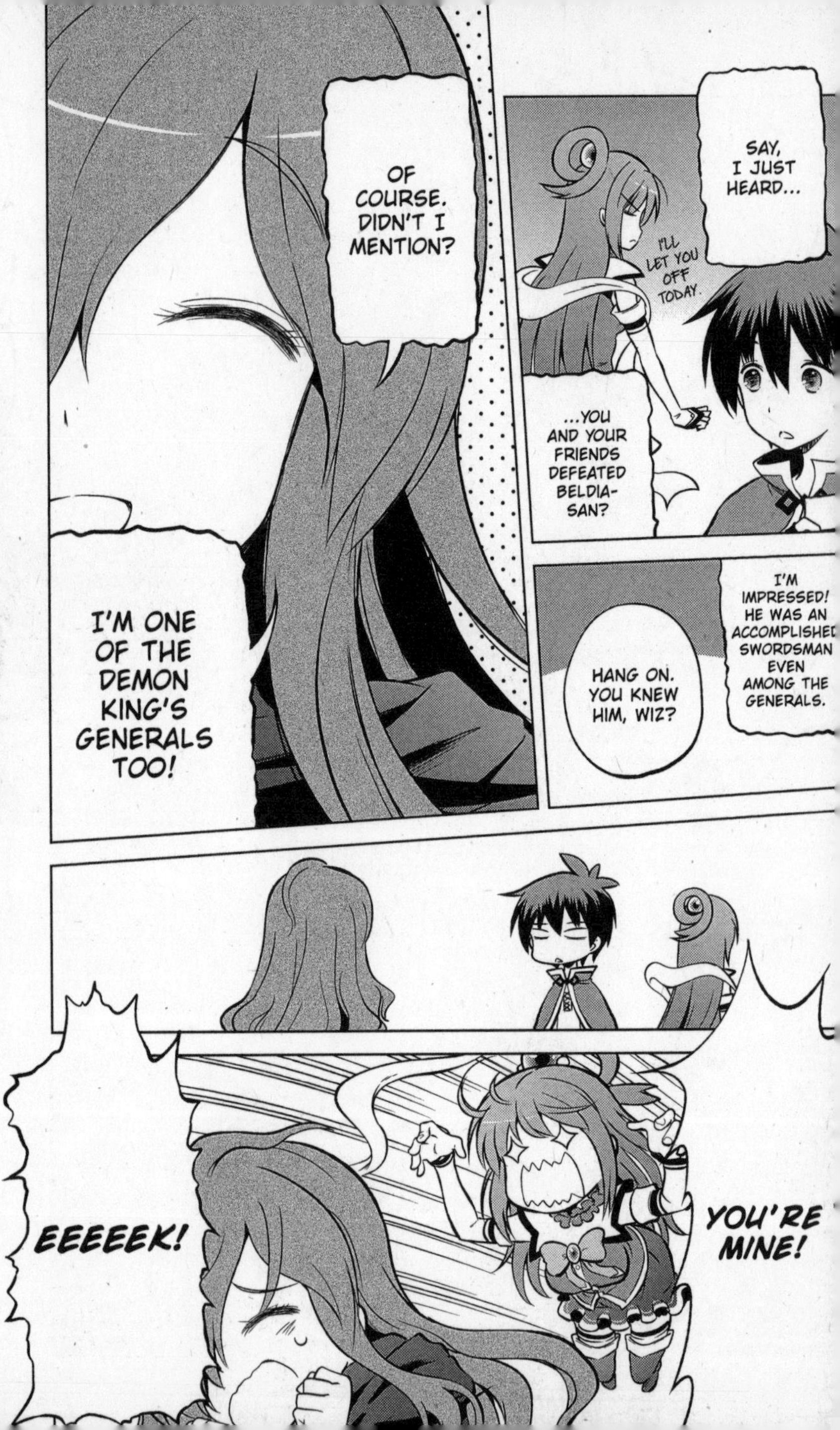
SAY, I JUST HEARD...
I'LL LET YOU OFF TODAY.
...YOU AND YOUR FRIENDS DEFEATED BELDIA-SAN?
I'M IMPRESSED! HE WAS AN ACCOMPLISHED SWORDSMAN EVEN AMONG THE GENERALS.
HANG ON. YOU KNEW HIM, WIZ?
OF COURSE. DIDN'T I MENTION?
I'M ONE OF THE DEMON KING'S GENERALS TOO!
YOU'RE MINE!
EEEEEK!

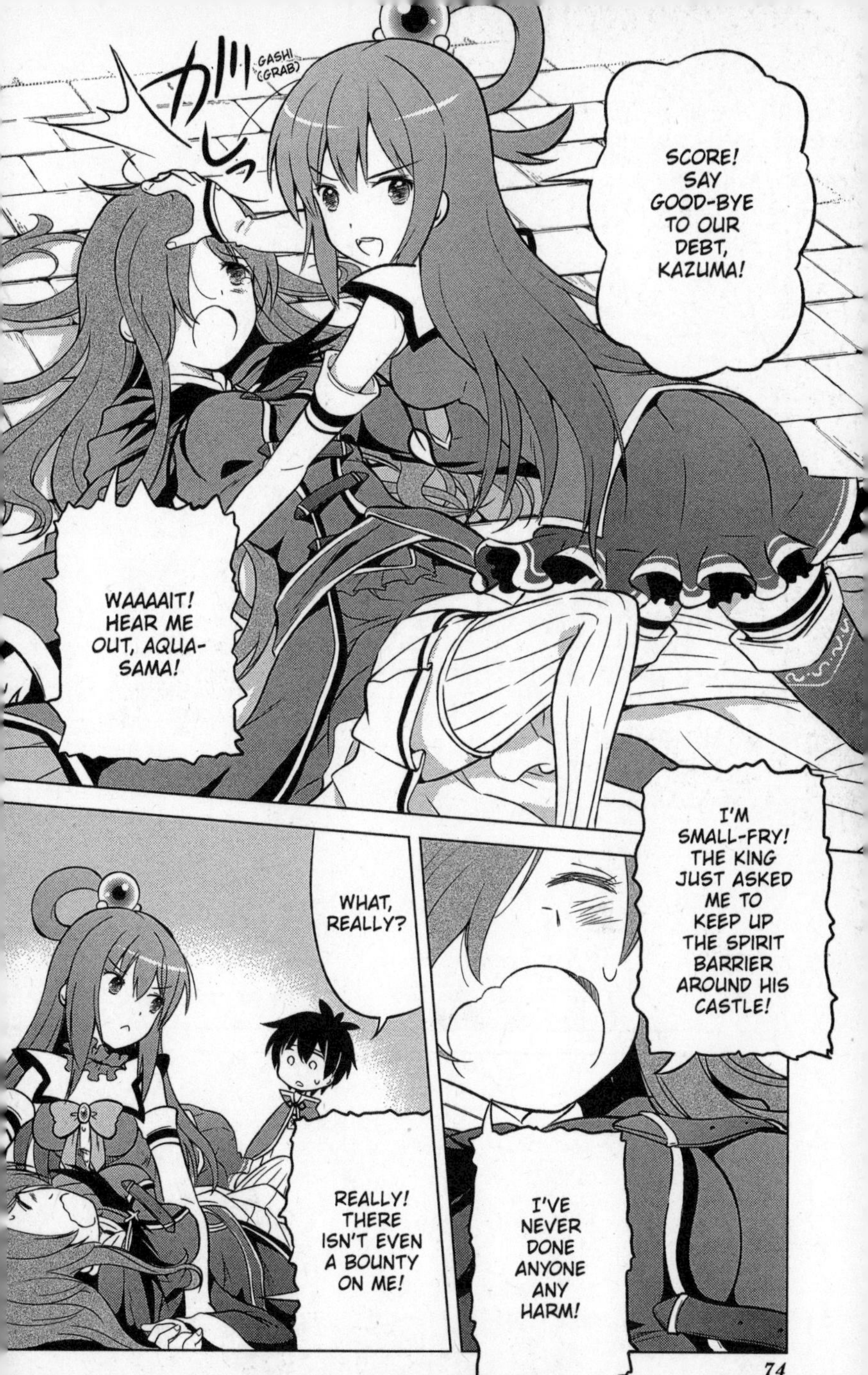
SCORE! SAY GOOD-BYE TO OUR DEBT, KAZUMA!
GASHI (GRAB)
WAAAAIT! HEAR ME OUT, AQUA-SAMA!
I'M SMALL-FRY! THE KING JUST ASKED ME TO KEEP UP THE SPIRIT BARRIER AROUND HIS CASTLE!
I'VE NEVER DONE ANYONE ANY HARM!
WHAT, REALLY?
REALLY! THERE ISN'T EVEN A BOUNTY ON ME!

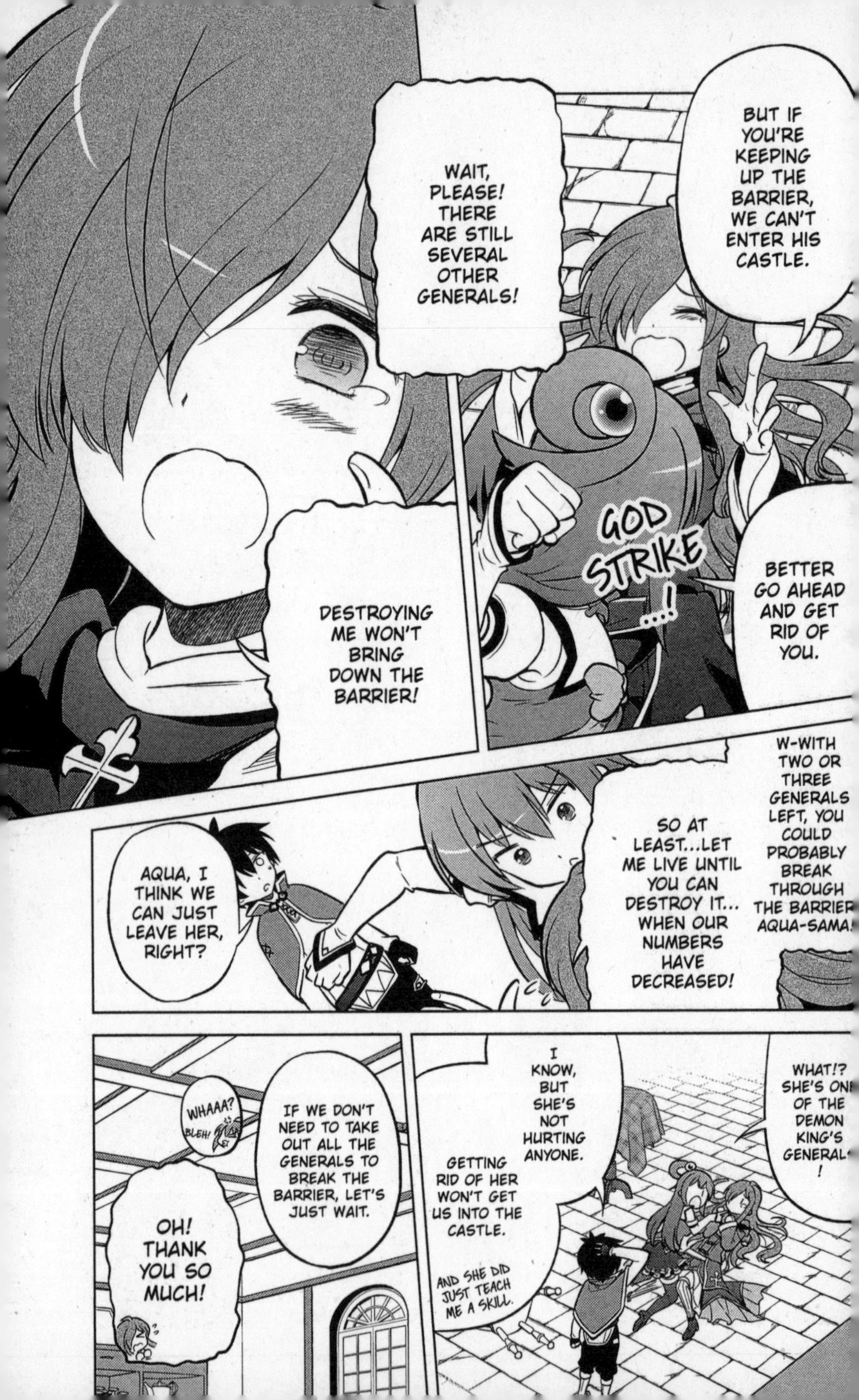
BUT IF YOU'RE KEEPING UP THE BARRIER, WE CAN'T ENTER HIS CASTLE.
BETTER GO AHEAD AND GET RID OF YOU.
GOD STRIKE ...!
WAIT, PLEASE! THERE ARE STILL SEVERAL OTHER GENERALS!
DESTROYING ME WON'T BRING DOWN THE BARRIER!
W-WITH TWO OR THREE GENERALS LEFT, YOU COULD PROBABLY BREAK THROUGH THE BARRIER AQUA-SAMA!
SO AT LEAST...LET ME LIVE UNTIL YOU CAN DESTROY IT... WHEN OUR NUMBERS HAVE DECREASED!
AQUA, I THINK WE CAN JUST LEAVE HER, RIGHT?
WHAT!? SHE'S ON OF THE DEMON KING'S GENERAL !
I KNOW, BUT SHE'S NOT HURTING ANYONE.
GETTING RID OF HER WON'T GET US INTO THE CASTLE.
AND SHE DID JUST TEACH ME A SKILL.
IF WE DON'T NEED TO TAKE OUT ALL THE GENERALS TO BREAK THE BARRIER, LET'S JUST WAIT.
WHAAA?
BLEH!
OH! THANK YOU SO MUCH!

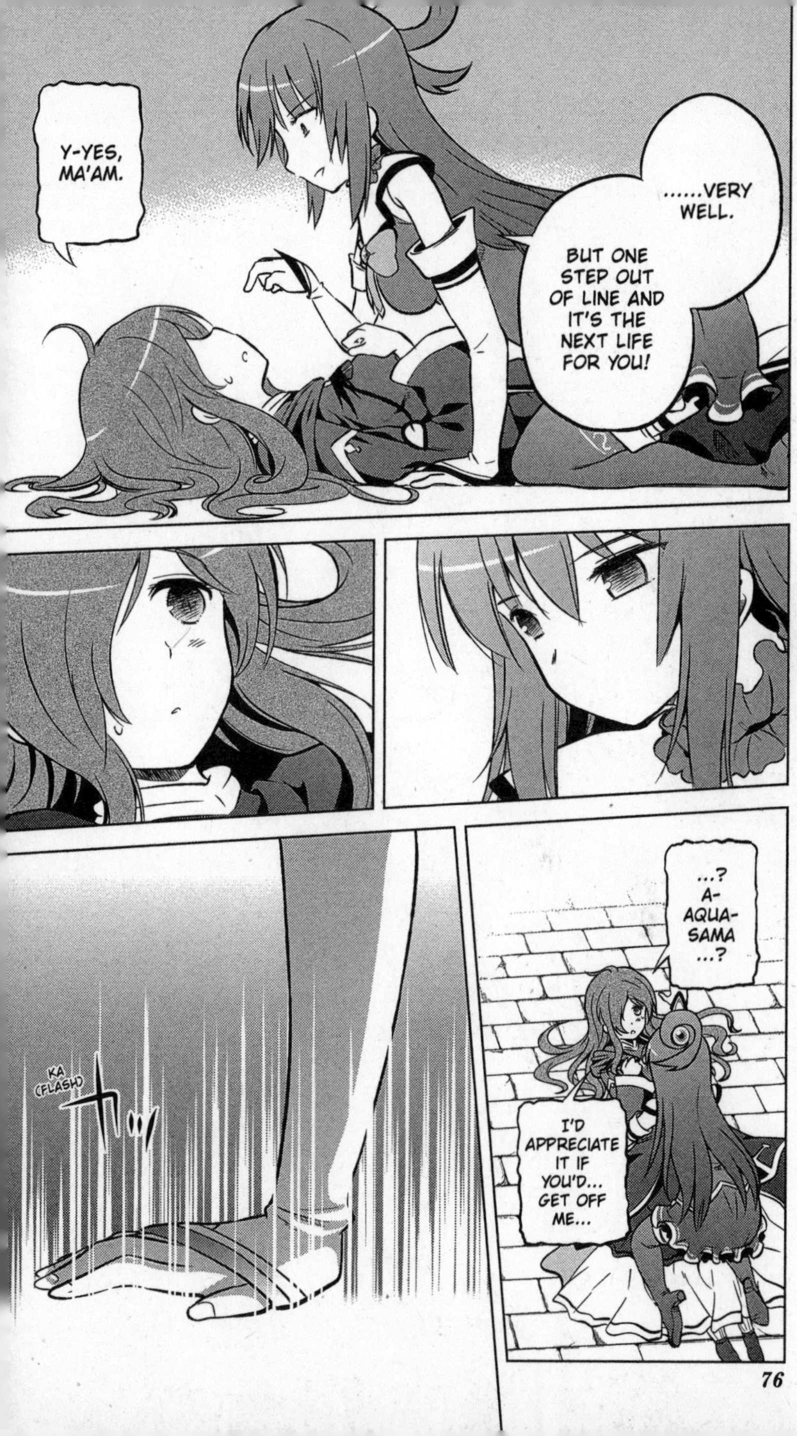
......VERY WELL.
BUT ONE STEP OUT OF LINE AND IT'S THE NEXT LIFE FOR YOU!
Y-YES, MA'AM.
...? A-AQUA-SAMA ...?
I'D APPRECIATE IT IF YOU'D... GET OFF ME...
KA (FLASH)

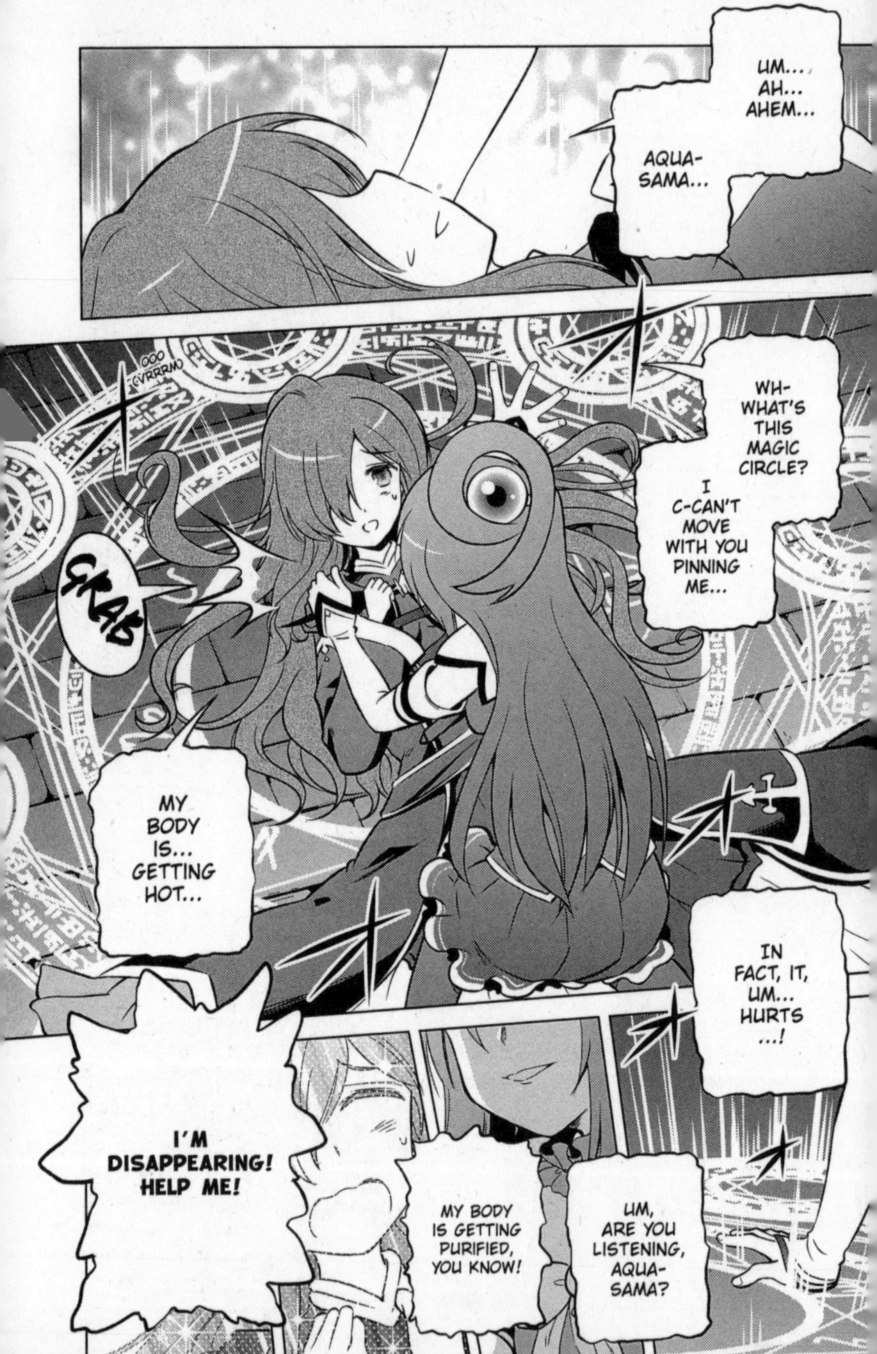
UM... AH... AHEM...
AQUA-SAMA...
OOO (VRRRM)
WH-WHAT'S THIS MAGIC CIRCLE?
I C-CAN'T MOVE WITH YOU PINNING ME...
GRAB
MY BODY IS... GETTING HOT...
IN FACT, IT, UM... HURTS ...!
UM, ARE YOU LISTENING, AQUA-SAMA?
MY BODY IS GETTING PURIFIED, YOU KNOW!
I'M DISAPPEARING! HELP ME!

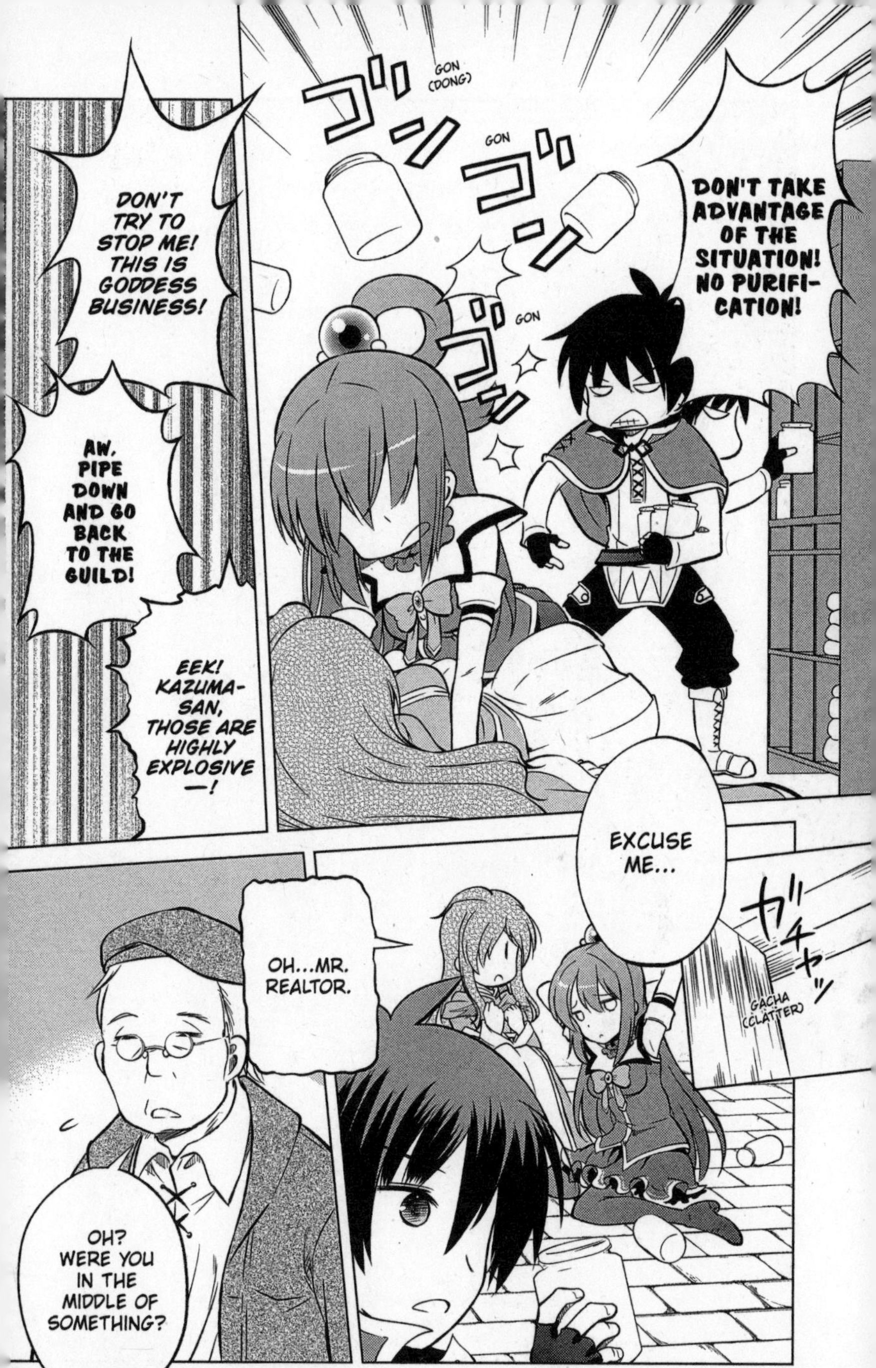
GON (DONG)
GON
GON
DON'T TAKE ADVANTAGE OF THE SITUATION! NO PURIFICATION!
DON'T TRY TO STOP ME! THIS IS GODDESS BUSINESS!
AW. PIPE DOWN AND GO BACK TO THE GUILD!
EEK! KAZUMA-SAN, THOSE ARE HIGHLY EXPLOSIVE—!
GACHA (CLATTER)
EXCUSE ME...
OH...MR. REALTOR.
OH? WERE YOU IN THE MIDDLE OF SOMETHING?

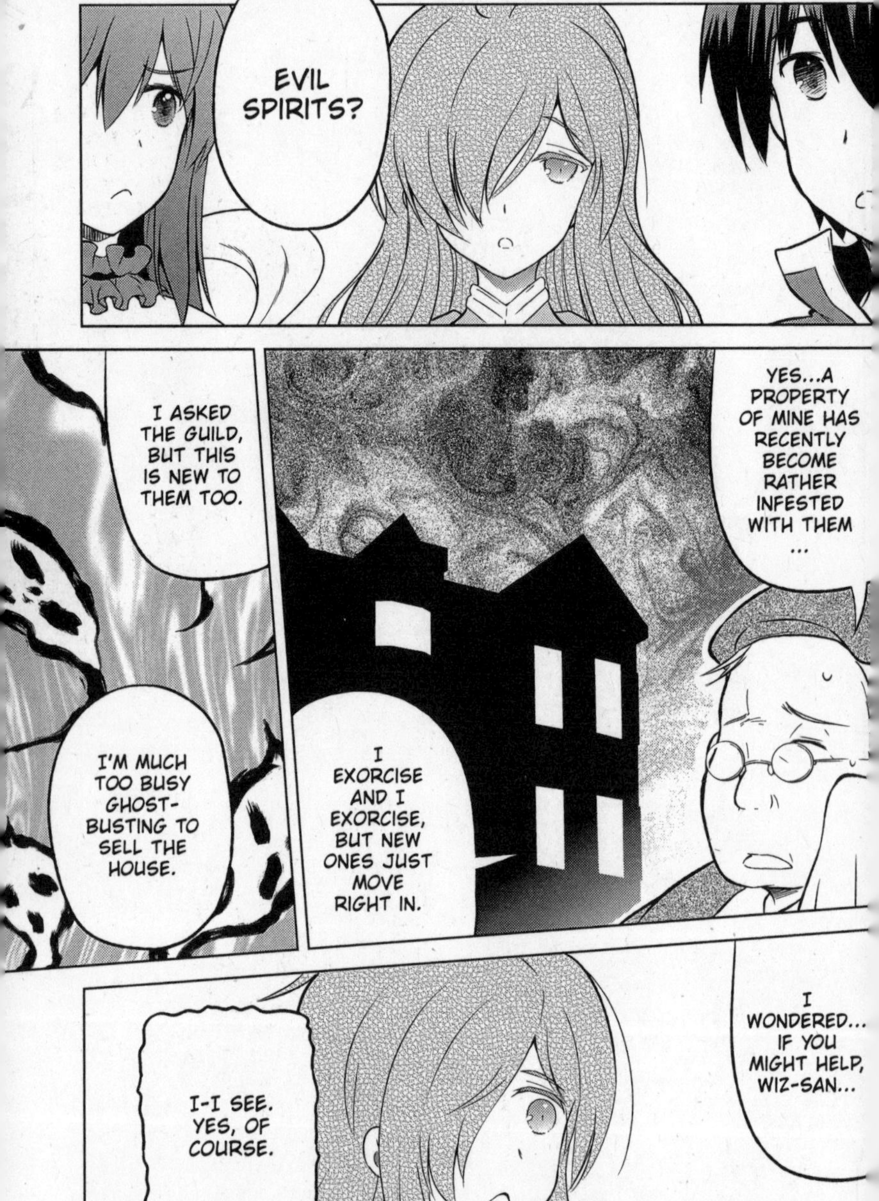
EVIL SPIRITS?
YES...A PROPERTY OF MINE HAS RECENTLY BECOME RATHER INFESTED WITH THEM ...
I EXORCISE AND I EXORCISE, BUT NEW ONES JUST MOVE RIGHT IN.
I ASKED THE GUILD, BUT THIS IS NEW TO THEM TOO.
I'M MUCH TOO BUSY GHOST-BUSTING TO SELL THE HOUSE.
I WONDERED... IF YOU MIGHT HELP, WIZ-SAN...
I-I SEE. YES, OF COURSE.

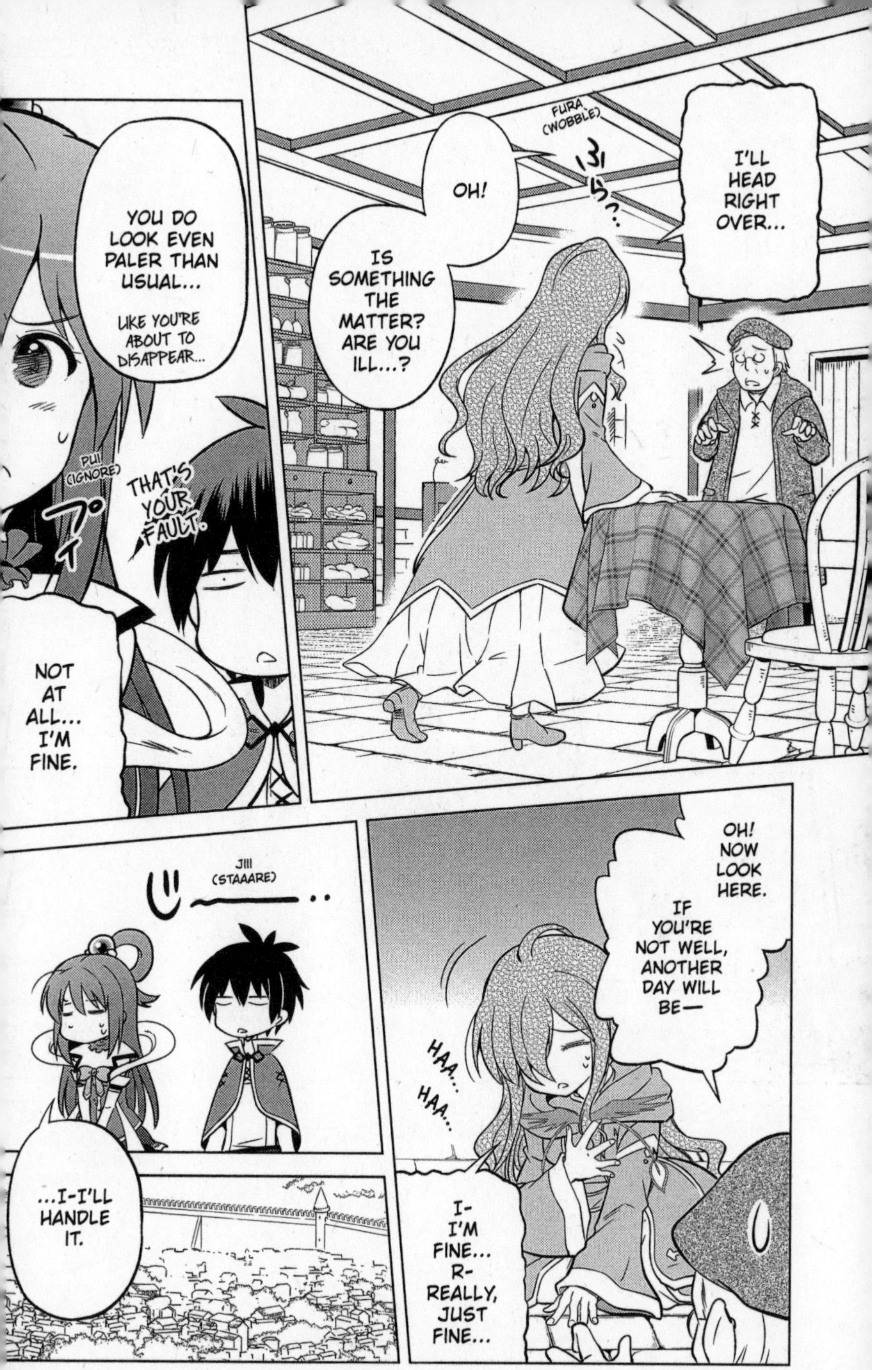
I'LL HEAD RIGHT OVER...
FURA (WOBBLE)
OH!
IS SOMETHING THE MATTER? ARE YOU ILL...?
YOU DO LOOK EVEN PALER THAN USUAL...
LIKE YOU'RE ABOUT TO DISAPPEAR...
PUI (IGNORE)
THAT'S YOUR FAULT.
NOT AT ALL... I'M FINE.
OH! NOW LOOK HERE.
IF YOU'RE NOT WELL, ANOTHER DAY WILL BE—
HAA... HAA...
I- I'M FINE... R-REALLY, JUST FINE...
JIII (STAAARE)
...I-I'LL HANDLE IT.

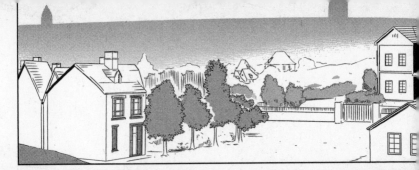

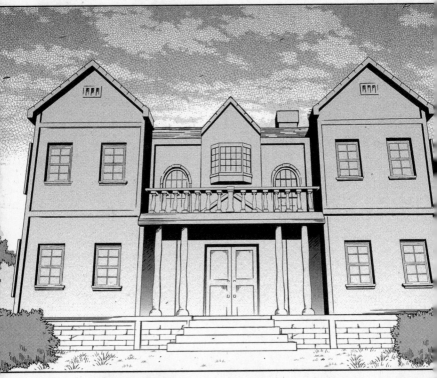

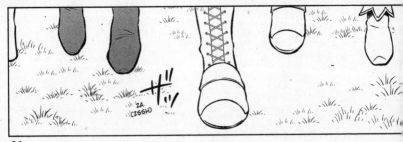

ZA
CISSHD

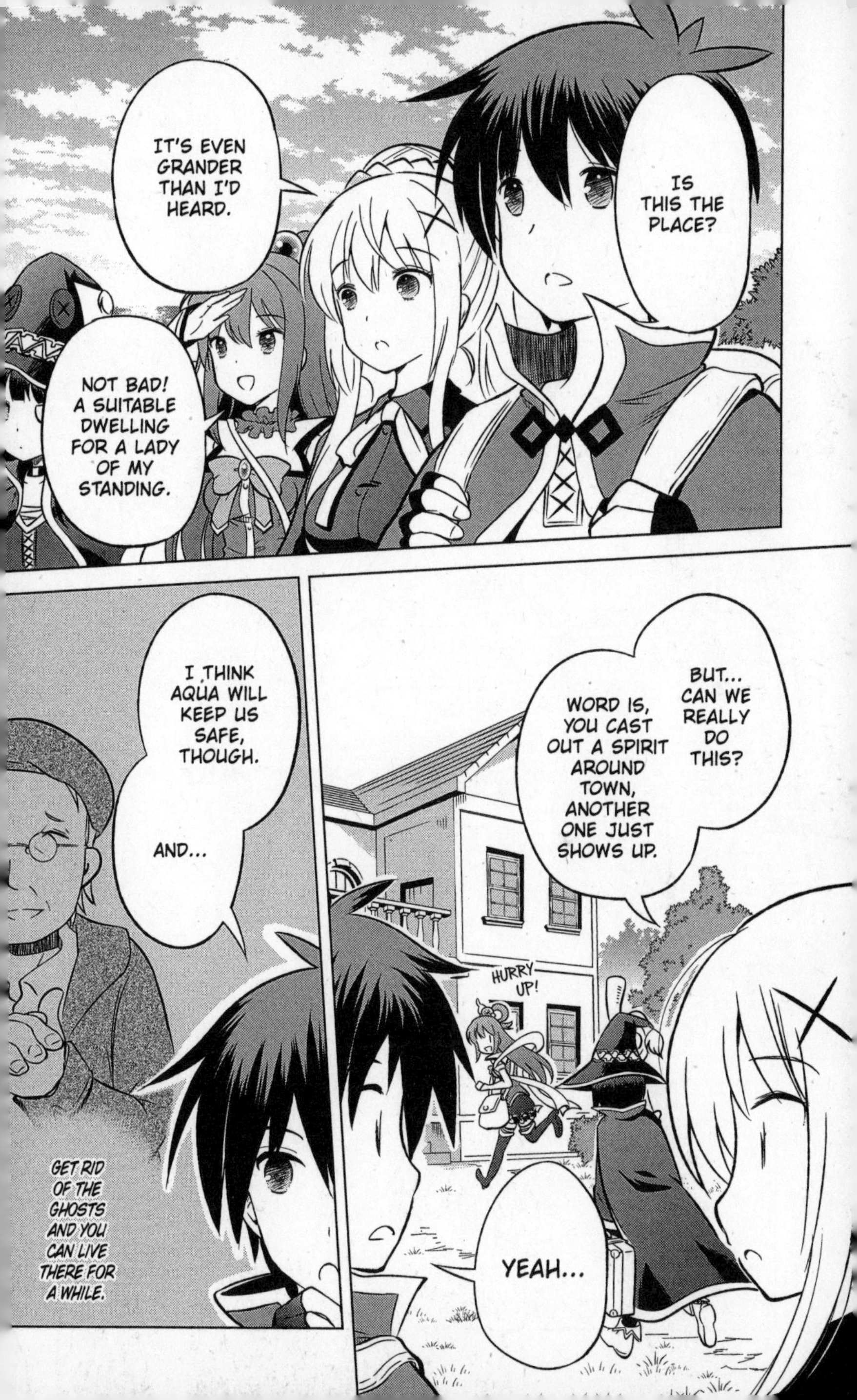
IS THIS THE PLACE?
IT'S EVEN GRANDER THAN I'D HEARD.
NOT BAD! A SUITABLE DWELLING FOR A LADY OF MY STANDING.
BUT... CAN WE REALLY DO THIS?
WORD IS, YOU CAST OUT A SPIRIT AROUND TOWN, ANOTHER ONE JUST SHOWS UP.
HURRY UP!
YEAH...
I THINK AQUA WILL KEEP US SAFE, THOUGH.
AND...
GET RID OF THE GHOSTS AND YOU CAN LIVE THERE FOR A WHILE.

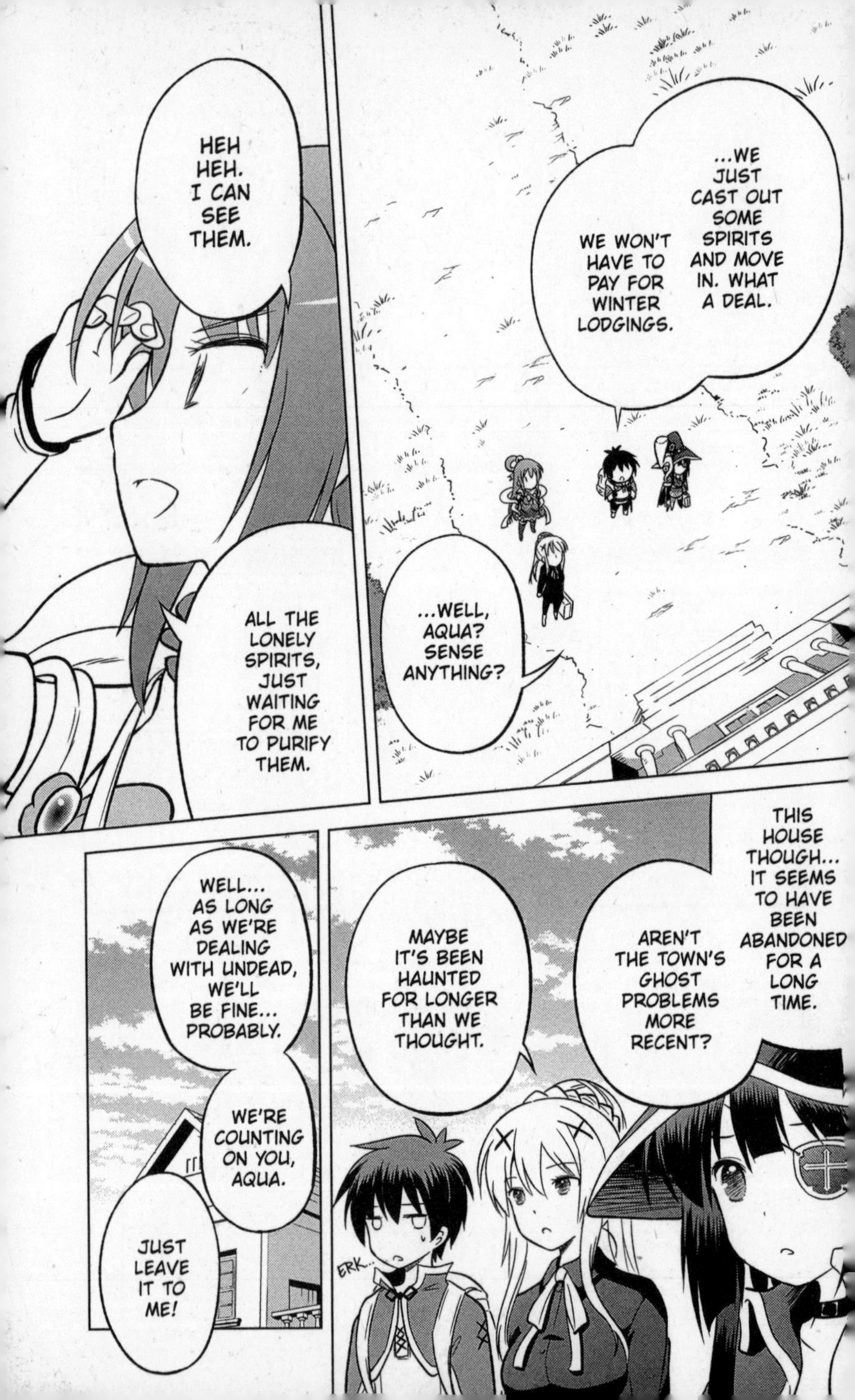
...WE JUST CAST OUT SOME SPIRITS AND MOVE IN. WHAT A DEAL.
WE WON'T HAVE TO PAY FOR WINTER LODGINGS.
...WELL, AQUA? SENSE ANYTHING?
HEH HEH. I CAN SEE THEM.
ALL THE LONELY SPIRITS, JUST WAITING FOR ME TO PURIFY THEM.
THIS HOUSE THOUGH... IT SEEMS TO HAVE BEEN ABANDONED FOR A LONG TIME.
AREN'T THE TOWN'S GHOST PROBLEMS MORE RECENT?
MAYBE IT'S BEEN HAUNTED FOR LONGER THAN WE THOUGHT.
ERK...
WELL... AS LONG AS WE'RE DEALING WITH UNDEAD, WE'LL BE FINE... PROBABLY.
WE'RE COUNTING ON YOU, AQUA.
JUST LEAVE IT TO ME!

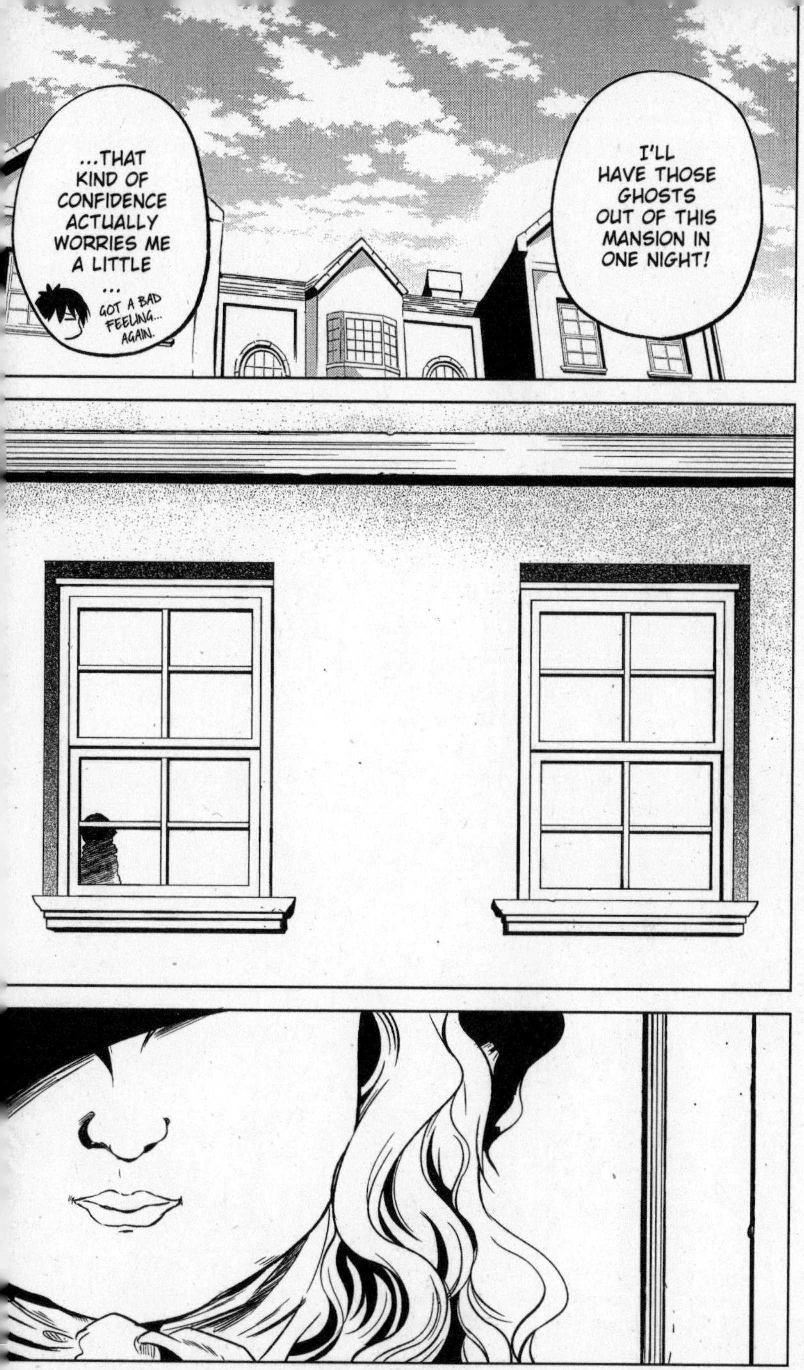
I'LL HAVE THOSE GHOSTS OUT OF THIS MANSION IN ONE NIGHT!
...THAT KIND OF CONFIDENCE ACTUALLY WORRIES ME A LITTLE ...
GOT A BAD FEELING... AGAIN.

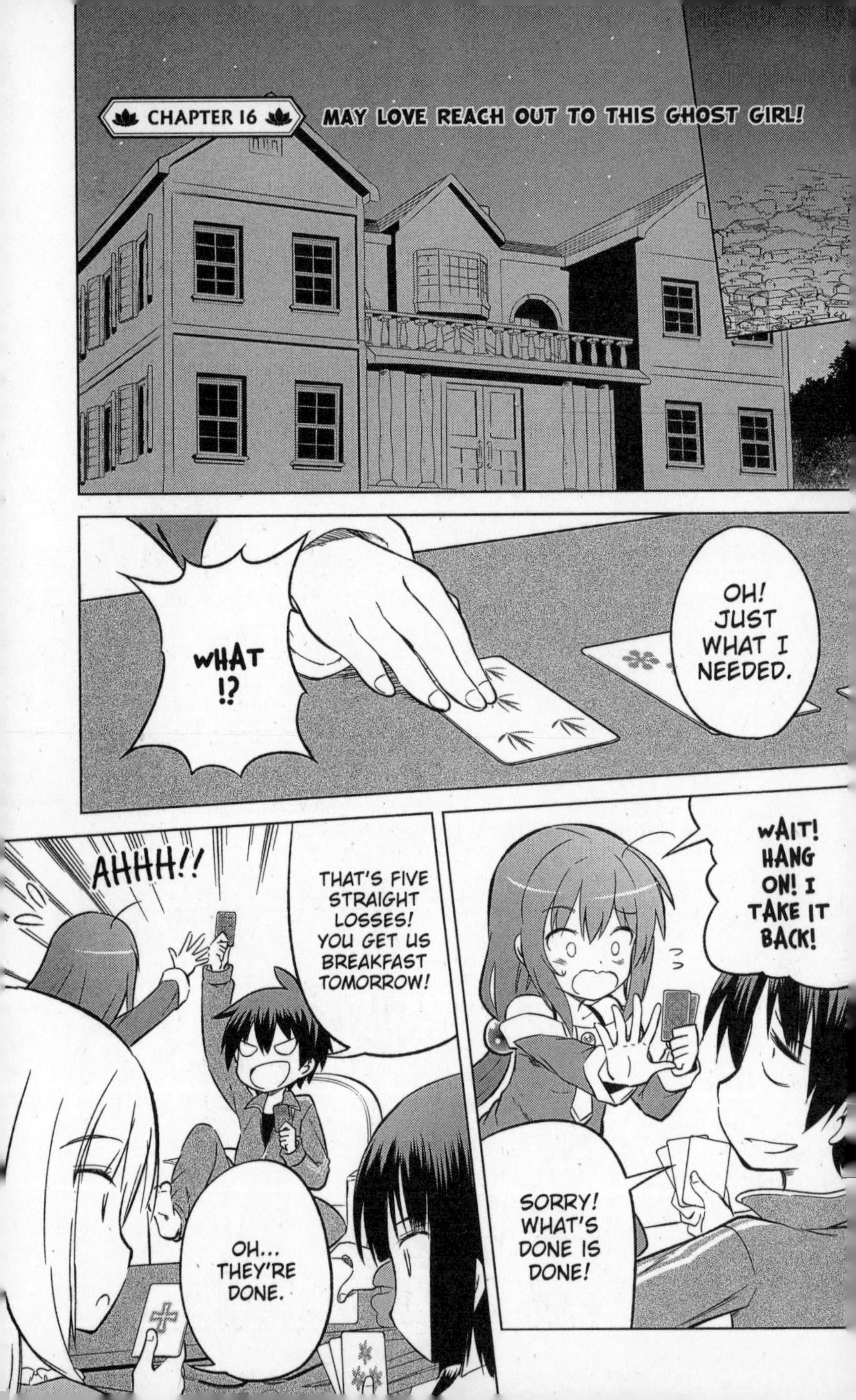
CHAPTER 16
MAY LOVE REACH OUT TO THIS GHOST GIRL!
OH! JUST WHAT I NEEDED.
WHAT !?
WAIT! HANG ON! I TAKE IT BACK!
SORRY! WHAT'S DONE IS DONE!
THAT'S FIVE STRAIGHT LOSSES! YOU GET US BREAKFAST TOMORROW!
AHHH!!
OH... THEY'RE DONE.

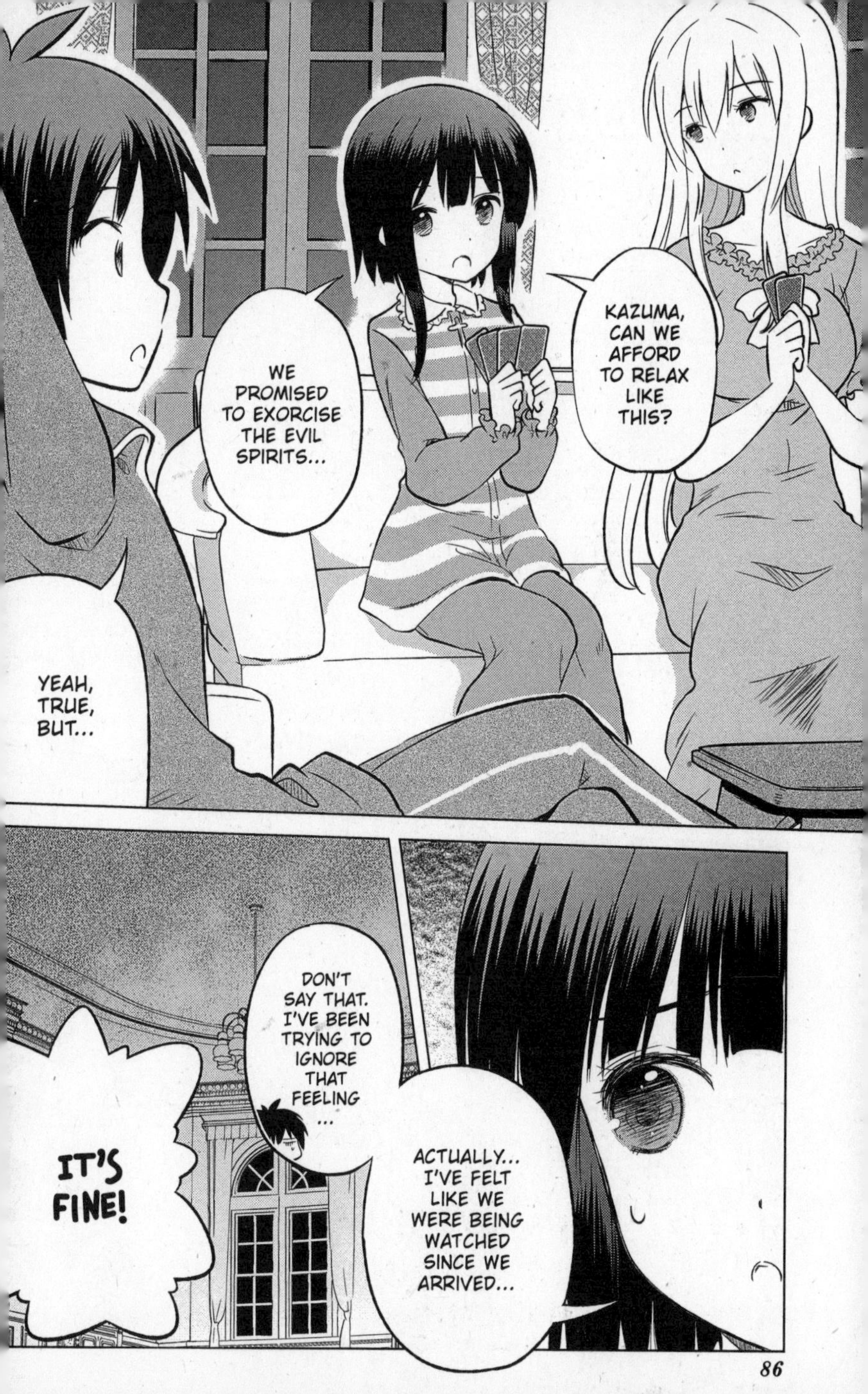
KAZUMA, CAN WE AFFORD TO RELAX LIKE THIS?
WE PROMISED TO EXORCISE THE EVIL SPIRITS...
YEAH, TRUE, BUT...
ACTUALLY... I'VE FELT LIKE WE WERE BEING WATCHED SINCE WE ARRIVED...
DON'T SAY THAT. I'VE BEEN TRYING TO IGNORE THAT FEELING...
IT'S FINE!

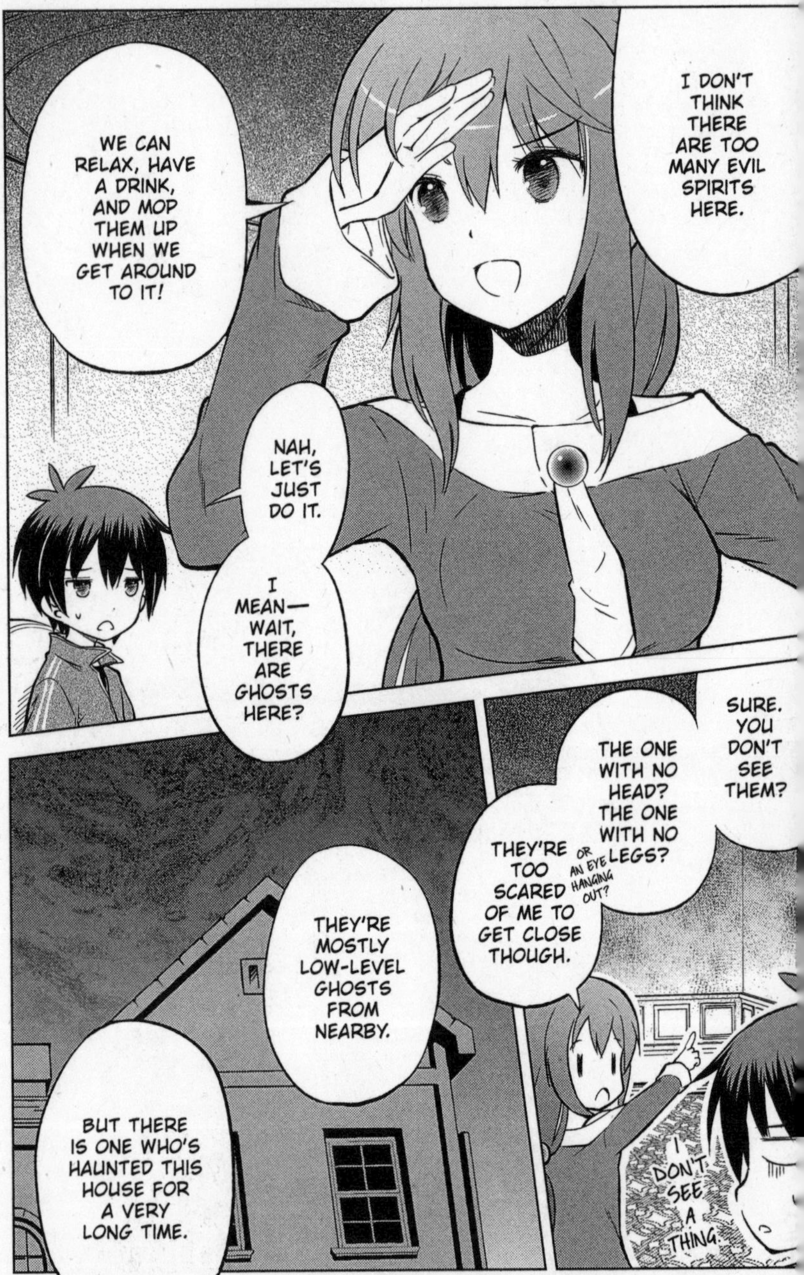
I DON'T THINK THERE ARE TOO MANY EVIL SPIRITS HERE.
WE CAN RELAX, HAVE A DRINK, AND MOP THEM UP WHEN WE GET AROUND TO IT!
NAH, LET'S JUST DO IT.
I MEAN—WAIT, THERE ARE GHOSTS HERE?
SURE. YOU DON'T SEE THEM?
THE ONE WITH NO HEAD? THE ONE WITH NO LEGS?
OR AN EYE HANGING OUT?
THEY'RE TOO SCARED OF ME TO GET CLOSE THOUGH.
I DON'T SEE A THING.
THEY'RE MOSTLY LOW-LEVEL GHOSTS FROM NEARBY.
BUT THERE IS ONE WHO'S HAUNTED THIS HOUSE FOR A VERY LONG TIME.

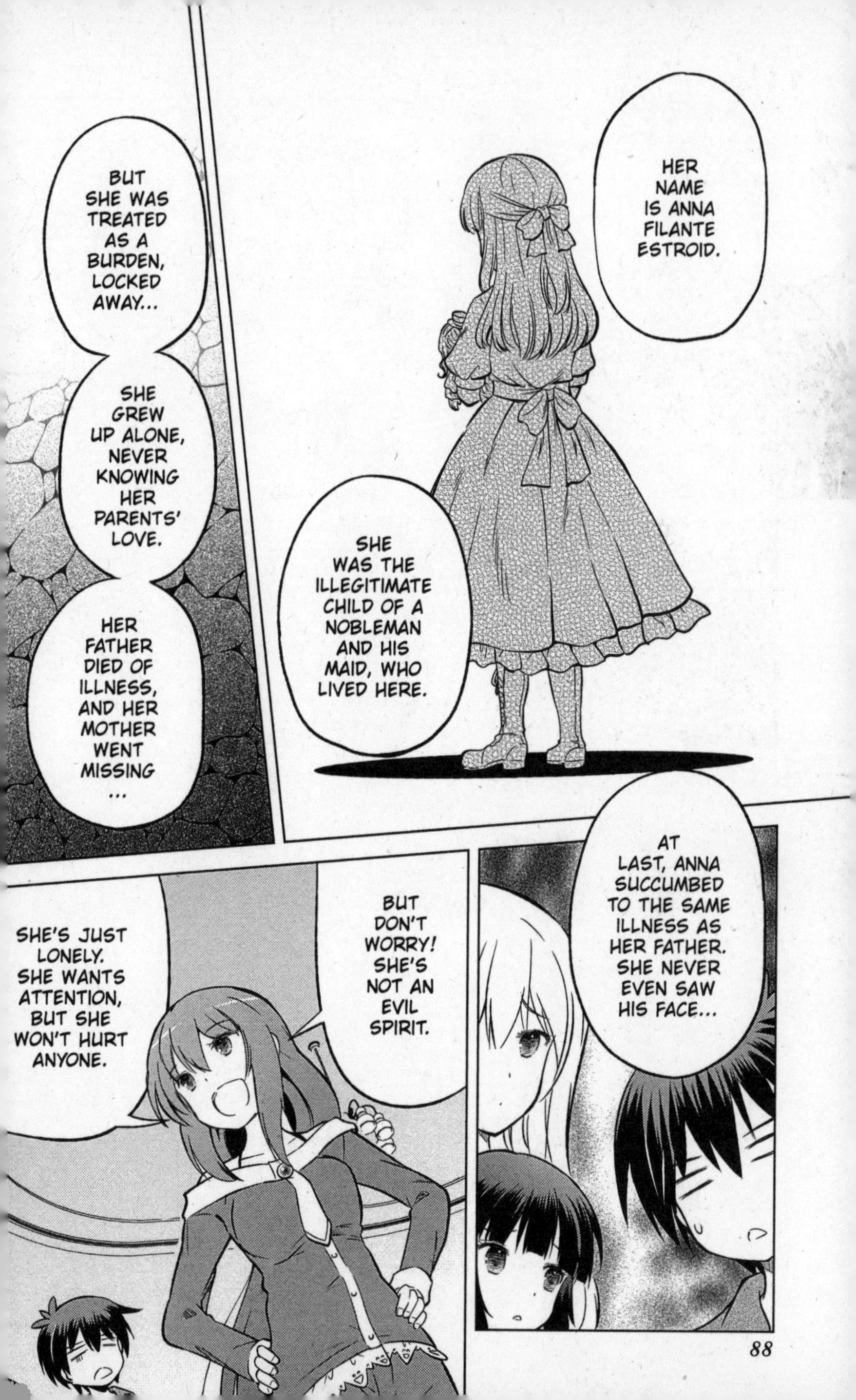
HER NAME IS ANNA FILANTE ESTROID.
SHE WAS THE ILLEGITIMATE CHILD OF A NOBLEMAN AND HIS MAID, WHO LIVED HERE.
BUT SHE WAS TREATED AS A BURDEN, LOCKED AWAY...
SHE GREW UP ALONE, NEVER KNOWING HER PARENTS' LOVE.
HER FATHER DIED OF ILLNESS, AND HER MOTHER WENT MISSING...
AT LAST, ANNA SUCCUMBED TO THE SAME ILLNESS AS HER FATHER. SHE NEVER EVEN SAW HIS FACE...
BUT DON'T WORRY! SHE'S NOT AN EVIL SPIRIT.
SHE'S JUST LONELY. SHE WANTS ATTENTION, BUT SHE WON'T HURT ANYONE.

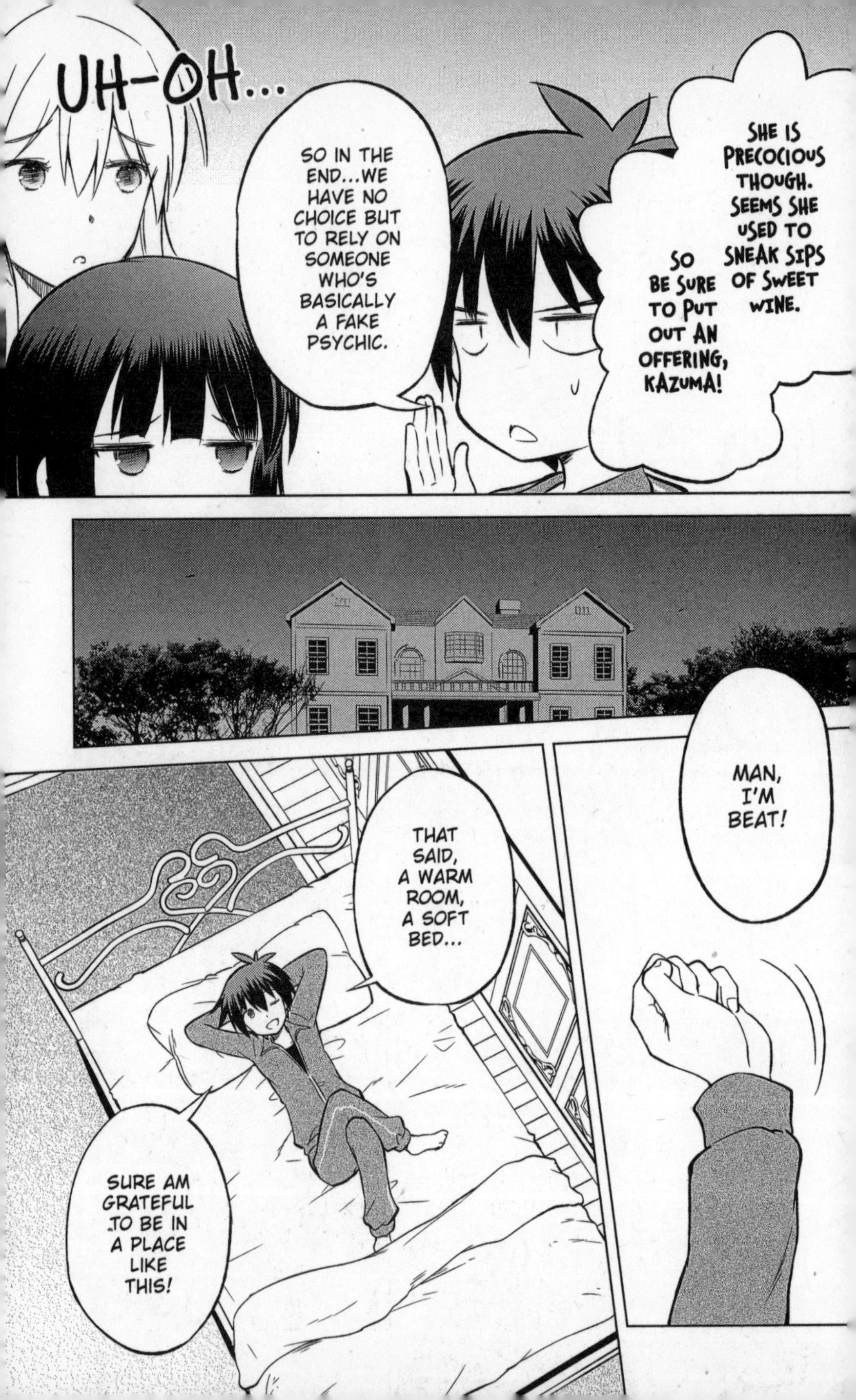
SHE IS PRECOCIOUS THOUGH. SEEMS SHE USED TO SNEAK SIPS OF SWEET WINE.
SO BE SURE TO PUT OUT AN OFFERING, KAZUMA!
SO IN THE END...WE HAVE NO CHOICE BUT TO RELY ON SOMEONE WHO'S BASICALLY A FAKE PSYCHIC.
UH-OH...
MAN, I'M BEAT!
THAT SAID, A WARM ROOM, A SOFT BED...
SURE AM GRATEFUL TO BE IN A PLACE LIKE THIS!

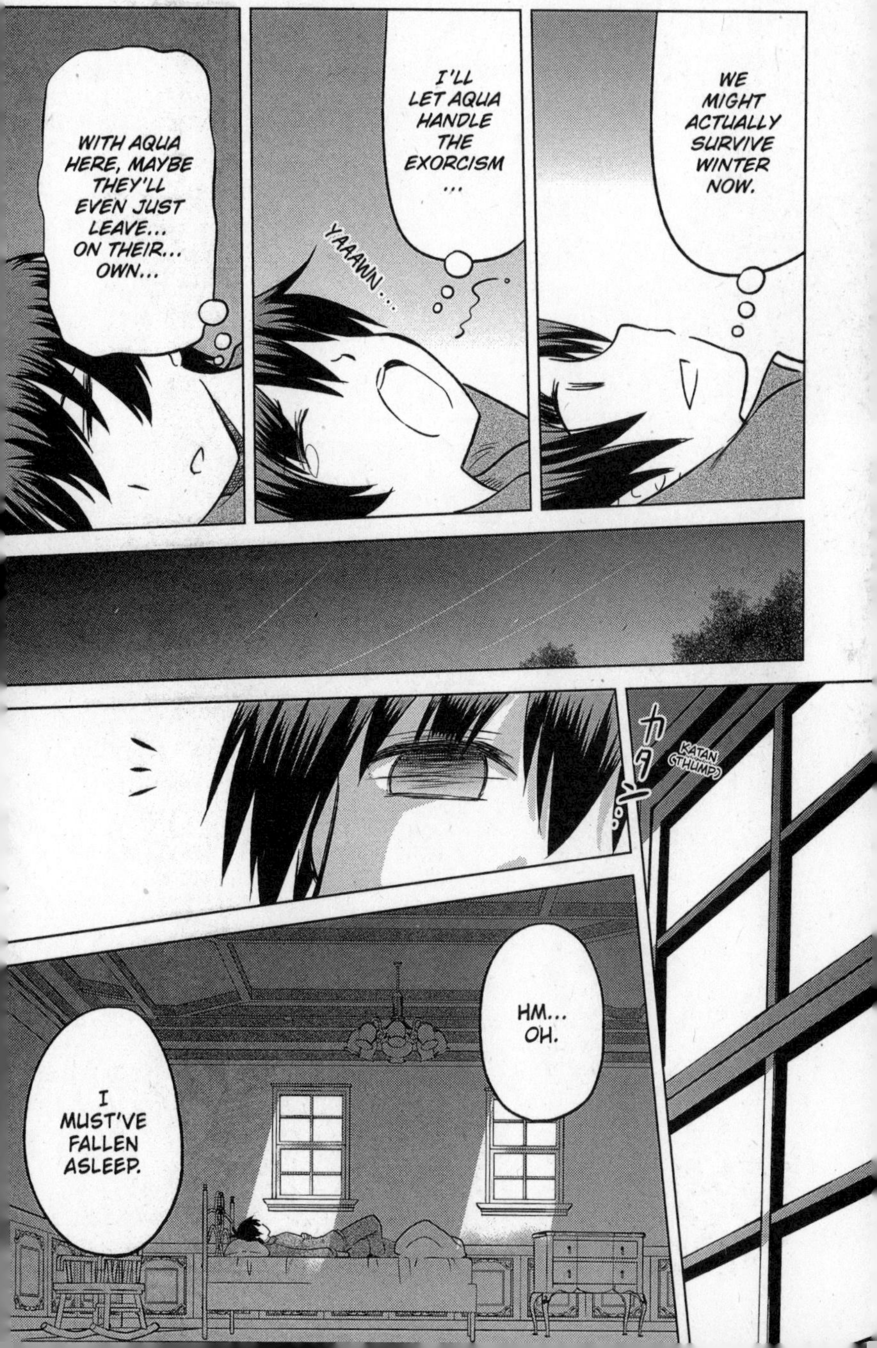
WE MIGHT ACTUALLY SURVIVE WINTER NOW.
I'LL LET AQUA HANDLE THE EXORCISM...
YAAAWN...
WITH AQUA HERE, MAYBE THEY'LL EVEN JUST LEAVE... ON THEIR... OWN...
KATAN (THUMP)
HM... OH.
I MUST'VE FALLEN ASLEEP.

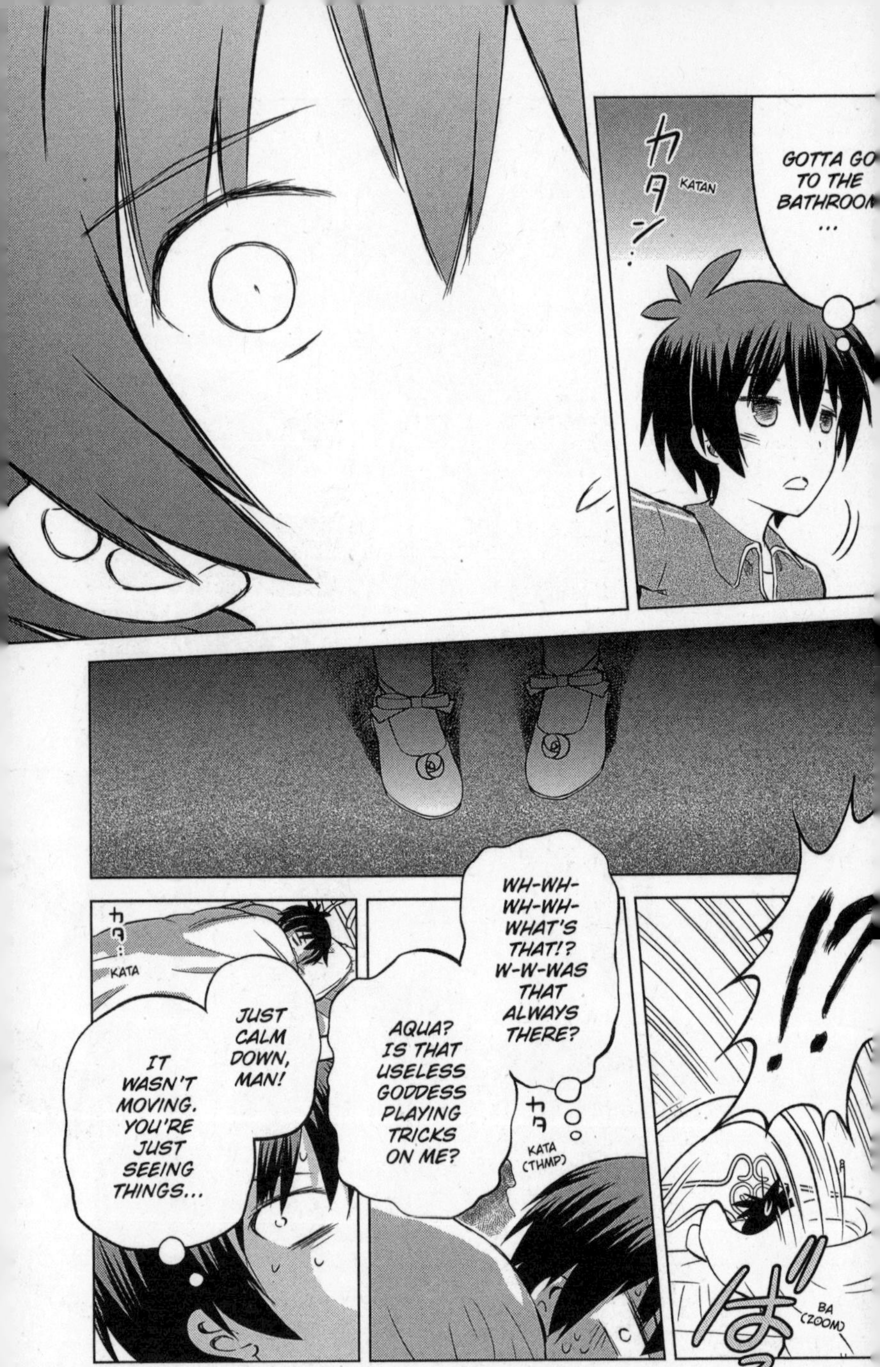
GOTTA GO TO THE BATHROOM...
カタン
KATAN
!?
ばっ
BA (ZOOM)
WH-WH-WH-WH-WHAT'S THAT!? W-W-WAS THAT ALWAYS THERE?
AQUA? IS THAT USELESS GODDESS PLAYING TRICKS ON ME?
カタ
KATA (THMP)
カタ…
KATA
JUST CALM DOWN, MAN!
IT WASN'T MOVING. YOU'RE JUST SEEING THINGS...

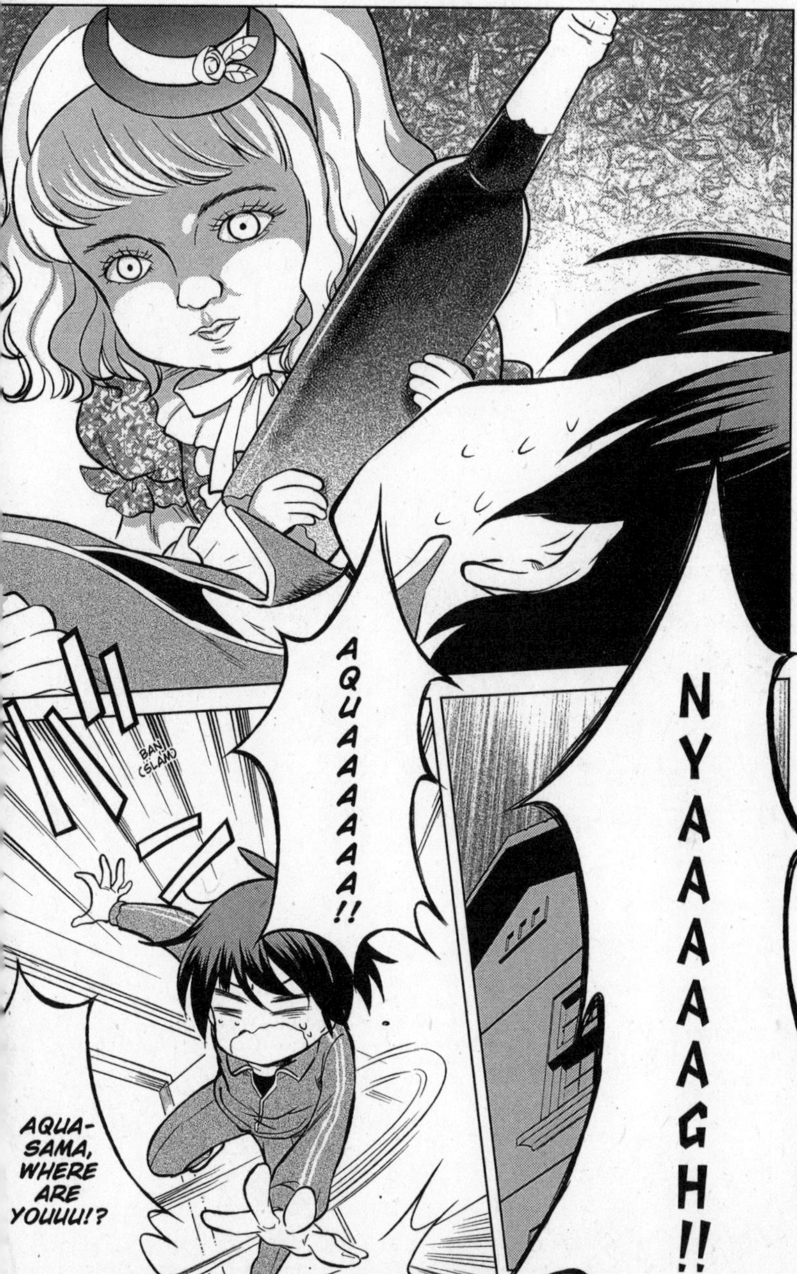
NYAAAAAGH!!
AQUAAAAAA!!
BAN (SLAM)
AQUA-SAMA, WHERE ARE YOUUU!?

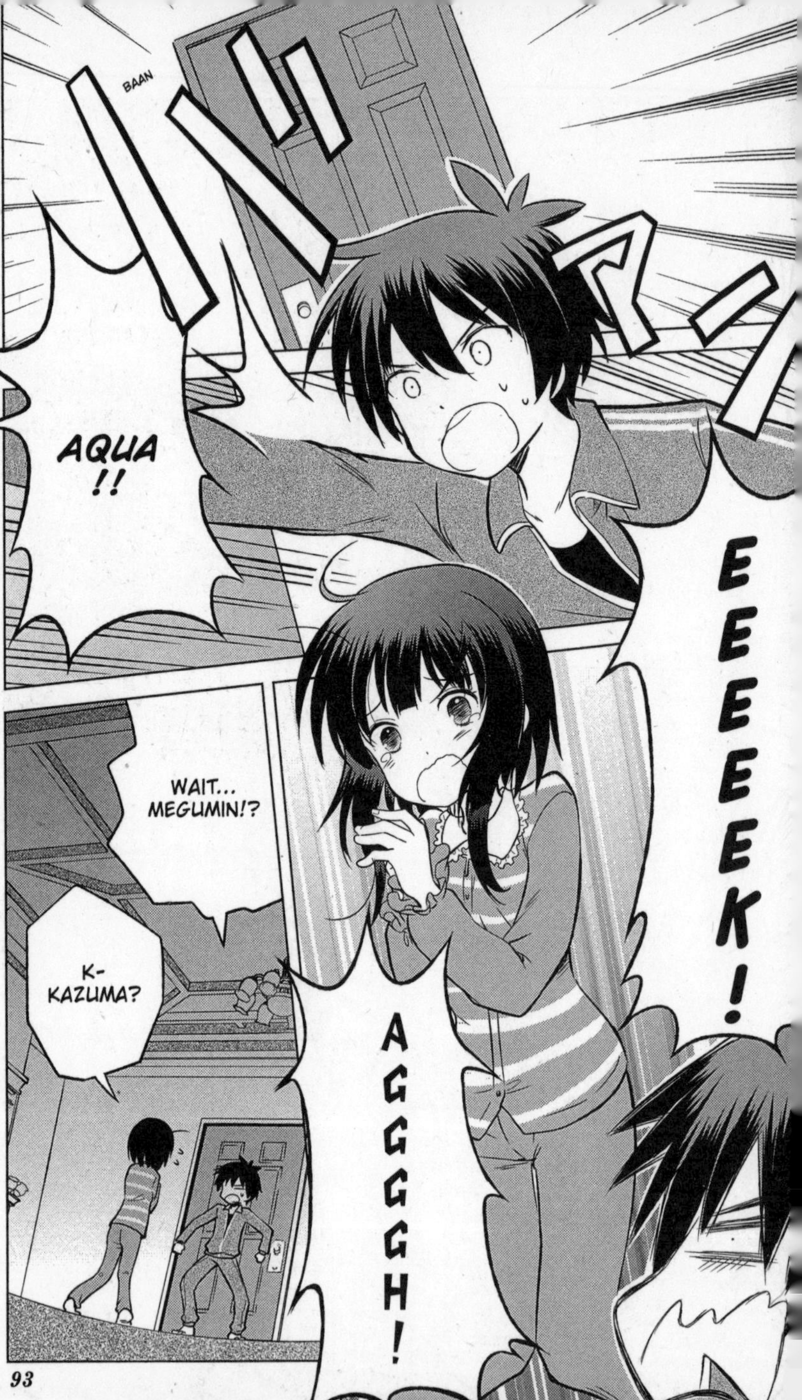
BAAN
AQUA!!
EEEEEK!
AGGGGH!
WAIT... MEGUMIN!?
K-KAZUMA?

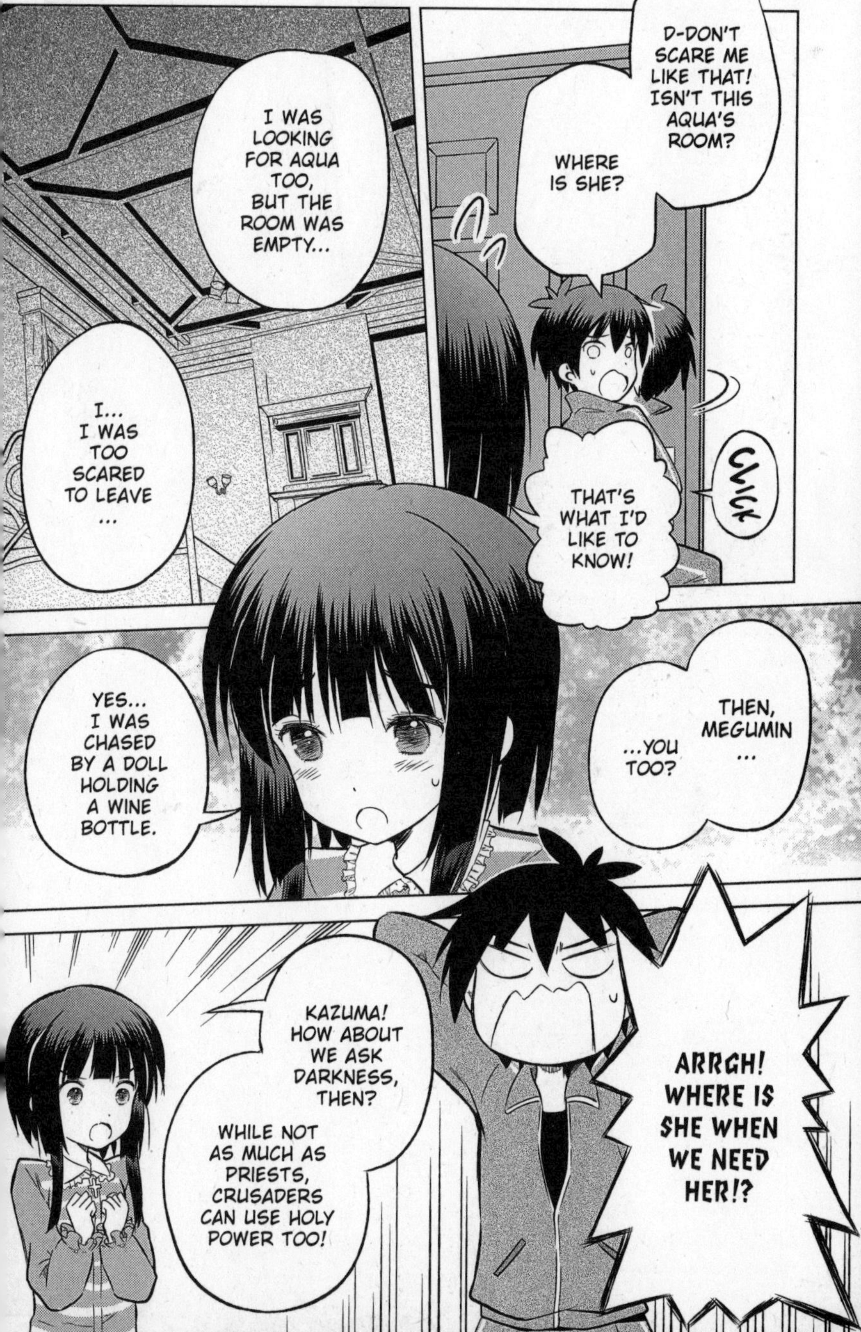
D-DON'T SCARE ME LIKE THAT! ISN'T THIS AQUA'S ROOM?
WHERE IS SHE?
CLICK
THAT'S WHAT I'D LIKE TO KNOW!
I WAS LOOKING FOR AQUA TOO, BUT THE ROOM WAS EMPTY...
I... I WAS TOO SCARED TO LEAVE ...
THEN, MEGUMIN ...
...YOU TOO?
YES... I WAS CHASED BY A DOLL HOLDING A WINE BOTTLE.
ARRGH! WHERE IS SHE WHEN WE NEED HER!?
KAZUMA! HOW ABOUT WE ASK DARKNESS, THEN?
WHILE NOT AS MUCH AS PRIESTS, CRUSADERS CAN USE HOLY POWER TOO!

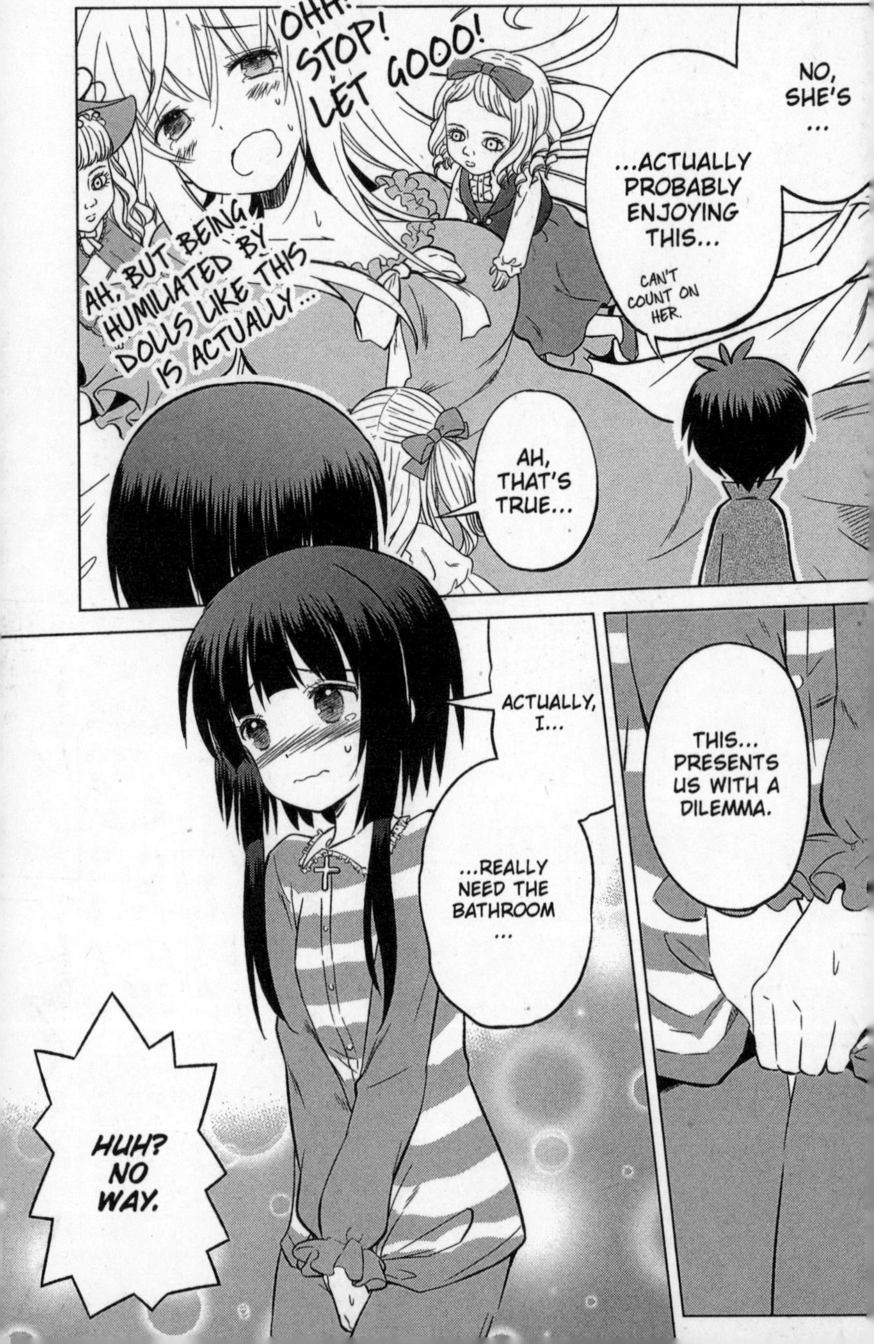
NO, SHE'S ...
...ACTUALLY PROBABLY ENJOYING THIS...
CAN'T COUNT ON HER.
OHH! STOP! LET GOOO!
AH, BUT BEING HUMILIATED BY DOLLS LIKE THIS IS ACTUALLY...
AH, THAT'S TRUE...
THIS... PRESENTS US WITH A DILEMMA.
ACTUALLY, I...
...REALLY NEED THE BATHROOM ...
HUH? NO WAY.

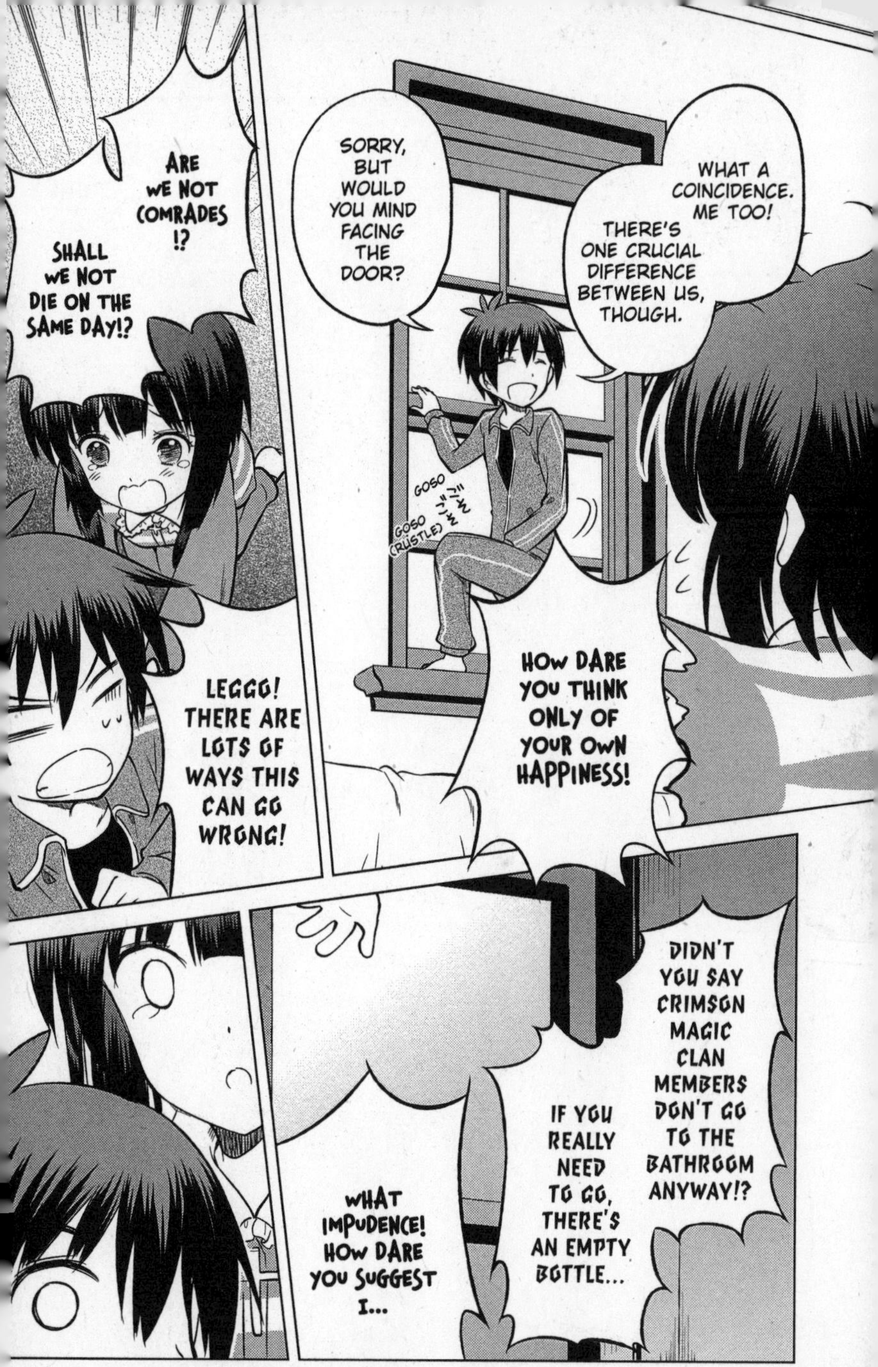
WHAT A COINCIDENCE. ME TOO!
THERE'S ONE CRUCIAL DIFFERENCE BETWEEN US, THOUGH.
SORRY, BUT WOULD YOU MIND FACING THE DOOR?
GOSO GOSO (RUSTLE)
HOW DARE YOU THINK ONLY OF YOUR OWN HAPPINESS!
ARE WE NOT COMRADES!?
SHALL WE NOT DIE ON THE SAME DAY!?
LEGGO! THERE ARE LOTS OF WAYS THIS CAN GO WRONG!
DIDN'T YOU SAY CRIMSON MAGIC CLAN MEMBERS DON'T GO TO THE BATHROOM ANYWAY!?
IF YOU REALLY NEED TO GO, THERE'S AN EMPTY BOTTLE...
WHAT IMPUDENCE! HOW DARE YOU SUGGEST I...

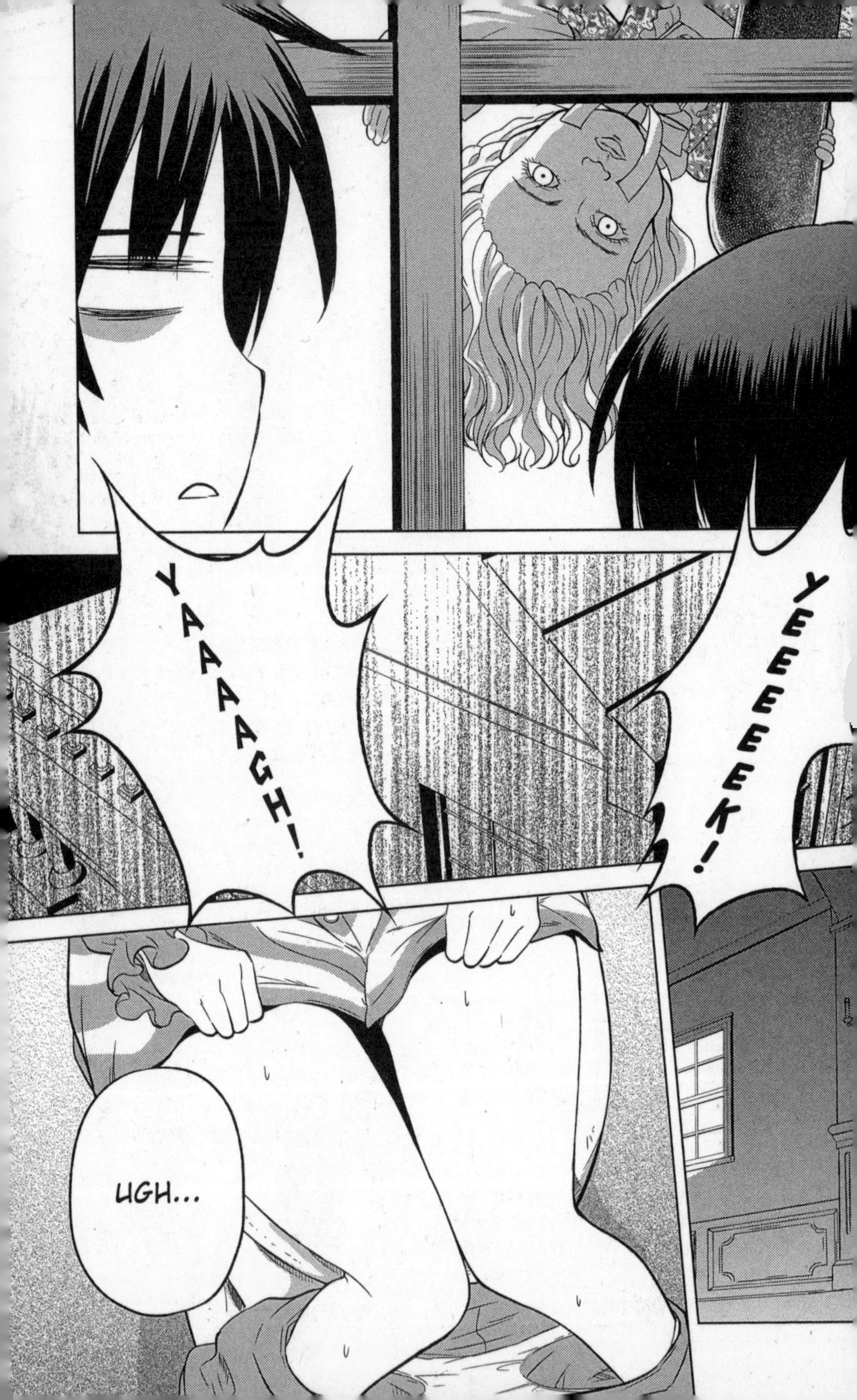
YEEEEEEK!
YAAAAGH!
UGH...

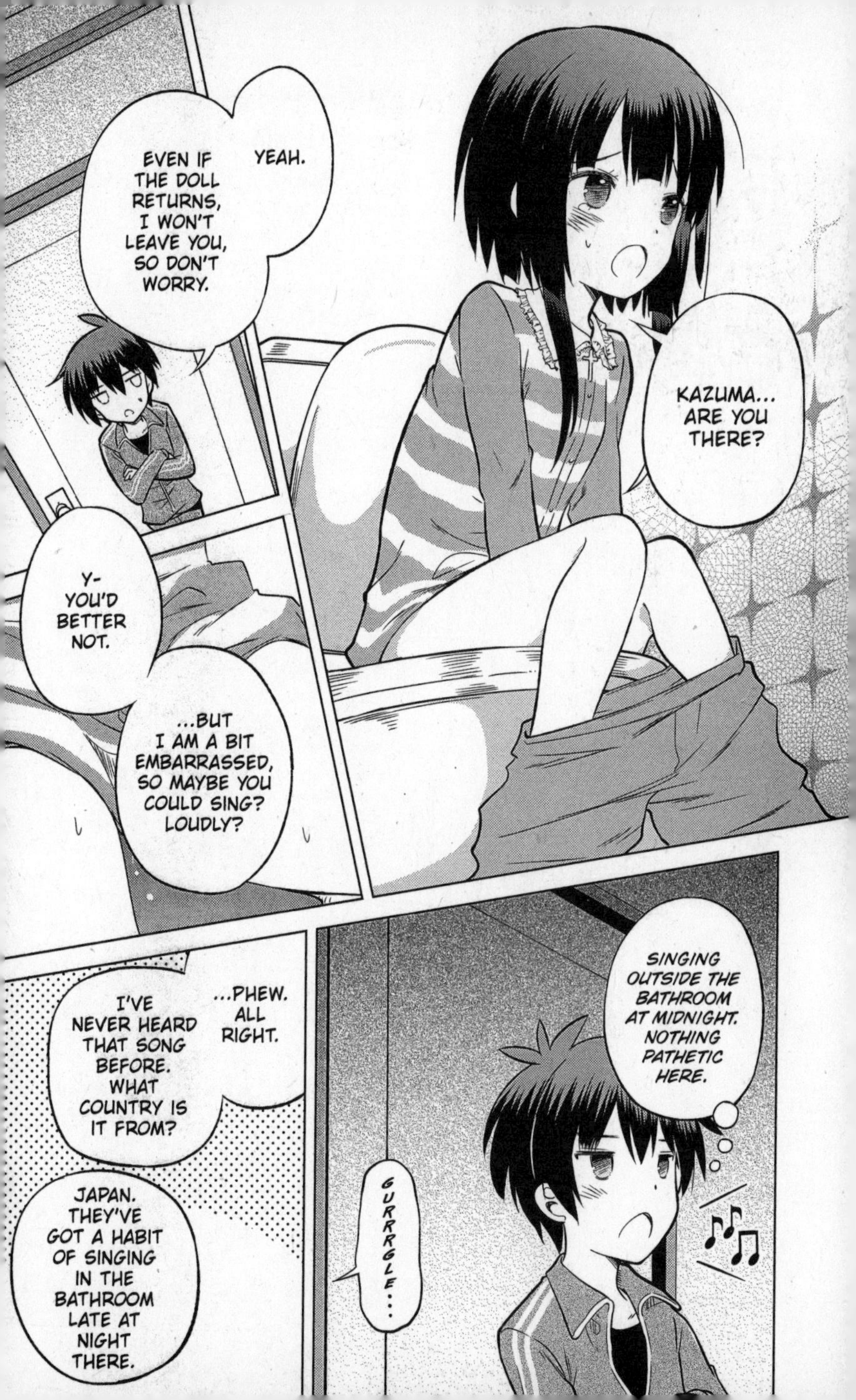
KAZUMA... ARE YOU THERE?
YEAH.
EVEN IF THE DOLL RETURNS, I WON'T LEAVE YOU, SO DON'T WORRY.
Y- YOU'D BETTER NOT.
...BUT I AM A BIT EMBARRASSED, SO MAYBE YOU COULD SING? LOUDLY?
SINGING OUTSIDE THE BATHROOM AT MIDNIGHT. NOTHING PATHETIC HERE.
GURRRGLE...
...PHEW. ALL RIGHT.
I'VE NEVER HEARD THAT SONG BEFORE. WHAT COUNTRY IS IT FROM?
JAPAN. THEY'VE GOT A HABIT OF SINGING IN THE BATHROOM LATE AT NIGHT THERE.

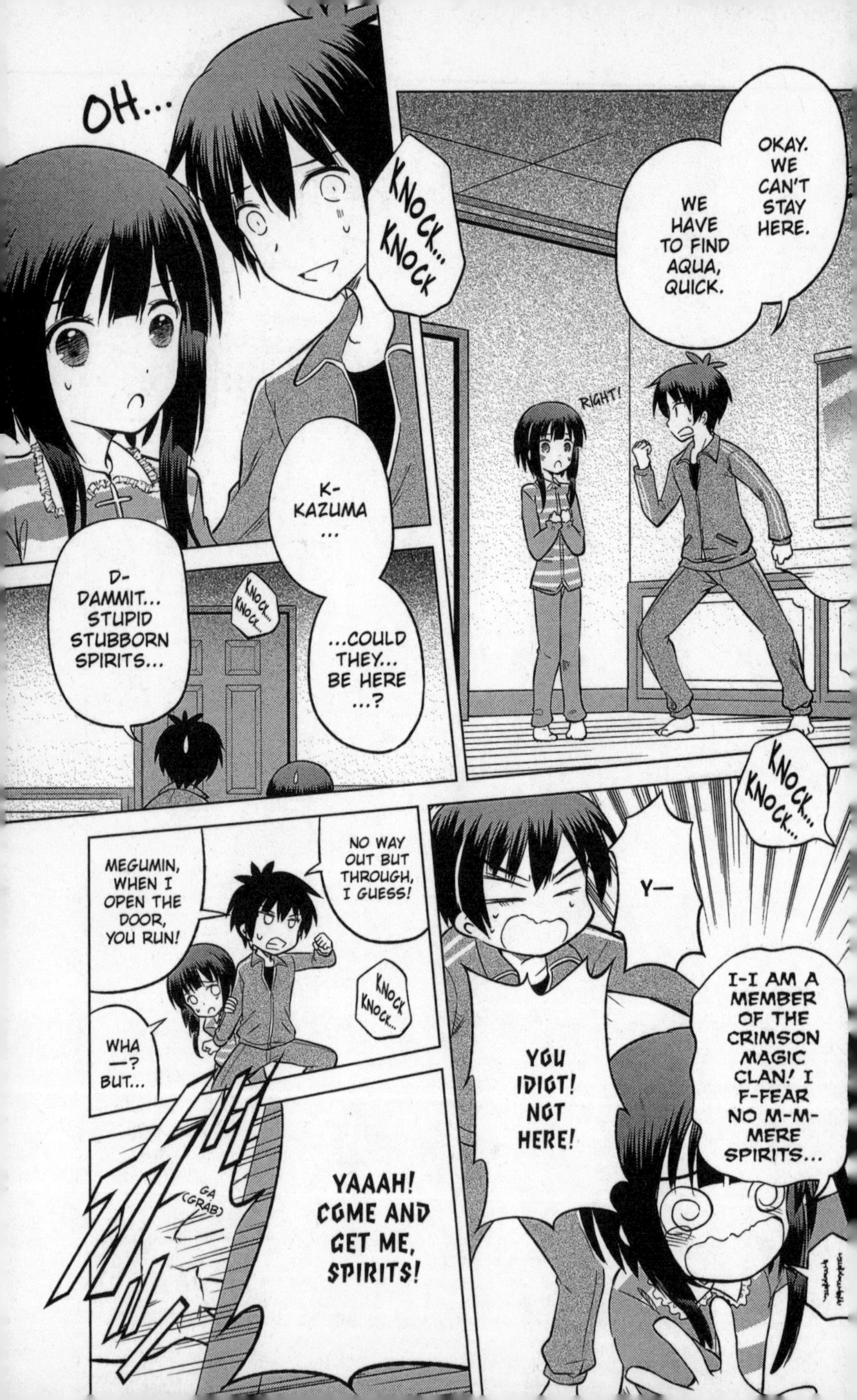
OKAY. WE CAN'T STAY HERE.
WE HAVE TO FIND AQUA, QUICK.
RIGHT!
OH...
KNOCK... KNOCK
K-KAZUMA...
D-DAMMIT... STUPID STUBBORN SPIRITS...
KNOCK... KNOCK...
...COULD THEY... BE HERE ...?
KNOCK... KNOCK...
Y—
I-I AM A MEMBER OF THE CRIMSON MAGIC CLAN! I F-FEAR NO M-M-MERE SPIRITS...
YOU IDIOT! NOT HERE!
NO WAY OUT BUT THROUGH, I GUESS!
MEGUMIN, WHEN I OPEN THE DOOR, YOU RUN!
KNOCK KNOCK...
WHA—? BUT...
YAAAH! COME AND GET ME, SPIRITS!
GA (GRAB)

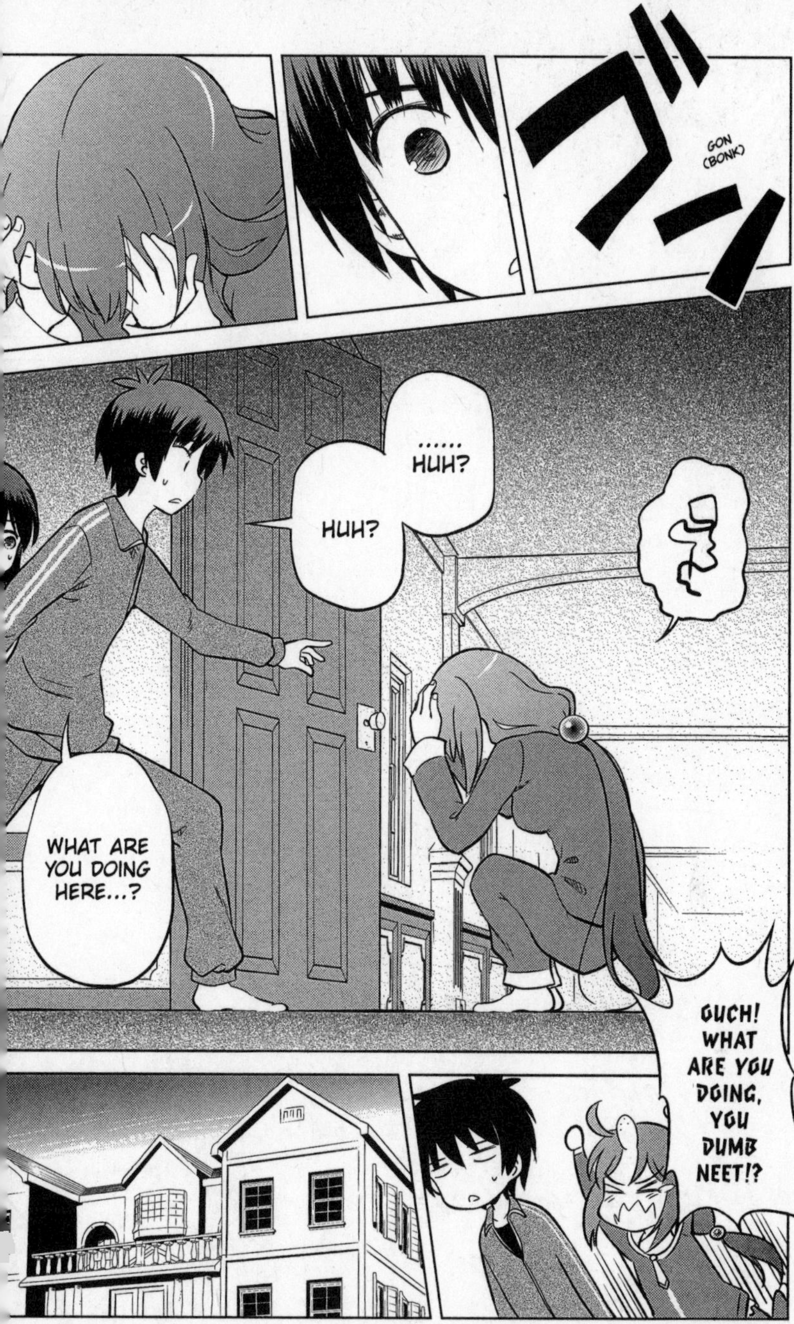
ゴン
GON (BONK)
...... HUH?
HUH?
WHAT ARE YOU DOING HERE...?
OUCH! WHAT ARE YOU DOING, YOU DUMB NEET!?

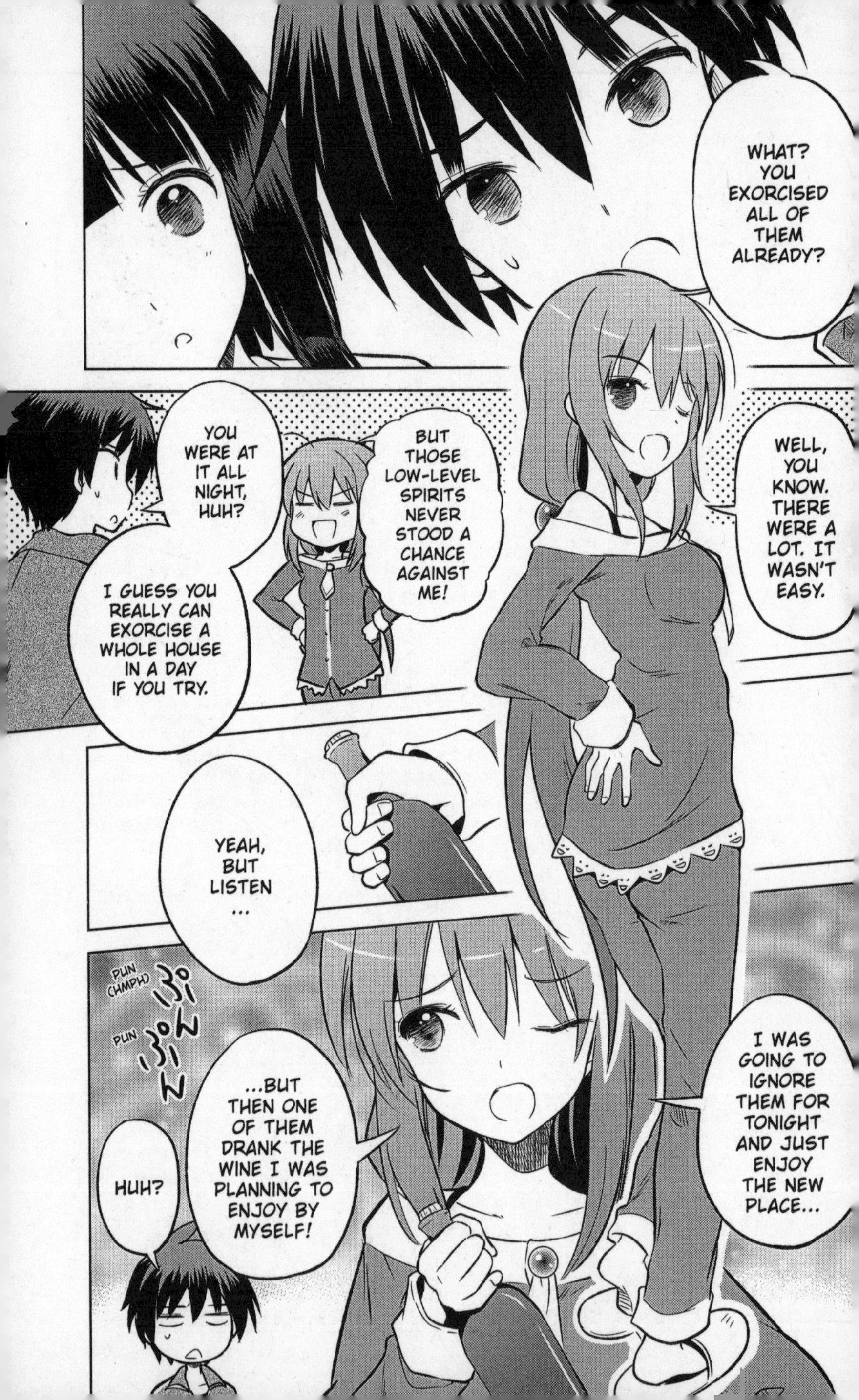
WHAT? YOU EXORCISED ALL OF THEM ALREADY?
WELL, YOU KNOW. THERE WERE A LOT. IT WASN'T EASY.
BUT THOSE LOW-LEVEL SPIRITS NEVER STOOD A CHANCE AGAINST ME!
YOU WERE AT IT ALL NIGHT, HUH?
I GUESS YOU REALLY CAN EXORCISE A WHOLE HOUSE IN A DAY IF YOU TRY.
YEAH, BUT LISTEN ...
I WAS GOING TO IGNORE THEM FOR TONIGHT AND JUST ENJOY THE NEW PLACE...
PUN (HMPH)
PUN
...BUT THEN ONE OF THEM DRANK THE WINE I WAS PLANNING TO ENJOY BY MYSELF!
HUH?

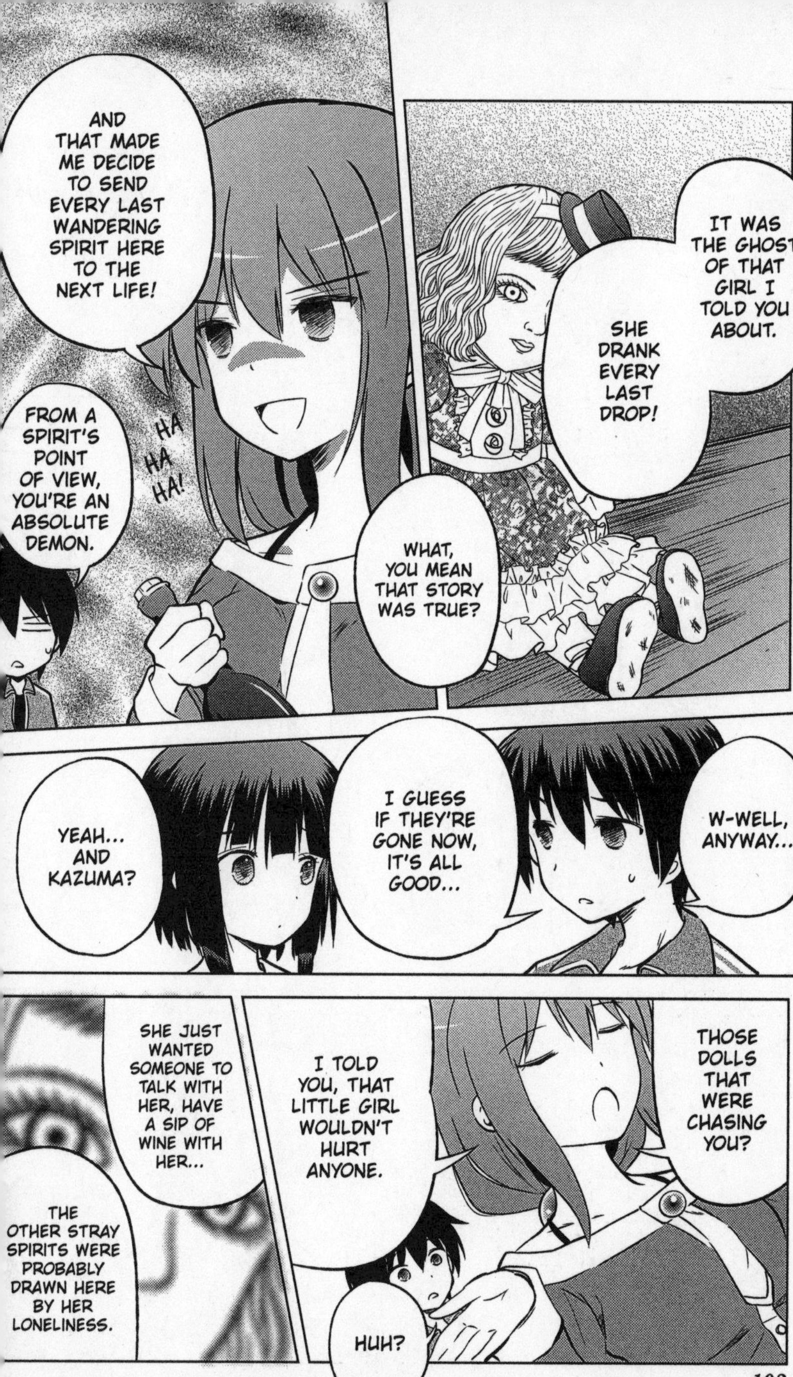
IT WAS THE GHOST OF THAT GIRL I TOLD YOU ABOUT.
SHE DRANK EVERY LAST DROP!
WHAT, YOU MEAN THAT STORY WAS TRUE?
AND THAT MADE ME DECIDE TO SEND EVERY LAST WANDERING SPIRIT HERE TO THE NEXT LIFE!
HA HA HA!
FROM A SPIRIT'S POINT OF VIEW, YOU'RE AN ABSOLUTE DEMON.
W-WELL, ANYWAY...
I GUESS IF THEY'RE GONE NOW, IT'S ALL GOOD...
YEAH... AND KAZUMA?
THOSE DOLLS THAT WERE CHASING YOU?
HUH?
I TOLD YOU, THAT LITTLE GIRL WOULDN'T HURT ANYONE.
SHE JUST WANTED SOMEONE TO TALK WITH HER, HAVE A SIP OF WINE WITH HER...
THE OTHER STRAY SPIRITS WERE PROBABLY DRAWN HERE BY HER LONELINESS.

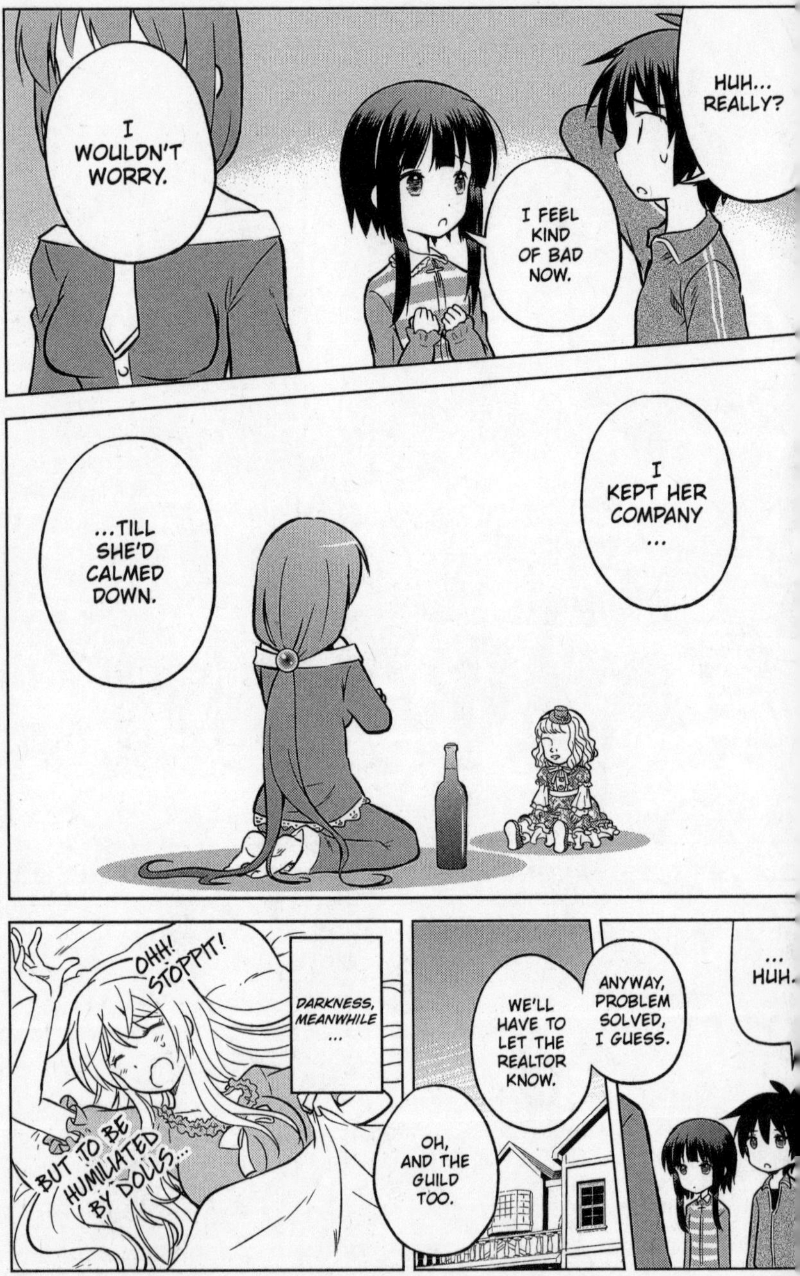
HUH... REALLY?
I FEEL KIND OF BAD NOW.
I WOULDN'T WORRY.
I KEPT HER COMPANY ...
...TILL SHE'D CALMED DOWN.
... HUH.
ANYWAY, PROBLEM SOLVED, I GUESS.
WE'LL HAVE TO LET THE REALTOR KNOW.
OH, AND THE GUILD TOO.
DARKNESS, MEANWHILE ...
OHH! STOPPIT!
BUT TO BE HUMILIATED BY DOLLS...

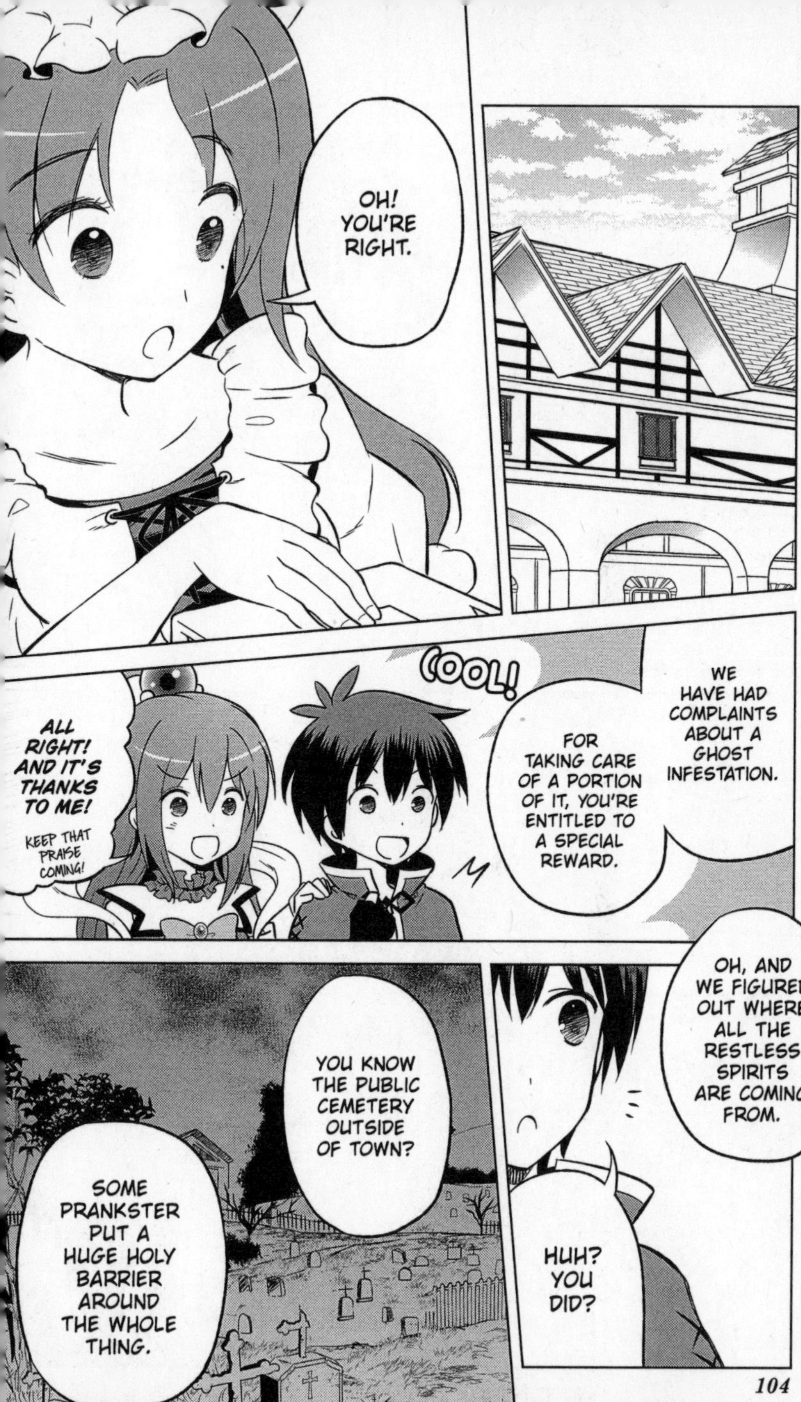
OH! YOU'RE RIGHT.
WE HAVE HAD COMPLAINTS ABOUT A GHOST INFESTATION.
FOR TAKING CARE OF A PORTION OF IT, YOU'RE ENTITLED TO A SPECIAL REWARD.
COOL!
ALL RIGHT! AND IT'S THANKS TO ME!
KEEP THAT PRAISE COMING!
OH, AND WE FIGURED OUT WHERE ALL THE RESTLESS SPIRITS ARE COMING FROM.
HUH? YOU DID?
YOU KNOW THE PUBLIC CEMETERY OUTSIDE OF TOWN?
SOME PRANKSTER PUT A HUGE HOLY BARRIER AROUND THE WHOLE THING.

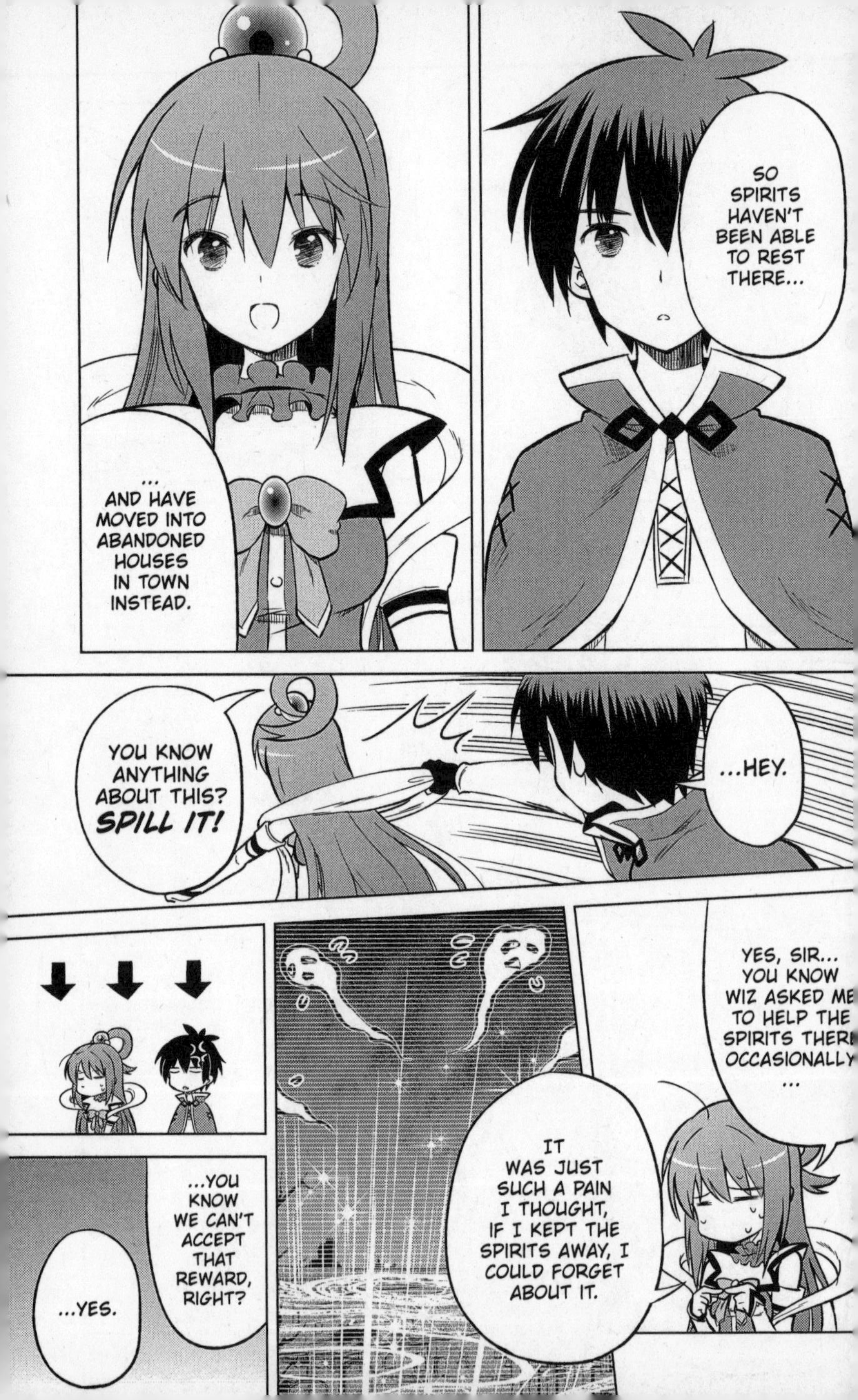
SO SPIRITS HAVEN'T BEEN ABLE TO REST THERE...
...AND HAVE MOVED INTO ABANDONED HOUSES IN TOWN INSTEAD.
...HEY.
YOU KNOW ANYTHING ABOUT THIS? **SPILL IT!**
YES, SIR... YOU KNOW WIZ ASKED ME TO HELP THE SPIRITS THERE OCCASIONALLY...
IT WAS JUST SUCH A PAIN I THOUGHT, IF I KEPT THE SPIRITS AWAY, I COULD FORGET ABOUT IT.
...YOU KNOW WE CAN'T ACCEPT THAT REWARD, RIGHT?
...YES.

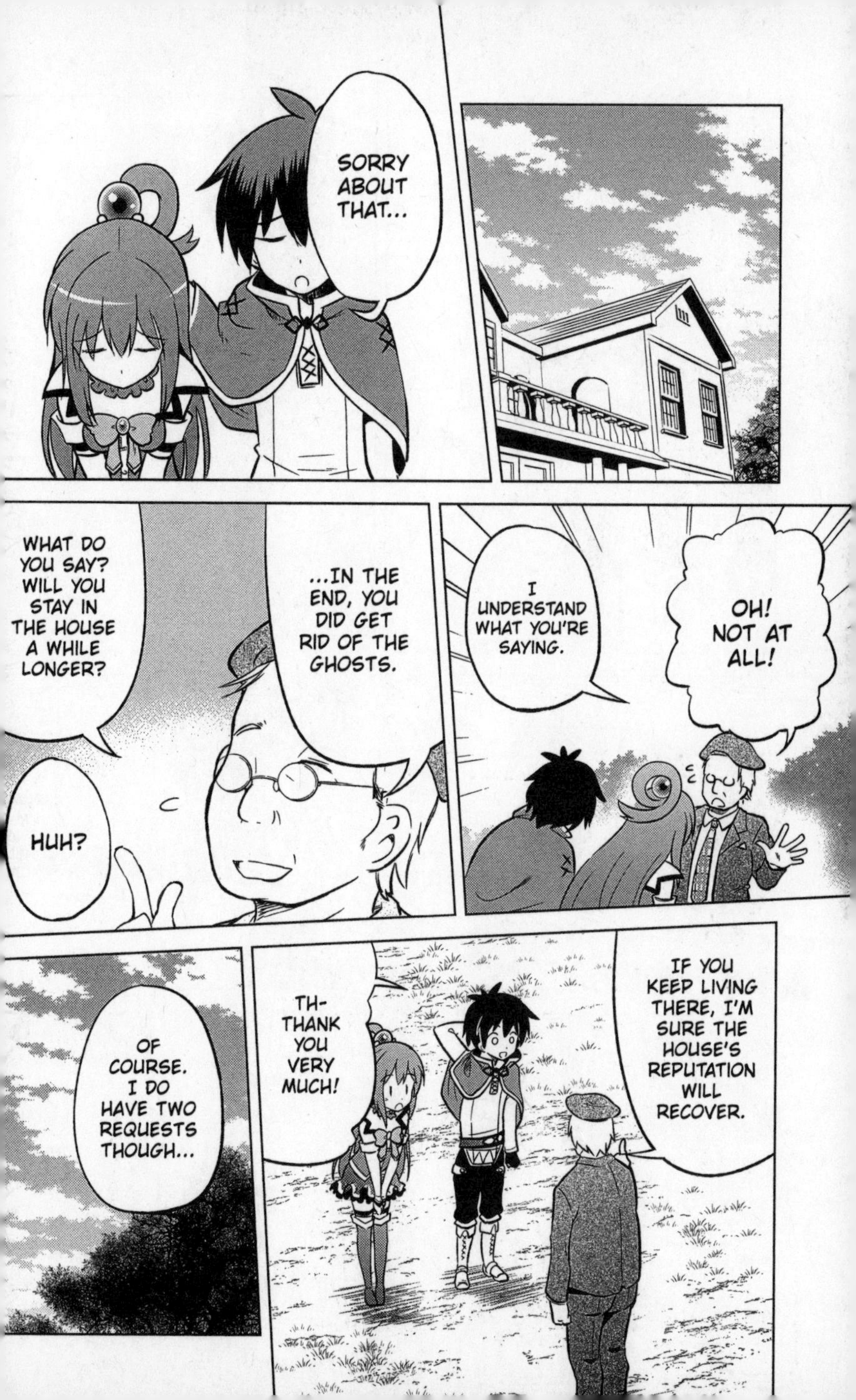
SORRY ABOUT THAT...
OH! NOT AT ALL!
I UNDERSTAND WHAT YOU'RE SAYING.
...IN THE END, YOU DID GET RID OF THE GHOSTS.
WHAT DO YOU SAY? WILL YOU STAY IN THE HOUSE A WHILE LONGER?
HUH?
IF YOU KEEP LIVING THERE, I'M SURE THE HOUSE'S REPUTATION WILL RECOVER.
TH-THANK YOU VERY MUCH!
OF COURSE. I DO HAVE TWO REQUESTS THOUGH...

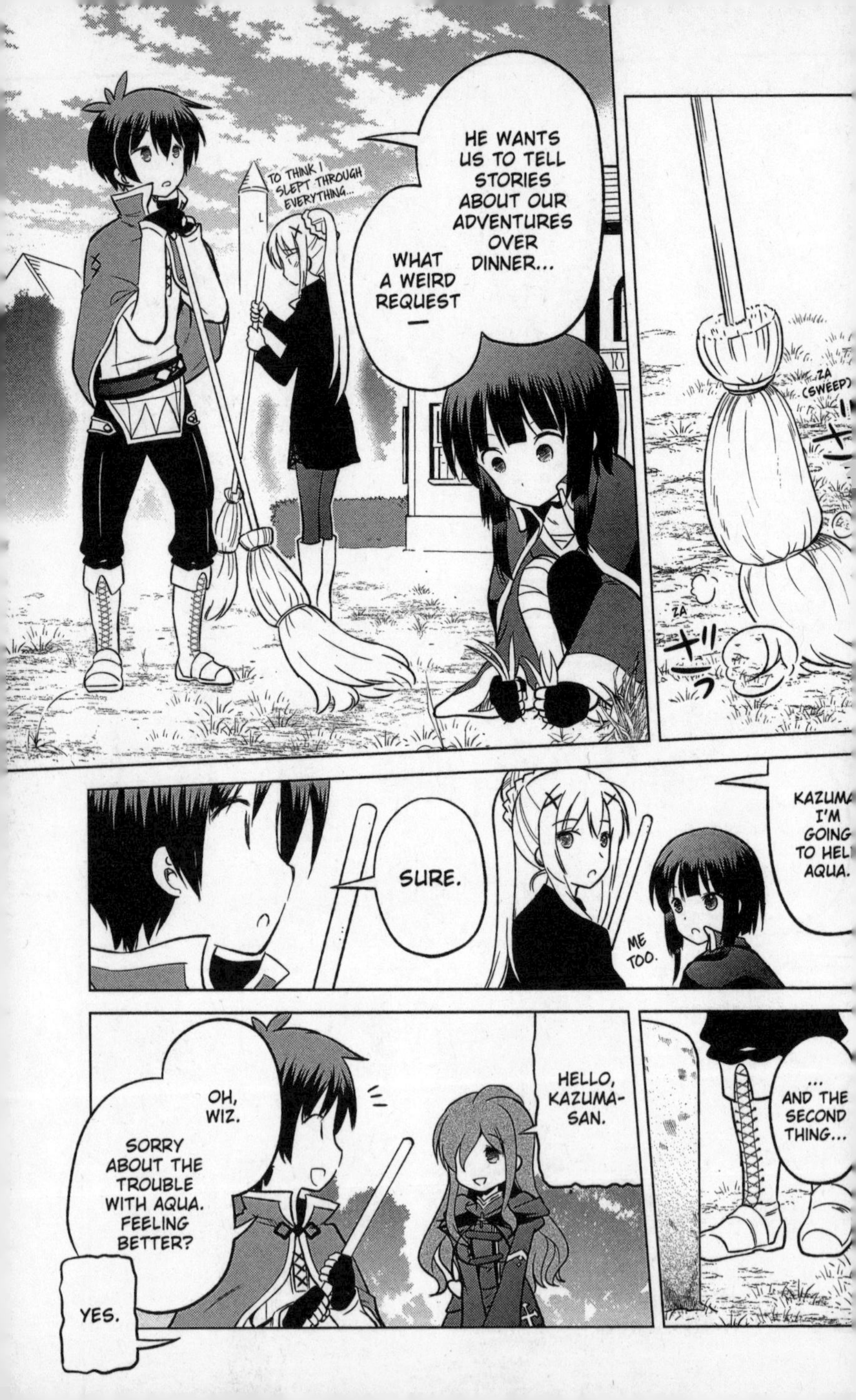
ZA (SWEEP)
ZA
HE WANTS US TO TELL STORIES ABOUT OUR ADVENTURES OVER DINNER...
WHAT A WEIRD REQUEST —
TO THINK I SLEPT THROUGH EVERYTHING...
KAZUMA I'M GOING TO HEL AQUA.
ME TOO.
SURE.
... AND THE SECOND THING...
HELLO, KAZUMA-SAN.
OH, WIZ.
SORRY ABOUT THE TROUBLE WITH AQUA. FEELING BETTER?
YES.

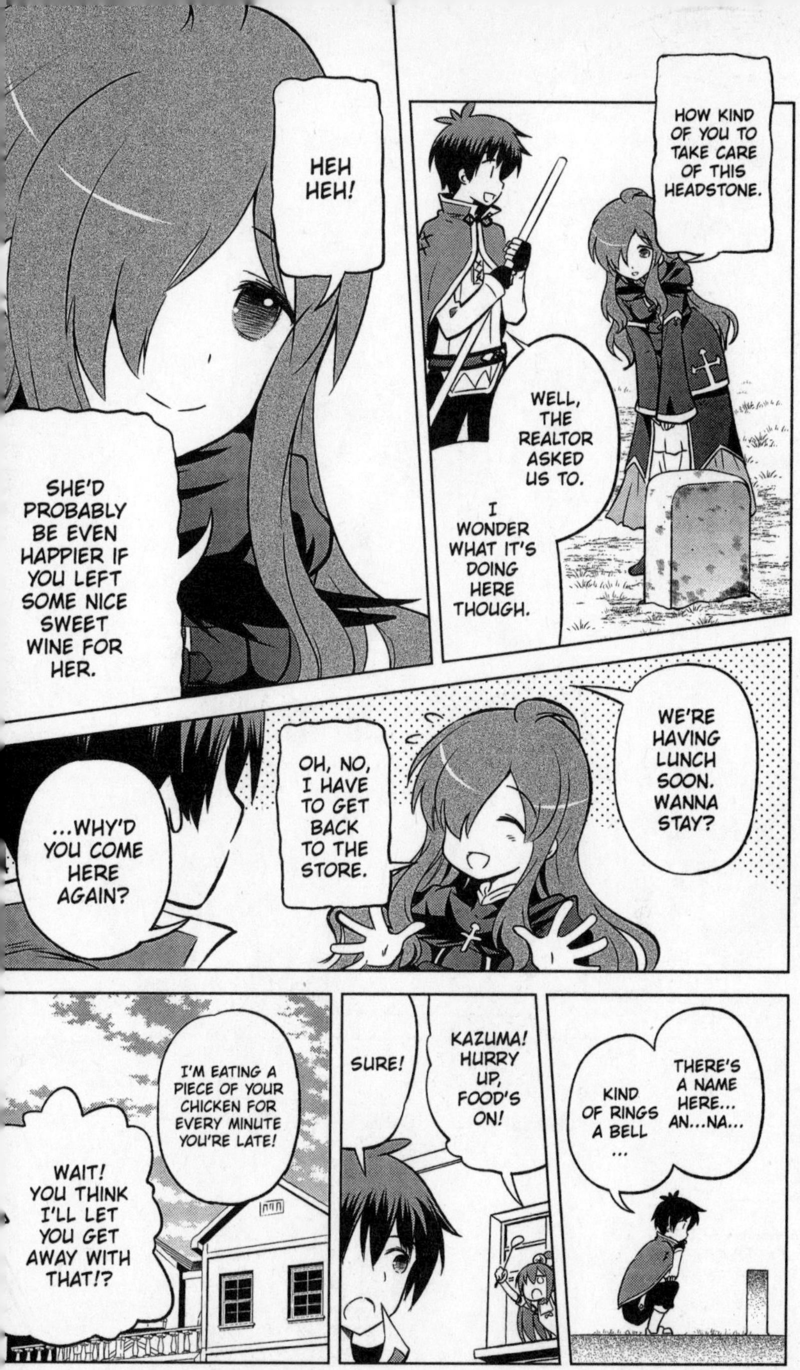
HOW KIND OF YOU TO TAKE CARE OF THIS HEADSTONE.
WELL, THE REALTOR ASKED US TO.
I WONDER WHAT IT'S DOING HERE THOUGH.
HEH HEH!
SHE'D PROBABLY BE EVEN HAPPIER IF YOU LEFT SOME NICE SWEET WINE FOR HER.
WE'RE HAVING LUNCH SOON. WANNA STAY?
OH, NO, I HAVE TO GET BACK TO THE STORE.
...WHY'D YOU COME HERE AGAIN?
THERE'S A NAME HERE... AN...NA...
KIND OF RINGS A BELL ...
KAZUMA! HURRY UP, FOOD'S ON!
SURE!
I'M EATING A PIECE OF YOUR CHICKEN FOR EVERY MINUTE YOU'RE LATE!
WAIT! YOU THINK I'LL LET YOU GET AWAY WITH THAT!?

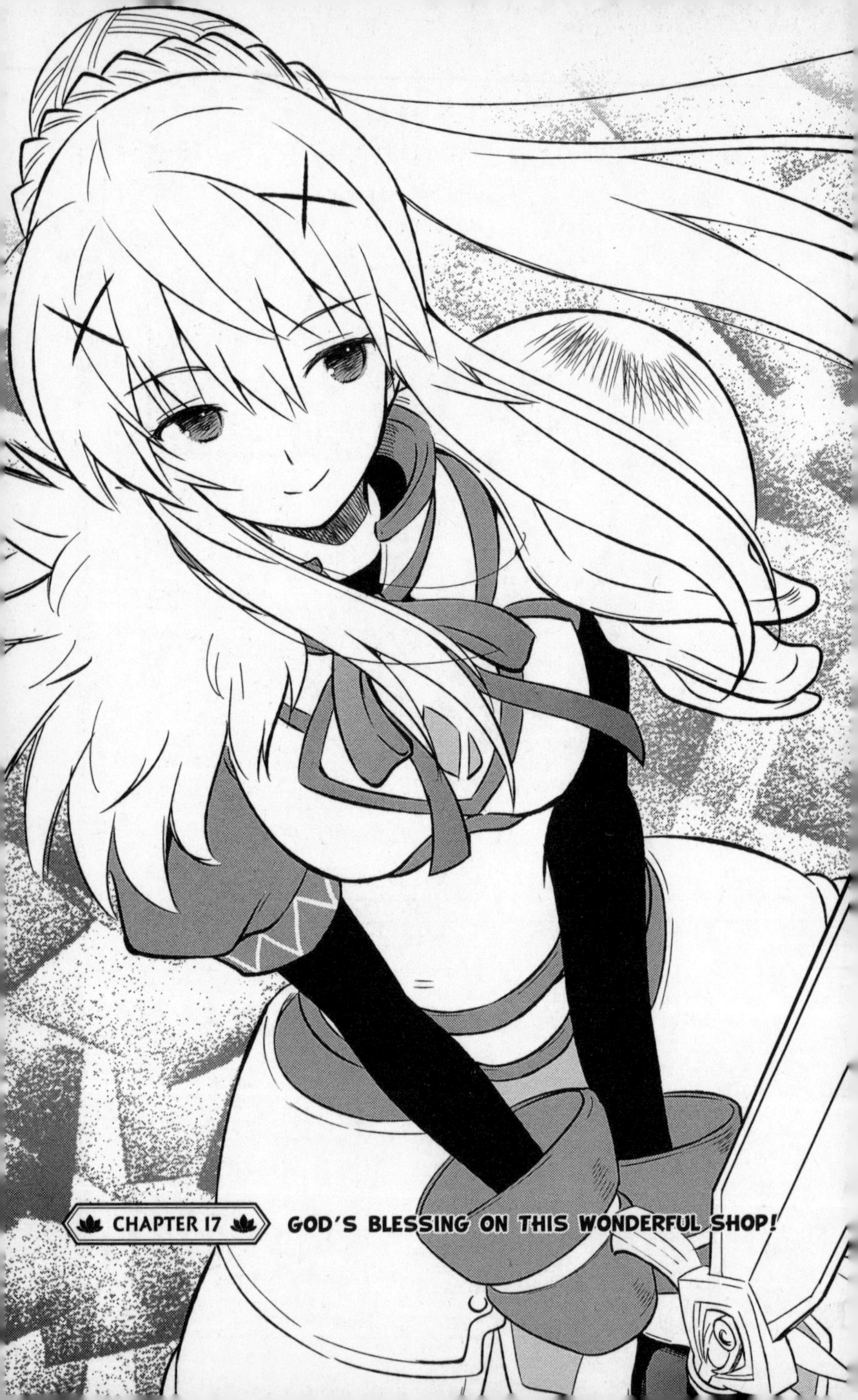

# CHAPTER 17 GOD'S BLESSING ON THIS WONDERFUL SHOP!

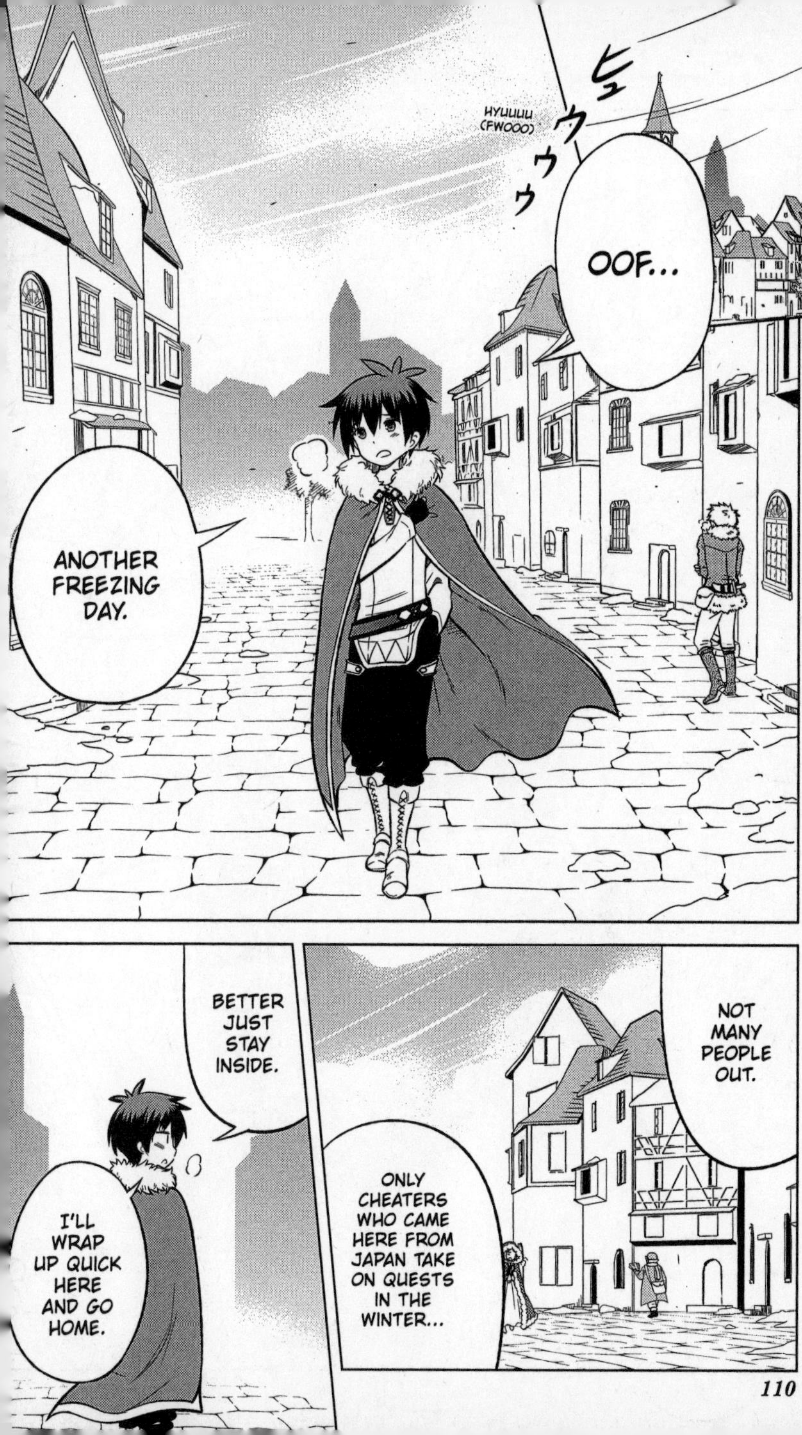
ヒュウウウ
HYUUUU (FWOOO)
OOF...
ANOTHER FREEZING DAY.
NOT MANY PEOPLE OUT.
ONLY CHEATERS WHO CAME HERE FROM JAPAN TAKE ON QUESTS IN THE WINTER...
BETTER JUST STAY INSIDE.
I'LL WRAP UP QUICK HERE AND GO HOME.

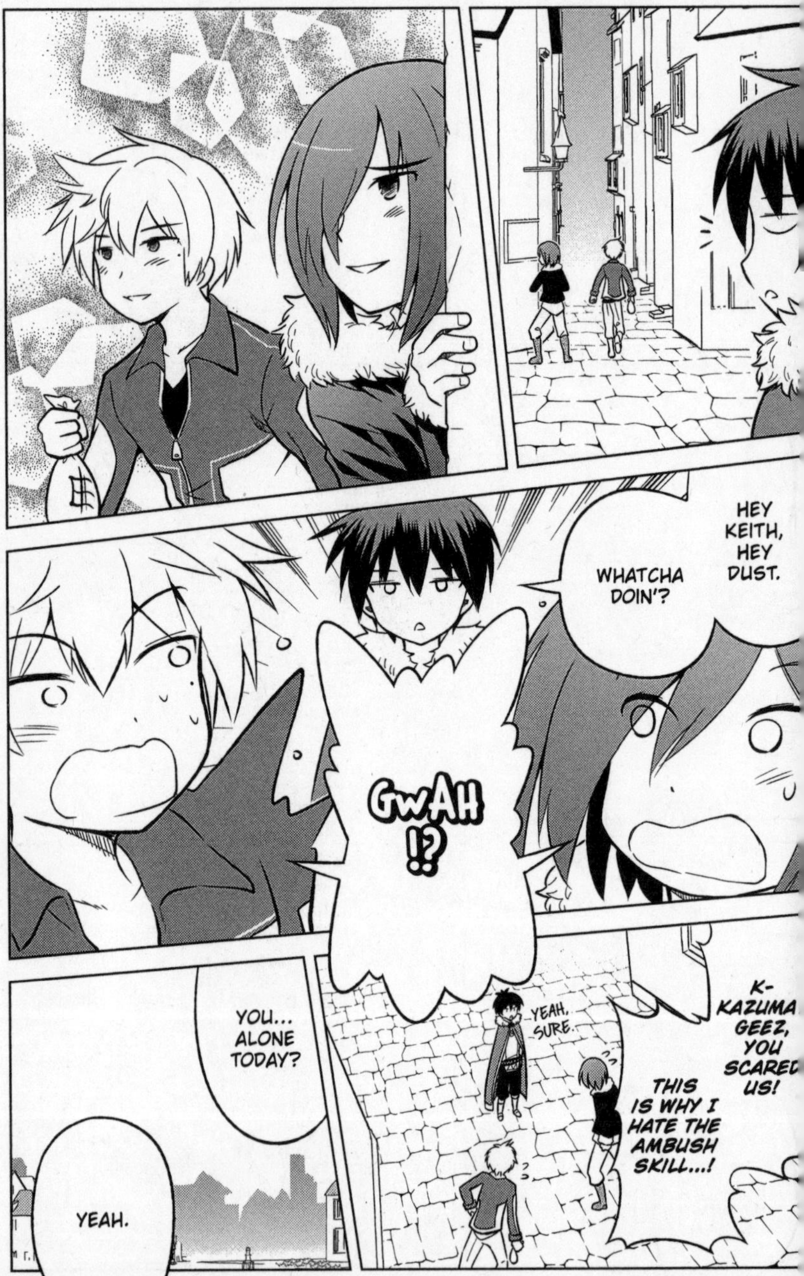
HEY KEITH, HEY DUST.
WHATCHA DOIN'?
GwAH !?
K-KAZUMA GEEZ, YOU SCARED US!
THIS IS WHY I HATE THE AMBUSH SKILL...!
YEAH, SURE.
YOU... ALONE TODAY?
YEAH.

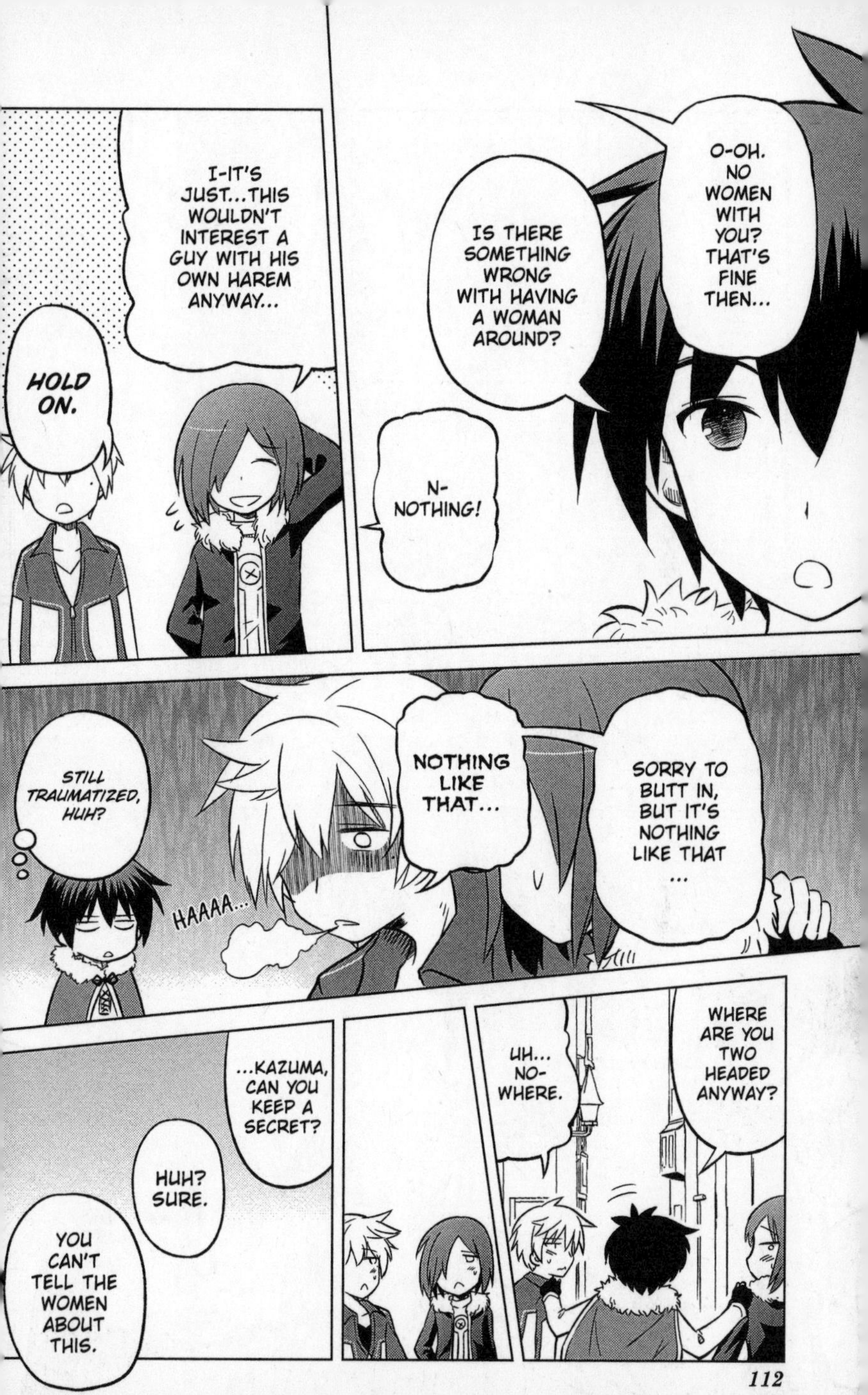
O-OH. NO WOMEN WITH YOU? THAT'S FINE THEN...
IS THERE SOMETHING WRONG WITH HAVING A WOMAN AROUND?
N-NOTHING!
I-IT'S JUST...THIS WOULDN'T INTEREST A GUY WITH HIS OWN HAREM ANYWAY...
HOLD ON.
SORRY TO BUTT IN, BUT IT'S NOTHING LIKE THAT...
NOTHING LIKE THAT...
HAAAA...
STILL TRAUMATIZED, HUH?
WHERE ARE YOU TWO HEADED ANYWAY?
UH... NO-WHERE.
...KAZUMA, CAN YOU KEEP A SECRET?
HUH? SURE.
YOU CAN'T TELL THE WOMEN ABOUT THIS.

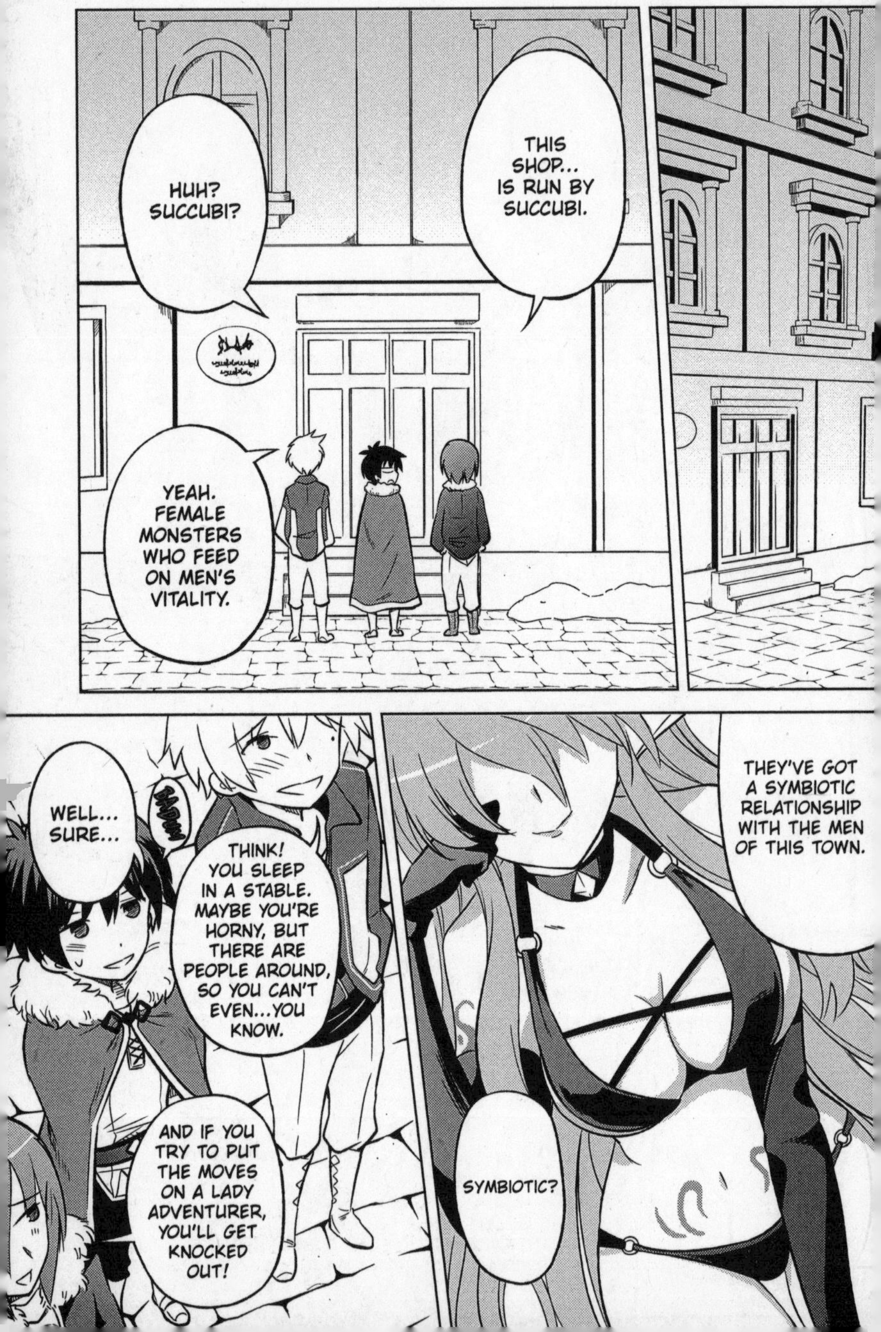
THIS SHOP... IS RUN BY SUCCUBI.
HUH? SUCCUBI?
YEAH. FEMALE MONSTERS WHO FEED ON MEN'S VITALITY.
THEY'VE GOT A SYMBIOTIC RELATIONSHIP WITH THE MEN OF THIS TOWN.
SYMBIOTIC?
THINK! YOU SLEEP IN A STABLE. MAYBE YOU'RE HORNY, BUT THERE ARE PEOPLE AROUND, SO YOU CAN'T EVEN...YOU KNOW.
WELL... SURE...
AND IF YOU TRY TO PUT THE MOVES ON A LADY ADVENTURER, YOU'LL GET KNOCKED OUT!

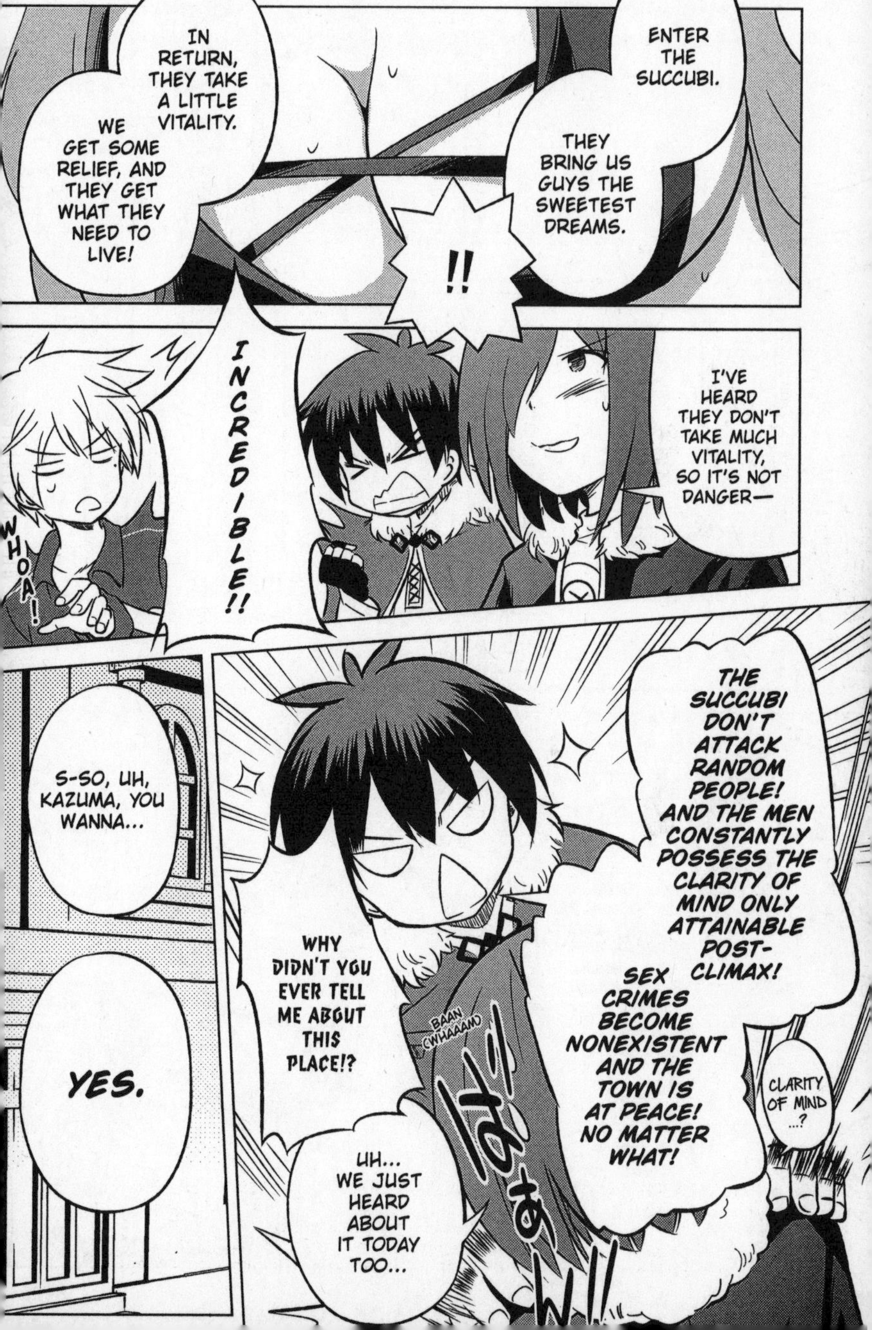
ENTER THE SUCCUBI.
THEY BRING US GUYS THE SWEETEST DREAMS.
IN RETURN, THEY TAKE A LITTLE VITALITY.
WE GET SOME RELIEF, AND THEY GET WHAT THEY NEED TO LIVE!
I'VE HEARD THEY DON'T TAKE MUCH VITALITY, SO IT'S NOT DANGER—
!!
INCREDIBLE!!
WHOA!
THE SUCCUBI DON'T ATTACK RANDOM PEOPLE! AND THE MEN CONSTANTLY POSSESS THE CLARITY OF MIND ONLY ATTAINABLE POST-CLIMAX!
SEX CRIMES BECOME NONEXISTENT AND THE TOWN IS AT PEACE! NO MATTER WHAT!
CLARITY OF MIND ...?
WHY DIDN'T YOU EVER TELL ME ABOUT THIS PLACE!?
BAAN (WHAAAM)
UH... WE JUST HEARD ABOUT IT TODAY TOO...
S-SO, UH, KAZUMA, YOU WANNA...
YES.

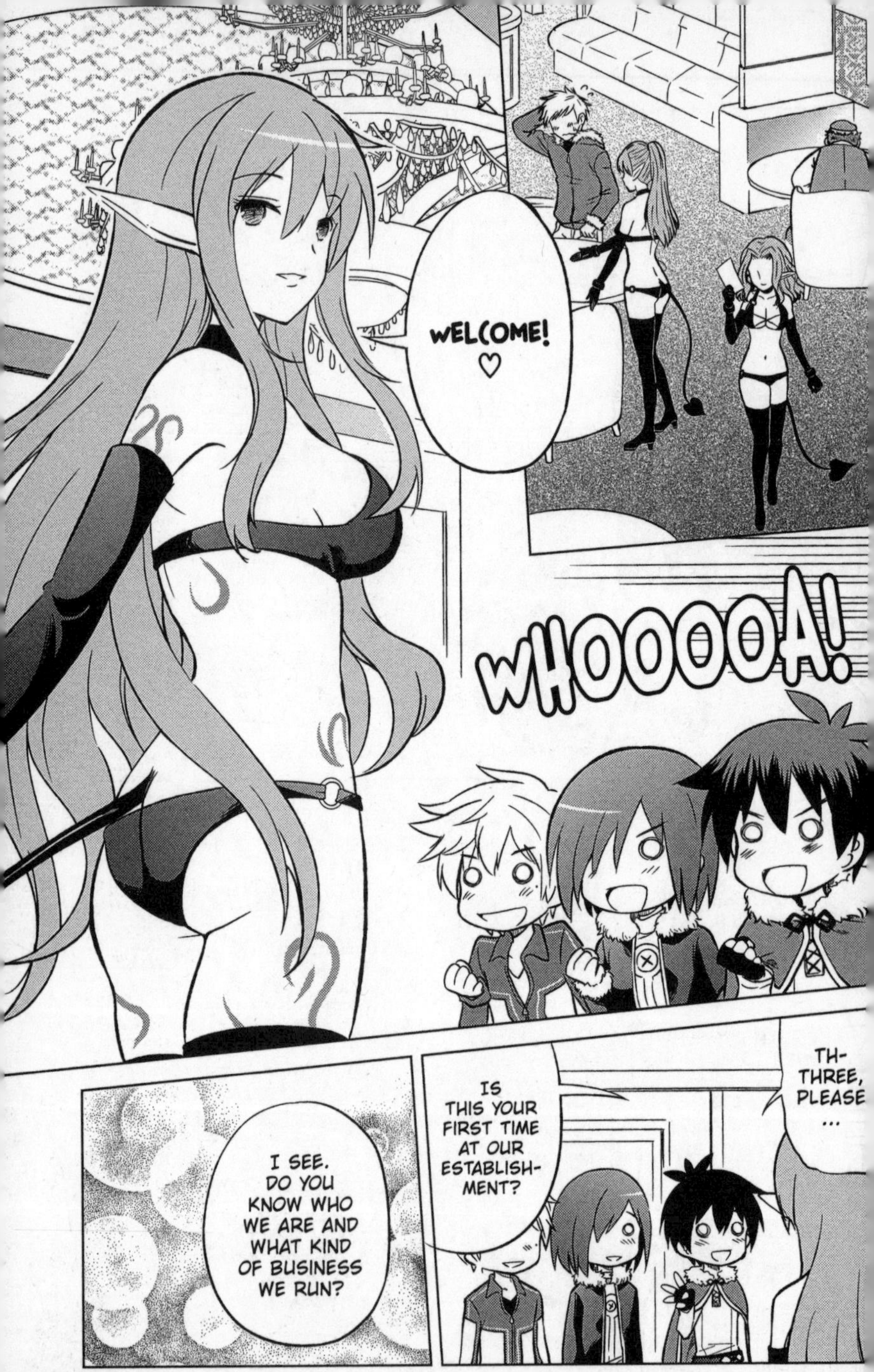
WELCOME! ♡
WHOOOOA!
TH-THREE, PLEASE...
IS THIS YOUR FIRST TIME AT OUR ESTABLISHMENT?
I SEE. DO YOU KNOW WHO WE ARE AND WHAT KIND OF BUSINESS WE RUN?

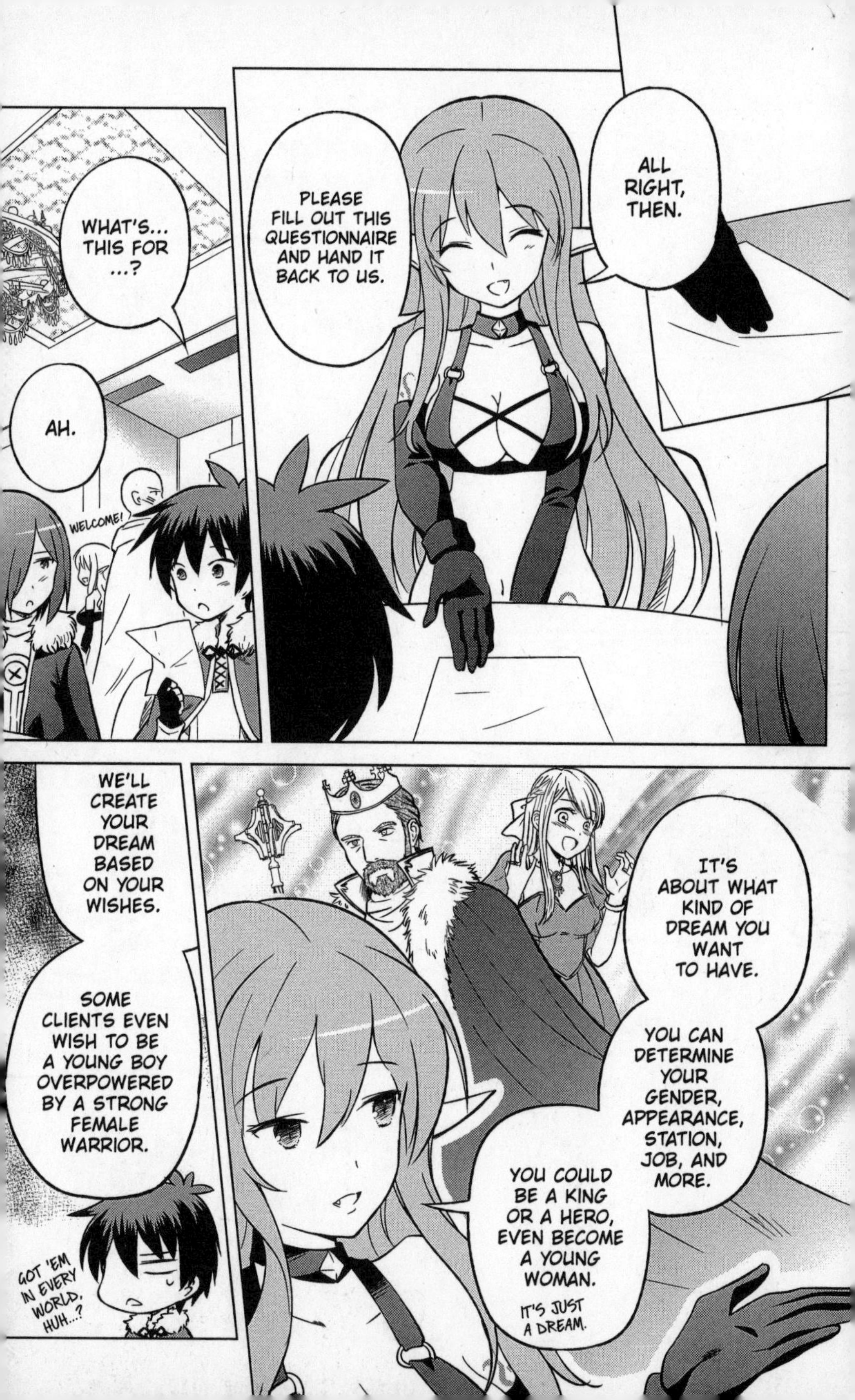
ALL RIGHT, THEN.
PLEASE FILL OUT THIS QUESTIONNAIRE AND HAND IT BACK TO US.
WHAT'S... THIS FOR ...?
AH.
WELCOME!
IT'S ABOUT WHAT KIND OF DREAM YOU WANT TO HAVE.
YOU CAN DETERMINE YOUR GENDER, APPEARANCE, STATION, JOB, AND MORE.
YOU COULD BE A KING OR A HERO, EVEN BECOME A YOUNG WOMAN.
IT'S JUST A DREAM.
WE'LL CREATE YOUR DREAM BASED ON YOUR WISHES.
SOME CLIENTS EVEN WISH TO BE A YOUNG BOY OVERPOWERED BY A STRONG FEMALE WARRIOR.
GOT 'EM IN EVERY WORLD, HUH...?

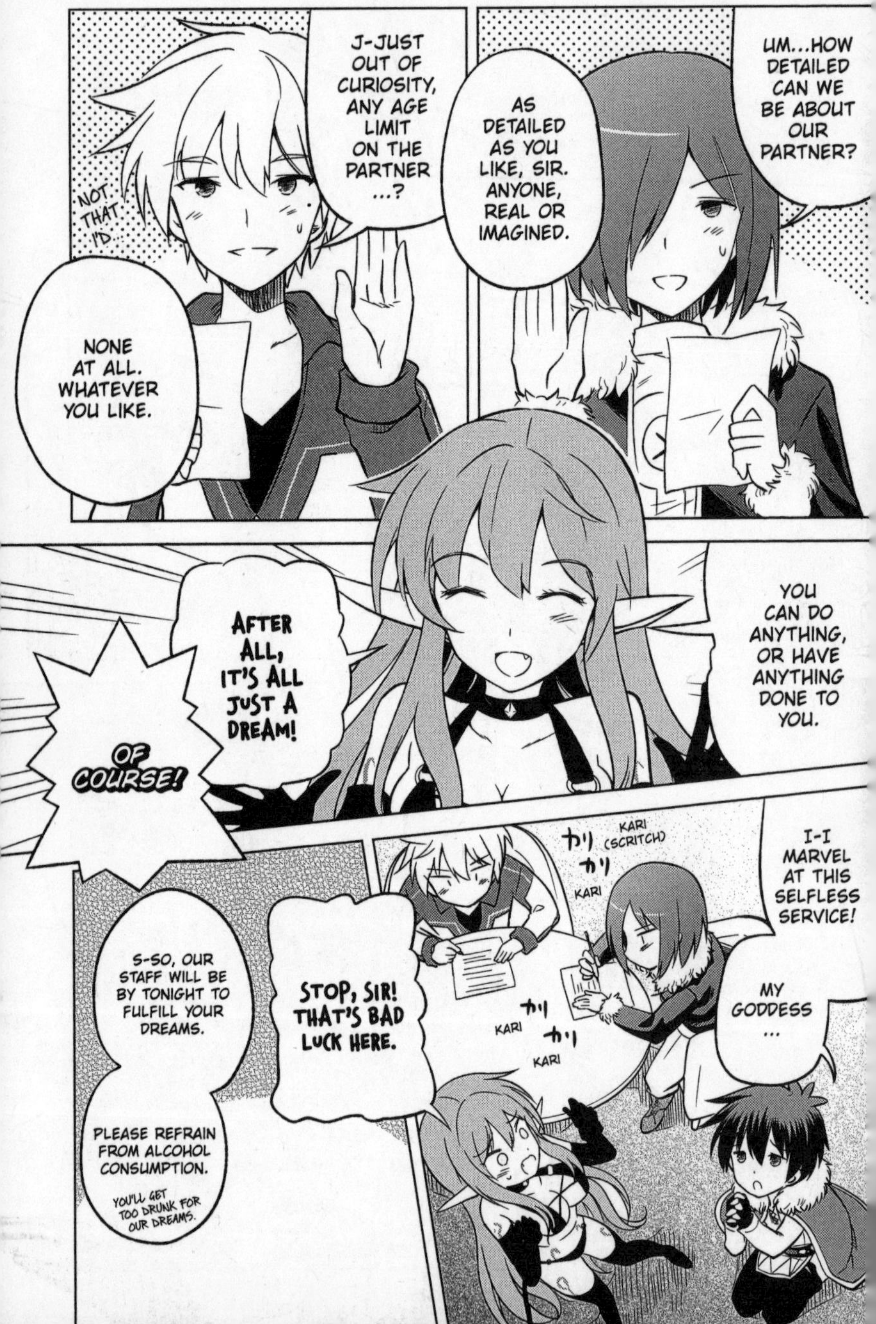
UM...HOW DETAILED CAN WE BE ABOUT OUR PARTNER?
AS DETAILED AS YOU LIKE, SIR. ANYONE, REAL OR IMAGINED.
J-JUST OUT OF CURIOSITY, ANY AGE LIMIT ON THE PARTNER ...?
NOT THAT I'D...
NONE AT ALL. WHATEVER YOU LIKE.
YOU CAN DO ANYTHING, OR HAVE ANYTHING DONE TO YOU.
AFTER ALL, IT'S ALL JUST A DREAM!
OF COURSE!
I-I MARVEL AT THIS SELFLESS SERVICE!
MY GODDESS ...
カリ KARI (SCRITCH)
カリ KARI
カリ KARI
カリ KARI
STOP, SIR! THAT'S BAD LUCK HERE.
S-SO, OUR STAFF WILL BE BY TONIGHT TO FULFILL YOUR DREAMS.
PLEASE REFRAIN FROM ALCOHOL CONSUMPTION.
YOU'LL GET TOO DRUNK FOR OUR DREAMS.

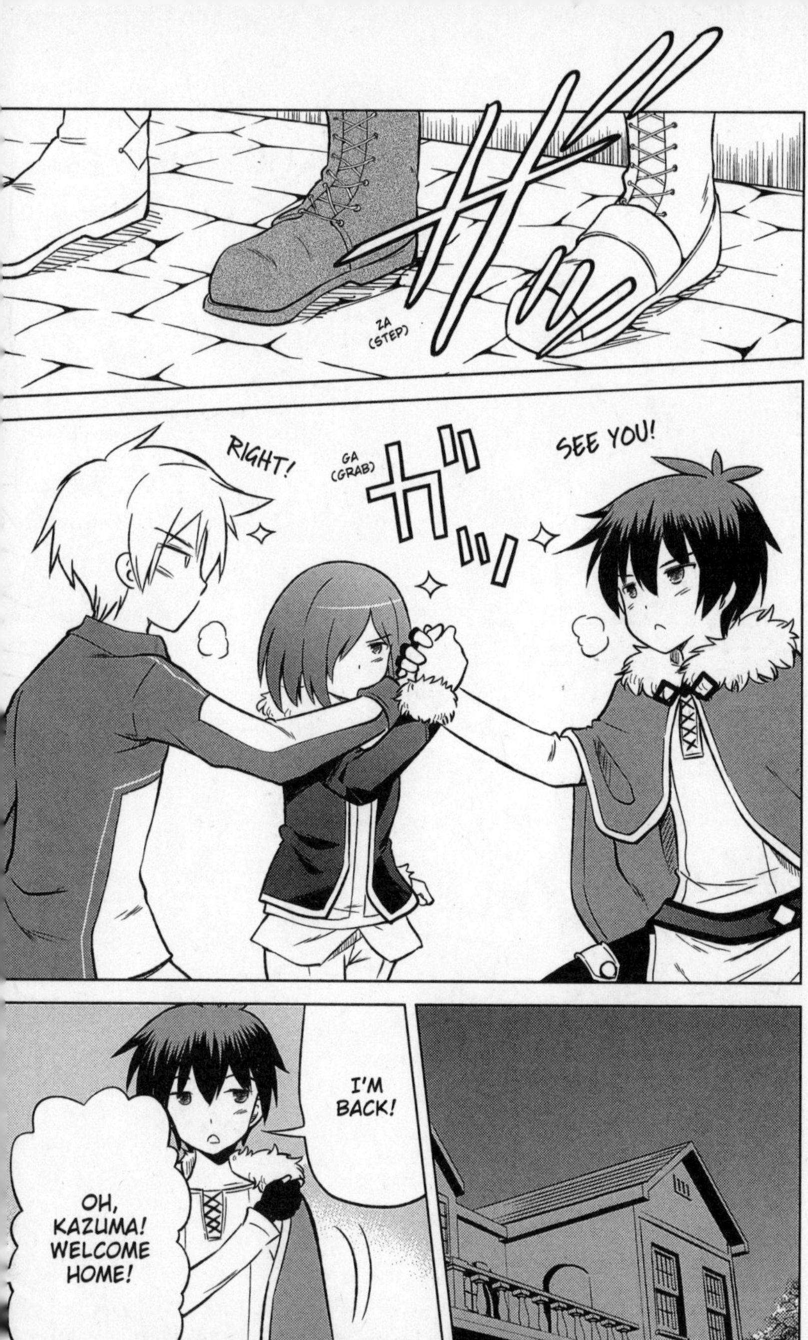
ZA
(STEP)
SEE YOU!
GA
(GRAB)
RIGHT!
I'M BACK!
OH, KAZUMA! WELCOME HOME!

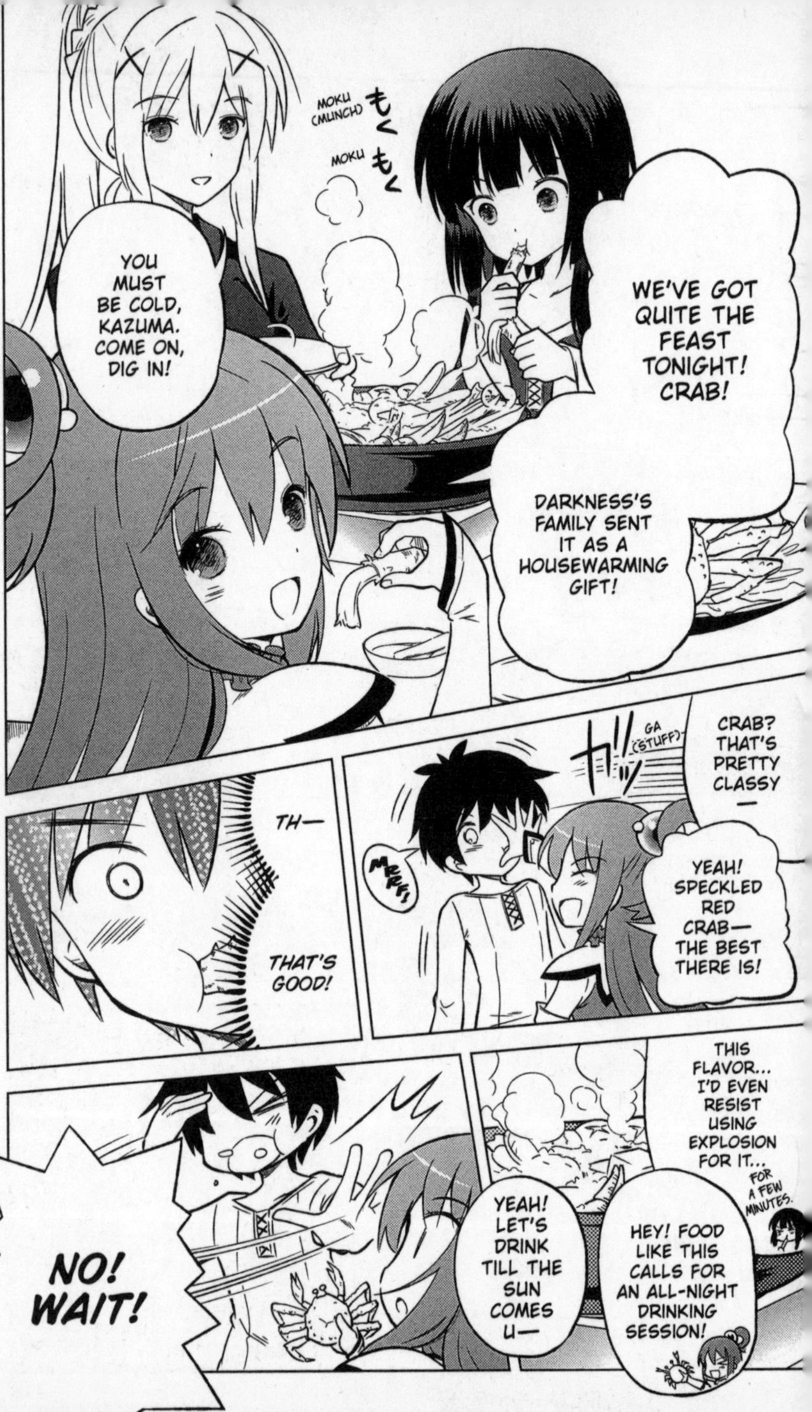
WE'VE GOT QUITE THE FEAST TONIGHT! CRAB!
DARKNESS'S FAMILY SENT IT AS A HOUSEWARMING GIFT!
MOKU (MUNCH) もく
MOKU もく
YOU MUST BE COLD, KAZUMA. COME ON, DIG IN!
CRAB? THAT'S PRETTY CLASSY—
GA (STUFF)
YEAH! SPECKLED RED CRAB—THE BEST THERE IS!
MRRF!
TH—
THAT'S GOOD!
THIS FLAVOR... I'D EVEN RESIST USING EXPLOSION FOR IT...
FOR A FEW MINUTES.
HEY! FOOD LIKE THIS CALLS FOR AN ALL-NIGHT DRINKING SESSION!
YEAH! LET'S DRINK TILL THE SUN COMES U—
NO! WAIT!

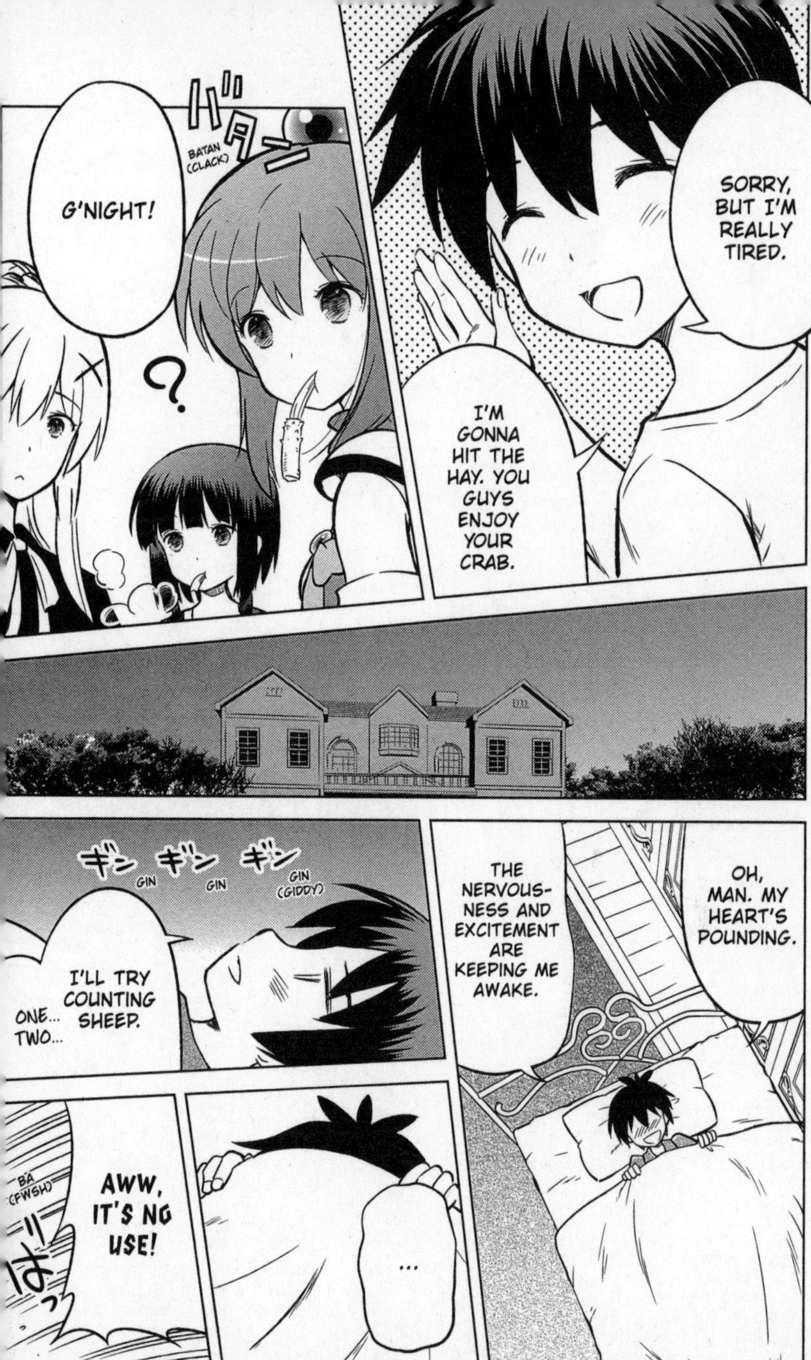
SORRY, BUT I'M REALLY TIRED.
I'M GONNA HIT THE HAY. YOU GUYS ENJOY YOUR CRAB.
BATAN (CLACK)
G'NIGHT!
?
OH, MAN. MY HEART'S POUNDING.
THE NERVOUS-NESS AND EXCITEMENT ARE KEEPING ME AWAKE.
GIN GIN GIN (GIDDY)
I'LL TRY COUNTING SHEEP.
ONE... TWO...
...
BA (FWSH)
AWW, IT'S NG USE!

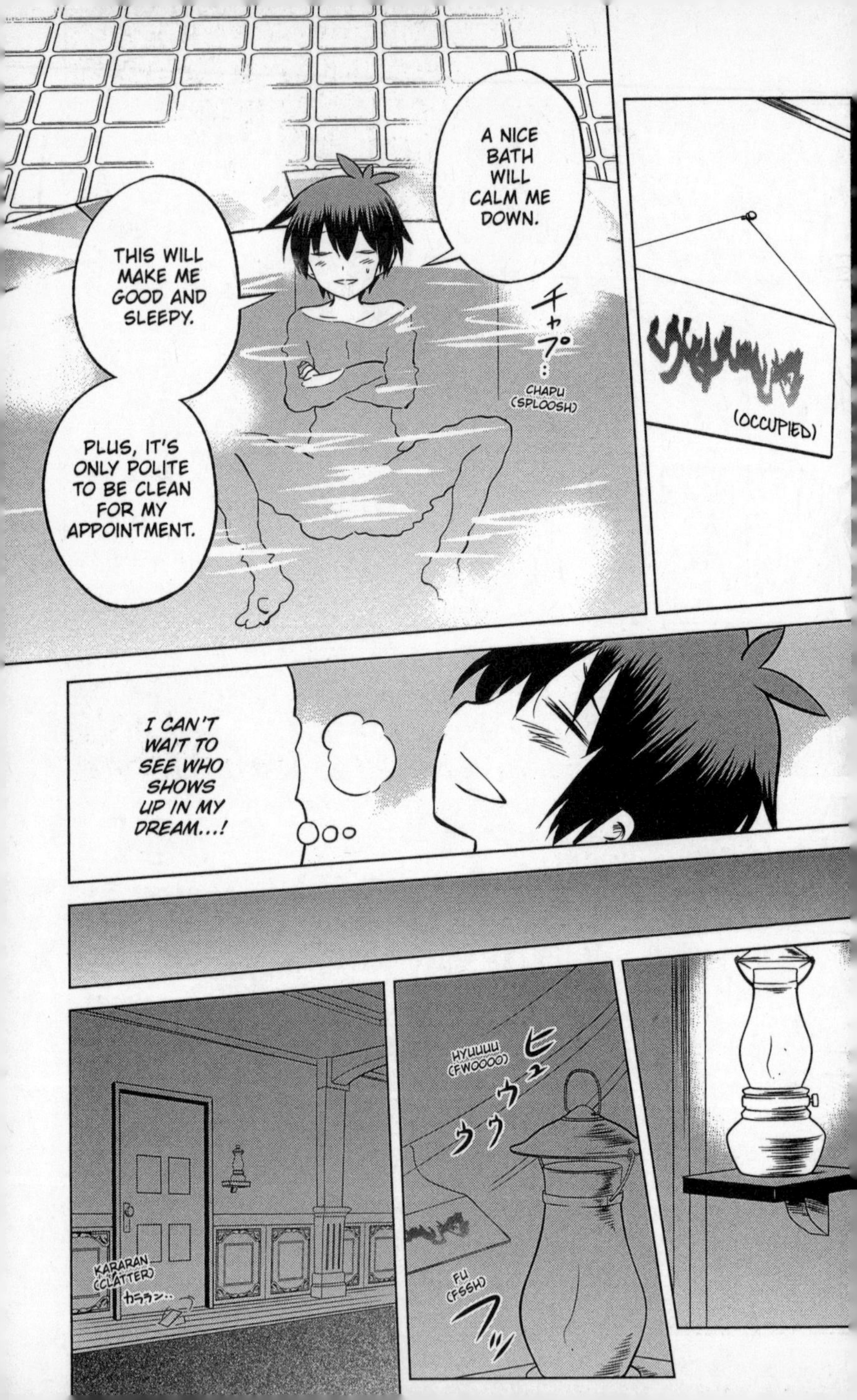
(OCCUPIED)
A NICE BATH WILL CALM ME DOWN.
チャプ…
CHAPU (SPLOOSH)
THIS WILL MAKE ME GOOD AND SLEEPY.
PLUS, IT'S ONLY POLITE TO BE CLEAN FOR MY APPOINTMENT.
I CAN'T WAIT TO SEE WHO SHOWS UP IN MY DREAM...!
ヒュウウウ
HYUUUU (FWOOOO)
フッ
FU (FSSH)
KARARAN (CLATTER)
カララン‥

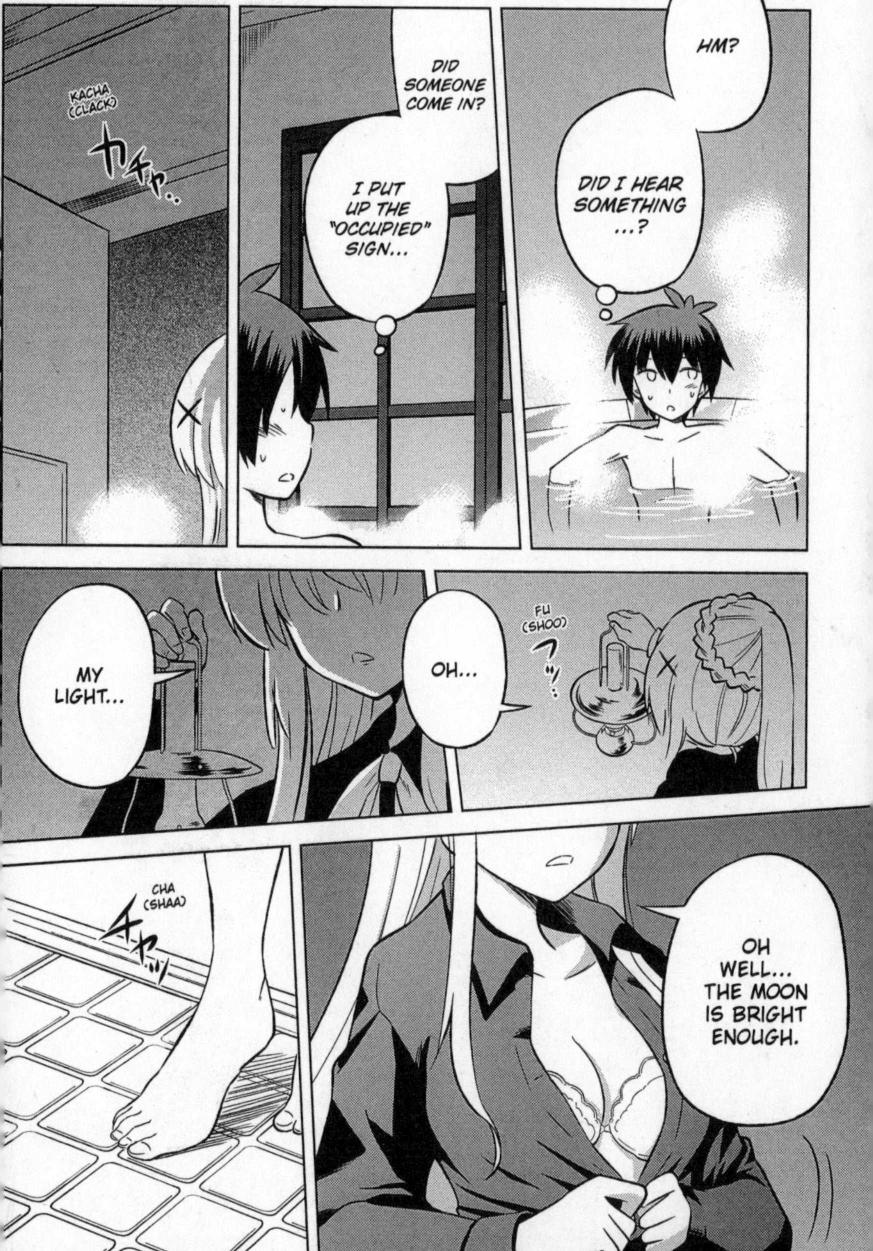
HM?
DID I HEAR SOMETHING ...?
DID SOMEONE COME IN?
I PUT UP THE "OCCUPIED" SIGN...
KACHA (CLACK)
FU (SHOO)
OH...
MY LIGHT...
OH WELL... THE MOON IS BRIGHT ENOUGH.
CHA (SHAA)

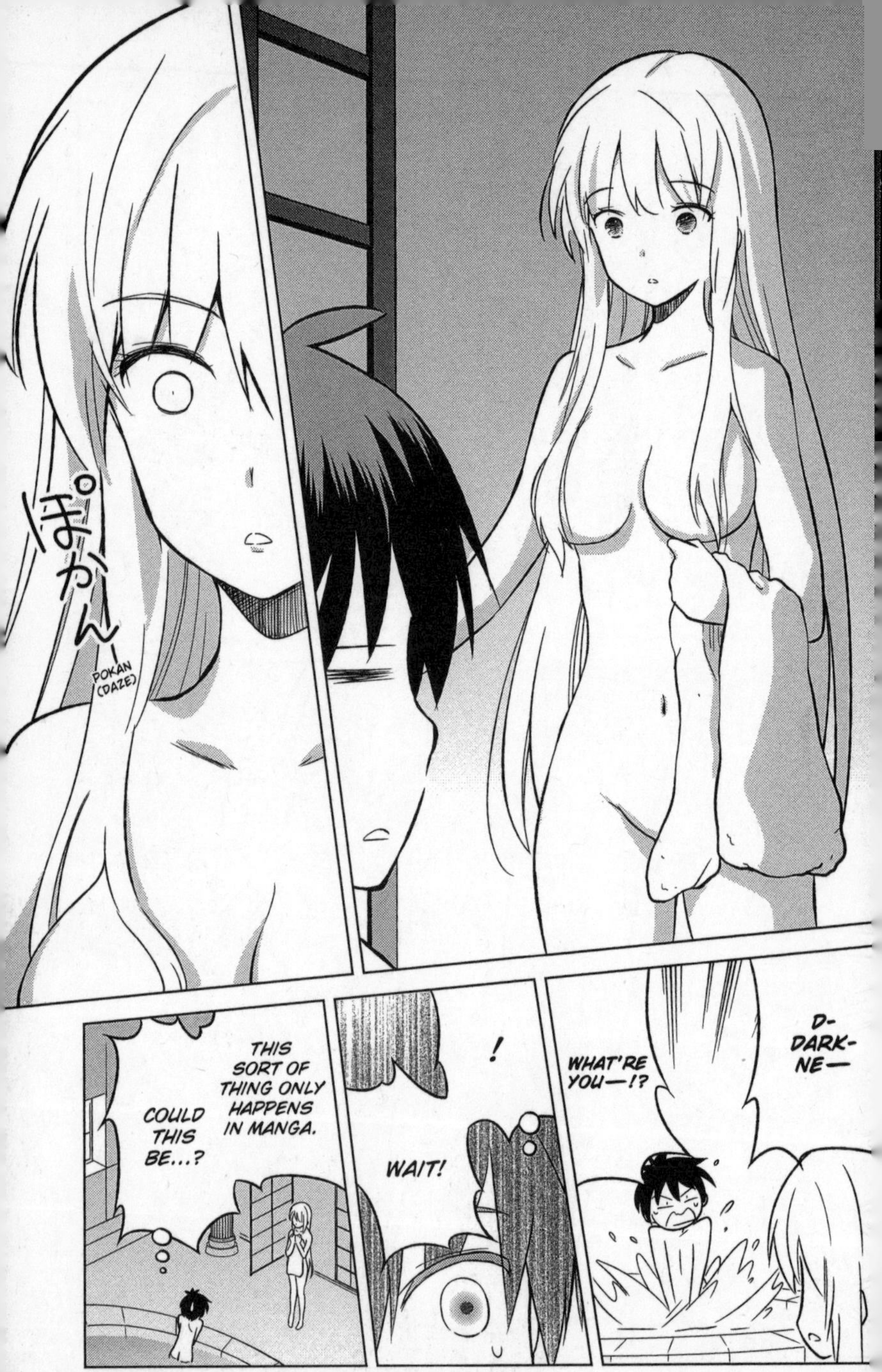
ぽかん
POKAN (DAZE)
D-DARK-NE—
WHAT'RE YOU—!?
!
WAIT!
THIS SORT OF THING ONLY HAPPENS IN MANGA.
COULD THIS BE...?

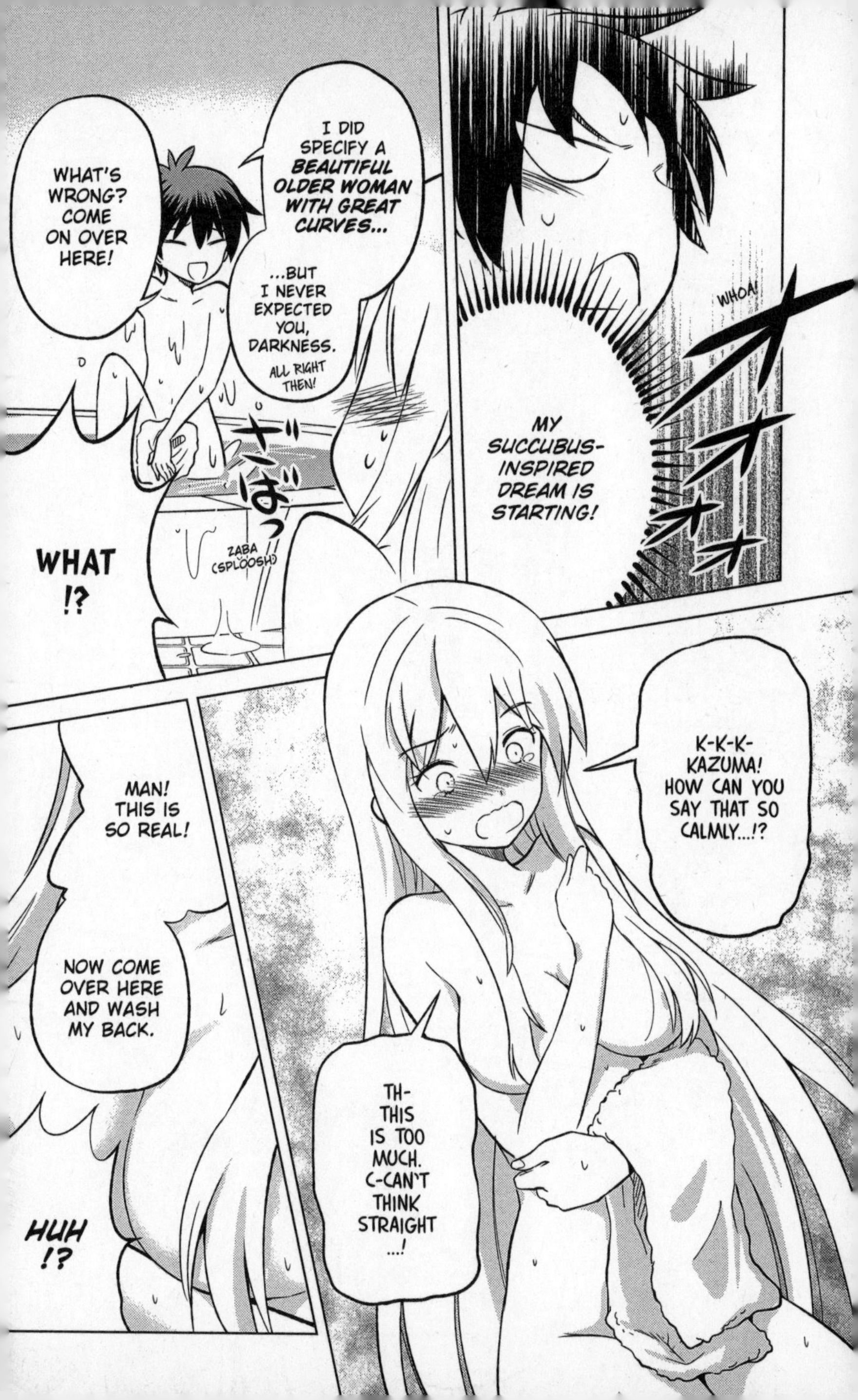
WHOA!
MY SUCCUBUS-INSPIRED DREAM IS STARTING!
I DID SPECIFY A BEAUTIFUL OLDER WOMAN WITH GREAT CURVES...
...BUT I NEVER EXPECTED YOU, DARKNESS.
ALL RIGHT THEN!
WHAT'S WRONG? COME ON OVER HERE!
ZABA (SPLOOSH)
WHAT !?
K-K-K-KAZUMA! HOW CAN YOU SAY THAT SO CALMLY...!?
TH-THIS IS TOO MUCH. C-CAN'T THINK STRAIGHT ...!
MAN! THIS IS SO REAL!
NOW COME OVER HERE AND WASH MY BACK.
HUH !?

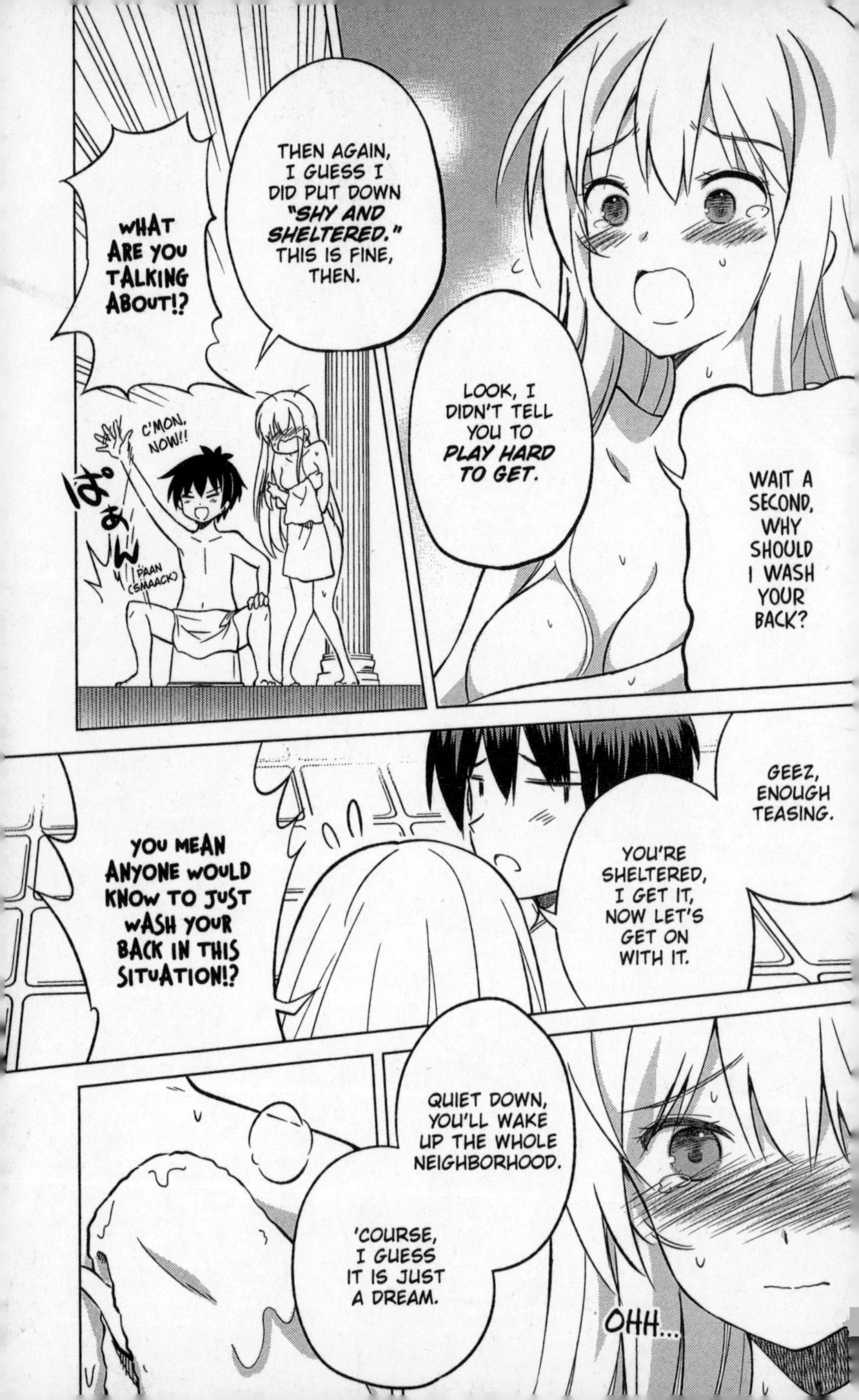
WAIT A SECOND, WHY SHOULD I WASH YOUR BACK?
LOOK, I DIDN'T TELL YOU TO ***PLAY HARD TO GET.***
THEN AGAIN, I GUESS I DID PUT DOWN ***"SHY AND SHELTERED."*** THIS IS FINE, THEN.
WHAT ARE YOU TALKING ABOUT!?
C'MON, NOW!!
ぱぁん
PAAN (SMAACK)
GEEZ, ENOUGH TEASING.
YOU'RE SHELTERED, I GET IT, NOW LET'S GET ON WITH IT.
YOU MEAN ANYONE WOULD KNOW TO JUST WASH YOUR BACK IN THIS SITUATION!?
QUIET DOWN, YOU'LL WAKE UP THE WHOLE NEIGHBORHOOD.
'COURSE, I GUESS IT IS JUST A DREAM.
OHH...

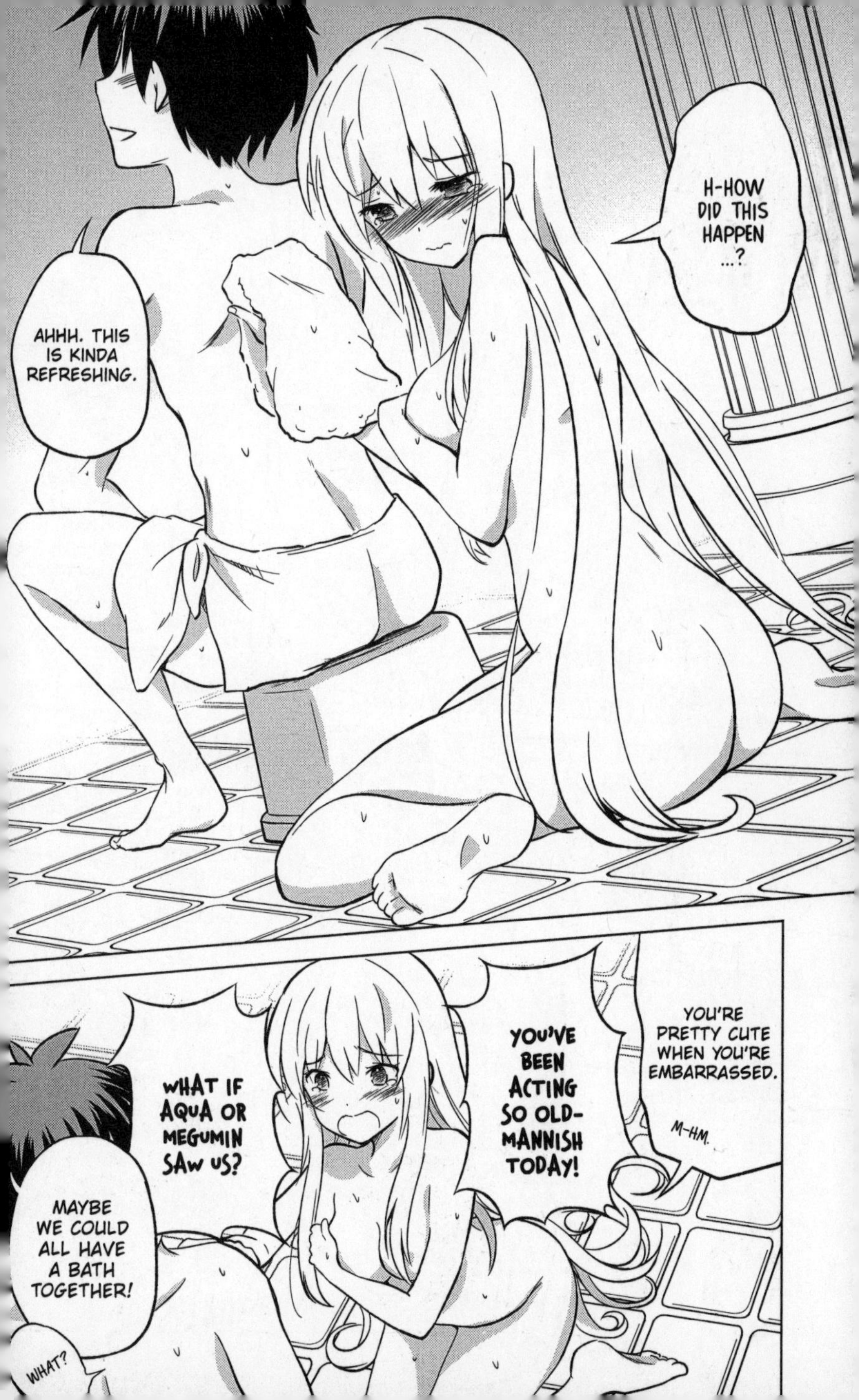
H-HOW DID THIS HAPPEN ...?
AHHH. THIS IS KINDA REFRESHING.
YOU'RE PRETTY CUTE WHEN YOU'RE EMBARRASSED.
M-HM.
YOU'VE BEEN ACTING SO OLD-MANNISH TODAY!
WHAT IF AQUA OR MEGUMIN SAW US?
MAYBE WE COULD ALL HAVE A BATH TOGETHER!
WHAT?

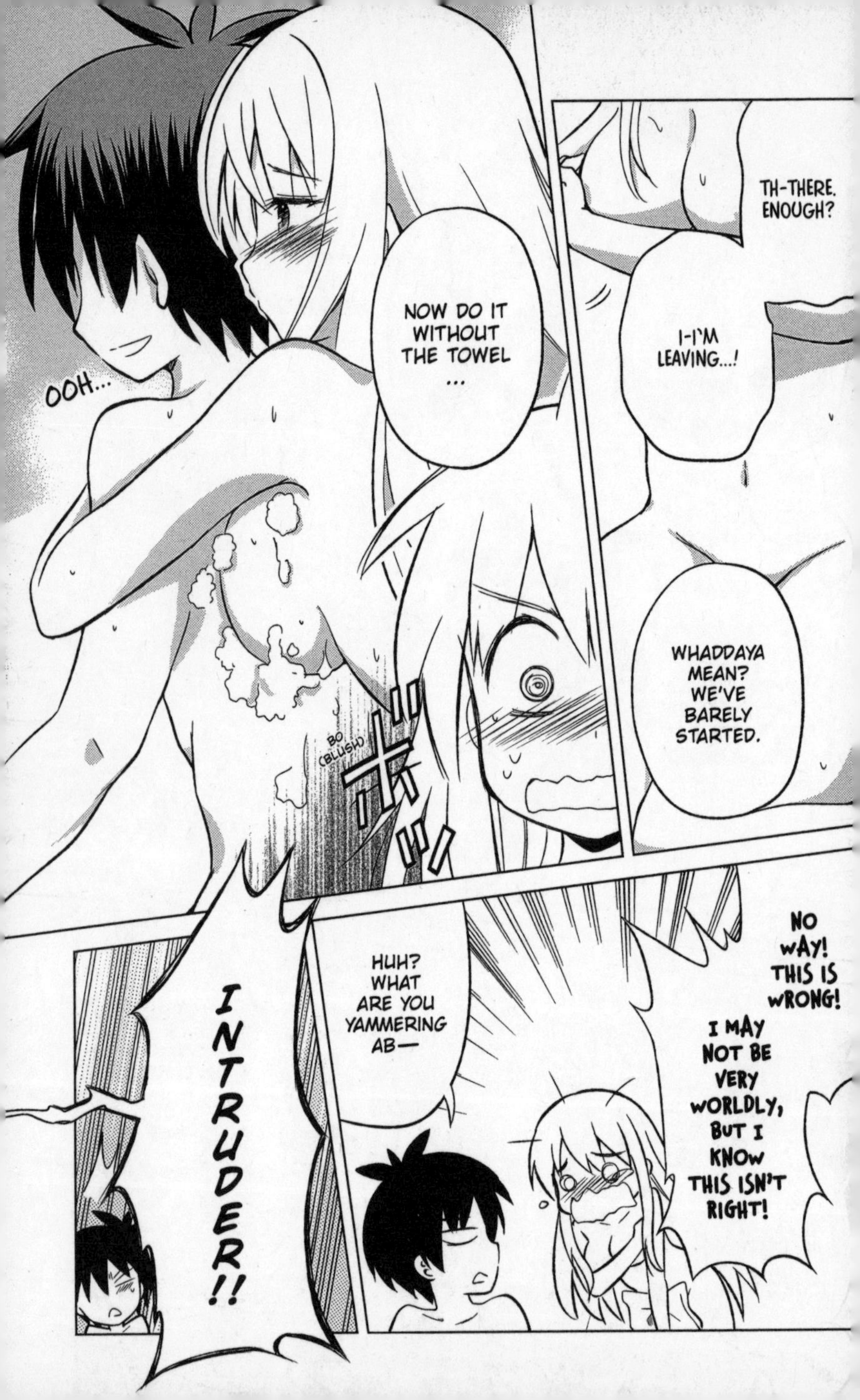
TH-THERE. ENOUGH?
I-I'M LEAVING...!
WHADDAYA MEAN? WE'VE BARELY STARTED.
NOW DO IT WITHOUT THE TOWEL ...
OOH...
BO (BLUSH)
NO WAY! THIS IS WRONG!
I MAY NOT BE VERY WORLDLY, BUT I KNOW THIS ISN'T RIGHT!
HUH? WHAT ARE YOU YAMMERING AB—
INTRUDER!!

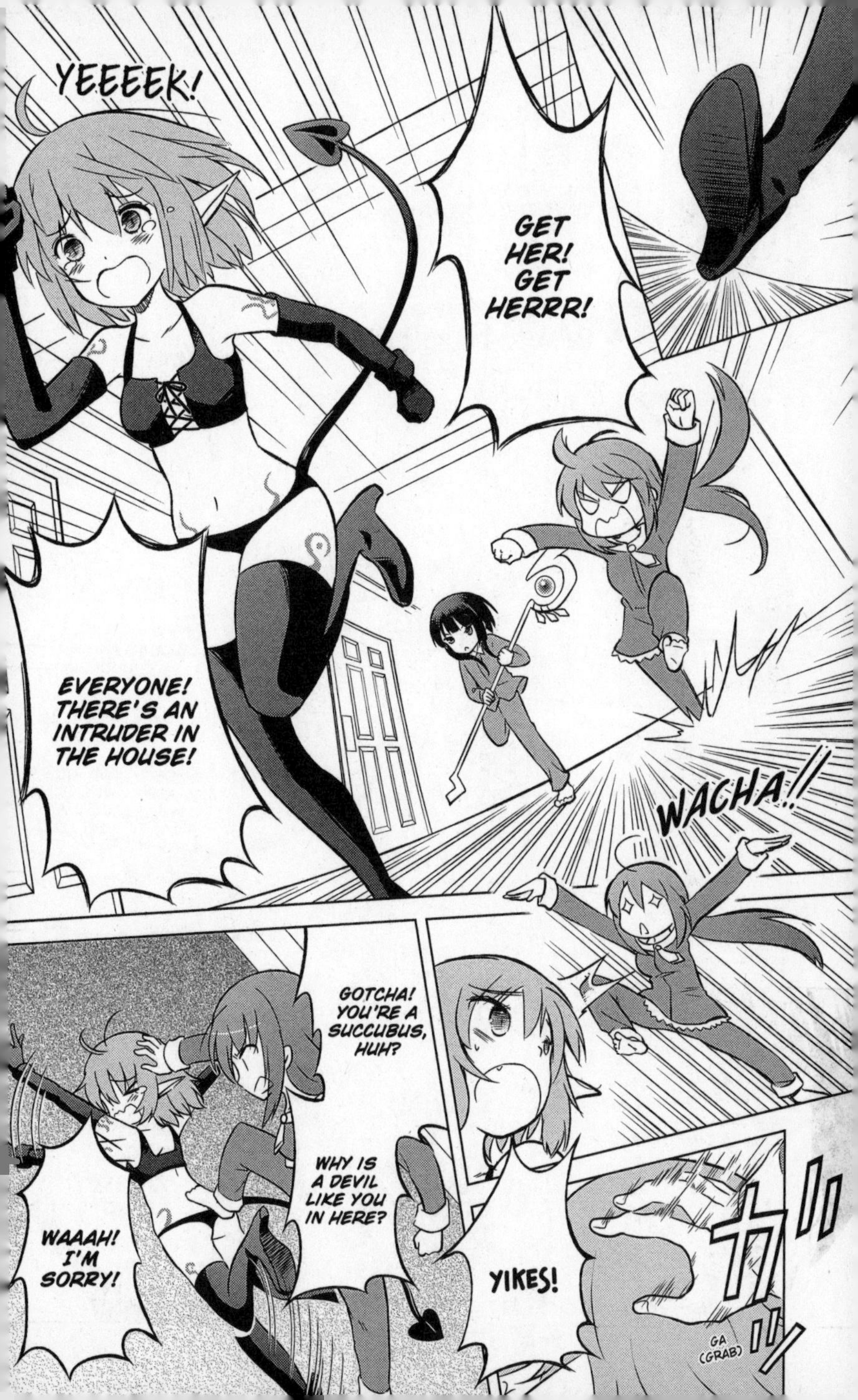
GET HER! GET HERRR!
YEEEEK!
EVERYONE! THERE'S AN INTRUDER IN THE HOUSE!
WACHA!!
YIKES!
ガッ
GA (GRAB)
GOTCHA! YOU'RE A SUCCUBUS, HUH?
WHY IS A DEVIL LIKE YOU IN HERE?
WAAAH! I'M SORRY!

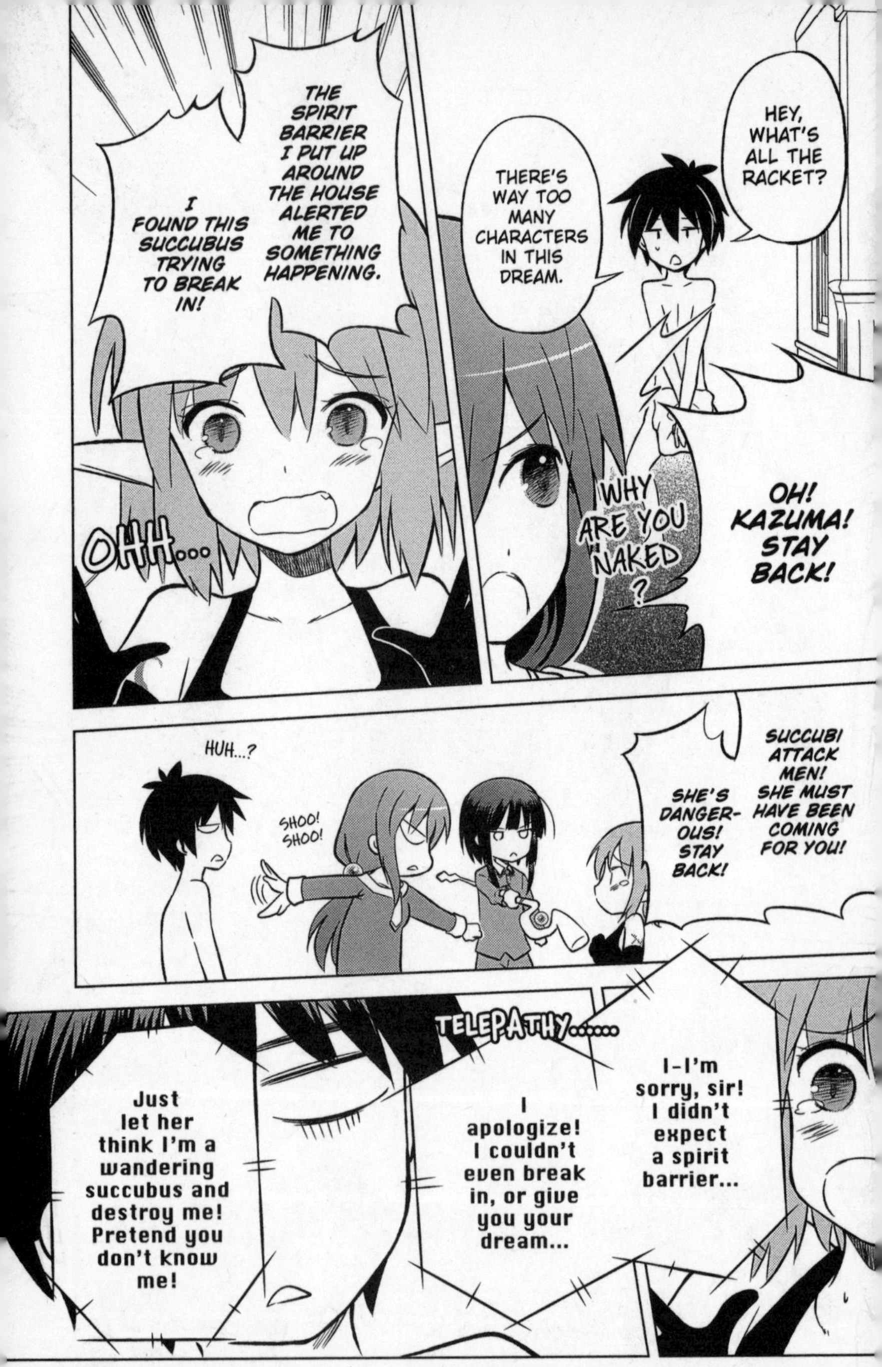
HEY, WHAT'S ALL THE RACKET?
THERE'S WAY TOO MANY CHARACTERS IN THIS DREAM.
OH! KAZUMA! STAY BACK!
WHY ARE YOU NAKED?
THE SPIRIT BARRIER I PUT UP AROUND THE HOUSE ALERTED ME TO SOMETHING HAPPENING.
I FOUND THIS SUCCUBUS TRYING TO BREAK IN!
OHH...
SUCCUBI ATTACK MEN! SHE MUST HAVE BEEN COMING FOR YOU!
SHE'S DANGER-OUS! STAY BACK!
HUH...?
SHOO! SHOO!
I-I'm sorry, sir! I didn't expect a spirit barrier...
I apologize! I couldn't even break in, or give you your dream...
TELEPATHY......
Just let her think I'm a wandering succubus and destroy me! Pretend you don't know me!

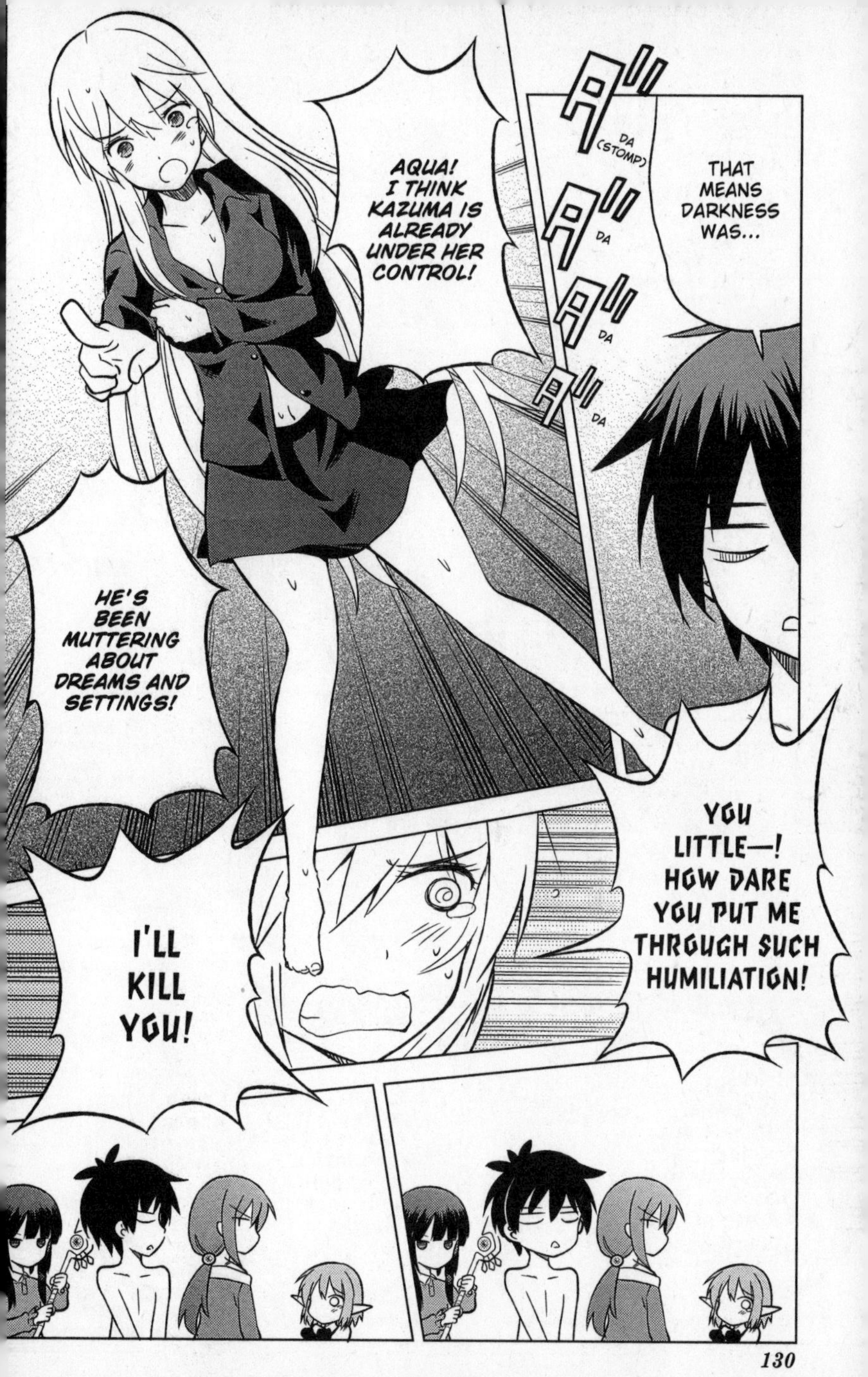
THAT MEANS DARKNESS WAS...
DA (STOMP)
DA
DA
DA
AQUA! I THINK KAZUMA IS ALREADY UNDER HER CONTROL!
HE'S BEEN MUTTERING ABOUT DREAMS AND SETTINGS!
YOU LITTLE—! HOW DARE YOU PUT ME THROUGH SUCH HUMILIATION!
I'LL KILL YOU!

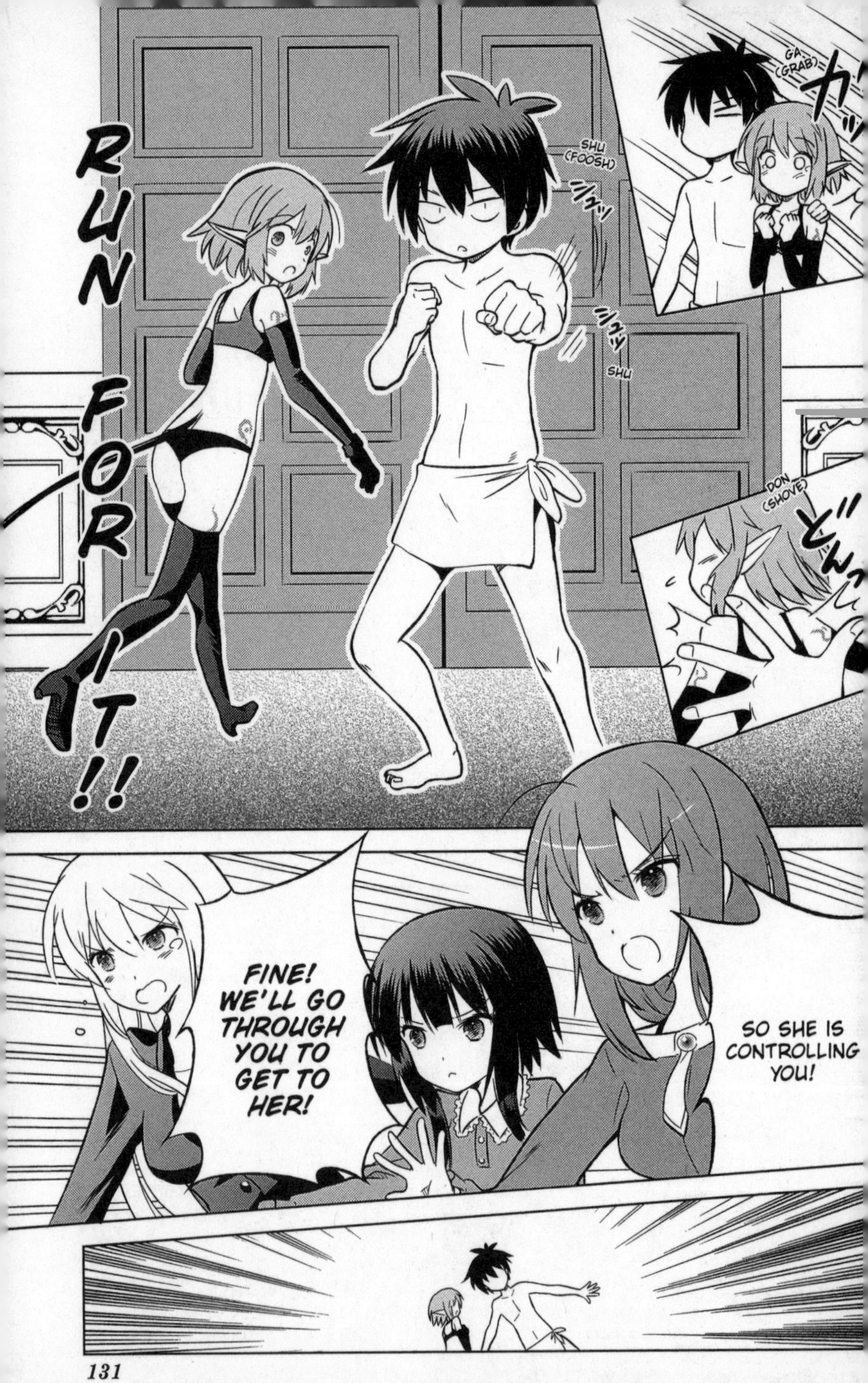
GA (GRAB)
DON (SHOVE)
SHU (FOOSH)
SHU
RUN FOR IT!!
SO SHE IS CONTROLLING YOU!
FINE! WE'LL GO THROUGH YOU TO GET TO HER!

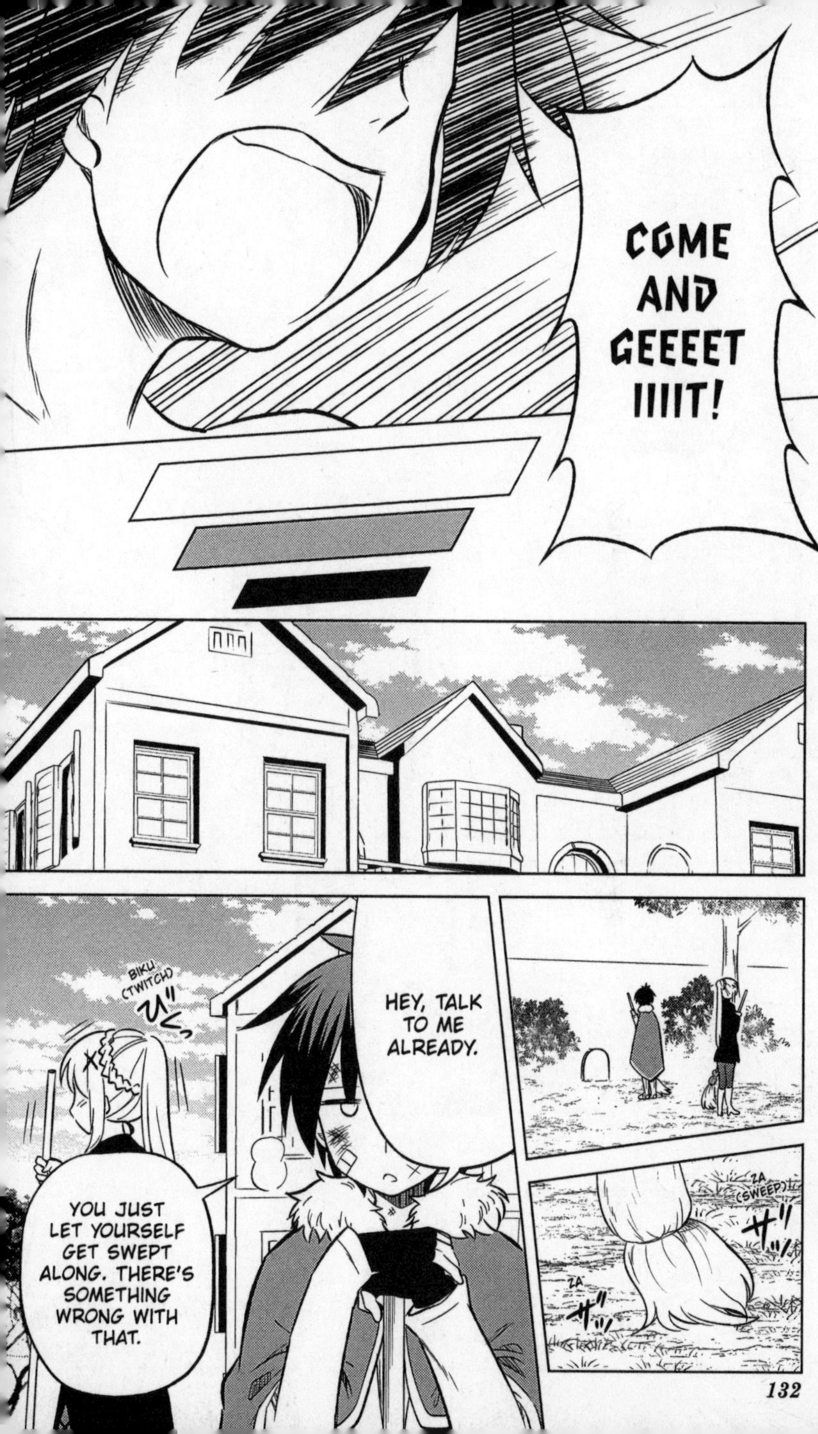

COME AND GEEEET IIIIT!
ZA (SWEEP)
ザッ
ZA
ザッ
HEY, TALK TO ME ALREADY.
BIKU (TWITCH)
びくっ
YOU JUST LET YOURSELF GET SWEPT ALONG. THERE'S SOMETHING WRONG WITH THAT.

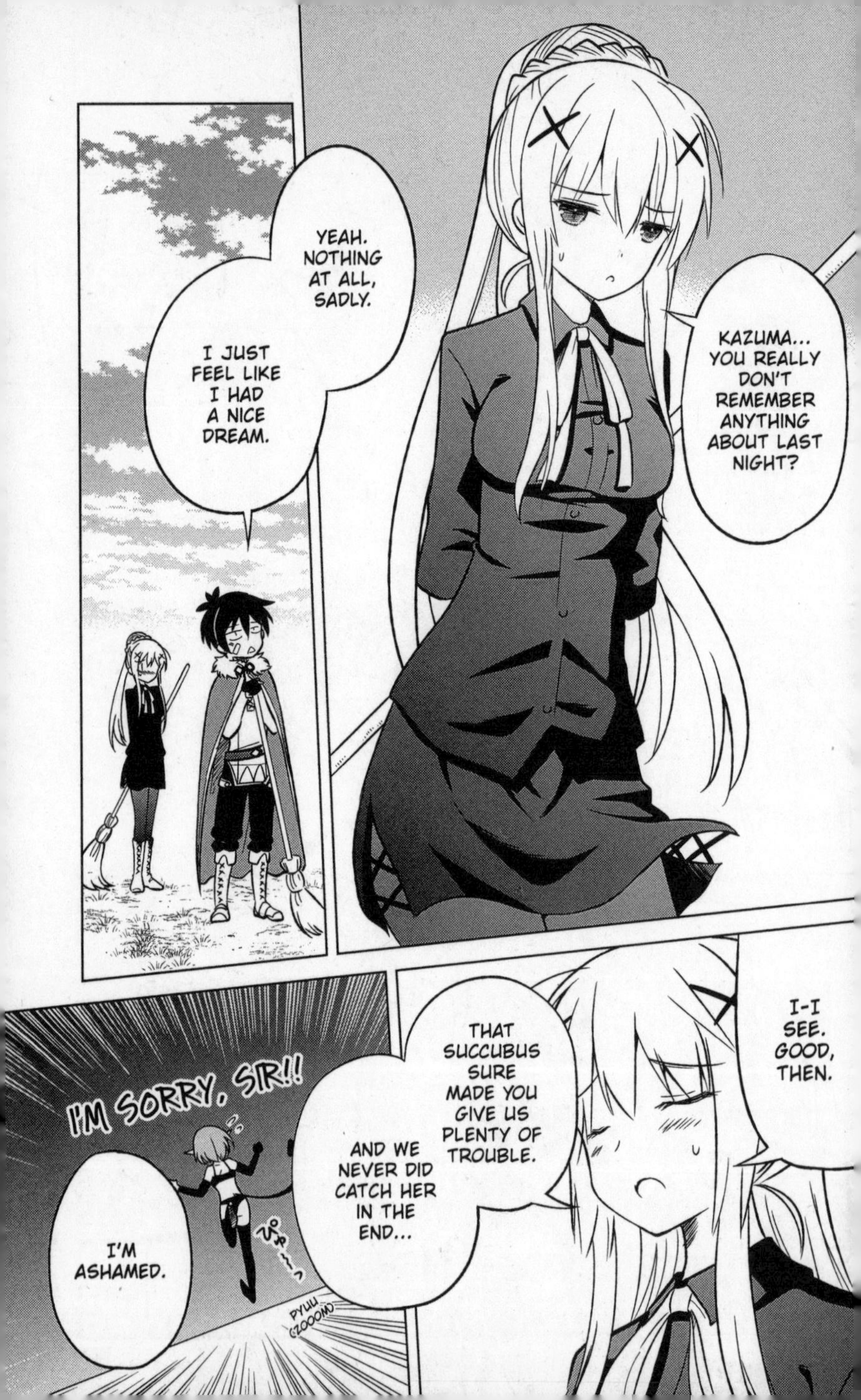
KAZUMA... YOU REALLY DON'T REMEMBER ANYTHING ABOUT LAST NIGHT?
YEAH. NOTHING AT ALL, SADLY.
I JUST FEEL LIKE I HAD A NICE DREAM.
I-I SEE. GOOD, THEN.
THAT SUCCUBUS SURE MADE YOU GIVE US PLENTY OF TROUBLE.
AND WE NEVER DID CATCH HER IN THE END...
I'M SORRY, SIR!!
I'M ASHAMED.
PYUU (ZOOOM)

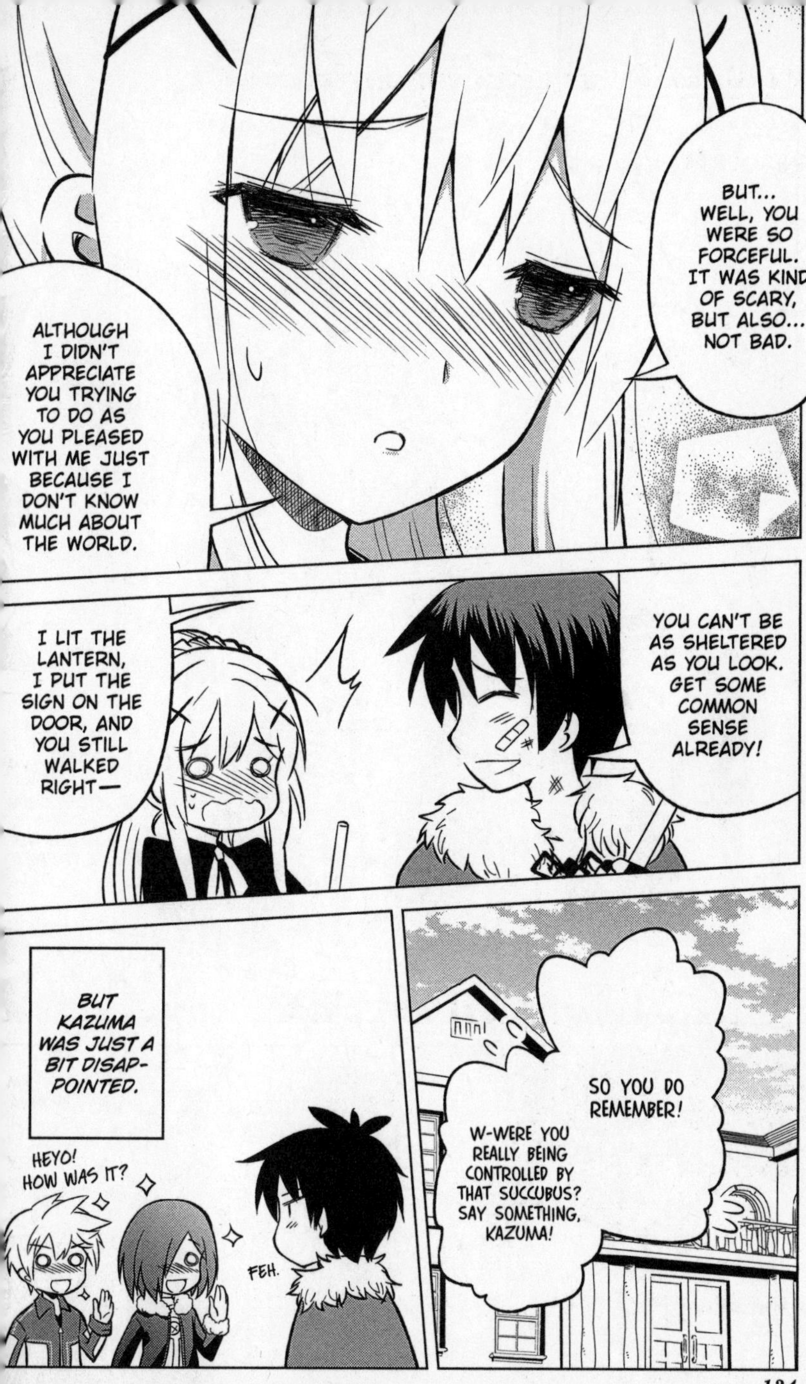
BUT... WELL, YOU WERE SO FORCEFUL. IT WAS KIND OF SCARY, BUT ALSO... NOT BAD.
ALTHOUGH I DIDN'T APPRECIATE YOU TRYING TO DO AS YOU PLEASED WITH ME JUST BECAUSE I DON'T KNOW MUCH ABOUT THE WORLD.
YOU CAN'T BE AS SHELTERED AS YOU LOOK. GET SOME COMMON SENSE ALREADY!
I LIT THE LANTERN, I PUT THE SIGN ON THE DOOR, AND YOU STILL WALKED RIGHT—
SO YOU DO REMEMBER!
W-WERE YOU REALLY BEING CONTROLLED BY THAT SUCCUBUS? SAY SOMETHING, KAZUMA!
BUT KAZUMA WAS JUST A BIT DISAP-POINTED.
HEYO! HOW WAS IT?
FEH.

## CHAPTER 18 HEY, LET'S VISIT ANOTHER WORLD!

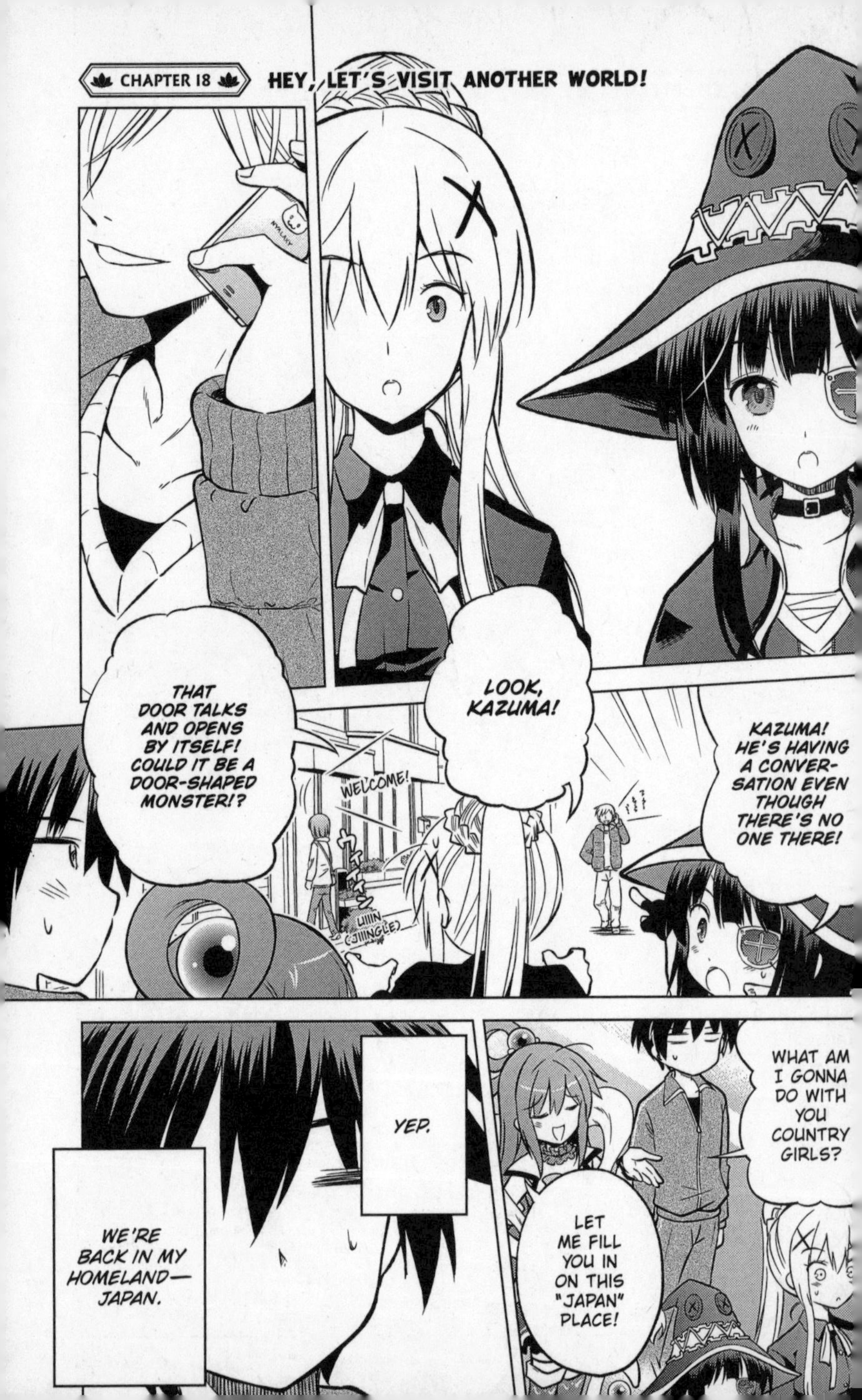

KAZUMA! HE'S HAVING A CONVERSATION EVEN THOUGH THERE'S NO ONE THERE!
LOOK, KAZUMA!
WELCOME!
LIIIN (JIIINGLE)
THAT DOOR TALKS AND OPENS BY ITSELF! COULD IT BE A DOOR-SHAPED MONSTER!?
WHAT AM I GONNA DO WITH YOU COUNTRY GIRLS?
LET ME FILL YOU IN ON THIS "JAPAN" PLACE!
YEP.
WE'RE BACK IN MY HOMELAND—JAPAN.

## CHAPTER 18 HEY, LET'S VISIT ANOTHER WORLD!

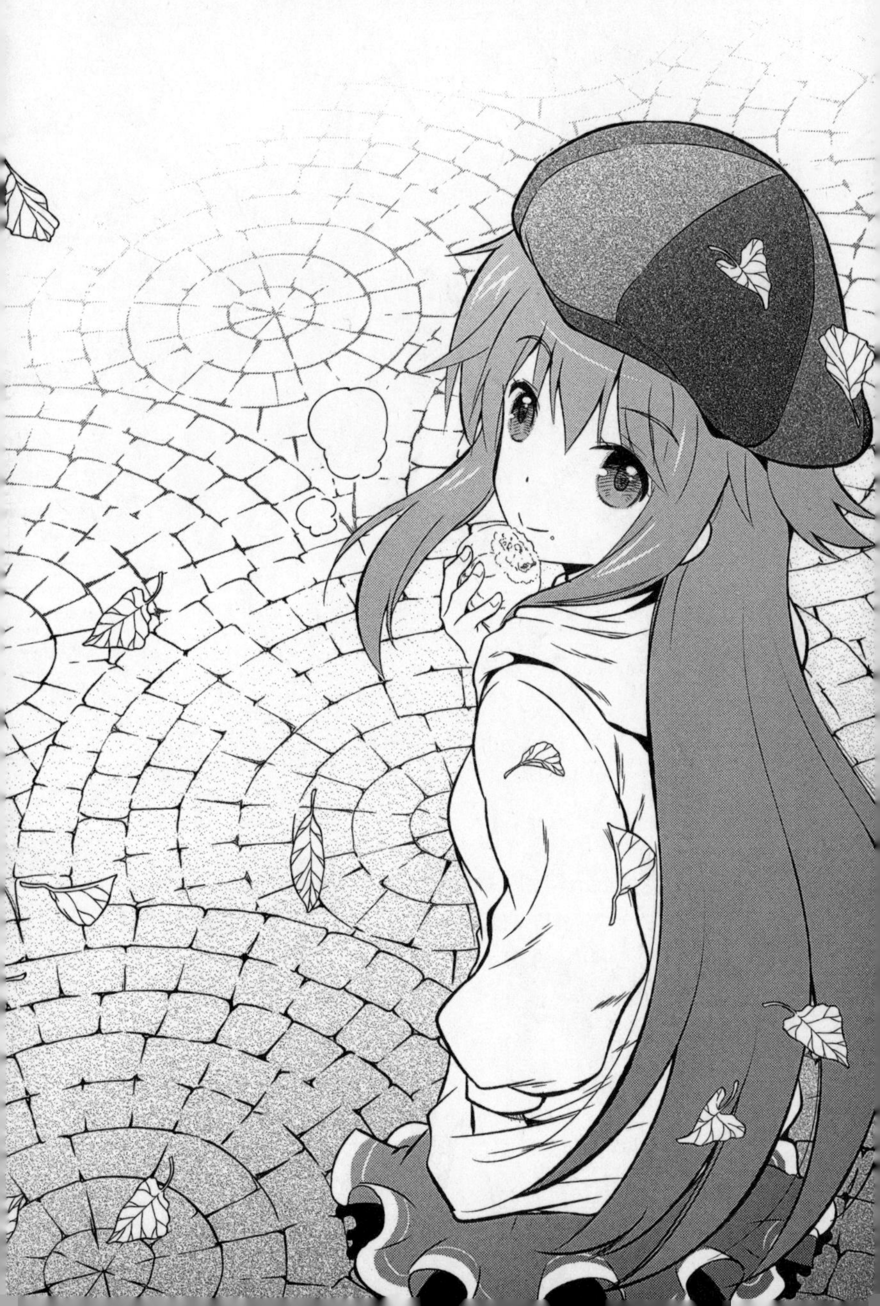

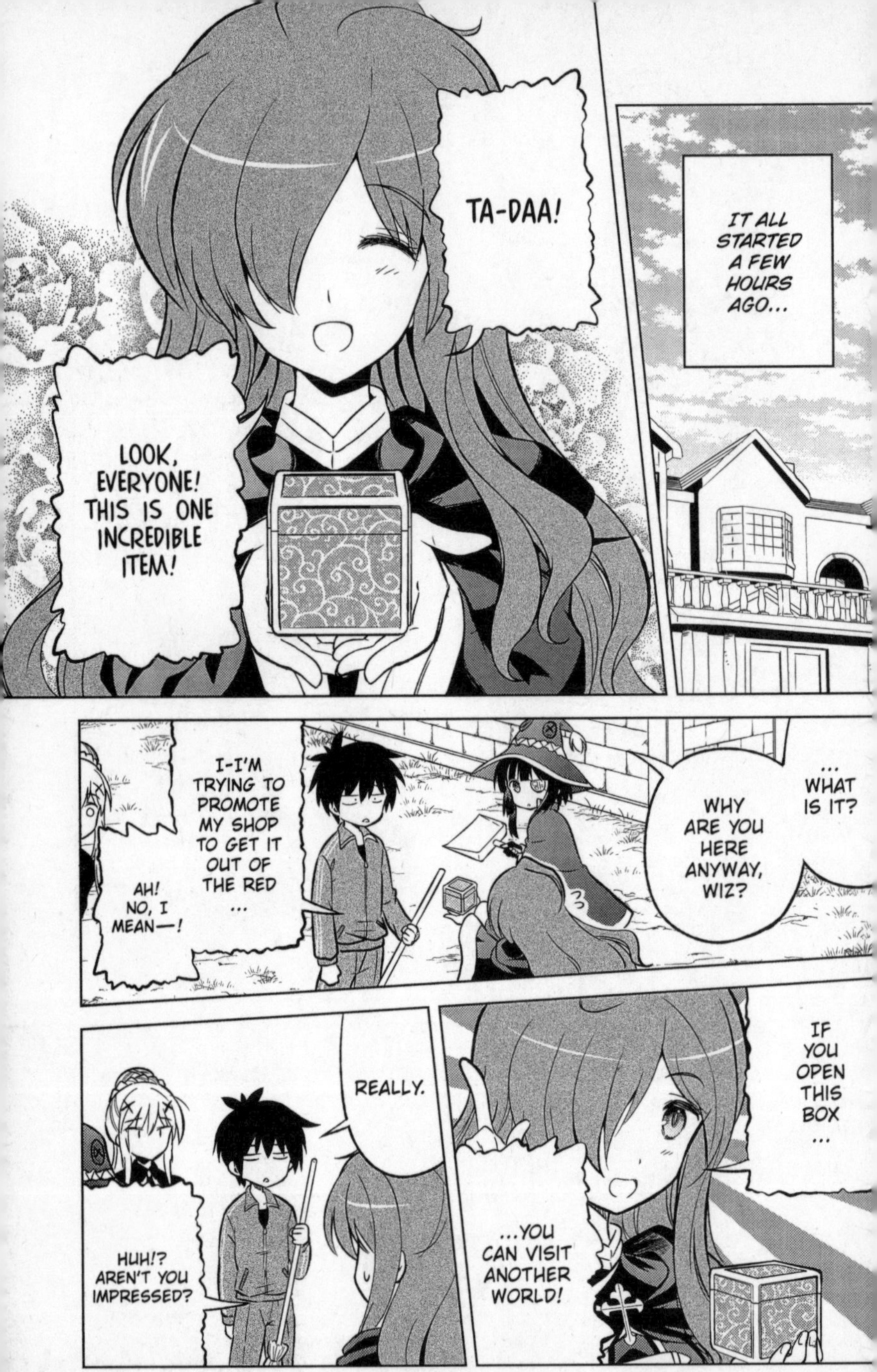
IT ALL STARTED A FEW HOURS AGO...
TA-DAA!
LOOK, EVERYONE! THIS IS ONE INCREDIBLE ITEM!
... WHAT IS IT?
WHY ARE YOU HERE ANYWAY, WIZ?
I-I'M TRYING TO PROMOTE MY SHOP TO GET IT OUT OF THE RED ...
AH! NO, I MEAN—!
IF YOU OPEN THIS BOX ...
...YOU CAN VISIT ANOTHER WORLD!
REALLY.
HUH!? AREN'T YOU IMPRESSED?

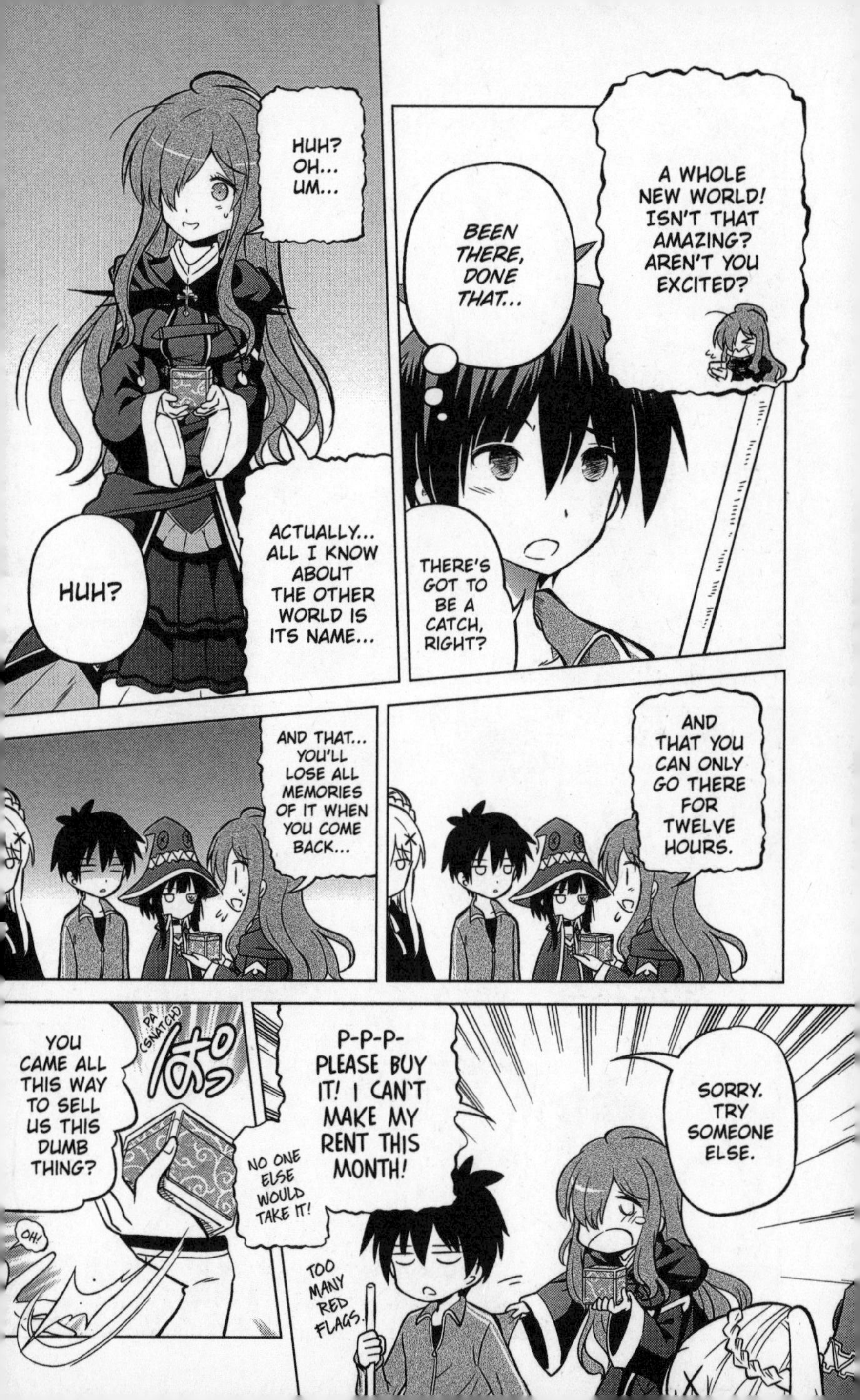
A WHOLE NEW WORLD! ISN'T THAT AMAZING? AREN'T YOU EXCITED?
BEEN THERE, DONE THAT...
THERE'S GOT TO BE A CATCH, RIGHT?
HUH? OH... UM...
ACTUALLY... ALL I KNOW ABOUT THE OTHER WORLD IS ITS NAME...
HUH?
AND THAT YOU CAN ONLY GO THERE FOR TWELVE HOURS.
AND THAT... YOU'LL LOSE ALL MEMORIES OF IT WHEN YOU COME BACK...
SORRY. TRY SOMEONE ELSE.
P-P-P-PLEASE BUY IT! I CAN'T MAKE MY RENT THIS MONTH!
NO ONE ELSE WOULD TAKE IT!
TOO MANY RED FLAGS.
ぱっ
PA (SNATCH)
YOU CAME ALL THIS WAY TO SELL US THIS DUMB THING?
OH!

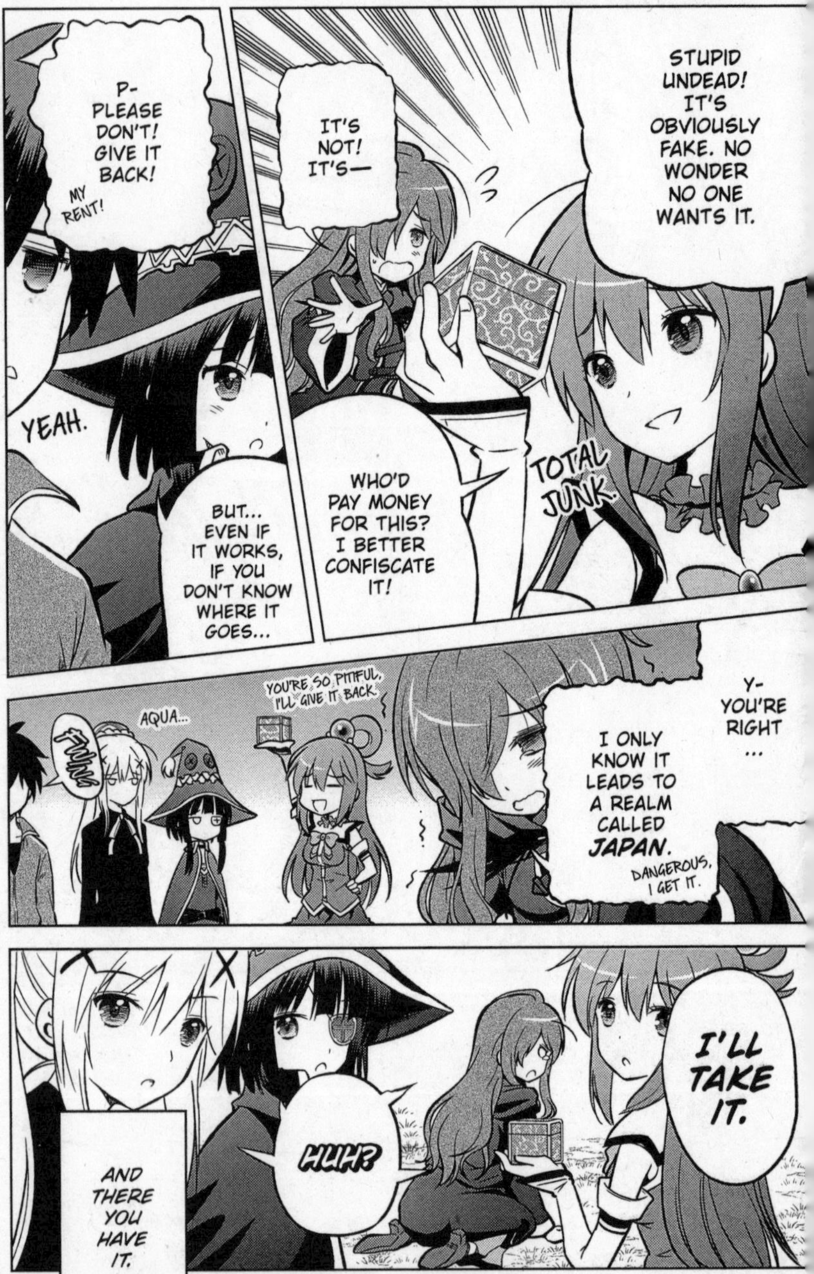
STUPID UNDEAD! IT'S OBVIOUSLY FAKE. NO WONDER NO ONE WANTS IT.
TOTAL JUNK.
IT'S NOT! IT'S—
WHO'D PAY MONEY FOR THIS? I BETTER CONFISCATE IT!
P-PLEASE DON'T! GIVE IT BACK!
MY RENT!
YEAH.
BUT... EVEN IF IT WORKS, IF YOU DON'T KNOW WHERE IT GOES...
Y-YOU'RE RIGHT...
I ONLY KNOW IT LEADS TO A REALM CALLED JAPAN.
DANGEROUS, I GET IT.
YOU'RE SO PITIFUL, I'LL GIVE IT BACK.
AQUA...
I'LL TAKE IT.
HUH?
AND THERE YOU HAVE IT.

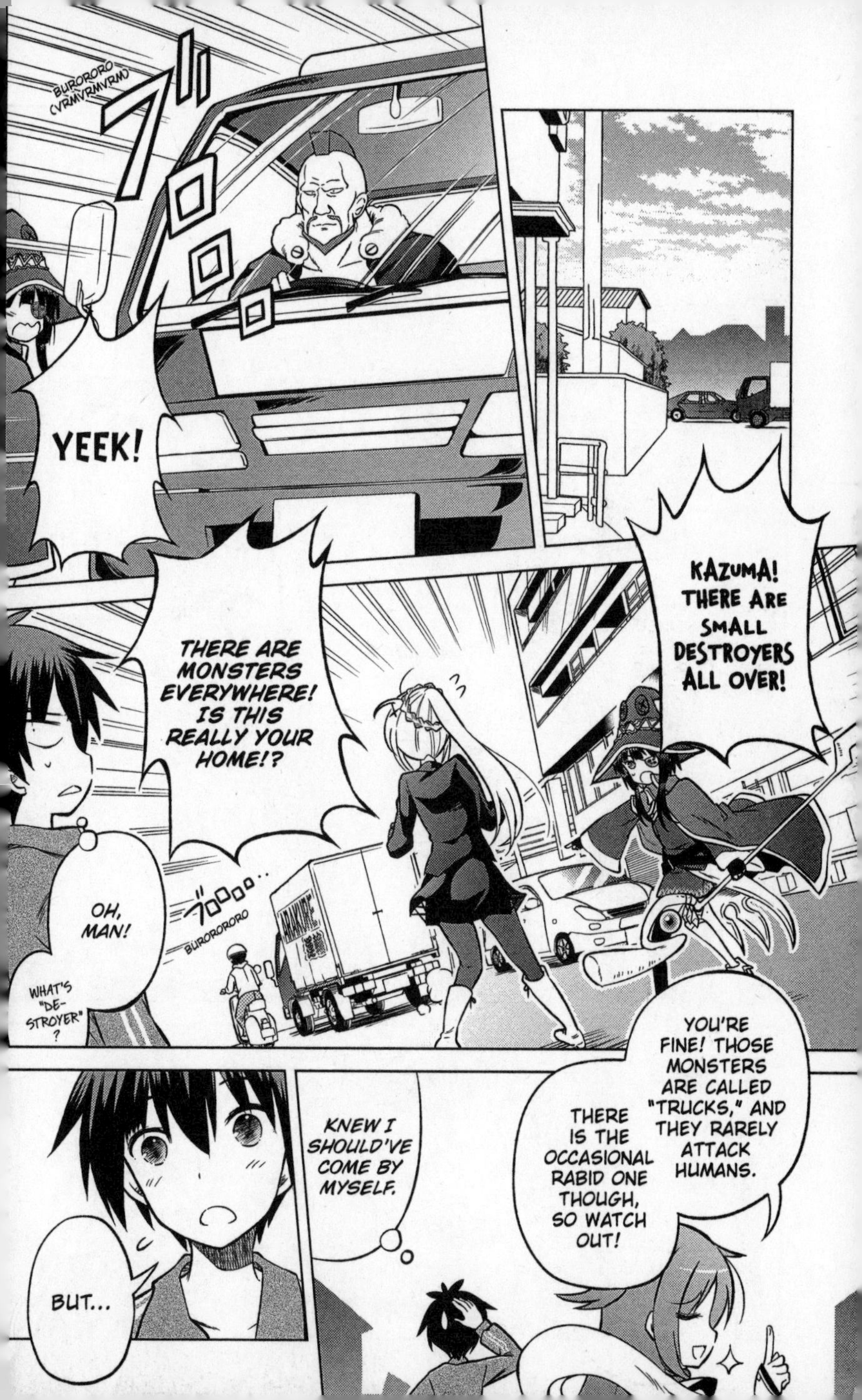

BURORORO (VRMVRMVRM)
YEEK!
KAZUMA! THERE ARE SMALL DESTROYERS ALL OVER!
THERE ARE MONSTERS EVERYWHERE! IS THIS REALLY YOUR HOME!?
BURORORO
OH, MAN!
WHAT'S "DE-STROYER"?
YOU'RE FINE! THOSE MONSTERS ARE CALLED "TRUCKS," AND THEY RARELY ATTACK HUMANS.
THERE IS THE OCCASIONAL RABID ONE THOUGH, SO WATCH OUT!
KNEW I SHOULD'VE COME BY MYSELF.
BUT...

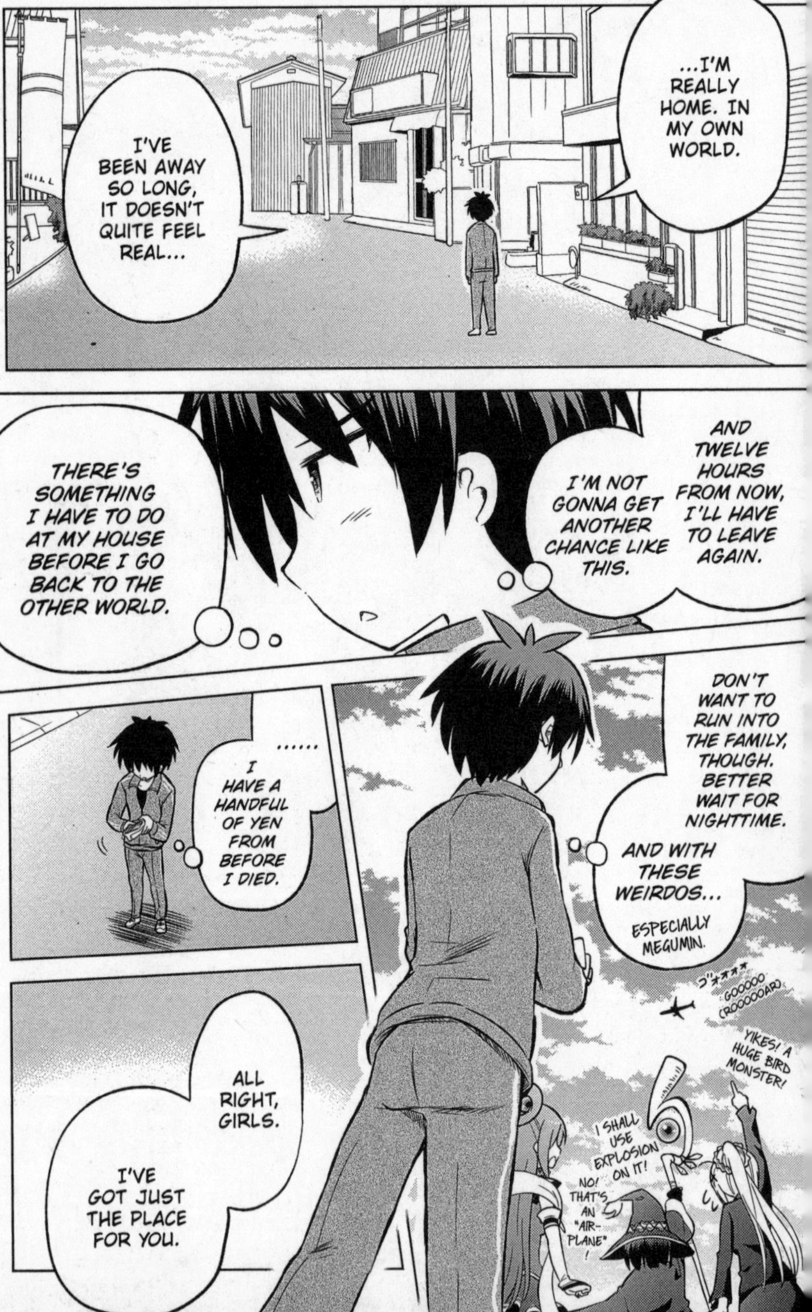
...I'M REALLY HOME. IN MY OWN WORLD.
I'VE BEEN AWAY SO LONG, IT DOESN'T QUITE FEEL REAL...
AND TWELVE HOURS FROM NOW, I'LL HAVE TO LEAVE AGAIN.
I'M NOT GONNA GET ANOTHER CHANCE LIKE THIS.
THERE'S SOMETHING I HAVE TO DO AT MY HOUSE BEFORE I GO BACK TO THE OTHER WORLD.
DON'T WANT TO RUN INTO THE FAMILY, THOUGH. BETTER WAIT FOR NIGHTTIME.
AND WITH THESE WEIRDOS...
ESPECIALLY MEGUMIN.
ゴオオオ GOOOOO (ROOOOOAR)
YIKES! A HUGE BIRD MONSTER!
I SHALL USE EXPLOSION ON IT!
NO! THAT'S AN "AIR-PLANE"!
......
I HAVE A HANDFUL OF YEN FROM BEFORE I DIED.
ALL RIGHT, GIRLS.
I'VE GOT JUST THE PLACE FOR YOU.

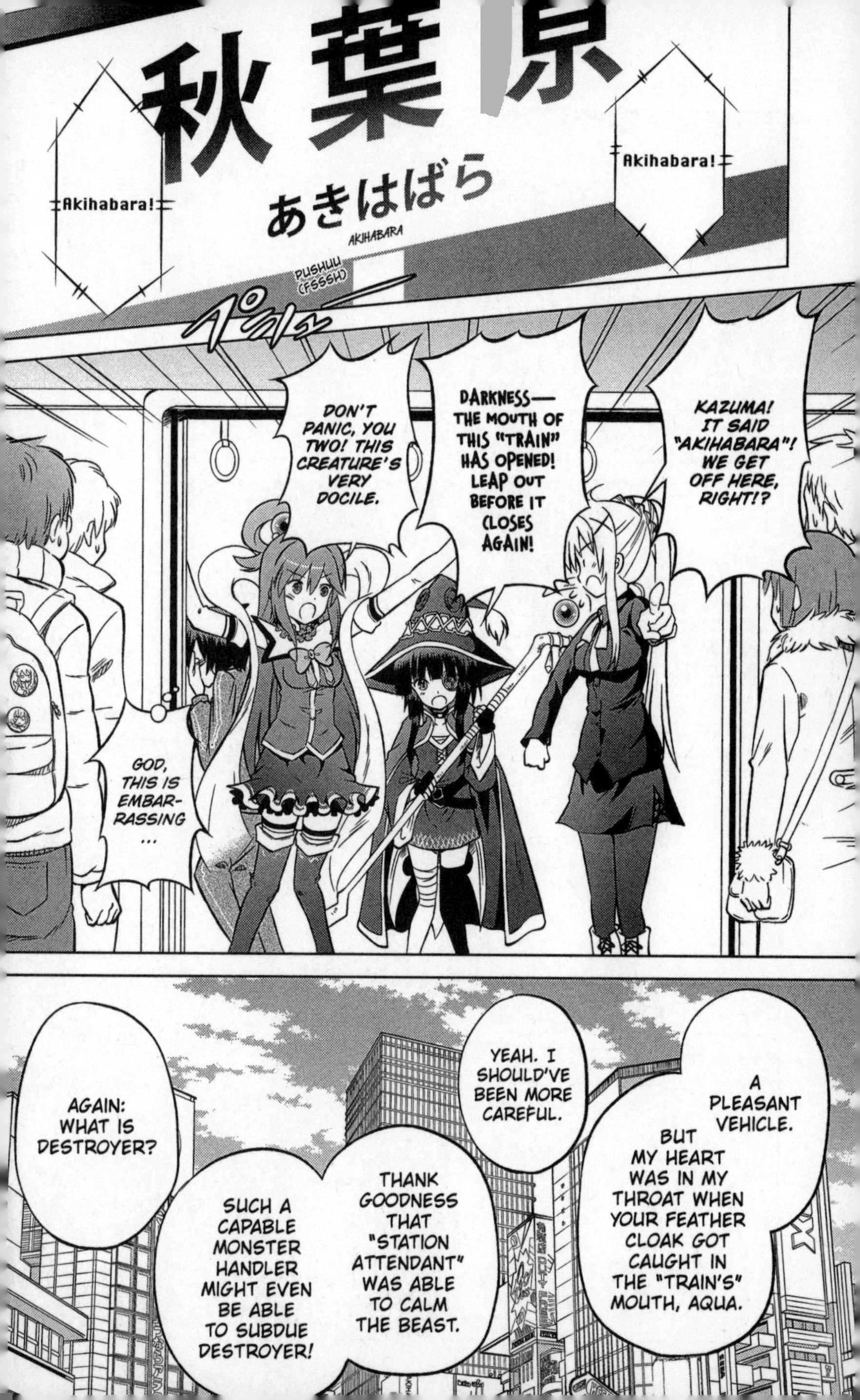

秋葉原
あきはばら
AKIHABARA
Akihabara!
Akihabara!
プシュー
PUSHUU (FSSSH)
KAZUMA! IT SAID "AKIHABARA"! WE GET OFF HERE, RIGHT!?
DARKNESS—THE MOUTH OF THIS "TRAIN" HAS OPENED! LEAP OUT BEFORE IT CLOSES AGAIN!
DON'T PANIC, YOU TWO! THIS CREATURE'S VERY DOCILE.
GOD, THIS IS EMBARRASSING...
A PLEASANT VEHICLE. BUT MY HEART WAS IN MY THROAT WHEN YOUR FEATHER CLOAK GOT CAUGHT IN THE "TRAIN'S" MOUTH, AQUA.
YEAH. I SHOULD'VE BEEN MORE CAREFUL.
THANK GOODNESS THAT "STATION ATTENDANT" WAS ABLE TO CALM THE BEAST.
SUCH A CAPABLE MONSTER HANDLER MIGHT EVEN BE ABLE TO SUBDUE DESTROYER!
AGAIN: WHAT IS DESTROYER?

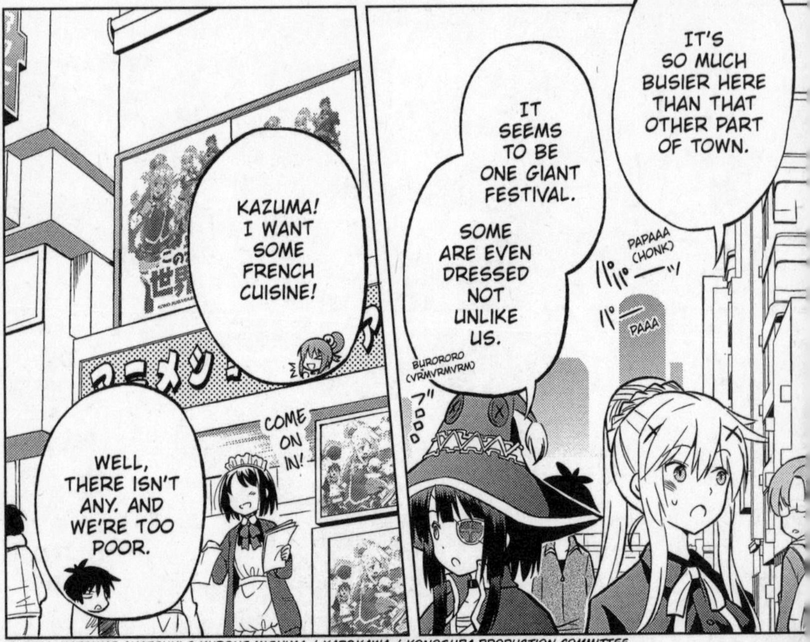
IT'S SO MUCH BUSIER HERE THAN THAT OTHER PART OF TOWN.
PAPAAA (HONK)
PAAA
IT SEEMS TO BE ONE GIANT FESTIVAL.
SOME ARE EVEN DRESSED NOT UNLIKE US.
BURORORO (VRMVRMVRM)
KAZUMA! I WANT SOME FRENCH CUISINE!
COME ON IN!
WELL, THERE ISN'T ANY. AND WE'RE TOO POOR.



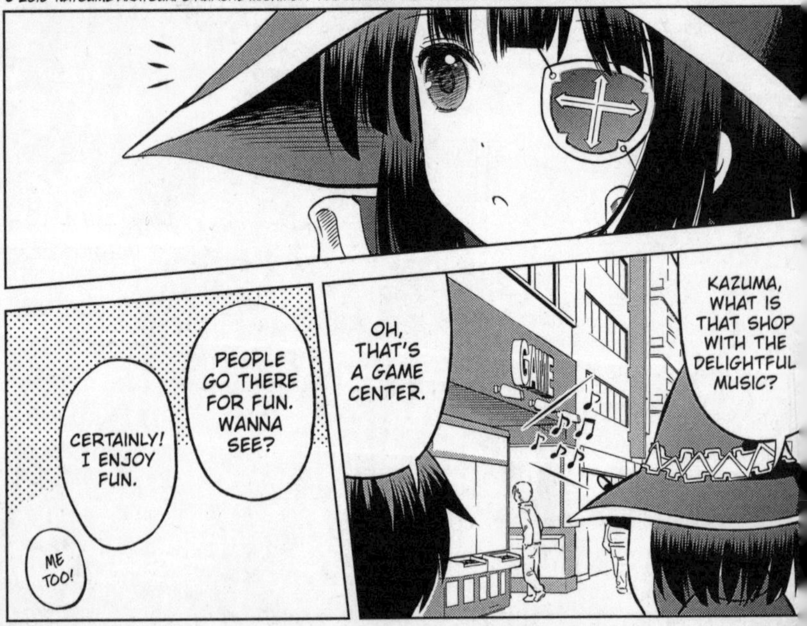
KAZUMA, WHAT IS THAT SHOP WITH THE DELIGHTFUL MUSIC?
GAME
OH, THAT'S A GAME CENTER.
PEOPLE GO THERE FOR FUN. WANNA SEE?
CERTAINLY! I ENJOY FUN.
ME TOO!

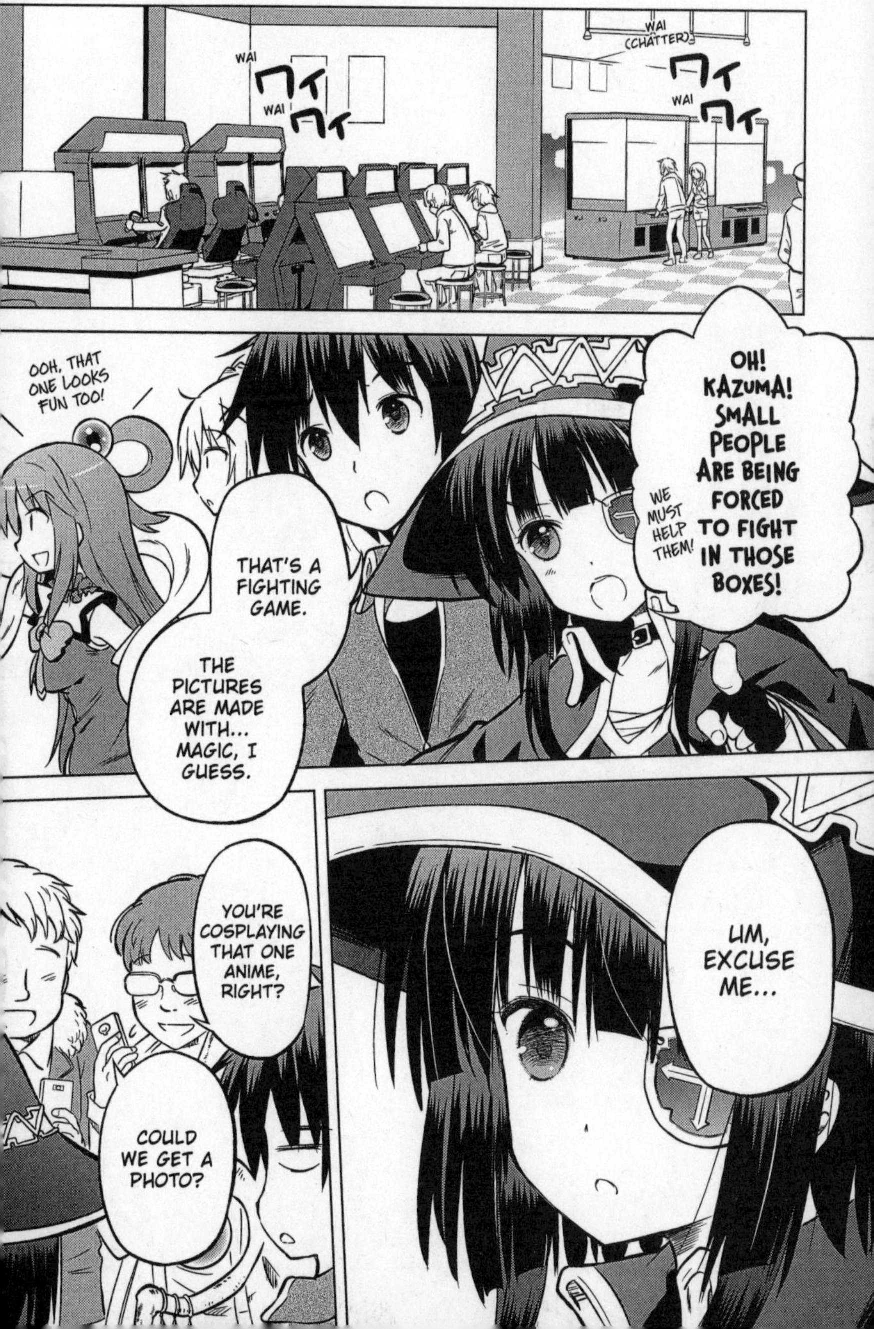
WAI (CHATTER)
ワイ
WAI
ワイ
WAI
ワイ
WAI
ワイ
OH! KAZUMA! SMALL PEOPLE ARE BEING FORCED TO FIGHT IN THOSE BOXES!
WE MUST HELP THEM!
THAT'S A FIGHTING GAME.
THE PICTURES ARE MADE WITH... MAGIC, I GUESS.
OOH, THAT ONE LOOKS FUN TOO!
UM, EXCUSE ME...
YOU'RE COSPLAYING THAT ONE ANIME, RIGHT?
COULD WE GET A PHOTO?

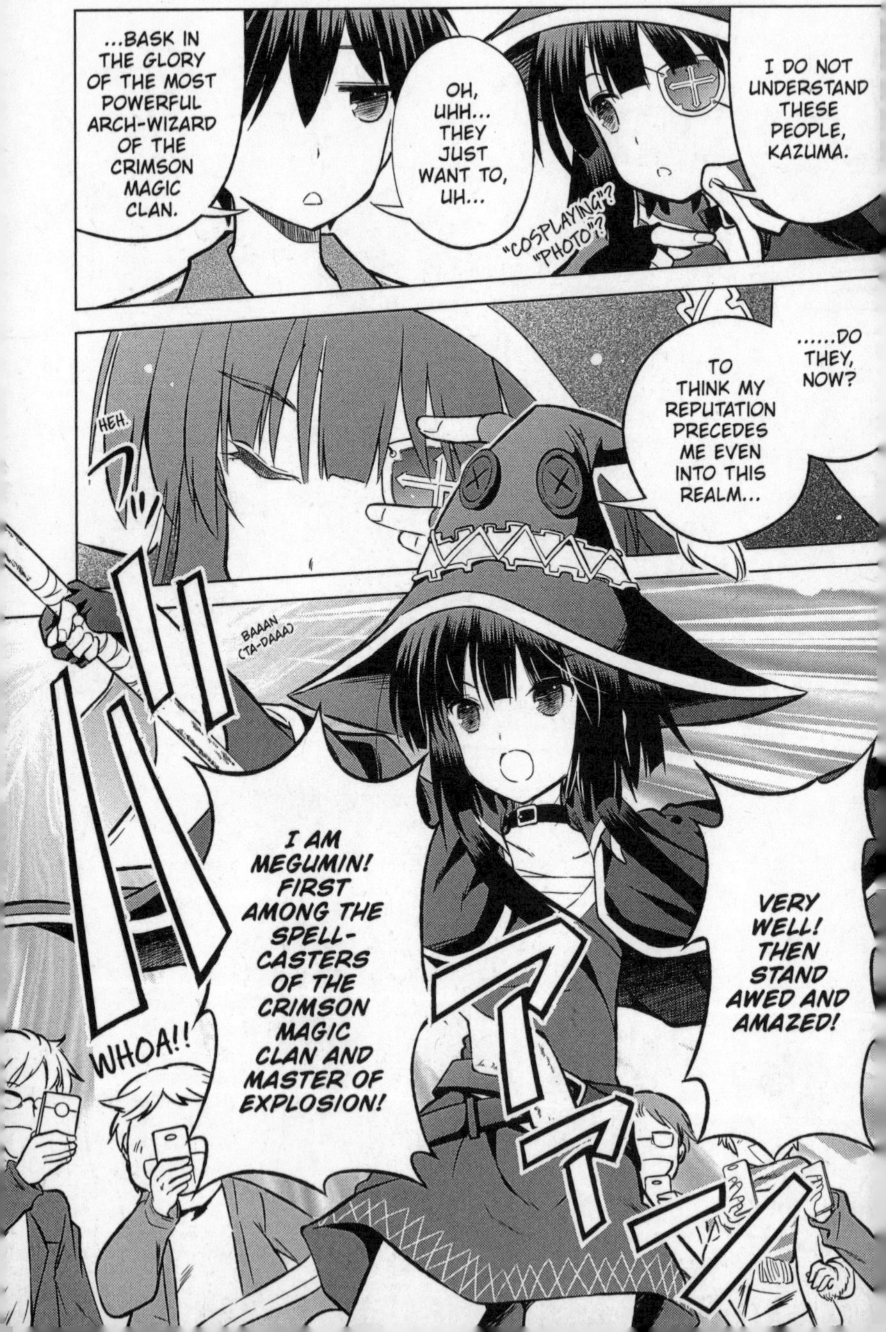
I DO NOT UNDERSTAND THESE PEOPLE, KAZUMA.
"COSPLAYING"? "PHOTO"?
OH, UHH... THEY JUST WANT TO, UH...
...BASK IN THE GLORY OF THE MOST POWERFUL ARCH-WIZARD OF THE CRIMSON MAGIC CLAN.
......DO THEY, NOW?
TO THINK MY REPUTATION PRECEDES ME EVEN INTO THIS REALM...
HEH.
VERY WELL! THEN STAND AWED AND AMAZED!
I AM MEGUMIN! FIRST AMONG THE SPELL-CASTERS OF THE CRIMSON MAGIC CLAN AND MASTER OF EXPLOSION!
BAAAN (TA-DAAA)
WHOA!!

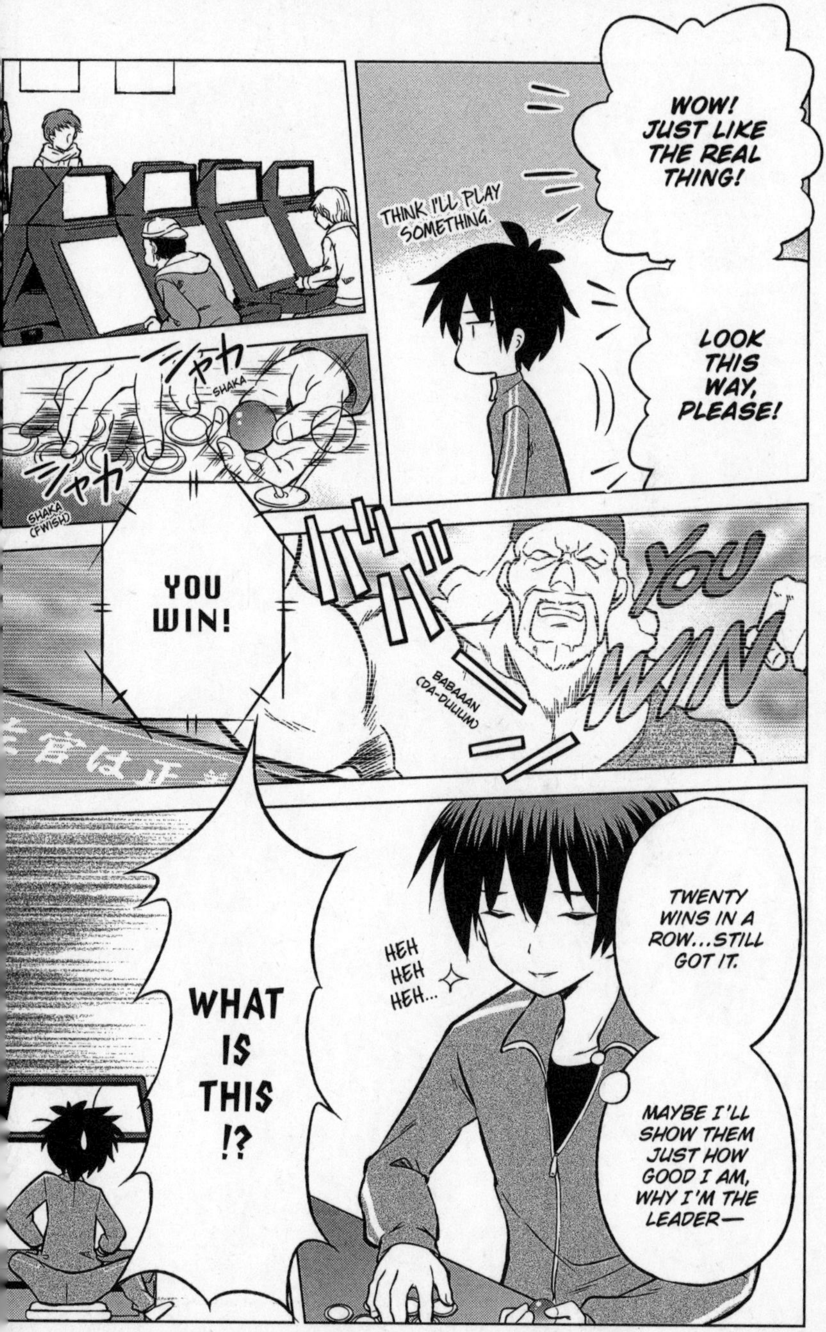
WOW! JUST LIKE THE REAL THING!
LOOK THIS WAY, PLEASE!
THINK I'LL PLAY SOMETHING.
シャカ
SHAKA
シャカ
SHAKA (FWISH)
YOU WIN
BABAAAN (DA-DUUUM)
YOU WIN!
TWENTY WINS IN A ROW...STILL GOT IT.
HEH HEH HEH...
MAYBE I'LL SHOW THEM JUST HOW GOOD I AM, WHY I'M THE LEADER—
WHAT IS THIS!?

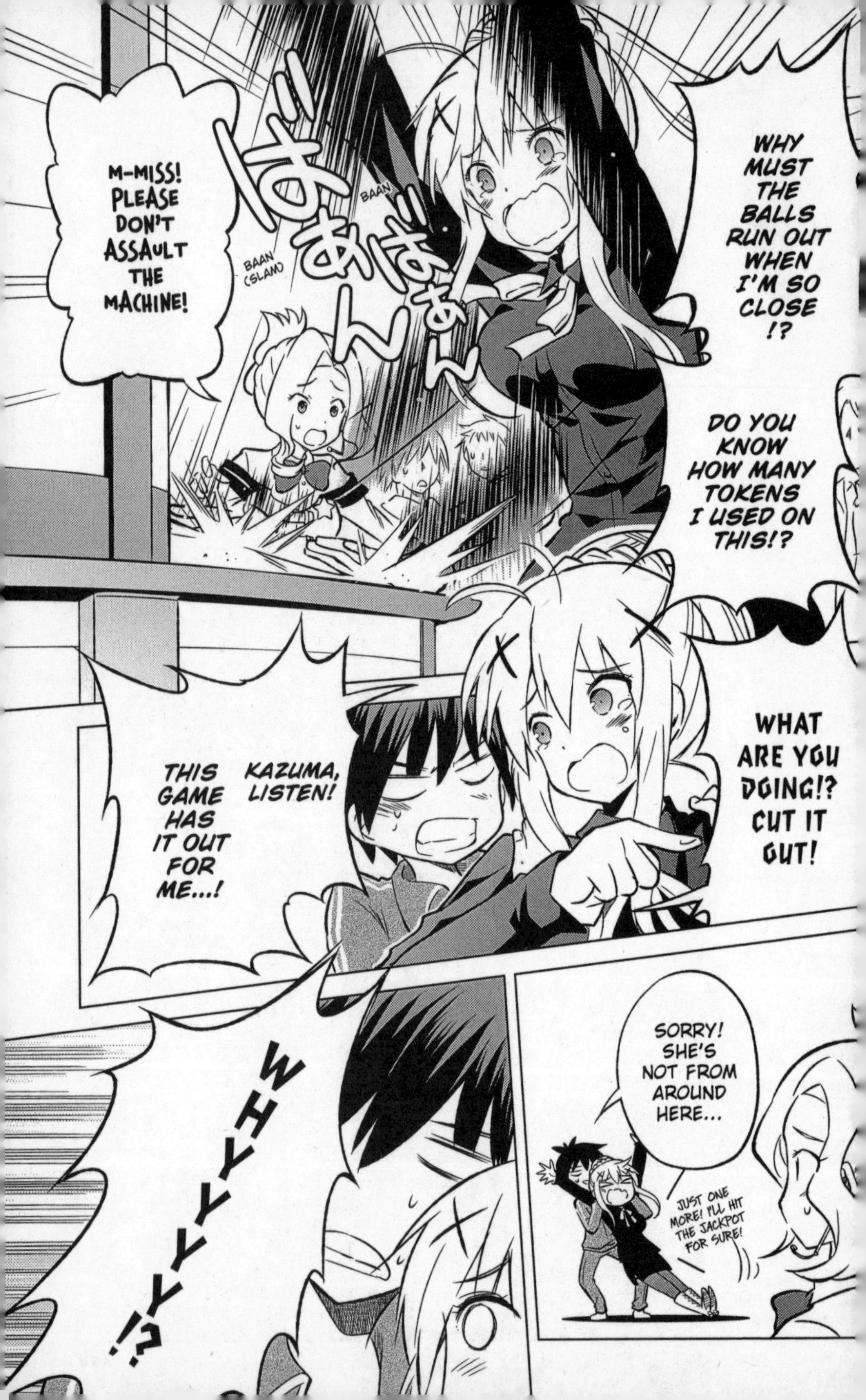
WHY MUST THE BALLS RUN OUT WHEN I'M SO CLOSE!?
DO YOU KNOW HOW MANY TOKENS I USED ON THIS!?
ばぁんばぁん
BAAN
BAAN (SLAM)
M-MISS! PLEASE DON'T ASSAULT THE MACHINE!
WHAT ARE YOU DOING!? CUT IT OUT!
KAZUMA, LISTEN!
THIS GAME HAS IT OUT FOR ME...!
SORRY! SHE'S NOT FROM AROUND HERE...
JUST ONE MORE! I'LL HIT THE JACKPOT FOR SURE!
WHYYYYYY!?

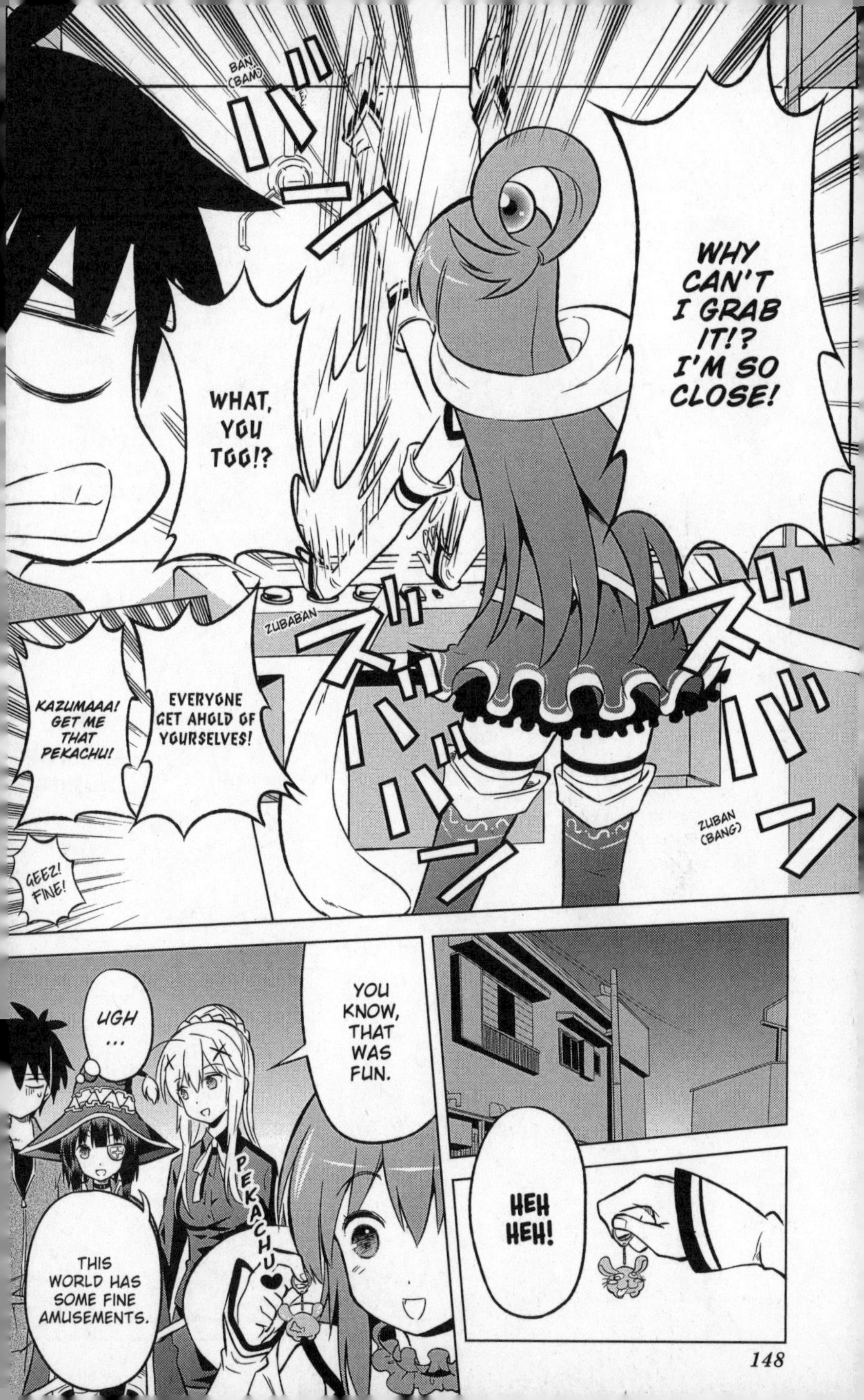
WHY CAN'T I GRAB IT!? I'M SO CLOSE!
BAN (BAM)
WHAT, YOU TOO!?
ZUBABAN
ZUBAN (BANG)
EVERYONE GET AHOLD OF YOURSELVES!
KAZUMAAA! GET ME THAT PEKACHU!
GEEZ! FINE!
HEH HEH!
YOU KNOW, THAT WAS FUN.
UGH ...
PEKACHU
THIS WORLD HAS SOME FINE AMUSEMENTS.

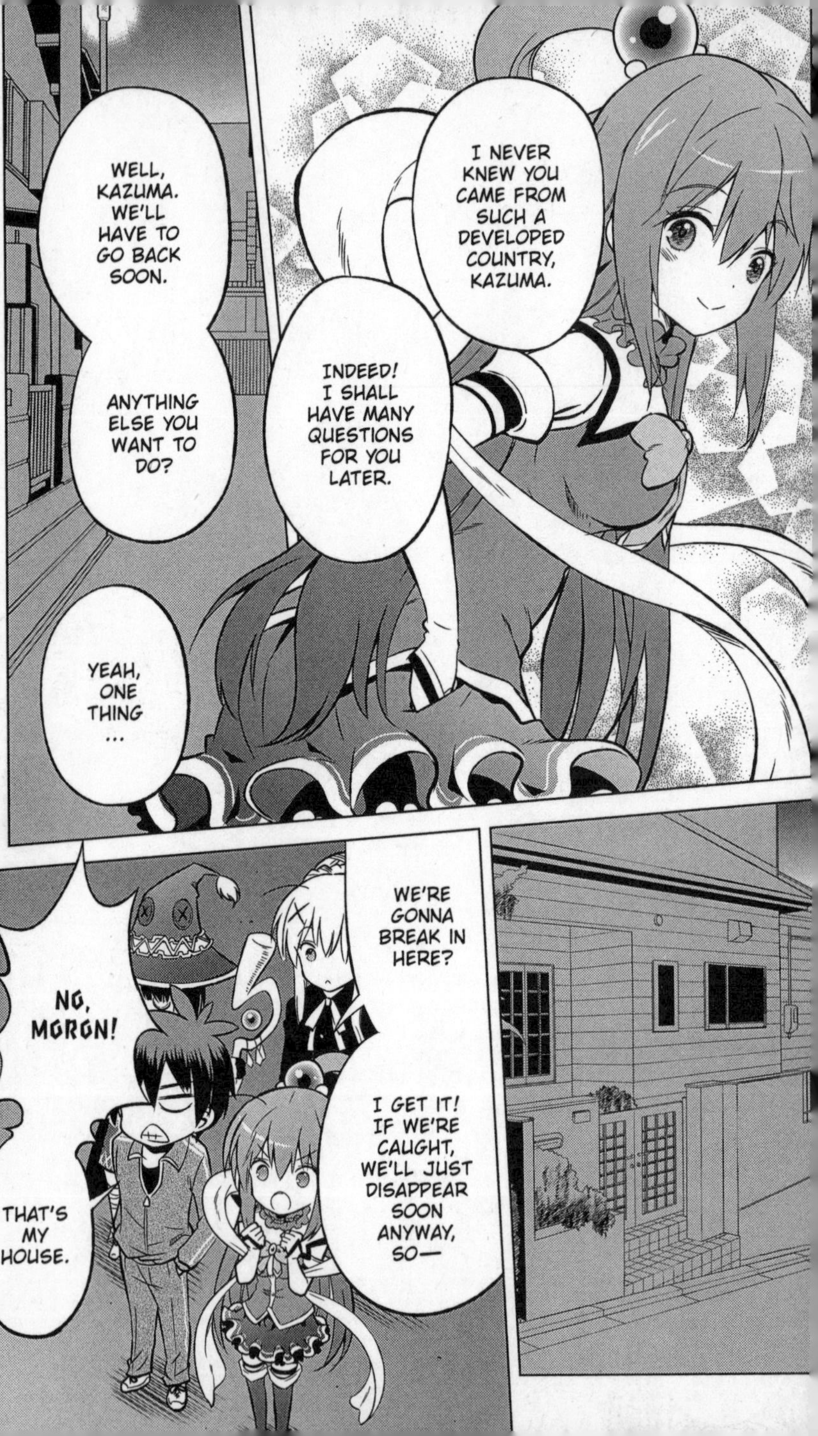
I NEVER KNEW YOU CAME FROM SUCH A DEVELOPED COUNTRY, KAZUMA.
INDEED! I SHALL HAVE MANY QUESTIONS FOR YOU LATER.
WELL, KAZUMA. WE'LL HAVE TO GO BACK SOON.
ANYTHING ELSE YOU WANT TO DO?
YEAH, ONE THING...
WE'RE GONNA BREAK IN HERE?
I GET IT! IF WE'RE CAUGHT, WE'LL JUST DISAPPEAR SOON ANYWAY, SO—
NO, MORON!
THAT'S MY HOUSE.

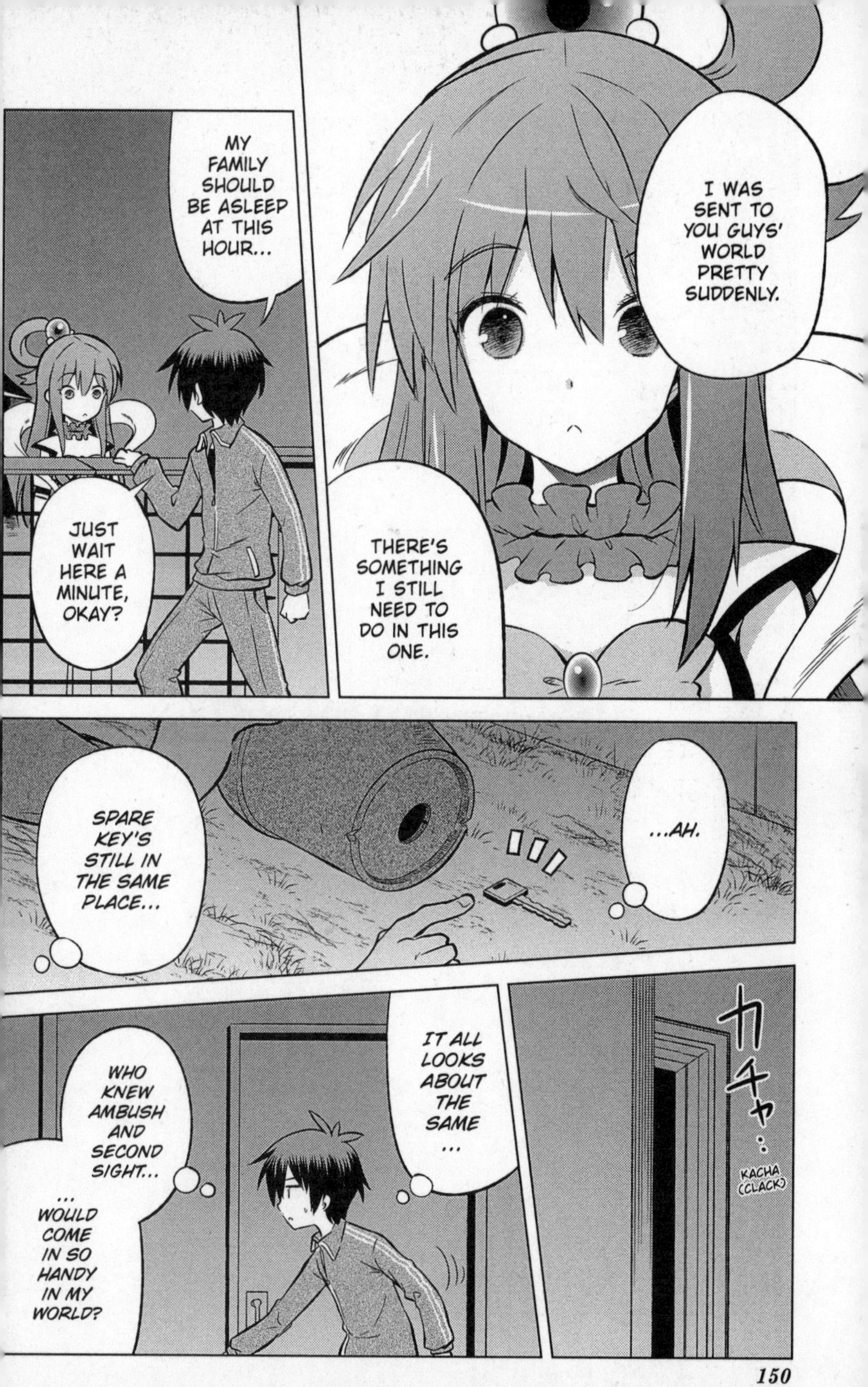
I WAS SENT TO YOU GUYS' WORLD PRETTY SUDDENLY.
THERE'S SOMETHING I STILL NEED TO DO IN THIS ONE.
MY FAMILY SHOULD BE ASLEEP AT THIS HOUR...
JUST WAIT HERE A MINUTE, OKAY?
...AH.
SPARE KEY'S STILL IN THE SAME PLACE...
カチャ
KACHA (CLACK)
IT ALL LOOKS ABOUT THE SAME...
WHO KNEW AMBUSH AND SECOND SIGHT...
...WOULD COME IN SO HANDY IN MY WORLD?

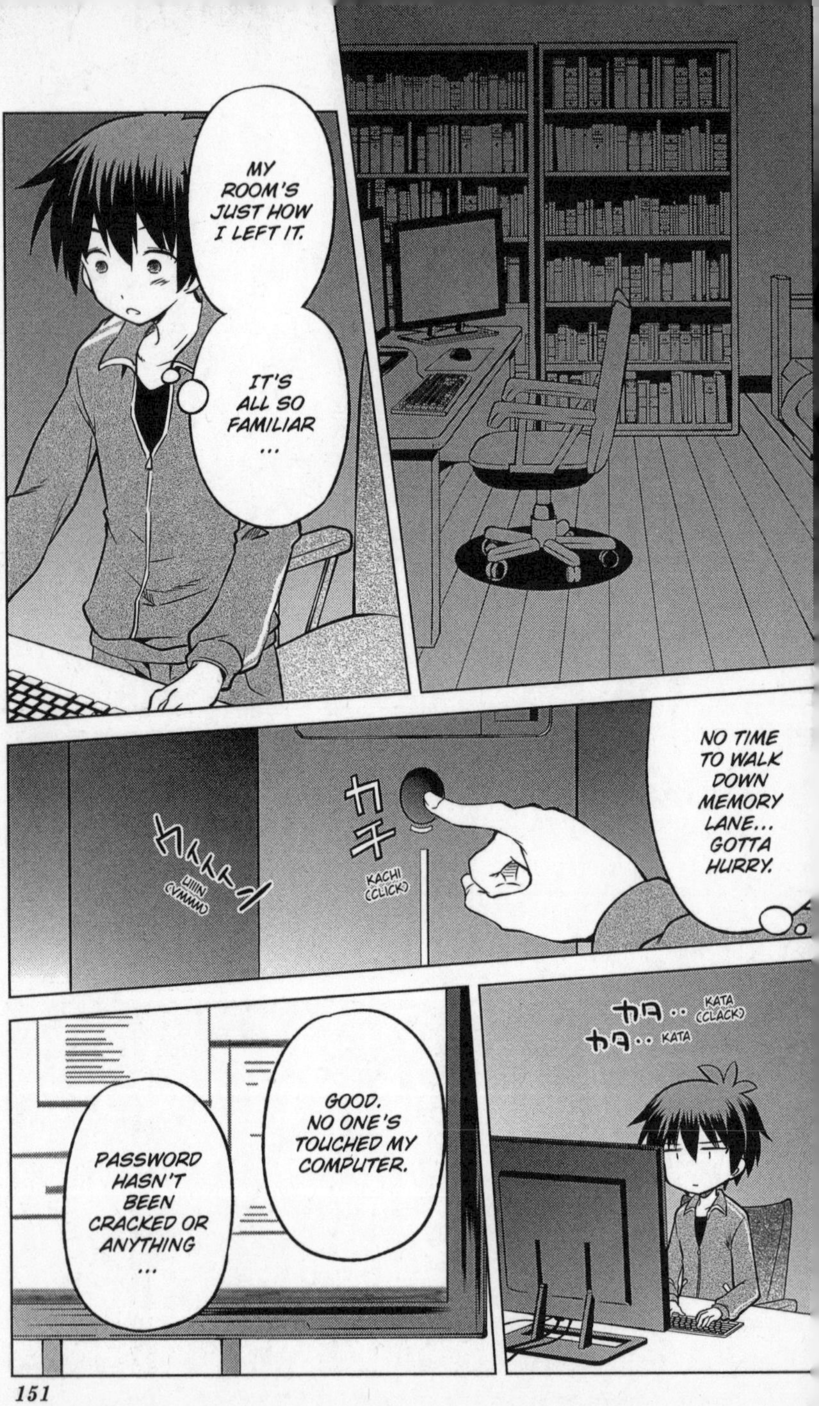
MY ROOM'S JUST HOW I LEFT IT.
IT'S ALL SO FAMILIAR ...
NO TIME TO WALK DOWN MEMORY LANE... GOTTA HURRY.
カチ
KACHI (CLICK)
ウィィィーン
UIIIN (VMMMM)
カタ..
KATA (CLACK)
カタ..
KATA
GOOD. NO ONE'S TOUCHED MY COMPUTER.
PASSWORD HASN'T BEEN CRACKED OR ANYTHING ...

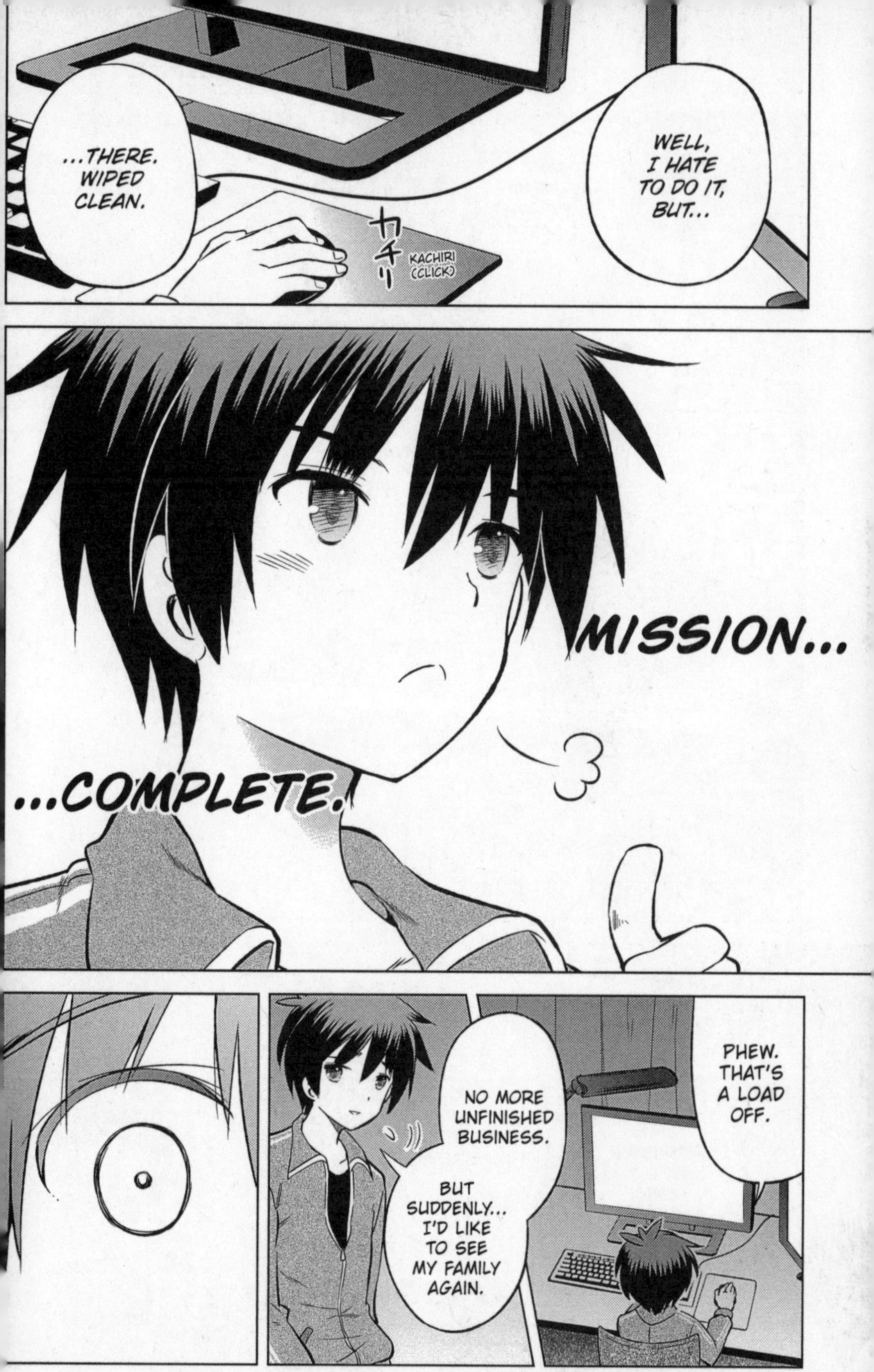
WELL, I HATE TO DO IT, BUT...
カチリ
KACHIRI (CLICK)
...THERE. WIPED CLEAN.
MISSION...
...COMPLETE.
PHEW. THAT'S A LOAD OFF.
NO MORE UNFINISHED BUSINESS.
BUT SUDDENLY... I'D LIKE TO SEE MY FAMILY AGAIN.

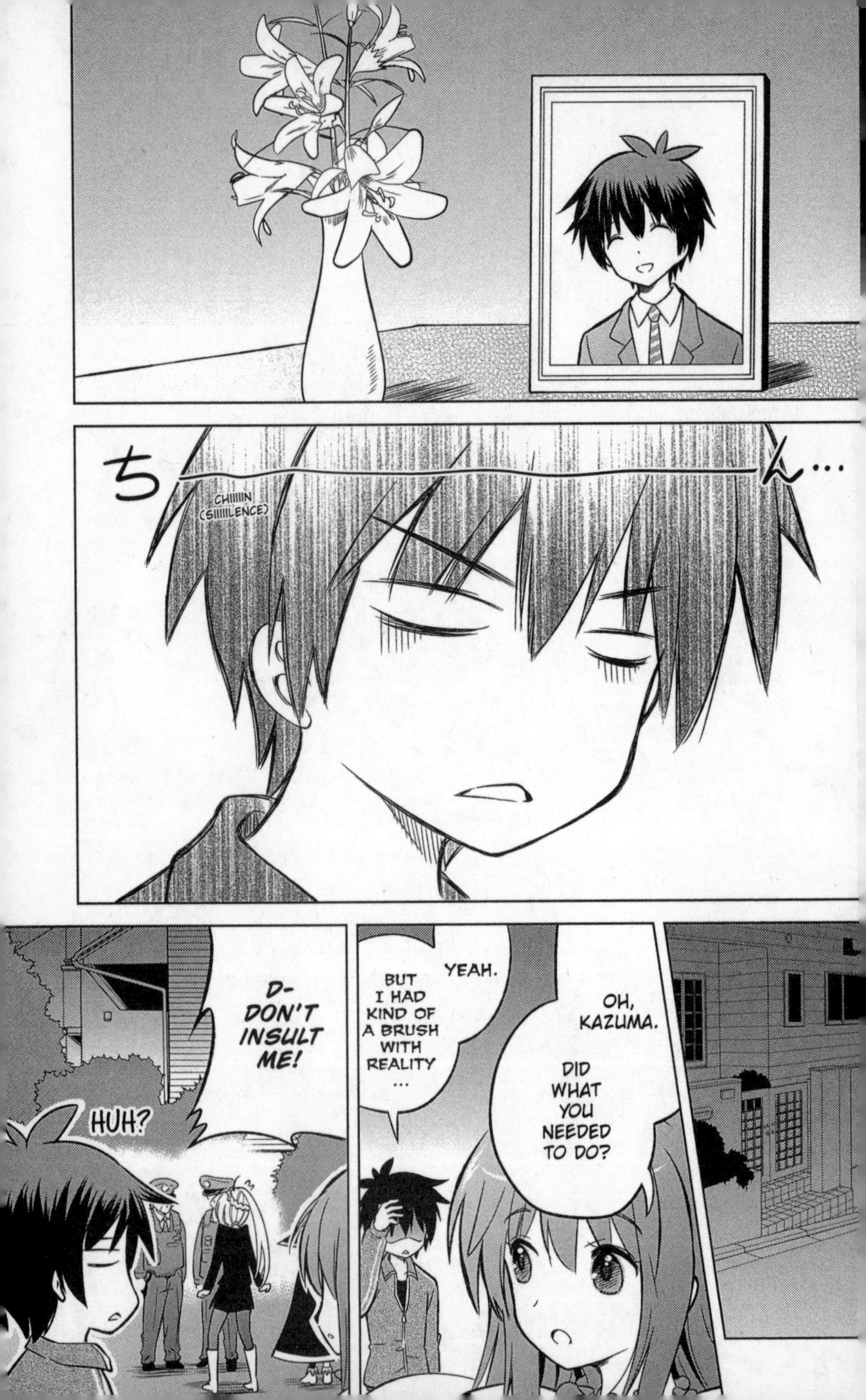
ち――――ん…
CHIIIIIN (SIIIIILENCE)
OH, KAZUMA.
DID WHAT YOU NEEDED TO DO?
YEAH.
BUT I HAD KIND OF A BRUSH WITH REALITY...
D-DON'T INSULT ME!
HUH?

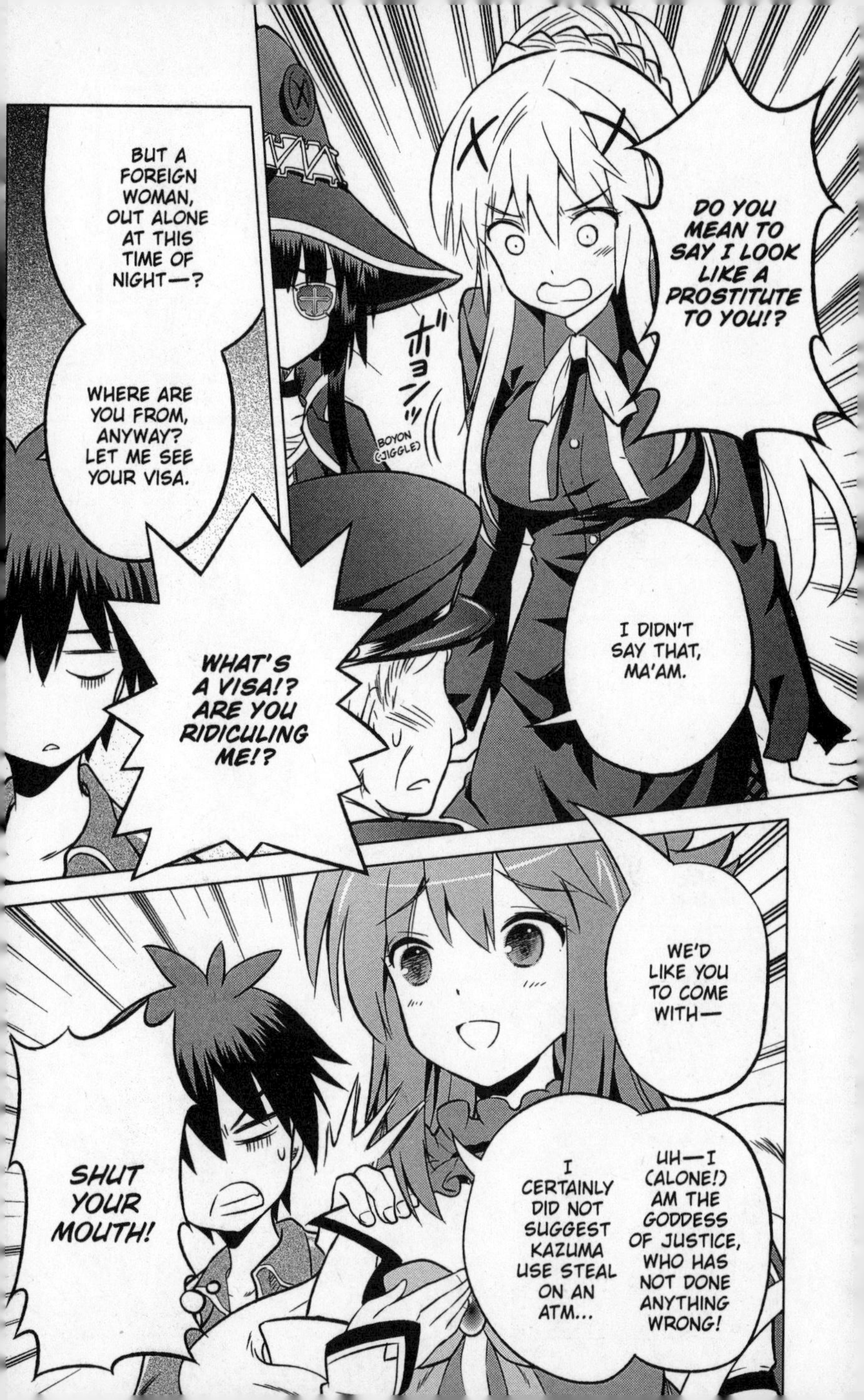
DO YOU MEAN TO SAY I LOOK LIKE A PROSTITUTE TO YOU!?
BOYON (JIGGLE)
BUT A FOREIGN WOMAN, OUT ALONE AT THIS TIME OF NIGHT—?
WHERE ARE YOU FROM, ANYWAY? LET ME SEE YOUR VISA.
I DIDN'T SAY THAT, MA'AM.
WHAT'S A VISA!? ARE YOU RIDICULING ME!?
WE'D LIKE YOU TO COME WITH—
UH—I (ALONE!) AM THE GODDESS OF JUSTICE, WHO HAS NOT DONE ANYTHING WRONG!
I CERTAINLY DID NOT SUGGEST KAZUMA USE STEAL ON AN ATM...
SHUT YOUR MOUTH!

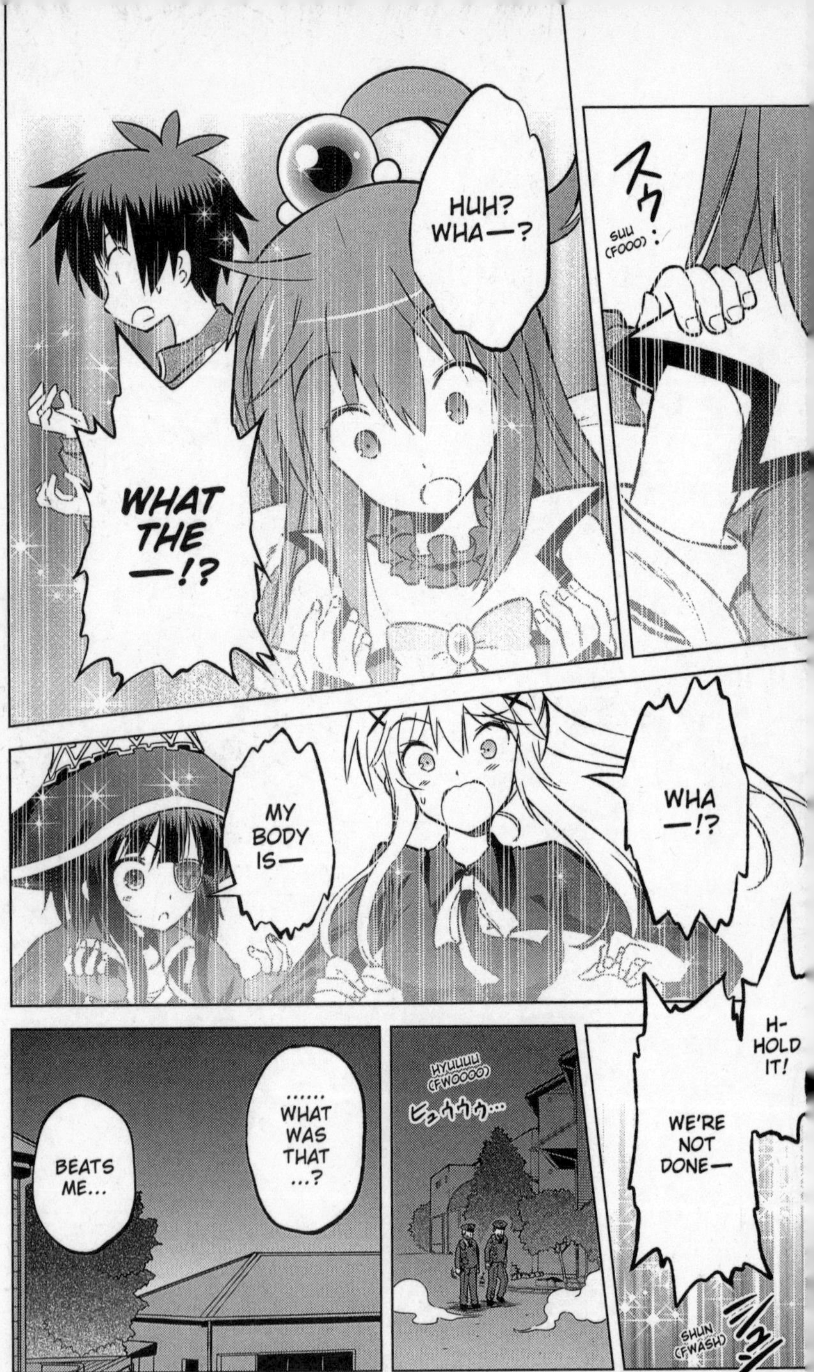

スゥ
SUU (FOOO)
HUH? WHA—?
WHAT THE—!?
WHA—!?
MY BODY IS—
H-HOLD IT!
WE'RE NOT DONE—
シュン
SHUN (FWASH)
ヒュウウウ…
HYUUUU (FWOOOO)
......WHAT WAS THAT...?
BEATS ME...

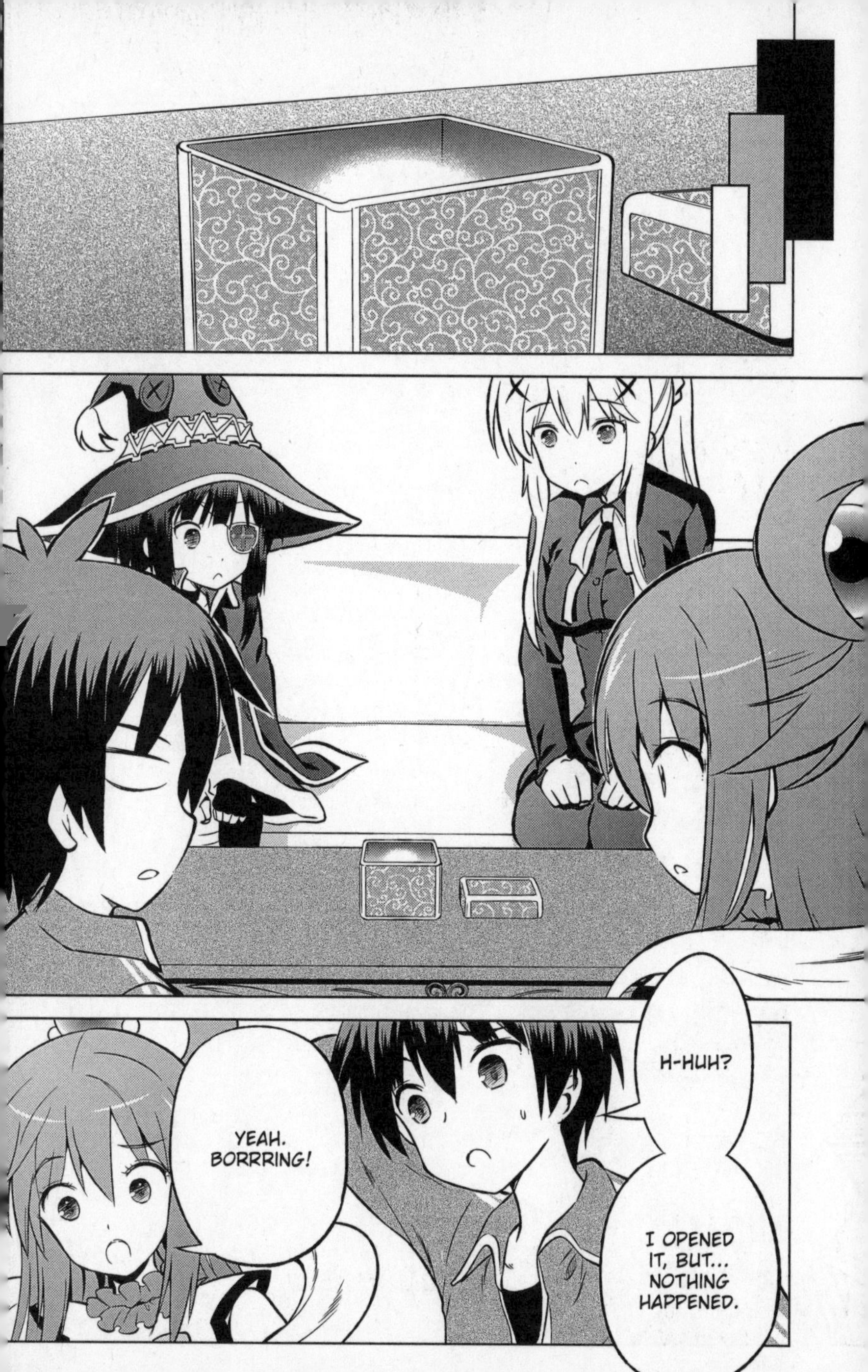
H-HUH?
I OPENED IT, BUT... NOTHING HAPPENED.
YEAH. BORRRING!

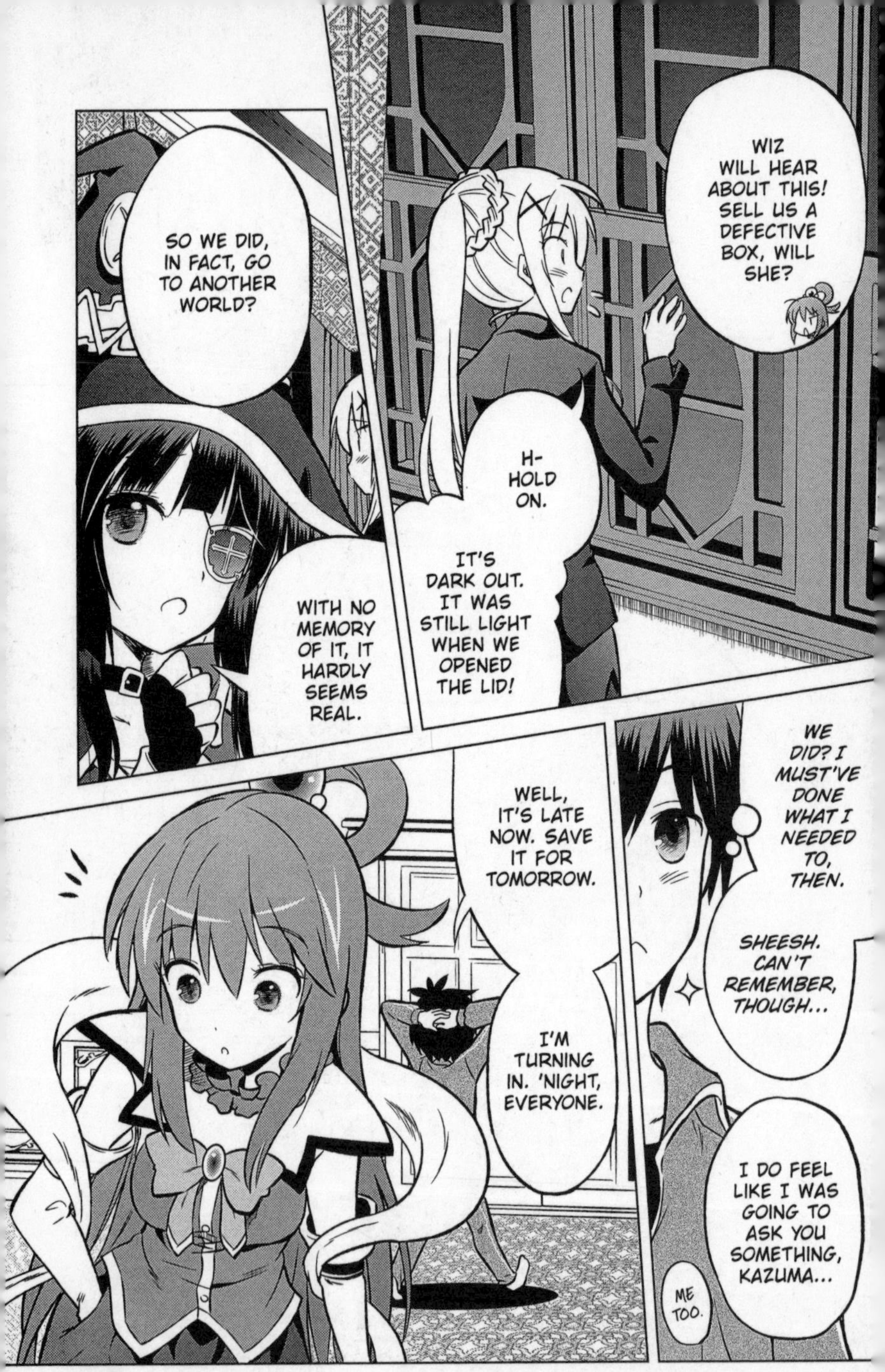
WIZ WILL HEAR ABOUT THIS! SELL US A DEFECTIVE BOX, WILL SHE?
H-HOLD ON.
IT'S DARK OUT. IT WAS STILL LIGHT WHEN WE OPENED THE LID!
SO WE DID, IN FACT, GO TO ANOTHER WORLD?
WITH NO MEMORY OF IT, IT HARDLY SEEMS REAL.
WE DID? I MUST'VE DONE WHAT I NEEDED TO, THEN.
SHEESH. CAN'T REMEMBER, THOUGH...
I DO FEEL LIKE I WAS GOING TO ASK YOU SOMETHING, KAZUMA...
ME TOO.
WELL, IT'S LATE NOW. SAVE IT FOR TOMORROW.
I'M TURNING IN. 'NIGHT, EVERYONE.

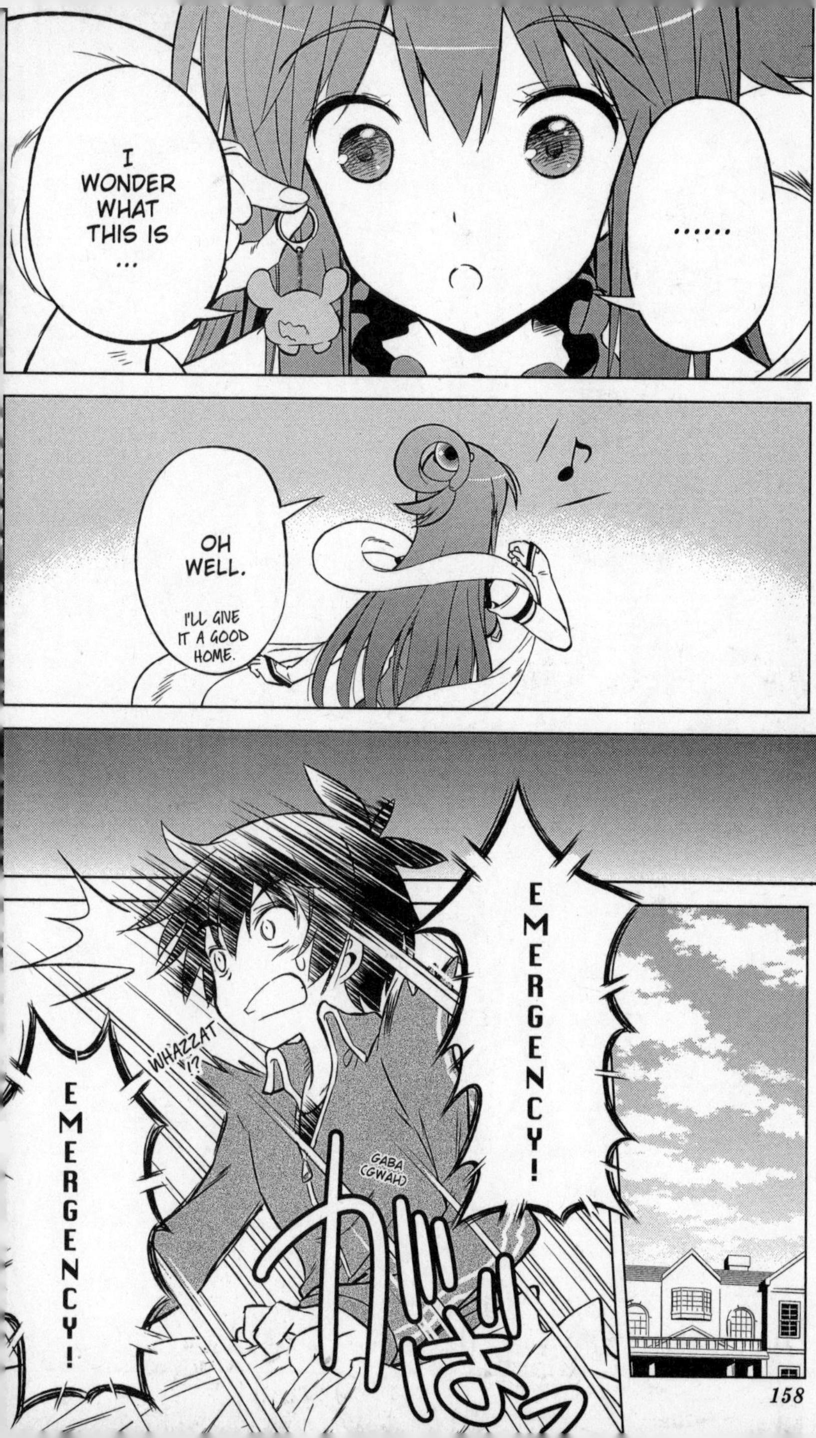
......
I WONDER WHAT THIS IS ...
OH WELL.
I'LL GIVE IT A GOOD HOME.
EMERGENCY!
WHAZZAT!?
GABA (GWAH)
EMERGENCY!

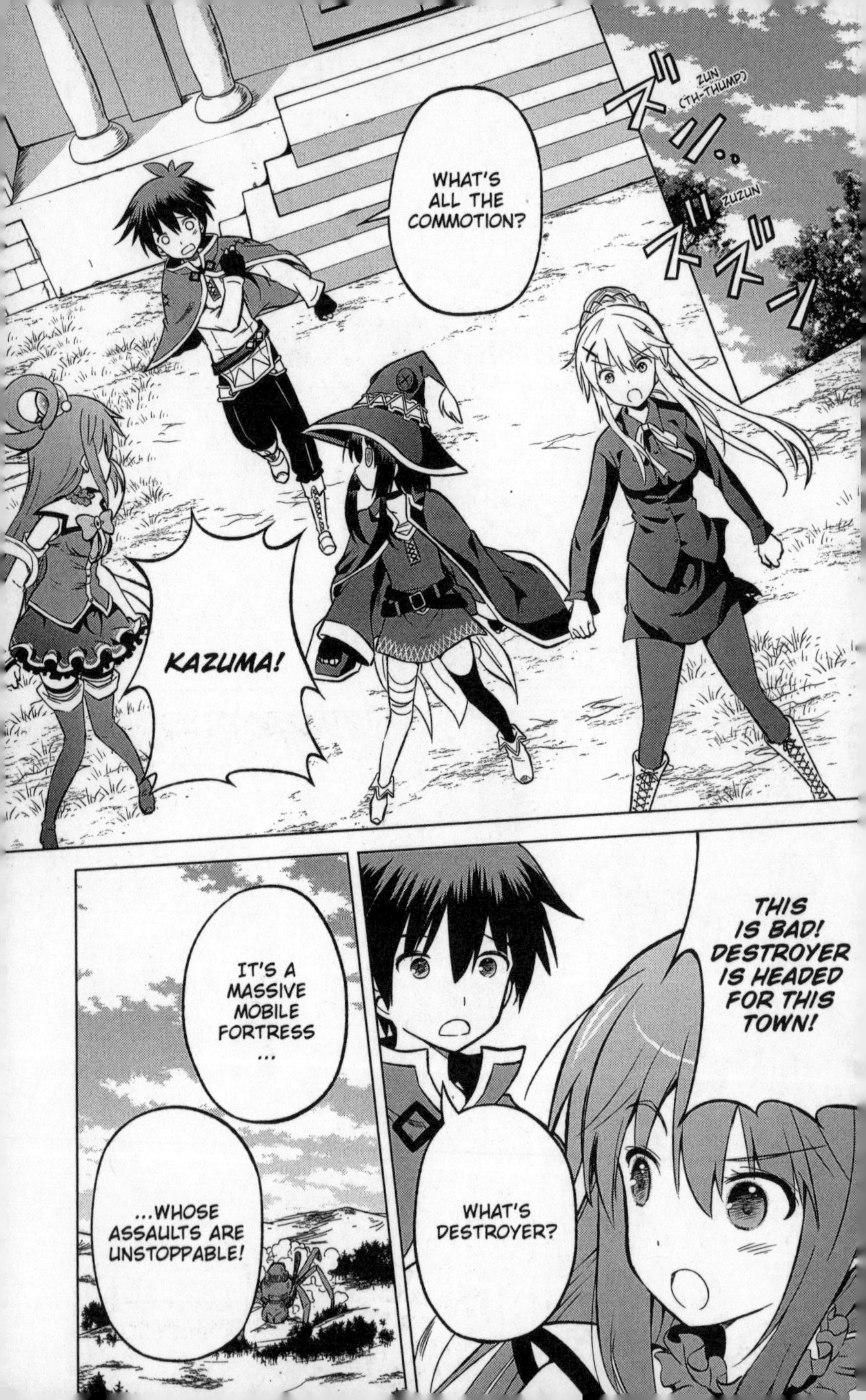
ZUN (TH-THUMP)
ZUZUN
WHAT'S ALL THE COMMOTION?
KAZUMA!
THIS IS BAD! DESTROYER IS HEADED FOR THIS TOWN!
WHAT'S DESTROYER?
IT'S A MASSIVE MOBILE FORTRESS ...
...WHOSE ASSAULTS ARE UNSTOPPABLE!

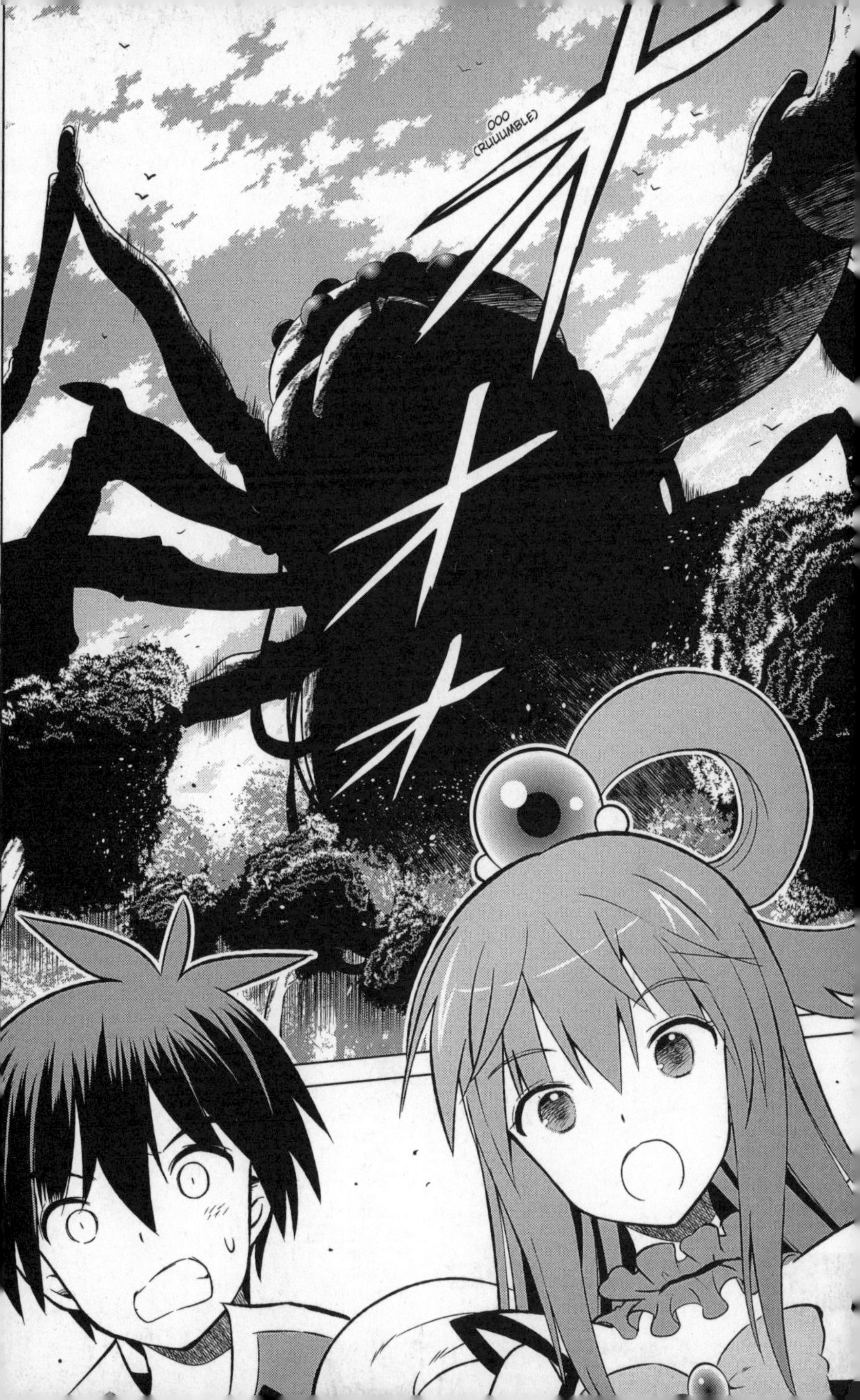
OOO
(RUUUMBLE)

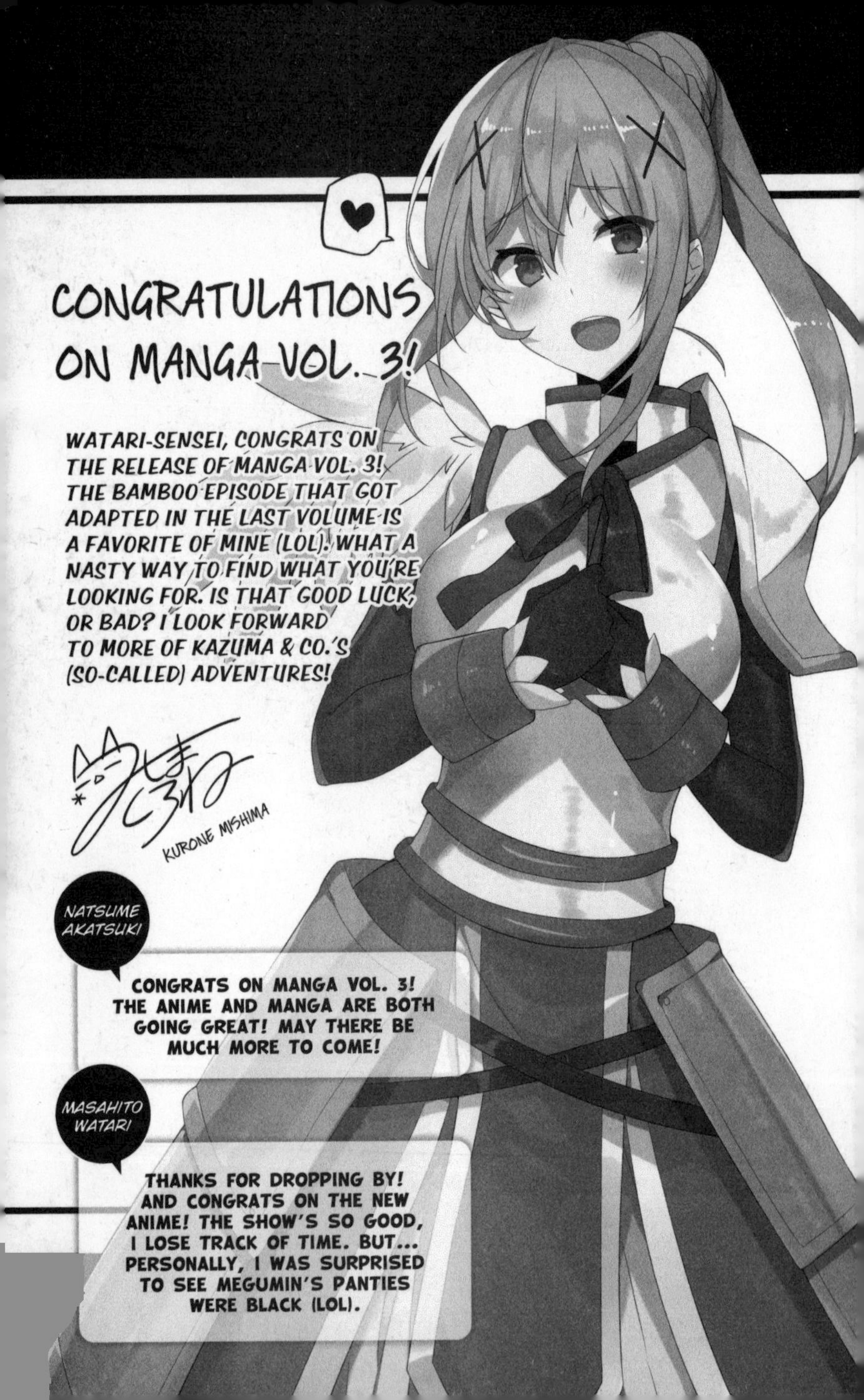
CONGRATULATIONS ON MANGA VOL. 3!
WATARI-SENSEI, CONGRATS ON THE RELEASE OF MANGA VOL. 3! THE BAMBOO EPISODE THAT GOT ADAPTED IN THE LAST VOLUME IS A FAVORITE OF MINE (LOL). WHAT A NASTY WAY TO FIND WHAT YOU'RE LOOKING FOR. IS THAT GOOD LUCK, OR BAD? I LOOK FORWARD TO MORE OF KAZUMA & CO.'S (SO-CALLED) ADVENTURES!
KURONE MISHIMA
NATSUME AKATSUKI
CONGRATS ON MANGA VOL. 3! THE ANIME AND MANGA ARE BOTH GOING GREAT! MAY THERE BE MUCH MORE TO COME!
MASAHITO WATARI
THANKS FOR DROPPING BY! AND CONGRATS ON THE NEW ANIME! THE SHOW'S SO GOOD, I LOSE TRACK OF TIME. BUT... PERSONALLY, I WAS SURPRISED TO SEE MEGUMIN'S PANTIES WERE BLACK (LOL).

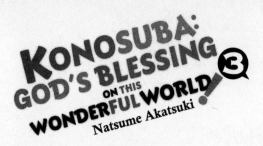

KONOSUBA:
GOD'S BLESSING
ON THIS
WONDERFUL WORLD! 3
Natsume Akatsuki

**TRANSLATION:** Kevin Steinbach 　 **LETTERING:** Bianca Pistillo

Kono subarashii sekai ni syukufuku wo! Volume 3
©MASAHITO WATARI 2016
©NATSUME AKATSUKI, KURONE MISHIMA 2016
First published in Japan in 2016 by Kadokawa Corporation, Tokyo. English translation rights arranged with KADOKAWA Corporation, Tokyo through Tuttle-Mori Agency, Inc., Tokyo.

English translation © 2017 by Yen Press, LLC

Yen Press
1290 Avenue of the Americas
New York, NY 10104

Visit us at yenpress.com
facebook.com/yenpress
twitter.com/yenpress
yenpress.tumblr.com
instagram.com/yenpress

First Yen Press Edition: April 2017

Yen Press is an imprint of Yen Press, LLC.
The Yen Press name and logo are trademarks of Yen Press, LLC.

The publisher is not responsible for websites (or their content) that are not owned by the publisher.

Library of Congress Control Number: 2016946112

ISBNs: 978-0-316-46933-3 (paperback)
　　　　978-0-316-55953-9 (ebook)

10 9 8 7 6 5 4 3

BVG

Printed in the United States of America